Study Guide to Accompany
Smith and Roberson's

BUSINESS LAW

Seventh Edition

Len Young Smith
G. Gale Roberson
Richard A. Mann
Barry S. Roberts

Prepared by
Peter T. Kahn
University of Minnesota

Dennis R. Hower
University of Minnesota

West Publishing Company
St. Paul   New York   Los Angeles   San Francisco

COPYRIGHT © 1988   by WEST PUBLISHING CO.
50 W. Kellogg Boulevard
P.O. Box 64526
St. Paul, MN 55164-1003

96 95 94 93 92 91 90 89   8 7 6 5 4 3 2 1

ISBN 0-314-81242-3

∞

Contents

Purpose of Study Guide

Students in college business law courses are often studying law for the first time. As with other demanding and challenging areas of study, law uses a specialized vocabulary to convey complicated theories, concepts and principles. Such semantic and doctrinal complexity poses difficulties and problems. Acquiring a working understanding of the American legal system and its related fields of specific study is not an easy task.

For legal knowledge presented in text materials and classroom lecture to have a value, students must develop an ability to apply their learning to everyday life. Clearly, the purpose of introductory law courses is not to train or prepare students to become legal experts, qualified to handle legal matters with the same degree of precision and expertise as an attorney. The realistic goals of "first-exposure" courses in law instead include presenting the law, its terminology and basic principles, in a manner that enables students to understand the legal system of which they are a part, apply the terms and concepts they have learned to their own lives, to consider law as a future career and to effectively seek professional legal assistance when the need arises.

This *Study Guide* was written to help students in introductory law courses achieve these goals by providing a useful learning aid. Used properly, the *Study Guide* will hopefully prove an invaluable learning tool in conjunction with textual readings and classroom instruction.

HOW TO USE STUDY GUIDE

The most beneficial use of the *Study Guide* will occur by students keeping pace with in-class lecture and text reading assignments with the related *Study Guide* chapters. By completing *Study Guide* assignments topically concurrent with classroom instruction and textual material, students will be aided in comprehending the text and will be provided a useful frame of reference for organizing class notes. The *Study Guide* assignments have also been written to facilitate exam review and preparation.

The *Study Guide* format has been designed to achieve the above purposes as effectively as possible. Each text chapter has a related study assignment in the *Study Guide*. Answer keys for *Study Guide* chapters are included at the end of the *Study Guide*.

Each *Study Guide* chapter opens with a brief review of the textbook materials upon which it is based. These introductory SCOPE NOTES explain the major theme of a chapter, how it relates to the preceding material, and how it introduces subsequent chapters. Following the introductory comments, EDUCATIONAL OBJECTIVES focus student attention on important concepts and doctrines to remember from the chapter, which can prove useful in exam preparation.

The next section of the *Guide* is a CHAPTER OUTLINE. Its purpose is not to supplant careful reading of the text but to assist reading and studying the text by summarizing and highlighting major concepts of each chapter.

The CHAPTER OUTLINE is followed by a series of objective questions presented to enhance student mastery of textual and classroom material. TRUE-FALSE questions have been written to facilitate understanding important legal doctrines and principles. To gain the most benefit from the TRUE-FALSE items, students should refrain from over analyzing or reading too much into them. Thoughts, interpretations or assumptions that are not in the question itself should not be addressed. To challenge understanding the legal principles from which the TRUE-FALSE questions are drawn, students should rephrase false statements to become true and vice-versa.

MATCHING EXERCISES are the next set of *Study Guide* objective questions. These items introduce key terms and phrases that are vital to understanding various legal doctrines. The third set of objective questions is made up of MULTIPLE CHOICE items. These questions are designed to enhance comprehension of the important components and interconnections among the various doctrines, principles and concepts being studied.

The *Study Guide* assignments close with CASE ANALYSIS problems. These are written to help students develop the ability to apply academic principles to factual situations. After conceptualizing the problem developed in the facts, students should identify the pertinent legal issues. Recalling relevant text and classroom material, students reach a solution to the problem supported by coherent reasoning. It is important to read the facts slowly and carefully while working through the short answer essay problems. This is the only way to precisely define the nature of the dispute, its relevant legal issues, and reach a proper decision. In this manner, students will achieve a real understanding of the legal topics discussed in the text.

After completing the *Study Guide* chapter assignments, answers may be checked with the ANSWER KEY at the end of the *Guide*. Failure to understand how and why some answers are incorrect will make our studying of law frustrating and fruitless.

The fifty-one text chapters are divided into ten separate study units. The *Study Guide* chapters that comprise a single study unit close with RESEARCH QUESTIONS drawn from the material for that unit. These QUESTIONS follow: Part One-Legal Environment of Business, Chapters 1-6; Part Two-Contracts, Chapters 7-16; Part Three-Agency, Chapters 17-18; Part Four-Sales, Chapter 19-23; Part Five-Commercial Paper, Chapters 24-28; Part Six-Partnership, Chapters 29-32; Part Seven-Corporations, Chapters 33-36; Part Eight-Debtor/Creditor Relations, Chapters 37-39; Part Nine-Regulation of Business, Chapters 40-45; and Part Ten-Property, Chapters 46-51. The RESEARCH QUESTIONS are designed to challenge student understanding of the basic principles, doctrines and concepts examined in the related text readings by asking students to apply such knowledge to broader, contemporary social issues and problems.

How to Study Law:
Text, Class and Exams

In response to the often asked question, "How should I study for a course of this nature?" the authors would like to offer some suggestions. First, be at ease with confusion. Since law is a difficult field of study, it is rare that a single reading of the text or attending class without taking notes will lead to an understanding of the material sufficient to handle exams adequately. Usually, the first reading of the text and noteless class attendance results in total confusion. What do these strange, seemingly foreign terms mean? How do these entangled, complicated legal principles and doctrines fit together? DON'T BECOME DISCOURAGED! Practicing attorneys and legal educators rarely grasp all the ramifications of a particular court decision, legislative enactment or administrative ruling after just one reading. It is only after many readings of the rule in question, prolonged study, review and discussion with colleagues, that the fog of analytic confusion begins to lift. Be cautioned, however, that this short-term apparent understanding will, in many cases, give way to long-term mystification as the future implications, meanings and interpretations of the principle in question become clouded with speculation and uncertainty associated with change.

WRESTLING WITH THE TEXT

Review the Preface, Table of Contents and Introduction. This provides an overall perspective on the course and the approach to the material taken by the authors. Noting the organization of the text and determining how the chapters relate to one another enables students to see how the textual material integrates with classroom lecture. The text chapters contain both narrative (definitional) and case (illustrative) material. The cases, since they are applications of the legal principles discussed in the preceding textual material, should be read after the narrative portion to reduce confusion and to enhance understanding of the terms and doctrines developed in the chapter.

WRESTLING WITH EXAMS

Proper preparation for tests is crucial. Do not fall behind in text reading or class attendance. Keep up with text and lecture material. This allows concentration on exam preparation over an extended period of time rather than attempting to cover the material for the first time shortly before the exam. Since we are dealing with complicated terms and concepts, last minute cramming often triggers a sense of panic which can lower concentration levels and, generally, detract from effective studying. To facilitate understanding the text, outlining, underlining and note-taking have all proved effective. Taking complete class notes and participating in class discussion are also effective learning tools. They help to maintain attention and concentration, as well as indicate the material that the instructor considers most important -- a probable clue to the content of an upcoming exam. Remember that most of the students in the class and, depending on the issue, the instructor as well, may be just as confused about certain topics as you are. Participating in class discussion contributes to overcoming this confusion.

Once an exam has begun, budget time carefully. Avoid spending too much time on a single question. Before answering an objective question (true-false, multiple choice, matching, etc.), make sure that its content is fully understood. Do not misread or overread a question. Read it slowly and carefully. Do not read into the question unstated interpretative information. Focus exclusively on the doctrine, principle or term addressed in the question.

For essay questions, several readings may be required. It might prove useful to diagram the facts. Make sure an answer addresses the significant legal issues and quotes relevant legal doctrines for their solutions. Be sure to develop the reasons for an answer. Don't make the exam grader read the exam writer's mind. Explain answers with full, pertinent information.

These suggestions are offered to assist understanding the material studied in your law course. Hopefully, they will make learning about the American legal system and its workings easier and more enjoyable. Happy reading in your journey through law.

Assistant Professor Peter T. Kahn, J.D.
Professor Dennis R. Hower, J.D.

CHAPTER 1

Introduction to Law

SCOPE NOTE

As modern life has become increasingly crowded, complicated and subject to fast-paced change, our everyday affairs have become more subject to legal scrutiny and regulation. Our daily activities carry profound legal implications. It is therefore important to gain a working understanding of this all-pervasive influencing force in our lives, the American legal system. Chapter One introduces basic terminology, concepts and principles relevant to the nature, origin, and growth of our system of laws. Through understanding the foundations of our legal identities (rights/duties), we will have a useful frame of reference when studying the specific areas of legal inquiry contained in the subsequent chapters. What is law? What is the legal reasoning process? What are the sources of law? These and other fundamental topics are the focus of discussion in Chapter One.

EDUCATIONAL OBJECTIVES

1. Define law and discuss the importance of the phrase, "a society governed by a system of laws."

2. Enumerate the function of and purposes served by law.

3. Discuss the "legal analysis" process.

4. Explain the interrelationships among law, morality and justice.

5. Differentiate among the various classifications of law.

6. Identify the law-making bodies within the American legal system.

7. Develop the importance of stare decisis in the formation of common law.

8. Trace the historical origins of America's system of laws.

9. Evaluate the significance of the movement towards uniform, codified laws in various arenas of legal regulation.

10.   Define and explain the significance of Equity.

CHAPTER OUTLINE

A.   Nature of Law
    1.   Definition of Law - "a rule of civil conduct prescribed by the supreme power of the state, commanding what is right, and prohibiting what is wrong."
    2.   Functions of Law - the primary function is to maintain stability in the social, political and economic system while at the same time permitting ordered change.
    3.   Legal Sanctions - the means by which the law enforces the decisions of the courts.
    4.   Law and Morals - they are NOT the same. Law and ethics are similar but they differ because rules of law have sanctions; rules of ethics do not.
    5.   Law and Justice - without law there can be no justice, but law is no guarantee of justice.
B.   Classification of Law
    1.   Substantive and Procedural Law - substantive laws create, define, and regulate legal rights and obligations; procedural law sets the rules for enforcing the rights which exist by substantive law.
    2.   Public and Private Law - public law consists of constitutional, administrative, and criminal law; private law includes civil and business law.
    3.   Civil and Criminal Law - civil law defines duties which if violated constitute a wrong against the party injured by the violation; criminal law establishes duties which if violated constitute a wrong against the whole community.
C.   Sources of Law
    1.   Constitutional Law - established by the U.S. Constitution and the individual State constitutions.
    2.   Judicial Law - established by Federal and State courts.
        a.   Common law - also called case law (judge-made decisions)
        b.   Equity - a supplementary court system to courts of law (common law) with its own remedies when no adequate remedy is available at common law.
        c.   Restatements of law - the authoritative statement of the common law of the United States.
    3.   Legislative law - established by Federal and State enactments (statutes).
        a.   Treaties - agreements between or among independent nations.
        b.   Executive orders - laws issued by the President or by governors of the States.
    4.   Administrative Law - rules and regulations created by Federal, State and local administrative agencies.
D.   Legal Analysis - the method of analyzing and briefing Federal and State judicial decisions.

TRUE-FALSE: Circle true or false.

Answers

T   F   1.   In order to survive, a civilized society must have an efficient legal system.

T   F   2.   Civil law is a wrong against an injured party while criminal law is a wrong against the whole community.

T   F   3.   Stare decisis is a doctrine based on present court decisions following previous ones, and it should never be overturned.

T   F   4.   A "maxim" is a general legal principle formulated over the years by courts of equity.

T   F   5.   The source of American law superior to all other sources within a state is the state statutes.

T   F   6.   The government has the burden of proving a defendant guilty of a crime beyond a reasonable doubt.

T   F   7.   The source of American law to which all other sources are subordinate is a President's executive order.

T   F   8.   The person who sues in a lawsuit is called the plaintiff, the person being sued is the defendant.

T   F   9.   The Uniform Commercial Code was prepared and developed to make the law governing commercial transactions uniform within the various jurisdictions of Minnesota.

T   F   10.   Legal sanctions are the means by which the law enforces the decisions of the courts.

T   F   11.   Statutory law results from the independent decisions of the state and federal courts.

T   F   12.   An authoritative statement of the common law of the United States can be found in the Restatements of Law.

KEY TERMS – MATCHING EXERCISE: Select the term which best completes each statement below and write the corresponding number in the ANSWERS column.

Column I	Column II	Answers
1. A public wrong committed against society or the state.	1. Federal Trade Commission	1. _____
		2. _____
2. The law that establishes rules for enforcing rights.	2. Federal statutes	3. _____
3. The remedy obtainable from a court of law.	3. Uniform Commercial Code	4. _____
		5. _____
4. A guiding principle whereby a court follows previous decisions in deciding the present case before it.	4. Crime	6. _____
	5. Substantive law	7. _____

5.   A new system of judicial relief that developed because of a lack of a proper remedy from the common law system.

6.   One type of remedy available only in a court of equity requiring a party to refrain from doing a specific act.

7.   The means by which the law enforces judgments.

8.   The supreme law of the land.

9.   The law that governs commercial transactions in most states.

10. The law that defines, creates, and regulates legal rights and duties.

11. An agreement between or among independent nations.

12. General legal principles formulated by equity courts.

13. Legislative laws passed by the Federal government.

14. A governor of a State may issue this source of law.

15. A remedy in equity in which a party is allowed to invalidate a contract.

6.   Procedural law

7.   Injunction

8.   Maxims

9.   Money judgment

10. U.S. Constitution

11. Tort law

12. Restatement of law

13. Legal sanctions

14. Equity

15. Stare decisis

16. Uniform Probate Code

17. Administrative law

18. Executive order

19. Rescission

20. Treaty

8.   _____

9.   _____

10. _____

11. _____

12. _____

13. _____

14. _____

15. _____

MULTIPLE CHOICE: Select the alternative which best completes each statement below and write the corresponding letter in the ANSWERS column.   **Answers**

1.   Equitable remedies include (a) specific performance (b) rescission (c) reformation (d) all of the above.

1.   _____

2.   Federal Court decisions are not found in which of the following? (a) Federal Reporter (b) Lawyers Edition (c) Federal Supplement (d) North Western Reporter.

2.   _____

3.   Of the following, the one with present authority over commercial transactions is the (a) Uniform Commercial Code (b) Uniform Sales Act (c) Uniform Bills of Lading Act (d) Bulk Sales Act.

                                                                    3.   _____

4.   Which of the following is most accurate? (a) all states have adopted the Uniform Commercial Code (b) the majority of states have adopted the Uniform Commercial Code (c) only one state has not adopted the entire Uniform Commercial Code (d) all the statements are false.

                                                                     4.   _____

5.   An example of a legal sanction for a criminal conviction is (a) a fine (b) capital punishment (c) imprisonment (d) all of the above.

                                                                    5.   _____

6.   The branch of public law that deals with regulatory functions of the government as performed and supervised by public officials or commissions is (a) judicial law (b) legislative law (c) administrative law (d) none of the above.

                                                                    6.   _____

7.   Which of the following is not a "maxim" of equity? (a) Equity will not suffer a wrong to be without a remedy (b) He who comes into equity must come with clean hands (c) He who seeks equity must do equity (d) Equity favors a forfeiture.

                                                                    7.   _____

8.   Law can best be classified into categories as (a) procedural or substantive (b) public or private (c) civil or criminal (d) all of the above.

                                                                    8.   _____

9.   That law that deals with the rights and powers of the government is (a) private law (b) public law (c) administrative law (d) tort law.

                                                                    9.   _____

10.   A source of law in our American legal system includes (a) the Federal Constitution (b) court decisions (c) municipal ordinances (d) all of the above.

                                                                   10. _____

11.   Torts and contracts are examples of (a) private law (b) public law (c) criminal law (d) all of the above.

                                                                    11. _____

12.   A remedy in equity in which a party to a contract is required to perform her obligations according to the contract is (a) an injunction (b) specific performance (c) reformation (d) rescission.

                                                                    12. _____

13.   Public law consists of (a) administrative law (b) constitutional law (c) criminal law (d) all of the above.

                                                                    13. _____

CASE PROBLEMS - SHORT ESSAY ANSWERS: Read each case problem carefully. When appropriate, answer by stating a Decision for the case and by explaining the rationale - Rule of Law - relied upon to support your decision.

1.   Sarah is in her first year of law school. The teaching method used at the school is the "case method" in which the students read and analyze the reports of court decisions or "cases." One such

case is <u>Brown v. Board of Education of Topeka</u>, 347 U.S. 686, 74 S. Ct. 686 (1954). Explain to Sarah how to find this case in a law library.

Decision: _____

_____

Rule of Law: _____

_____

2.   Harold signs a contract to buy Maude's home. Although he has the funds, Harold breaches the contract. Maude sues, asking for the remedy of specific performance. Harold demands a jury trial. Is he entitled to one? Explain.

Decision: _____

_____

Rule of Law: _____

_____

3.   Nathanial Horn was walking along the street when he was arrested and booked for arson. At his trial, the state brought evidence showing that Horn was indeed in the immediate area when the fire purportedly began. Has the state proven its case against Horn?

Decision: _____

_____

Rule of Law: _____

_____

4.   Anita wins a civil suit against Baker for damages of $10,000. Anita is unable to satisfy the judgment (receive payment) by collecting money from Baker. In order to be paid, what other possible remedy is available to Anita?

Decision: _____

_____

Rule of Law: _____

_____

5.   John Powers, one of the best-known swimmers in America, was walking near a river one day when he saw Mollie drowning. John, who was wearing a brand new shirt, didn't feel like getting wet. Would the State have a criminal action against John for not attempting to rescue Mollie? Explain.

Decision: _____

_____

Rule of Law: _____

_____

CHAPTER 2

Legal Process

SCOPE NOTE

Over the past decades, increased demands have been placed on our legal system to solve a multitude of previously non-existent societal and individual problems. Courts, informal dispute settling processes, and administrative bodies have been called upon not only to resolve such conflicts, but to carve out new directions in social, political and economic policy. As individuals and groups continue to make greater use of the legal process, knowledge of its operational dynamics becomes vital. Chapter Two introduces students to the principles and practices of the part of the American legal system responsible for dispute settling -- courts. How does a particular dispute move through the American civil law trial process? What are the rights/duties of parties to litigation? These and other concerns are focused upon in the context of our two basic court systems, State and Federal, as well as from the perspective of the overriding concern for fairness (Due Process) in these dispute settling arenas. Of major concern is understanding how courts apply legal principles to the facts of a controversy in performing a conflict resolving function.

EDUCATIONAL OBJECTIVES

1. Outline the organization of and the types of cases heard by State and Federal courts.

2. Chart the passage of a case through the judicial process, from the pleadings stage through an appeal of an adverse judgment.

3. Define and identify the basic elements of jurisdiction.

4. Develop the importance of venue.

5. Explain conflict of law problems from both a State and Federal court perspective.

6. Discuss the importance of arbitration as a court substitute for resolving conflict.

CHAPTER OUTLINE
A. The Court System

    1.   The Federal Courts
        a.   District courts - the trial courts of general jurisdiction in the Federal system.
        b.   Courts of Appeals - the Federal courts that primarily hear appeals from Federal district courts and administrative agencies.
        c.   The Supreme Court - the nation's highest court consisting of nine justices whose principal function is to review decisions of the Federal Courts of Appeals and the highest State courts.
        d.   Special courts - includes the U.S. Claims Court, the Tax Court, the U.S. Bankruptcy Courts, and the U.S. Court of Appeals for the Federal Circuit.
    2.   State Courts
        a.   Inferior trial courts - decide the least serious criminal and civil cases. Small claims courts - decide only civil cases involving a limited amount of money.
        b.   Trial courts - State trial courts of general jurisdiction over civil and criminal cases. Appellate courts - includes the highest court of each State whose decisions are often final.

B.   Jurisdiction
    1.   Subject Matter Jurisdiction - the authority of a particular court to adjudicate a controversy of a particular kind.
        a.   Exclusive Federal jurisdiction - Federal courts have exclusive jurisdiction over Federal criminal cases, bankruptcy, antitrust, patent, trademark, and copyright cases.
        b.   Concurrent Federal jurisdiction - cases that may be heard by either State or Federal courts.
        c.   Exclusive State jurisdiction - jurisdiction over all other cases.
        d.   Stare decisis in the dual court system - only decisions of the U.S. Supreme Court are binding on all other courts, Federal and State.
    2.   Jurisdiction Over the Parties - jurisdiction over the parties involved in the dispute.
        a.   In personam jurisdiction - jurisdiction of the court over the parties to a lawsuit.
        b.   In rem jurisdiction - jurisdiction over property.
        c.   Attachment jurisdiction - quasi in rem jurisdiction over property.
        d.   Venue - the location where a lawsuit should be brought.

C.   Civil Procedure
    1.   The Pleadings - the purpose of pleadings is to establish the issues of fact and law presented and disputed.
    2.   Pretrial Procedure - each party has the right to obtain evidence from the other party by discovery.
    3.   Trial - the proceeding to determine the outcome of a case with or without a jury trial.
    4.   Appeal - the purpose is to determine whether the trial court committed prejudicial error.

D.   Alternative Dispute Resolution
    1.   Arbitration - the disputing parties select a third person who renders a binding decision.
    2.   Conciliation and Mediation - methods of resolving disputes by use of a conciliator or a mediator.

TRUE-FALSE: Circle true or false.

T   F   1.   Venue is the power and authority of a court to hear and decide a case.

T   F   2.   A court may not render a binding decision unless it has jurisdiction over the dispute and over the parties to that dispute.

T   F   3.   The only court expressly created by the Federal Constitution is the U.S. Supreme Court.

T   F   4.   The decisions of a State Supreme Court are always final.

T   F   5.   The purpose of discovery is to enable each party to be informed of the evidence so there will be no surprises at the trial.

T   F   6.   A decision of the U.S. Supreme Court on Federal questions is binding on all other courts, Federal or State.

T   F   7.   In arbitration, the decision of the arbitrator is generally binding on the parties involved in the dispute.

T   F   8.   Generally speaking, appellate courts hear the same witnesses' testimony as the trial court.

T   F   9.   The United States has a dual court system: separate State and Federal courts.

T   F   10.   The examination or questioning of potential jurors in the jury selection process is called voir dire.

T   F   11.   The membership of the U.S. Supreme Court consists of nine justices.

T   F   12.   Disputes involving public employees such as police officers or fire fighters may require compulsory arbitration as stated in the U.S. Constitution.

KEY TERMS - MATCHING EXERCISE: Select the term which best completes each statement below and write the corresponding number in the ANSWERS column.

Column I	Column II	Answers
1. The type of jurisdiction the U.S. Supreme Court has in cases affecting ambassadors.	1. Pleadings	1. _____
	2. Writ of certiorari	2. _____
2. The place (county) where the lawsuit should be filed or has to be tried.	3. Mediator	3. _____
		4. _____
3. The "charges" given by the judge for the purpose of aiding the jury in reaching its decision.	4. Discovery	5. _____
	5. Venue	6. _____

4.   The jury's decision.

5.   The use of a neutral person selected by the disputing parties to decide the dispute.

6.   Pre-trial testimony under oath taken out of court which may be used at the trial.

7.   The claims of the plaintiff which, when filed, commences a civil lawsuit.

8.   The pre-trial procedure by which each party has the right to obtain evidence, or facts that might lead to evidence, from the other party.

9.   A method of appealing a case to the U.S. Supreme Court.

10.   The power or authority a court must have to hear and decide a case.

11.   A claim by the defendant in a civil lawsuit that she has been damaged and claims compensation (money).

12.   Written questions submitted to the opposing party in a civil lawsuit requiring written answers made under oath but before the trial.

13.   A person who proposes possible solutions to disputing parties that are not binding.

14.   The decision of an arbitrator.

15.   Notice to a defendant that a civil lawsuit has been brought against the defendant.

6.   Original jurisdiction

7.   Appellate jurisdiction

8.   Complaint

9.   Summons

10.   Arbitration

11.   Depositions

12.   Counterclaim

13.   Jurisdiction

14.   Instructions

15.   Verdict

16.   Conciliator

17.   Award

18.   Mediation

19.   Judgment

20.   Interrogatories

7.   _____

8.   _____

9.   _____

10.   _____

11.   _____

12.   _____

13.   _____

14.   _____

15.   _____

MULTIPLE CHOICE: Select the alternative which best completes each statement below and write the corresponding letter in the ANSWERS column.

1.   Diversity of citizenship exists when (a) the plaintiff and defendant are citizens of different states (b) a foreign country brings an action against U.S. citizens (c) a dispute is between U.S. citizens and citizens of a foreign country (d) all of the above.   1. _____

2.   The trial court of general jurisdiction in the Federal court system is the (a) Federal district court (b) Court of Appeals (c) U.S. Supreme Court (d) Court of Claims.   2. _____

3.   A motion made by the losing party in a civil action to the judge after the jury's verdict is a (a) directed verdict (b) judgment (c) judgment n.o.v. (d) writ of execution.   3. _____

4.   The majority of appellate cases that reach the U.S. Supreme Court come from (a) a State court declaring a Federal statute invalid (b) a State court declaring a treaty invalid (c) all appeals reach the U.S. Supreme Court (d) a writ of certiorari.   4. _____

5.   The Federal Courts of Appeals (a) exist within judicial circuits in the United States (b) have nine justices who decide the cases (c) hear only cases from administrative agencies (d) all of the above.   5. _____

6.   Which type of case would the U.S. Supreme Court handle under its original jurisdiction? (a) traffic arrest (b) murder (c) controversy between two states (d) equity.   6. _____

7.   Under its appellate jurisdiction, the U.S. Supreme Court (a) must hear and decide every case appealed to the court (b) hears all cases appealed to the court by writ of certiorari (c) hears only those cases in which a State court declares a Federal statute invalid (d) none of the above.   7. _____

8.   The special Federal court that hears claims against the Federal government is the (a) Tax Court (b) Claims Court (c) Customs Court (d) none of the above.   8. _____

9.   In order for a court to proceed with a lawsuit, it must have jurisdiction over the (a) plaintiff (b) defendant (c) subject matter of the case (d) all of the above.   9. _____

10.   In a civil lawsuit the defendant's answer to the plaintiff's complaint may contain (a) admissions or denials (b) affirmative defenses (c) counterclaims (d) all of the above.   10. _____

11.   The Federal courts have exclusive jurisdiction over cases involving (a) patents (b) bankruptcy (c) copyrights (d) all of the above.   11. _____

12. The purpose of this type of jurisdiction is to resolve conflicting claims to property (a) attachment jurisdiction (b) in personam jurisdiction (c) in rem jurisdiction (d) none of the above.

12. _____

13. Alternative dispute resolutions include (a) arbitration (b) conciliation (c) mediation (d) all of the above.

13. _____

CASE PROBLEMS - SHORT ESSAY ANSWERS: Read each case problem carefully. When appropriate, answer by stating a Decision for the case and by explaining the rationale - Rule of Law - relied upon to support your decision.

1. In a civil action, Mary Swift sues James Swanson in a State district court for negligently damaging her property. Mary wins, and James appeals to the State Supreme Court. The Supreme Court remands the decision of the district court. What does remand mean and, according to the rules of civil procedure, what happens to this case? Explain.

Decision: _____

Rule of Law: _____

2. Carla Marx, an ambassador, feeling that she wasn't being fully compensated by her home country, was caught holding up the Chase Manhattan Bank. Bank robbery is both a State and Federal crime. Could the U.S. Supreme Court try this case? Explain.

Decision: _____

Rule of Law: _____

3. A Georgia Supreme Court decision in a civil law paternity suit favors the defendant -- father. If a case involving the same facts was brought before a Texas court, would the Texas court be obligated to follow the Georgia decision under the "stare decisis" doctrine? Explain.

Decision: _____

Rule of Law: _____

4. While on vacation in Colorado, Amy Burns negligently struck Malcolm Morris with her ski, causing Malcolm to lose his sight in one eye. Amy is a resident of (or domiciled in) the State of Minnesota. Can this case be heard in Federal district court? Explain.

Decision: _____

Rule of Law: _____

5. Karla Johnson, a resident of Iowa, appeals a case to the Eighth Circuit Court of Appeals and wins. If a case involving the same facts was brought on appeal to the Fourth Circuit Court of Appeals, must that circuit court follow the decision of the Eighth Circuit? Explain.

Decision: _____

_____

Rule of Law: _____

_____

CHAPTER 3

Constitutional and Administrative Law

SCOPE NOTE

The "founding fathers" of the American government feared powerful, centralized and unitary government. They were committed to a political philosophy that stressed "limited government." The Federal Constitution, as the blueprint for governing authority, embodies the principles of "limited government" in its separation of powers, checks and balances, federalism, and other structural restrictions. Chapter Three examines the purpose and functions of the fundamental law of American society, the Federal Constitution.

Also examined in this Chapter is administrative law, sometimes referred to as the "fourth" branch of government. In the complex, crowded, urban society that constitutes present day America, many complicated socio-economic problems arise that demand attention and expertise beyond the capacity of traditional lawmakers, courts and legislatures. Chapter Three closes with a discussion of the growth of administrative law as the primary responder to such complex problems. How administrative agencies function is examined. Students should remember that the Federal agencies focused upon reflect the types of activities engaged in by similar lawmakers in their own states and towns.

EDUCATIONAL OBJECTIVES

1.   Discuss policy underlying concepts of constitutional and administrative law.

2.   Identify fundamental doctrines characterizing the U.S. Constitution.

3.   Outline major powers held by the Federal government.

4.   Explain activities pursued by administrative lawmakers.

5.   Distinguish among significant Federal administrative lawmakers.

CHAPTER OUTLINE

I.   Constitutional Law

A.   Basic Principles of Constitutional Law
  1.   Federal supremacy and preemption - all law in the United States is subject to the U.S. Constitution which is the supreme law of the land.
  2.   Judicial review - the process by which the courts examine governmental actions to determine whether they conform to the U.S. Constitution.
  3.   Separation of powers - our Constitution establishes three distinct and independent branches of government - executive, legislative, and judicial.
  4.   State action - includes any actions of the Federal and State governments according to the Constitution.

B.   Powers of Government
  1.   Federal commerce power - the Constitution gives Congress the power to regulate commerce with other Nations and among the States.
  2.   State regulation of commerce - the commerce clause of the Constitution also restricts the States' power to regulate activities if the result obstructs interstate commerce.
       a.   Regulations - the U.S. Supreme Court decides the extent of permissible State regulation affecting interstate commerce.
       b.   Taxation - the commerce clause in conjunction with the import-export clause also limits the power of the States to tax.
  3.   Federal fiscal powers - including the power to tax, to borrow and coin money, and the power of eminent domain.
       a.   Taxation and spending - the Constitution grants Congress broad powers to tax and spend which is an important way the Federal government regulates the economy.
       b.   Borrowing and coining money - this enables the Federal government to establish a national banking system, the Federal Reserve System.
       c.   Eminent domain - the government's power to take private property for public use.

C.   Limitations Upon Government
  1.   Contract clause - this clause of the Constitution restricts States from retroactively modifying public charters and private contracts.
  2.   First Amendment - the protection of free speech with some limits.
       a.   Commercial speech - is the expression related to the economic interests of the speaker and its audience, e.g., advertisements of a product or service.
       b.   Defamation - a tort consisting of a false communication that injures a person's reputation.
  3.   Due process - the Fifth and Fourteenth Amendments prohibit the Federal and State governments from depriving any person of life, liberty, or property without due process of law.
       a.   Substantive due process - involves a court's determination of whether a particular governmental action is compatible with individual liberties.
       b.   Procedural due process - pertains to the governmental decision-making process that results in depriving a person of life, liberty, or property.
  4.   Equal protection - the guarantee of equal protection requires that similarly situated persons be treated similarly by govermental actions.
       a.   Rational relationship test - a standard of review used by the Supreme Court to determine whether legislation satisfies the equal protection guarantee.
       b.   Strict scrutiny test - another standard of review.
       c.   Intermediate test - a third standard of review.

II.   Administrative Law

    A.   Operation of Administrative Agencies - most of these agencies perform three basic functions: they make rules, enforce the law, and adjudicate controversies.

       1.   Rulemaking - is the process by which an administrative agency promulgates rules of law.

       2.   Enforcement - agencies determine whether their rules have been violated.

       3.   Adjudication - an agency may use informal or formal methods to resolve disputes.

    B.   Limits on Administrative Agencies

       1.   Judicial review - acts as a control or check by a court on a particular rule or order of an administrative agency.

       2.   Legislative control - is exercised over administrative agencies through budget control or even by completely eliminating the agency.

       3.   Control by Executive Branch - by the President's power to appoint and remove the chief administrator of the agency.

TRUE-FALSE: Circle true or false.

Answers

T   F   1.   Public law is concerned with the rights and powers of government and its relation to individuals or groups.

T   F   2.   The Constitution of the United States was adopted in Washington, D.C. on August 1, 1776.

T   F   3.   The Federal commerce clause grants virtually complete power to the individual States to regulate the economy and business.

T   F   4.   The Federal government regulates the nation's economy by its power to spend money.

T   F   5.   The U.S. Supreme Court ruled that the contract clause of the Federal Constitution precludes the States from exercising eminent domain or their police powers.

T   F   6.   All administrative agencies receive their authority from the judicial branch of the Federal government.

T   F   7.   When a decision of a controversy is made by an administrative agency, that decision may be appealed to the appropriate State or Federal court.

T   F   8.   The adjudication of a controversy between an individual and one of the Federal administrative agencies is presided over by an administrative law judge.

T   F   9.   In the adjudication of a controversy between an individual and a Federal administrative agency, the agency serves as both prosecutor and decision maker.

T   F   10.   An example of the Federal government's fiscal powers is the prosecution of crimes that violate Federal law.

T   F   11.   The legislative branch of the U.S. government has the power to declare war and ratify treaties.

T   F   12.   Nominations by the President of persons to sit on the U.S. Supreme Court must be confirmed by the members of the House of Representatives.

KEY TERMS – MATCHING EXERCISES: Select the term which best completes each statement below and write the corrsponding number in the ANSWERS column.

	Column I		Column II		Answers
1.	The landmark Supreme Court decision that verified the supremacy of the Constitution over every other source of law.	1.	Administrative law	1.	_____
2.	The power of the government to take private property for public use.	2.	Marbury v. Madison	2.	_____
		3.	McCulloch v. Maryland	3.	_____
3.	The clause of the U.S. Constitution that grants complete power to Congress to regulate the economy.	4.	Bill of Rights	4.	_____
4.	The Federal power that allows the Federal government to tax and to spend, borrow, and coin money.	5.	Import-export clause	5.	_____
		6.	Eminent domain	6.	_____
5.	A tort that consists of a communication that injures a person's reputation.	7.	Defamation	7.	_____
6.	The right to a fair hearing (trial) before the government can deprive a person of life, liberty, or property.	8.	Chief Justice	8.	_____
		9.	Procedural due process	9.	_____
7.	The procedure by which a President can be removed from office by Congress.	10.	Equal Protection clause	10.	_____
		11.	Impeachment	11.	_____
8.	The Amendment to the Constitution that protects the right of free speech.	12.	Federal Commerce clause	12.	_____
		13.	Federal fiscal powers	13.	_____
9.	Public law that governs the powers and procedures of administrative agencies.	14.	Judicial review	14.	_____
		15.	First Amendment	15.	_____
		16.	Tenth Amendment		

10.   The guarantee that requires that similarly situated persons be treated the same by governmental actions.

11.   The first ten Amendments to the U.S. Constitution.

12.   The formal procedure by which an administrative agency resolves a case.

13.   The person who has the power to appoint and remove the chief administrator of an agency.

14.   The person who presides over an administrative agency hearing.

15.   The process by which courts determine whether governmental actions conform to the U.S. Constitution.

17.   President

18.   Constitutional Law

19.   Administrative law judge

20.   Adjudication

MULTIPLE CHOICE: Select the alternative which best completes each statement below and write the corresponding letter in the ANSWERS column.

Answers

1.   The source of law which is the "supreme law of the land" is (a) U.S. Supreme Court decisions (b) Federal statutes (c) the U.S. Constitution (d) none of the above.

1. _____

2.   The final arbiter of the constitutionality of any law in the U.S. is (a) the Federal Constitution (b) Congress (c) the President (d) the U.S. Supreme Court.

2. _____

3.   The doctrine that divides the U.S. government into three branches, e.g., executive, legislative, and judicial is the (a) separation of powers principle (b) Bill of Rights (c) Judicial Review (d) Federalist doctrine.

3. _____

4.   Public law consists of all of the following except (a) criminal law (b) tort law (c) constitutional law (d) administrative law.

4. _____

5.   Administrative agencies (a) create more legal rules than Congress (b) adjudicate more controversies than our State and Federal courts (c) have increased in numbers tremendously in the past fifty years (d) all of the above.

5. _____

6.   Administrative agencies do not (a) make rules and regulations (b) create
     statutes (c) enforce the agency's rules (d) adjudicate controversies.

     6. _____

7.   The standard the U.S. Supreme Court uses in determining whether
     legislation satisfies the equal protection guarantee is the (a) strict scrutiny
     test (b) rational relationship test (c) both a and b above (d) none of the
     above.

     7. _____

8.   The equal protection guarantee (a) applies when governmental action
     involves classification of people (b) requires that persons similarly situated
     be treated similarly by the government (c) is included in the Fourteenth
     Amendment to the Constitution (d) all of the above.

     8. _____

9.   Activities of the numerous administrative agencies are referred to as the (a)
     legislative process (b) judicial process (c) administrative process (d) none of
     the above.

     9. _____

10. Procedural due process considers "property" to include (a) real property (b)
     personal property (c) social security payments and food stamps (d) all of
     the above.

     10. _____

11. The branch of the U.S. government that has the power to pardon persons
     convicted of major crimes is the (a) executive branch (b) legislative branch
     (c) judicial branch (d) none of the above.

     11. _____

12. The branch of the U.S. government that has the power to reject executive
     appointments is the (a) executive branch (b) legislative branch (c) judicial
     branch (d) none of the above.

     12. _____

13. The "one person, one vote" rule decided by the U.S. Supreme Court is an
     example of the Court's use of the (a) rational relationship test (b) due
     process test (c) intermediate test (d) strict scrutiny test.

     13. _____

CASE PROBLEMS - SHORT ESSAY ANSWERS: Read each case problem carefully. When
appropriate, answer by stating a Decision for the case and by explaining the rationale - Rule of Law -
relied upon to support your decision.

1.   Explain the reason President Richard Nixon's claim of executive privilege was denied by the U.S.
     Supreme Court resulting in the requirement that certain Presidential tapes be produced and
     ultimately in President Nixon's resignation. [See United States v. Nixon, 418 U.S. 683 (1974).]

     Decision: _____
     _____

     Rule of Law: _____
     _____

2.   The State of Minnesota places an import tax on all foreign cars arriving at its international port

city of Duluth. The Datsun Company of Japan refuses to pay the State tax. If a lawsuit between these parties commences, who would prevail? Explain.

Decision: _____

_____

Rule of Law: _____

_____

3.   Mai Thai Fong has immigrated to the United States. She asks you to explain the separation of powers doctrine, one of the fundamental principles upon which our government is based. What would be your response?

Decision: _____

_____

Rule of Law: _____

_____

4.   The powers of the Federal government are superior to any and all of our fifty states. Yet each State has its own constitution and sovereignty over its own courts and citizens. Which Amendment to the U.S. Constitution expressly grants this right of sovereignty to the states?

Decision: _____

_____

Rule of Law: _____

_____

5.   Explain the strict scrutiny test used by the U.S. Supreme Court in its decision in the Brown v. Board of Education of Topeka case concerning the equal protection guarantee of the Fourteenth Amendment.

Decision: _____

_____

Rule of Law: _____

_____

CHAPTER 4

Criminal Law

SCOPE NOTE

The preceding materials have examined the American legal system from the perspective of civil law usually involving disputes between private individuals. This Chapter undertakes a different approach. That aspect of the American legal process which addresses disruptions of the public interest and society at large, criminal law, is discussed. The significant concepts

EDUCATIONAL OBJECTIVES

1.   Evaluate various policy assumptions underlying American criminal law.

2.   Distinguish tort law from criminal law.

3.   Differentiate civil from criminal procedure.

4.   Identify sources of criminal law.

5.   Explain major classifications of criminal law.

6.   Discuss major, definitional elements to criminal behavior.

7.   Outline prosecutorial burden of proof requisites for various specific crimes.

8.   Explain common defenses to criminal charges.

9.   Discuss criminal procedure.

CHAPTER OUTLINE

A.   Nature of Crimes
    1.   Essential elements – of a crime consists of two elements: the wrongful or overt act and the

criminal intent.

2. Classification - of crimes from the most serious, felony, to misdemeanor to petty crimes.
3. White-collar crime - defined as nonviolent crime involving deceit, corruption, or breach of trust.
  a. Liability of the employer - is imposed upon one person for the acts of another person.
  b. Liability of the corporation - today a corporation may be convicted of a criminal offense and can be punished by a fine.
  c. Computer crime - includes the use of a computer to steal money or services.
  d. Racketeering Influenced and Corrupt Organizations Act - its purpose is to stop the infiltration by organized crime into legitimate business.

B. Offenses Against the Person
 1. Homicide - the unlawful taking of another's life.
  a. Murder - the killing of another with malice aforethought.
  b. Manslaughter - the killing of another without malice aforethought.
 2. Assault and battery - are two distinct crimes although the term assault is frequently used in criminal law to cover both crimes.

C. Offenses Against Property
 1. Larceny - is the trespassory taking and carrying away of personal property of another with the intent to deprive the victim permanently of the goods.
 2. Embezzlement - is the improper taking of another's property by one who was in lawful possession of it.
 3. False pretenses - is a crime enacted to close a loophole in the requirements of larceny.
 4. Robbery - is a larceny in which the property is forceably taken from the victim.
 5. Extortion and bribery - extortion is blackmail while bribery is the offer of money or property to a public official to influence a decision by the official.
 6. Burglary - according to modern law, is an entry into a building with the intent to commit a felony.
 7. Forgery - is the intentional falsification of a document to defraud another person.
 8. Bad checks - is knowingly writing a check with insufficient funds in the account to cover the check.

D. Criminal Defenses
 1. Defense of person or property
  a. Self-defense - the right to use force to protect oneself.
  b. Defense of another - the use of reasonable force in defense of another believed to be in immediate danger of unlawful bodily harm.
  c. Defense of property - the use of reasonable force to protect one's property.
 2. Incapacity
  a. Insanity - the traditional test for insanity is the M'Naghten test.
  b. Infancy - minors under eighteen are brought before a juvenile court, not an adult criminal court.
  c. Intoxication - the majority position is that voluntary intoxication is not a defense.
 3. Other defenses
  a. Duress - is a valid defense to criminal conduct other than murder.
  b. Mistake of fact - an honest and reasonable mistake may justify the defendant's conduct.
  c. Entrapment - arises when a law officer induces a person to commit a crime when that person would not have done so otherwise.

E. Criminal Procedure
 1. Steps in criminal prosecution.

2.   Fourth Amendment - protects individuals against unreasonable searches and seizures.
3.   Fifth Amendment - protects persons against self-incrimination, double jeopardy, and being charged with a capital crime except by grand jury indictment.
4.   Sixth Amendment - provides the accused with a speedy and public jury trial and the right to counsel for her defense.

TRUE-FALSE: Circle true or false.

Answers

T   F   1.   The standard the government has to prove the defendant guilty of a crime is "guilt by a preponderance of the evidence."

T   F   2.   The same act (conduct) may constitute both a tort and a crime.

T   F   3.   The distinction between the crimes of larceny and false pretenses is that in the latter possession of the personal property taken is voluntarily transferred to the thief.

T   F   4.   All jurisdictions (States), except Nevada, have passed legislation making it a crime to issue bad checks.

T   F   5.   All criminal law defenses are valid against both crimes against the person and crimes against property.

T   F   6.   A "bench trial" is a trial tried by a judge without a jury.

T   F   7.   In order to obtain a search warrant, the judge or magistrate issuing the warrant must believe that probable cause exists that the search will reveal evidence of a crime.

T   F   8.   Civil law is private law; criminal law is public law.

T   F   9.   Computer crime is an example of one type of white-collar crime.

T   F   10. Extortion and bribery are identical crimes.

T   F   11. Federal crimes are exclusively covered by statutory law.

T   F   12. A corporation cannot be found guilty of a crime because it cannot be imprisoned.

KEY TERMS - MATCHING EXERCISE: Select the term which best completes each statement below and write the corresponding number in the ANSWERS column.

Column I	Column II	Answers
1. The unlawful killing of another without malice aforethought.	1. White-collar crime	1. _____

2.   The crime for which duress is not a valid defense.

3.   The criminal intent required for a crime to exist.

4.   The type or classification of crime punishable by death or imprisonment.

5.   The type of nonviolent crime involving deceit or breach of trust.

6.   The right to a fair hearing (trial) before the government can deprive a person of life, liberty, or property.

7.   The wrongful act which is a necessary element of a crime.

8.   The traditional and majority test for insanity when it is being used as a defense in a criminal case.

9.   The kind of force that is generally never reasonable to use to protect property.

10.   A grand jury's decision to indict the defendant in a criminal case.

11.   The formal accusation of a crime brought by a county prosecutor.

12.   The hearing at which the accused is informed of the charge against him and a plea is entered.

13.   A document that allows a legal search of a person's home.

2.   Search warrant

3.   Non-deadly force

4.   True bill

5.   Murder

6.   Manslaughter

7.   Defamation

8.   Deadly force

9.   Due process

10.   Equal Protection

11.   Actus reus

12.   Mens rea

13.   Felony

14.   Misdemeanor

15.   M'Naghten test

16.   Durham test

17.   Arraignment

18.   Entrapment

19.   Duress

20.   Information

2. _____

3. _____

4. _____

5. _____

6. _____

7. _____

8. _____

9. _____

10. _____

11. _____

12. _____

13. _____

14. _____

15. _____

14.   A criminal defense when a law
        officer induces a person to
        commit a crime that the person
        would have otherwise not
        committed.

15.   A criminal defense in which a
        person is threatened with serious
        bodily harm unless the person
        participates in committing a
        crime.

MULTIPLE CHOICE: Select the alternative which best completes each statement below and write the corresponding letter in the ANSWERS column.

Answers

1.   The amendment to the U.S. Constitution that prohibits double jeopardy in
        criminal cases is the (a) Eighth Amendment (b) Sixth Amendment (c)
        Fourth Amendment (d) Fifth Amendment.   1. _____

2.   Robbery differs from larceny in that the stolen property may be taken (a)
        directly from the victim (b) by force (c) by the threat of deadly force (d)
        all of the above.   2. _____

3.   The purpose of the exclusionary rule is to (a) deter all police activity (b)
        hinder the search for the truth in the case (c) protect individual liberty (d)
        none of the above.   3. _____

4.   The privilege against self-incrimination as guaranteed by the Fifth
        Amendment protects the accused from being forced to (a) testify against
        himself (b) stand in a "line up" for identification purposes (c) provide a   4. _____
        handwriting sample (d) take a blood test.

5.   A search warrant is not necessary (a) to search a person's luggage (b) when
        voluntary consent to search is given (c) to search a person's home (d) all of
        the above.   5. _____

6.   The accused in a serious criminal case (a) is not always entitled to a jury
        trial (b) if found guilty, may request probation (c) if acquitted, must allow
        the State the right to appeal the acquittal to a higher court (d) must be   6. _____
        proven guilty by a preponderance of the evidence.

7.   Punishment for criminal conduct does not include (a) fines (b)
        imprisonment (c) a lawsuit for money damages (d) the death penalty.   7. _____

8. The following persons may lack the capacity to form the criminal intent to commit a crime (a) minors (b) insane persons (c) intoxicated persons (d) all of the above.   8. _____

9. The amendment of the U.S. Constitution that protects individuals from unreasonable searches and seizures is the (a) First Amendment (b) Second Amendment (c) Fourth Amendment (d) Fifth Amendment.   9. _____

10. The U.S. Supreme Court has ruled that juries deciding criminal cases (a) may consist of twelve jurors (b) may consist of six jurors (c) need not reach unanimous verdicts in all State court cases (d) all of the above.   10. _____

11. The membership of a grand jury consists of not more than (a) six persons (b) twelve persons (c) twenty-three persons (d) none of the above.   11. _____

12. Criminal liability imposed upon one person for the criminal acts of another person is (a) computer crime (b) racketeering (c) voluntary manslaughter (d) vicarious liability.   12. _____

13. The amendment to the U.S. Constitution that provides for the assistance of counsel (an attorney) for the person accused of a crime is the (a) Fourth Amendment (b) Fifth Amendment (c) Sixth Amendment (d) Eighth   13. _____
Amendment.

CASE PROBLEMS - SHORT ESSAY ANSWERS: Read each case problem carefully. When appropriate, answer by stating a Decision for the case and by explaining the rationale - Rule of Law - relied upon to support your decision.

1. Allen Johnson, an undercover F.B.I. agent, convinces Melvin Howard, an industrialist whose company is in financial trouble, to participate in the purchase and re-sale of narcotics. If Melvin is arrested, what defense would you recommend for him? Explain.

   Decision: _____
   _____
   Rule of Law: _____
   _____

2. Carol Olson is convicted by a six member jury of the crime of embezzlement from the bank in which she is employed. Carol appeals her conviction on the grounds she was wrongfully deprived of a jury of twelve persons in violation of her Constitutional rights. What result? Explain.

   Decision: _____
   _____
   Rule of Law: _____
   _____

3. Karla Johnson is arrested for first degree murder in her home through the use of an arrest warrant together with an "information" of the charge at the time of the arrest. What other method could

be used to initiate prosecution of Karla for this crime? Explain.

Decision: _____

Rule of Law: _____

_____

4.   Howard Jensen has a party in which he serves all the liquor. Howard drinks to excess and
      becomes intoxicated. While driving to the local liquor store for more beer, Howard "runs" a red
      light and smashes into another car killing one of its passengers. When arrested and charged with a
      crime, Howard, as a defense, pleads that his intoxication made it impossible for him to form the
      necessary criminal intent required of a crime and therefore he should not be found guilty. How
      would this case be decided?

Decision: _____

Rule of Law: _____

_____

5.   In a famous Supreme Court case, Gideon v. Wainwright, 372 U.S. 335, 9 L. Ed. 799 (1963), the
      defendant, Gideon, charged with the commission of a felony, was unable to afford a lawyer for
      his defense, and the trial court denied his request to appoint a lawyer for him. Gideon was found
      guilty, and he was imprisoned. On appeal, the U.S. Supreme Court reversed the conviction and
      ordered his release. On what grounds did the Court make its decision?

Decision: _____

Rule of Law: _____

_____

Intentional Torts

SCOPE NOTE

Causing harm to people and property, apart from possible criminal implications, can often result in the injured party (victim) having a right of civil recovery against the wrongdoer. Torts is that area of the law which concerns injury causing conduct and compensation to a victim. The vocabulary and principles of private, civil wrongs, stemming from breaches of legal duties to act without danger to others, is focused on in Chapters Five and Six. Because tort law is essentially an exercise in loss-shifting (the recovering victim transfers to the injury-causer the financial liability for the loss suffered through the injury), our attention will be directed towards those types of acts which trigger the loss-shifting mechanism: deliberate, intentional harm to others, discussed in Chapters Five and Six; careless conduct resulting in accidental harm and the concept of "strict liability," both focused on in Chapter Six.

Chapter Five introduces the terminology and basic concepts of intentional torts. What various acts constitute the deliberate injuring of another person or their property? What excuses or justifications for such conduct are recognized that absolve the actor from liability? These and other concerns are addressed in relation to the overriding purpose of tort law, compensation
to the injured party.

EDUCATIONAL OBJECTIVES

1.   Be familiar with the range of conflicts brought to tort law for resolution.

2.   Differentiate among the various legal/equitable remedies available to a tort victim.

3.   Identify and distinguish among the various acts recognized as intentional harm to business, property or person.

4.   Discuss the plaintiff's burden of proof in the context of intentional torts.

5.   Enumerate the various valid defenses and their respective definitional elements associated with an intentional tort theory of recovery.

CHAPTER OUTLINE

I.   Intent
      A.   Injury or Damage to the Person
            1.   Battery - an intentional infliction of harmful or offensive bodily contact.
            2.   Assault - intentional conduct toward another person that puts him in fear of immediate bodily harm.
            3.   False imprisonment - or false arrest is the intentional confining of a person against her will.
            4.   Malicious prosecution - wrongful use of civil or criminal proceedings without probable cause.
            5.   Infliction of emotional distress - atrocious, intolerable conduct beyond all bounds of decency.
            6.   Defamation - false communication that injures a person's reputation.
                  a.   Libel and slander - written and spoken defamation.
                  b.   Defenses - truth and privilege are defenses to defamation.
            7.   Invasion of privacy - consists of four distinct torts.
                  a.   Appropriation - of a person's name or likeness.
                  b.   Intrusion - unreasonable and offensive interference with the seclusion of another.
                  c.   Public disclosure of private facts - offensive publicity of private information.
                  d.   False light - unreasonable publicity which places another in a false light in the public eye.
                  e.   Defenses - absolute, conditional, and constitutional privilege.
      B.   Interference with Property Rights
            1.   Real property - land and anything attached to it such as buildings, trees, and minerals.
                  a.   Trespass - entering on, remaining on, and failing to leave land in possession of another.
                  b.   Nuisance - a non-trespassory invasion of another's interest in the use and enjoyment of land.
            2.   Personal property - or chattel is any property other than an interest in land.
                  a.   Trespass - an intentional taking or unauthorized use of another's personal property.
                  b.   Conversion - control over another's property that justly requires the payment of full value for the property.
      C.   Interference with Economic Interests
            1.   Interference with contractual relations - intentional interference with the performance of another's contract with a third person.
            2.   Disparagement - publication of false statements about the title or quality of another's property or products.
            3.   Fraudulent misrepresentation - a misrepresentation of fact, opinion, or law to induce another to act or to refrain from action.
II.   Defenses to Intentional Torts
      A.   Consent - willingness that an act shall occur that negates the wrongfulness of the act.
            1.   Exceeding consent - is limited to conduct to which the plaintiff consents.
            2.   Consent to a criminal act - may or may not be a valid defense.
      B.   Privilege
            1.   Self-defense - action taken to prevent harm to oneself.
            2.   Defense of others - action taken to prevent harm to another.

3.   Defense of property - reasonable force, not intended or likely to cause death or serious bodily harm, to protect real or personal property.

TRUE-FALSE: Circle true or false.

Answers

T   F   1.   A tort is a private wrong generally resulting in personal injury or in property damage or destruction.

T   F   2.   Battery is the threat of bodily harm by the tortfeasor.

T   F   3.   An example of the tort of emotional distress is rude and abusive language.

T   F   4.   An obvious defense to the tort of trespass is that the trespasser mistakenly was unaware of the trespassing.

T   F   5.   Any force by an owner, including deadly force, can be used to prevent a trespass across the owner's property.

T   F   6.   One defense to the commission of an intentional tort is the plaintiff's consent to the defendant's conduct.

T   F   7.   If the accused in a criminal case is found not guilty, that person can sue the public prosecutor for malicious prosecution.

T   F   8.   Like other subject matter areas of the law such as contracts, tort law is static, i.e., it never changes.

T   F   9.   Truth is the only complete defense to a lawsuit for defamation.

T   F   10.   The privilege of self-defense to prevent harm to oneself may exist whether or not danger actually exists.

T   F   11.   Tort law is primarily based upon common law.

T   F   12.   The law protects the rights of the possessor of real property to its exclusive use and quiet enjoyment.

KEY TERMS - MATCHING EXERCISE: Select the term which best completes each statement below and write the corresponding number in the ANSWERS column.

Column I	Column II	Answers
1. The kind of conduct that furthers an important social interest and creates immunity from tort liability.	1. Tort	1. _____
	2. Slander	2. _____

2. A wrongful act causing personal injury or property damage or destruction.

3. A threat to do immediate bodily harm.

4. Interference with a person's right to unrestricted movement without an available alternative exit.

5. An unjust commencement of a civil lawsuit without probable cause and for an improper purpose.

6. Like the defense of truth, this type of privilege protects the defendant from liability for defamation regardless of motive or intent.

7. Another name for personal property.

8. A non-trespassory invasion of another's interest in the use and enjoyment of land.

9. Interference with another's right to the use and enjoyment of personal property.

10. False statements intended to cast doubt upon the quality of another's products.

11. Another name for punitive damages.

12. The type of defamatory communication that is written.

13. The use of the plaintiff's name or photograph for the benefit of the defendant.

14. The type of invasion of privacy that is the unreasonable and highly offensive interference with the solitude of another.

3. Battery   3. _____

4. Assault   4. _____

5. Disparagement   5. _____

6. Chattel   6. _____

7. Privileged   7. _____

8. False Imprisonment   8. _____

                              9. _____

9. Malicious Prosecution   10. _____

10. Conditional Privilege   11. _____

                              12. _____

11. Absolute Privilege   13. _____

12. Nuisance   14. _____

13. Conversion   15. _____

14. Duress

15. Defamation

16. Intrusion

17. Appropriation

18. False light

19. Libel

20. Exemplary

15.   The type of defamatory communi-
      cation that is oral.

MULTIPLE CHOICE: Select the alternative which best completes each statement below and write the corresponding letter in the ANSWERS column.

Answers

1.   Which of the following are responsible for their intentional torts? (a) adults (b) minors (c) incompetent persons (d) all of the above.

1. _____

2.   The tort of defamation includes (a) libel and slander (b) assault and battery (c) trespass and public nuisance (d) all of the above.

2. _____

3.   A person may commit the tort of trespass (a) on land (b) beneath the ground (c) above the surface of the land (d) all of the above.

3. _____

4.   Concerning chattels, the measure of damages (a) for the tort of trespass is the amount of damage for the actual harm to the chattel (b) for the tort of conversion is the full value of the chattel (c) for both trespass and conversion is the amount of damages for the loss of possession of the chattel (d) only a and b above.

4. _____

5.   An example of a tort that is not intentional is (a) defamation (b) negligence (c) invasion of privacy (d) emotional distress.

5. _____

6.   The tort of invasion of privacy does not include (a) the appropriation of a person's name (b) the unreasonable publication of private facts (c) trespassing on another's property (d) entering of another's home uninvited.

6. _____

7.   Interference with the performance of a contract by another may be (a) by the use of physical force (b) by threats (c) by an offer of higher pay for the performer (d) all of the above.

7. _____

8.   Consent to conduct, resulting in damage to the consenter's property but no liability, is valid if made by (a) an adult (b) a minor (c) an incompetent (d) an intoxicated person.

8. _____

9.   The privilege of self-defense exists (a) but not as an act of revenge (b) provided the defendant reasonably believed that it was necessary (c) even if the defendant could avoid the threatened contact by retreating (d) all of the above.

9. _____

10.   A fraudulent misrepresentation that induces another to enter a written agreement could involve a lawsuit within the law of (a) torts (b) contracts (c) both torts and contracts (d) none of the above.

10. _____

11. The type of invasion of privacy that imposes liability for false publicity which places another in a position that is highly offensive is (a) intrusion (b) appropriation (c) false light (d) all of the above.

11. _____

12. Privilege is a defense to intentional torts and it includes (a) defense of property (b) defense of other persons (c) self-defense (d) all of the above.

12. _____

13. Intentional interference with property rights includes the torts of (a) trespass to real or personal property (b) conversion (c) nuisance (d) all of the above.

13. _____

CASE PROBLEMS - SHORT ESSAY ANSWERS: Read each case problem carefully. When appropriate, answer by stating a Decision for the case and by explaining the rationale - Rule of Law - relied upon to support your decision.

1. While playing ice hockey, A knocks B down and continues to slam B's head against the ice. B's right eye is injured, and B sues. A argues that everyone knows hockey is a "violent" sport and that B's consent to play the game discharges any liability of A to B. Who wins? Explain.

Decision: _____

Rule of Law: _____

2. A says to B, "I'm going to beat you up." There is no way B can avoid the fight. A starts the fight. B grabs a rock and smashes A's head with it. A is seriously injured. What kind of tort liability, if any, would B have in this case? Explain.

Decision: _____

Rule of Law: _____

3. A newspaper prints a photograph of A with a caption stating that A has been accused of rape. In fact, the newspaper printed a photograph of the wrong person. Have the torts of defamation and invasion of privacy both been committed? Explain.

Decision: _____

Rule of Law: _____

4. A says to B that C has a venereal disease. A's statement is not true. C learns of A's comment and sues. What tort has been committed? Explain.

Decision: _____

Rule of Law: _____

5.   As a practical joke, A calls B on the phone and tells B that B's child has been hit by a car and is
      in the hospital. B sues A. Who wins? Explain.

      Decision: _____

      _____

      Rule of Law: _____

      _____

Negligence and Strict Liability

SCOPE NOTE

The basic elements associated with recovery to the victim of careless conduct (negligence) or ultra-hazardous behavior (strict liability) are the focus of attention in Chapter Six. What is negligence? How does the law determine whether an accident was unavoidable (no victim recovery) or avoidable (negligence)? What types of behavior fall within the strict liability category? These and other issues developed in Chapter Six close out our discussion of tort law.

EDUCATIONAL OBJECTIVES

1.   Define and discuss the basic elements of negligence.

2.   Distinguish among the various sources of duty of care.

3.   Develop the meaning and significance of the Res Ipsa Loquitur doctrine vis-a-vis the burden of proof of the victim-plaintiff.

4.   Define and explain the importance of proximate causation.

5.   Differentiate among the various defenses to a complaint of negligence.

6.   Enumerate the types of harm falling under strict liability.

7.   Develop the defenses which can be successfully asserted in response to a strict liability complaint.

CHAPTER OUTLINE

I.   Negligence
    A.   Duty of Care
        1.   Reasonable man standard - the degree of care which a reasonable person would exercise in a given situation.

        a.   Children - a child's conduct must conform to that of a child of like age, intelligence and experience.

        b.   Physical disability - a disabled person's conduct must conform to that of a reasonable person under like disability.

        c.   Mental deficiency - a mentally deficient person is held to the reasonable man standard.

        d.   Superior skill or knowledge - professionals must exercise the care and skill of members in good standing within their profession.

        e.   Emergencies - the standard is still the reasonable man but under the emergency circumstances.

        f.   Violation of statute - the reasonable man standard of conduct may be established by statute.

    2.   Duty of affirmative action - generally, no one is required to aid another in peril.

    3.   Special duties of possessors of land

        a.   Duty to trespassers - generally, none.

        b.   Duty to licensees - the possessor of land owes a higher duty of care to licensees than to trespassers.

        c.   Duty to invitees - duty to exercise reasonable care to protect invitees against dangerous conditions.

    4.   Res Ipsa Loquitur - a rule that permits the jury to infer both negligent conduct and causation from the mere occurence of certain types of events.

B.   Proximate Cause

    1.   Causation in fact - the defendant's conduct was the actual cause of the injury.

    2.   Limitations upon causation in fact

        a.   Unforeseeable consequences - may negate the defendant's liability for negligence.

        b.   Superseding cause - an intervening act that relieves the defendant's liability to the plaintiff.

C.   Injury

D.   Defenses to Negligence

    1.   Contributory negligence - both parties contribute to the negligence that causes the harm.

    2.   Comparative negligence - damages are apportioned between the parties in proportion to their degree of negligence.

    3.   Assumption of risk - a plaintiff who voluntarily and knowingly assumes the risk of harm arising from the negligence of the defendant cannot recover from such harm.

II.   Strict Liability

A.   Activities Giving Rise to Strict Liability

    1.   Abnormally dangerous activities - for harm resulting from such activities strict liability is imposed.

    2.   Keeping of animals

        a.   Trespassing animals - owners are strictly liable for harm caused by trespass of their animals.

        b.   Nontrespassing animals - keepers of wild animals are strictly liable for damage they cause.

    3.   Products liability - a form of strict liability upon manufacturers and merchants who sell goods in a defective condition.

B.   Defenses to Strict Liability

    1.   Contributory negligence - is not a defense to strict liability.

2.   Comparative negligence - some States apply this doctrine to products liability cases.

3.   Assumption of risk - is a defense to an action based upon strict liability.

TRUE-FALSE: Circle true or false.

Answers

T   F   1.   The basis of liability for negligence is the failure to exercise reasonable care for the safety of other persons or their property.

T   F   2.   Generally, the burden of proof in a civil action for negligence is on the plaintiff.

T   F   3.   A physically disabled person and a mentally deficient person are held to the standard of conduct of a reasonable man with like disabilities or deficiencies.

T   F   4.   Manufacturers and merchants who sell defective goods that are unreasonably dangerous to a consumer are strictly liable regardless of due care.

T   F   5.   Keepers (owners) of dangerous and domestic animals are strictly liable for the injuries the animals cause only if the keeper is aware that the animals are dangerous.

T   F   6.   Keepers of domestic animals are only liable for the injuries caused by their animal to other people.

T   F   7.   Strict liability refers to a defendant's absolute liability without regard to negligence or intent on the part of the tortfeasor (defendant).

T   F   8.   No one is under an affirmative duty to aid another who is in danger under any circumstances.

T   F   9.   It is possible for a person to be injured by another without the latter having any liability.

T   F   10.   The courts have traditionally allowed recovery for negligently inflicted emotional distress.

T   F   11.   Parents are liable for all of the torts committed by their minor children.

T   F   12.   The reasonable man standard means that a reasonable person is always careful, prudent, and never negligent.

KEY TERMS – MATCHING EXERCISE: Select the term which best completes each statement below and write the corresponding number in the ANSWERS column.

Column I	Column II	Answers

Column I

1. Conduct that falls below the standard established by law for protection of others against unreasonable risk of harm.

2. The term that identifies the dangerous inclination of a domestic animal to cause injury.

3. The doctrine that apportions damages between parties in proportion to the degree (percentage) of fault.

4. A person privileged to enter upon land only with consent of the lawful possessor.

5. The rule that means "the thing speaks for itself."

6. A widely applied test for causation in fact.

7. A standard of conduct involving the duty of care and imposed by law.

8. A plumber who enters a home for the purpose of making repairs.

9. A common law defense available in negligence cases in which the plaintiff and defendant are both at fault and neither can recover damages.

10. A person who enters on the land of another without permission.

11. An invitee who enters the premises to engage in private business.

Column II

1. Res ipsa loquitur
2. Reasonable man
3. Strict liability
4. Licensee
5. Trespasser
6. Negligence
7. Invitee
8. Contributory negligence
9. Products liability
10. Assumption of risk
11. Comparative negligence
12. Act of God
13. Propensity
14. But for rule
15. Proximate case
16. Last clear chance
17. Conversion
18. Substantial factor test
19. Superseding cause
20. Business visitor

Answers

1. _____
2. _____
3. _____
4. _____
5. _____
6. _____
7. _____
8. _____
9. _____
10. _____
11. _____
12. _____
13. _____
14. _____
15. _____

12. An intervening event that may
     relieve the defendant of liability.

13. Another name for absolute
     liability or liability without
     fault.

14. A valid defense to a charge of
     negligence that prohibits the
     plaintiff's recovery because of
     the plaintiff's consent to
     encounter a known danger.

15. A form of strict liability imposed
     on manufacturers who sell de-
     fective goods.

MULTIPLE CHOICE: Select the alternative which best completes each statement below and write the corresponding letter in the ANSWERS column.

Answers

1. Which of the following is not a defense to strict liability? (a) contributory
    negligence (b) comparative negligence (c) assumption of risk (d) all of the
    above.   1. _____

2. The possessor of land owes a duty of care to (a) a child trespasser (b)
    licensees (c) business visitors (d) all of the above.
                                                                                       2. _____

3. Domestic animals that are generally considered safe to mankind include (a)
    cats and dogs (b) horses and sheep (c) cattle (d) all of the above.
                                                                                       3. _____

4. Dangerous animals, whose keepers are held strictly liable for the harm they
    cause, include all of the following except (a) lions (b) bulls (c) monkeys (d)
    raccoons.   4. _____

5. Which of the following is not a defense to a charge of negligence? (a)
    assumption of risk (b) contributory negligence (c) proximate cause (d)
    comparative negligence.   5. _____

6. The reasonable man standard (a) is what a judge or jury determines that a
    reasonable person would have done in specific circumstances (b) requires a
    child who drives a boat or car to be held to the standard of care of a child
    of like age, intelligence and experience under the same circumstances (c)
    does not hold insane persons responsible for their negligent acts (d) all of   6. _____
    the above.

7. Which of the following professional or skilled persons would not be
    required to exercise special care and skill normally possessed by those
    practicing their professions or trade? (a) doctors and attorneys (b) teachers
    and professors (c) carpenters and electricians (d) architects and engineers.   7. _____

8.   The duty of affirmative action is not imposed on a defendant to aid or protect the plaintiff if the parties are (a) parent and child (b) employer and employee (c) best friends and neighbors (d) innkeeper and guest.   8. _____

9.   Strict liability will be imposed regardless of intent or negligence for (a) crop dusting that kills other life (b) faulty merchandise that results in injury (c) the use of dynamite in populated areas (d) all of the above.   9. _____

10.   If the plaintiff is aware of the dangerous or negligent conduct of the defendant and ignores it and is subsequently injured, the plaintiff cannot recover damages due to the doctrine of (a) contributory negligence (b) comparative negligence (c) assumption of risk (d) last clear chance.   10. _____

11.   A parent is responsible for the torts of her minor children if the parent (a) authorizes the tort (b) ratifies the tort (c) does not properly control her child's behavior (d) all of the above.   11. _____

12.   The possessor of land owes a duty of care to (a) licensees (b) child trespassers (c) business visitors (d) all of the above.   12. _____

13.   Which of the following is not a factor that imposes limitations on the causal connection between the defendant's negligence and the plaintiff's injury? (a) foreseeable events (b) superseding causes (c) unforeseeable consequences (d) none of the above.   13. _____

CASE PROBLEMS - SHORT ESSAY ANSWERS: Read each case problem carefully.   When appropriate, answer by stating a Decision for the case and by explaining the rationale - Rule of Law - relied upon to support your decision.

1.   While flying her airplane and performing various stunts, Joelene Brady loses control of the plane and crashes into Sarah Johnson's home. Sarah sues. Joelene claims it was an unintentional accident. Who wins? Explain.

       Decision: _____
       _____

       Rule of Law: _____
       _____

2.   Mark Benson is taking care of five-year-old Kathy Walsh while Kathy's mother is in the hospital. Kathy wanders from the house onto a nearby railroad track. Mark sees her on the track, and a train is approaching. To avoid liability, must Mark make an attempt to rescue Kathy at the risk of his own life? Explain.

       Decision: _____
       _____

       Rule of Law: _____
       _____

3.   While crossing a street, Abner and Baker meet in the middle of the street, have an argument, and

begin fighting. Abner knocks Baker down causing him to strike his head on the pavement and rendering him unconscious. Abner walks away. Carol unavoidably runs over the unconscious Baker with her car, seriously injuring him. Was the intervening force (Carol's car striking Baker) a superseding cause that relieves Abner of liability? Explain.

Decision: _____

Rule of Law: _____

_____

4. In a State that has a comparative negligence statute, a jury determines that the plaintiff, Susan, has sustained damages of $50,000 and that the percentages of fault of the parties to the case, Susan and the defendant, Michael, are: plaintiff - 10% negligent; defendant - 90% negligent. What would be Susan's judgment award in damages in this case?

Decision: _____

Rule of Law: _____

_____

5. The Swanberg Soup Company has shipped cases of its soup that are contaminated with botulism food poisoning to its retailers. Matthew purchases a can of the soup, eats some of it, and becomes very sick. Explain the type of liability the company has to Matthew in this case.

Decision: _____

Rule of Law: _____

_____

Introduction to Contracts

SCOPE NOTE

Contracts is an area of law that touches nearly all other branches of business law. Understanding contract law provides a useful foundation for learning and applying principles associated with other specific fields of business law. Chapter Seven focuses on basic concepts of contract law, the various types of binding agreements recognized by courts and important introductory terminology. This knowledge provides a crucial frame of reference for the successful study of the principles and vocabulary which comprise the specific areas of contract law which will occupy our further inquiry into the arena of binding agreements.

EDUCATIONAL OBJECTIVES

1. Discuss the importance of contracts in business.

2. Identify present day controlling sources of contract law.

3. Define what is meant by "contract."

4. Differentiate the various classifications of contracts based on such factors as extent of performance, validity, method of creation and type of use.

5. Enumerate the particular elements which make up a contract.

6. List examples of contract that you have entered into during recent weeks.

CHAPTER OUTLINE

A. Development of the Law of Contracts
    1. Common law - contracts are primarily governed by State common law.
    2. Uniform Commercial Code - governs all sales contracts concerning personal property.
    3. Types of contracts outside the Code - general contract law governs these contracts.
B. Nature of a Contract - the true nature is the relationship between the parties to the contract and

their mutual rights and duties.

C.   Definition of a Contract - a contract is a set of promises which the courts will enforce.

D.   Classification of Contracts

      1.   Express and implied contracts - contracts created either by express language or by conduct of the parties.

      2.   Unilateral and bilateral contracts - contracts created by a promise for an act or by an exchange of promises.

      3.   Void, voidable and unenforceable contracts - contracts classified according to their enforceability.

      4.   Executed and executory contracts - contracts that are completed or unperformed.

      5.   Formal and informal contracts - contracts based upon a particular form or those which are not dependent upon formality for their validity.

E.   Quasi Contracts - are implied-in-law contracts.

F.   Essentials of a Contract - there are four essential elements of a binding contract and each will be discussed in future chapters.

TRUE-FALSE: Circle true or false.

Answers

T   F   1.   Contract law could be referred to as the law of enforceable promises.

T   F   2.   A source of law upon which much of contract law is based is State common law.

T   F   3.   The Uniform Commercial Code (U.C.C.) is the sole source of contract law in the United States today.

T   F   4.   According to the U.C.C., all contracts are promises and all promises are contracts.

T   F   5.   A bilateral contract results from the exchange of one promise for another.

T   F   6.   When it is not clear whether a unilateral or bilateral contract has been formed, a unilateral contract will be presumed by the courts.

T   F   7.   Both the defrauded and fraudulent parties to a contract may declare the contract void.

T   F   8.   A void contract may be enforceable.

T   F   9.   To be executed, a contract must be fully performed by all parties.

T   F   10.   A quasi contract may be considered an obligation imposed by law and based upon equitable principles.

T   F   11.   In a bilateral contract there are always two promisors and two promisees.

T   F   12.   Only written contracts, not oral ones, are binding and enforceable.

KEY TERMS – MATCHING EXERCISE: Select the term which best completes each statement below and write the corresponding number in the ANSWERS column.

	Column I		Column II		Answers
1.	The U.C.C. term for movable, tangible personal property.	1.	Common law	1.	_____
2.	An enforceable contract formed by conduct.	2.	Uniform Commercial Code	2.	_____
3.	A contract created by a promise for a performance.	3.	Voidable	3.	_____
4.	The primary source of contract law.	4.	Bilateral	4.	_____
5.	A contract that either may be avoided or enforced.	5.	Implied	5.	_____
6.	Formal acknowledgements of indebtedness made in court.	6.	Executory	6.	_____
7.	A promise not to do an act.	7.	Recognizances	7.	_____
8.	A contract in which there are one or more unperformed promises.	8.	Forbearance	8.	_____
9.	A contract imposed by law where there has been no expressed assent.	9.	Quasi	9.	_____
10.	The source of contract law governing the sale of personal property.	10.	Assumpsit	10.	_____
11.	The failure to properly perform a contract.	11.	Void	11.	_____
12.	The person who makes a promise.	12.	Unilateral	12.	_____
13.	The person to whom the promise is made.	13.	Executed	13.	_____
14.	A contract created by an exchange of promises.	14.	Fraudulent	14.	_____
		15.	Goods	15.	_____
		16.	Promisor		
		17.	Formal		
		18.	Breach		
		19.	Informal		
		20.	Promisee		

15.   Simple contracts that do not depend
        upon formality for their legal
        validity.

MULTIPLE CHOICE: Select the alternative which best completes each statement below and write the corresponding letter in the ANSWERS column.

Answers

1.   The U.C.C. modifies contract law and applies to a type of contract
        involving (a) the transfer of title to goods from seller to buyer for a price
        (b) employment contracts (c) contracts for the sale of patents and
        copyrights (d) all of the above.   1. _____

2.   Contracts may be (a) oral (b) written (c) implied from the parties' conduct
        (d) all of the above.   2. _____

3.   An example of a formal contract is (a) a promise under seal (b) a
        negotiable instrument (c) a recognizance (d) all of the above.   3. _____

4.   A says to B, "If you paint my garage, I will pay you one hundred dollars."
        B paints the garage. This creates a (a) bilateral contract (b) unilateral
        contract (c) void contract (d) all of the above.   4. _____

5.   A contract induced by fraud is (a) void (b) express (c) voidable (d)
        unenforceable.   5. _____

6.   An essential element of all contracts is (a) manifestation of mutual assent
        (b) consideration (c) legality of the object (d) all of the above.   6. _____

7.   The party entitled to elect to avoid a contract induced by fraud is called (a)
        a minor (b) the defrauded party (c) the fraudulent party (d) none of the
        above.   7. _____

8.   The law of contracts is also basic to which of the following fields of law
        (a) agency (b) commercial paper (c) sales (d) all of the above.   8. _____

9.   An authoritative reference book which gives an orderly presentation of the
        law of contracts is the (a) Reporter (b) American Law Institute (c)
        Restatement (d) none of the above.   9. _____

10.   The only State that has not adopted all sections of the U.C.C. is (a)
        Minnesota (b) Georgia (c) Louisiana (d) Arizona.   10. _____

11.   General contract law governs all of the following except (a) sales of
        personal property (b) sales of real property (c) insurance contracts (d)
        service contracts.   11. _____

12.   A contract that fails to satisfy the requirements of the Statute of Frauds is
        classified as (a) valid (b) unenforceable (c) void (d) voidable.   12. _____

13.   An oral or written contract in which all the terms have been definitely
       stated and agreed upon by the parties is an (a) informal contract (b)
       implied contract (c) express contract (d) none of the above.   13. _____

CASE PROBLEMS - SHORT ESSAY ANSWERS: Read each case problem carefully.   When
appropriate, answer by stating a Decision for the case and by explaining the rationale - Rule of Law -
relied upon to support your decision.

1.   When Sara became ill, Mary performed housekeeping services for Sara without any agreement that
       Mary be paid. Sara requested the services, and Mary expected to be paid. Sara died. In a lawsuit
       seeking compensation for Mary, the court ruled a contract existed. What kind of contract is it?
       Explain.

       Decision: _____
       _____
       Rule of Law: _____
       _____

2.   Julie plans a summer trip to Europe. Her best friend, Karen, has been accepted to medical school
       in the fall. Karen says, "Julie, while on your trip, if you buy a microscope for me, I will give you
       $100.00." Julie buys the microscope in Europe and returns home. Does a contract exist? Explain.

       Decision: _____
       _____
       Rule of Law: _____
       _____

3.   Barry says to Arnold, "I will sell you my motorcycle for $400." Arnold replies, "O.K." Neither
       party used the word promise in their negotiation. Was a bilateral contract created? Explain.

       Decision: _____
       _____
       Rule of Law: _____
       _____

4.   Michael lied to Joyce about important terms of their contract.   On the basis of Michael's
       statement, Joyce agreed to the terms and signed the contract. How would such a contract be
       classified? Explain.

       Decision: _____
       _____
       Rule of Law: _____
       _____

5.   An employee of Harold's Hardware and Appliances Store delivers a T.V. set to Mary Martin mistakenly believing she had ordered it. Would the hardware store be entitled to the return of the set? Explain the legal concept of contract law involved in this case.

Decision: _____

_____

Rule of Law: _____

_____

CHAPTER 8

Mutual Assent

SCOPE NOTE

An agreement (meeting of the minds) is the basis for a contract. All contracts must be agreements but all agreements are not contracts. The first and most important area of contract study is how the parties to a contract reached an agreement. Meeting of the minds, as a primary factor in creating a legally valid and enforceable agreement, concerns the process by which the parties come to an understanding of the crucial terms which embody an agreement.

EDUCATIONAL OBJECTIVES

1.   Identify the acts which together form an agreement.

2.   Discuss the various requirements for a valid offer and acceptance.

3.   Discuss the types of conduct of the parties and events which bring the life of an offer to an end.

4.   Enumerate the significance of silence at the agreement formation stage.

CHAPTER OUTLINE

I.   Offer
    A.   Essentials of an Offer
        1.   Communication - mutual assent to form a contract requires that the offeree must have knowledge of the offer that was made by the offeror to the offeree.
        2.   Intent - to have legal effect, an offer must manifest an intent to enter into a contract.
            a.   Invitations seeking offers - are not valid offers that can create a contract.
            b.   Objective standard for intent - jokes and promises made in excitement are not offers.
        3.   Definiteness - the terms of a contract must be reasonably certain.
            a.   Open terms under the Code - the Code provides standards by which omitted terms may be determined.

        b.   Output, requirements and exclusive dealings - are enforceable agreements under the Code when based upon the good faith of the parties.

    B.   Duration of Offers

        1.   Lapse of time - an offer will terminate after a reasonable time.

        2.   Revocation - an offer may be revoked any time before it is accepted.

            a.   Option contracts - the offeror is bound to hold open for a specified time.

            b.   Firm offers under the Code - are those made by a merchant in writing and signed.

            c.   Statutory irrevocability - certain offers are irrevocable by statute.

        3.   Rejection - a refusal of the offer terminates it.

        4.   Counter-offer - is a counter-proposal that also terminates the original offer.

        5.   Death or incompetency - of either party terminates the offer.

        6.   Destruction of subject matter - of an offer terminates the offer.

        7.   Subsequent illegality - discharges the obligations of both parties under the contract.

II.   Acceptance

    A.   Definiteness of Acceptance - an acceptance must be positive and unequivocal.

    B.   Effective Moment - a contract is formed when the last act necessary to its formation is done.

        1.   Authorized means - the means expressly authorized by the offeror.

        2.   Unauthorized means - if the medium of communication used by the offeree is unauthorized, it still may be effective.

        3.   Stipulated provisions in the offer - of the means of acceptance must be satisfied.

        4.   Acceptance following a prior rejection - must be received by the offeror prior to the receipt of the rejection.

        5.   Defective acceptances - do not create a contract.

    C.   Mode of Acceptance

        1.   Silence as acceptance - is not generally a valid acceptance.

        2.   Contract formed by conduct - may be accomplished.

        3.   Auction sales - invite offers to buy, but are not themselves offers.

TRUE-FALSE: Circle true or false.

Answers

T   F   1.   One of the essentials of a contract is the agreement between the two or more parties.

T   F   2.   Parties usually manifest their mutual assent by means of an offer and an acceptance.

T   F   3.   An auction sale is a binding offer to sell the property being auctioned.

T   F   4.   It is essential to the contractual relationship that the offeree have knowledge of the offer.

T   F   5.   After rejecting an offer, the offeree no longer has the power to bind the parties by accepting.

T   F   6.   Illegality subsequent to the formation of a contract will discharge the contractual obligations of the parties.

T   F   7.   The acceptance of an offer can create a contract only if the offer was communicated
                              to a specifically named offeree.

T   F   8.   As a general rule, silence on the part of a person to whom an offer is made is
                              considered an acceptance of the offer.

T   F   9.   After an offer has expired, there can be no acceptance of it.

T   F   10.   An authorized means of communicating an acceptance is the method stated by the
                              offeror in the offer or, if none is stated, it is the method used by the offeror.

T   F   11.   Retail prices listed by merchants on items in a clothing or appliance store are not
                              considered offers made by the merchants that a customer may accept.

T   F   12.   The incompetency of either the offeror or the offeree ordinarily terminates an offer.

KEY TERMS - MATCHING EXERCISE: Select the term which best completes each statement below
and write the corresponding number in the ANSWERS column.

	Column I		Column II	Answers
1.	An overt act by the offeree that manifests assent to the terms of the offer.	1.	Offeree	1. _____
2.	An act by the offeree that will terminate the offer yet indicates a willingness to contract.	2.	Offeror	2. _____
		3.	Option	3. _____
3.	Inaction by the offeree that may result in an acceptance under special circumstances.	4.	Mirror Image Rule	4. _____
4.	The person who makes the offer in a contractual dealing.	5.	Definiteness	5. _____
		6.	Revocation	6. _____
5.	A circumstance where one may lack the required intent to form a contract.	7.	Alternative	7. _____
		8.	Firm Offer	8. _____
6.	The person to whom an offer is made.	9.	Inverted Unilateral Contract	9. _____
7.	This term is defined as "honesty in fact in the conduct of the transaction concerned."	10.	Jest	10. _____
		11.	Counter-offer	11. _____
8.	A contract in which the offeror is bound to keep open an offer for a specified time.	12.	Good faith	12. _____
		13.	Auctioneer	13. _____
				14. _____
				15. _____

9.   A contract created by an act for a promise.

10.   No contract exists under common law because similar terms of agreement, contained in printed forms used by both buyers and sellers, are not present.

11.   An agreement of a buyer to purchase the entire output of a seller's factory.

12.   The person who is bound to keep a written offer to buy or sell goods open for up to three months.

13.   The promise to refrain from doing an act.

14.   The withdrawal of an offer that occurs before the offer is accepted.

15.   A contract created by a promise exchanged for an act.

14.   Silence

15.   Acceptance

16.   Exclusive dealing

17.   Invitation

18.   Unilateral contract

19.   Merchant

20.   Forbearance

MULTIPLE CHOICE: Select the alternative which best completes each statement below and write the corresponding letter in the ANSWERS column.

Answers

1.   The terms of an offer may be accepted by (a) spoken words (b) a letter (c) a telegram (d) all of the above.

1. _____

2.   An offer may terminate by (a) revocation (b) rejection (c) death of either party (d) all of the above.

2. _____

3.   A definite contractual proposal requesting a forbearance and made by one person to another is (a) an offer (b) an invitation (c) an acceptance (d) a quasi contract.

3. _____

4.   To create a contract, an offer must (a) be definite and certain (b) be communicated (c) have contractual intent (d) all of the above.

4. _____

5.   When the auctioneer brings the hammer down on the bidding, the result is (a) a withdrawal (b) an offer (c) a manifestation (d) a contract.

5. _____

6.   If the offeror has the power to terminate the offer before acceptance, the offeror has (a) rejection power (b) the power to lapse (c) irrevocable options (d) the power of revocation.

6. _____

7. The manifestation of an unwillingness to accept an offer is called a (a) revocation (b) rejection (c) withdrawal (d) counter-offer.

    7. _____

8. An offer (a) may be a promise for a promise (b) must manifest intent to create a contract (c) that consists of a statement indicating a willingness to offer is not itself a binding offer (d) all of the above.

    8. _____

9. The following is generally effective upon being sent (dispatched): (a) an offer (b) an acceptance (c) a rejection (d) a revocation.

    9. _____

10. The standard the law applies to determine if a manifestation of mutual assent has occurred by the words or acts of the parties is (a) an objective standard (b) a subjective standard (c) a relative standard (d) none of the above.

    10. _____

11. An offer (a) may be a promise for an act (b) may be in the form of an act for a promise (c) requires an offeror and an offeree (d) all of the above.

    11. _____

12. Lapse of time of an offer (a) may terminate the offer (b) will terminate the offer after a reasonable period of time if no time for termination is stated (c) may be for one day if perishable goods are involved (d) all of the above.

    12. _____

13. A counter-offer (a) has no effect on the original offer (b) indicates a total rejection of the original offer (c) operates like a rejection (d) none of the above.

    13. _____

CASE PROBLEMS - SHORT ESSAY ANSWERS: Read each case problem carefully. When appropriate, answer by stating a Decision for the case and by explaining the rationale - Rule of Law - relied upon to support your decision.

1. Sam sent a registered letter to Jerome offering Jerome the exclusive rights to a certain line of goods. Sam requested a reply by registered mail. Jerome telegraphed Sam that he would accept. Sam refused to comply, and Jerome brings suit. Who prevails? Explain.

    Decision: _____

    _____

    Rule of Law: _____

    _____

2. A mailed a box of candy to B, stating that if B wanted to keep the candy, it would cost $5. B never requested the candy. B keeps the candy but refuses to pay. What result?

    Decision: _____

    _____

    Rule of Law: _____

    _____

3. A pays B $1,000 for a one year option to buy five acres of land. Ten months later the value of

the land has doubled, and B suddenly dies. B's executor refuses to honor the option, alleging B's death as a termination of the offer. Who prevails? Explain.

Decision: _____

_____

Rule of Law: _____

_____

4. William, whose child is trapped in his burning house, screams hysterically that he will pay $100,000 to anyone who will save the child. Sharon, a bystander, hears William and, at the risk of her life, rescues the child. Was William's statement an offer? Explain.

Decision: _____

_____

Rule of Law: _____

_____

5. Suppose that A mailed B a letter stating, "I wish I could find someone to buy my cattle for $10,000." B knows that $10,000 is a reasonable price. Therefore, B mails a letter to A stating, "I will buy your cattle for $10,000." Does a contract exist? Explain.

Decision: _____

_____

Rule of Law: _____

_____

CHAPTER 9

Conduct Invalidating Assent

SCOPE NOTE

This Chapter focuses upon factors that distinguish an enforceable contract from a voidable or unenforceable contract due to unfairness/inequality in the manner in which the parties reached their agreement. Contracts which seem on the face to be valid because essential formation elements are apparently present may, however, be voidable as a result of "contaminations" (misconduct of the parties) in the negotiation (agreement formation) process. What are the "wrongful acts" or misdeeds that remove "Reality of Consent" from the meeting of the minds process? What remedies are available to contracting parties when "Reality of Consent" is absent?

EDUCATIONAL OBJECTIVES

1. Define and identify the essential elements of fraud and discuss the consequences of fraud.

2. Differentiate fraud from innocent misrepresentation and discuss the significance of the latter.

3. Define and identify examples of and discuss the differences between duress and undue influence.

4. Distinguish between and discuss the significance of unilateral and bilateral mistakes.

5. Identify situations where a contracting party faces a duty of disclosure and the consequences of failing to meet that duty.

CHAPTER OUTLINE

A. Duress - the law will not enforce any contract induced by improper physical or mental coercion.
B. Undue Influence - is taking unfair advantage of a person by reason of a dominant position based upon a confidential relationship.
C. Fraud
   1. Fraud in the execution - a misrepresentation that deceives the defrauded person as to the nature of the contract.

2. Fraud in the inducement - an intentional misrepresentation of a material fact on which the defrauded person enters the contract in reliance upon the misrepresentation. The five requisite elements of fraud in the inducement are:
   a. False representation
   b. Fact
   c. Materiality
   d. Knowledge of falsity and intention to deceive
   e. Justifiable reliance

D. Non-Fraudulent Misrepresentation - a majority of courts permit a rescission of a contract for negligent or innocent (non-negligent) misrepresentation if all of the remaining elements of fraud are present.

E. Mistake - the understanding or belief that is not in accord with existing fact.
   1. Existence or identity of subject matter - the rule that if no subject matter exists, no contract is created.
   2. Nature of subject matter - the court would allow a rescission due to a mutual mistake of a material fact.
   3. Failure to read document - generally, a party is held to what she signs.
   4. Mistake of law - in the absence of fraud, a party cannot obtain a release from contractual liability on the ground that he did not understand the legal effect of the contract.

TRUE-FALSE: Circle true or false.

T F 1. When undue influence is the issue in a legally challenged contract, the law presumes that advantage was taken by the dominant party.

T F 2. Sellers are allowed some leeway to puff their goods to the public.

T F 3. Forcing a person to create a contract against the person's will is called fraud.

T F 4. All fraudulent contracts are void.

T F 5. Generally, when a person signs a contract without reading it, the person is bound by its terms.

T F 6. Duress is always either a tort or a crime.

T F 7. An example of duress is a threat to sue another for civil damages.

T F 8. Most courts today allow a rescission of a contract even if the false misrepresentation of a material fact which induces the plaintiff to enter the contract is innocently done.

T F 9. If there is a mutual mistake between the parties concerning the existence of the subject matter, the contract may be avoided.

T F 10. If a contracting party makes a mistake as to the value of the subject matter, the court will rescind the contract.

T F 11. To establish fraud the misrepresentation must be known by the fraudulent party to be false and must be made with an intent to deceive.

T   F   12.   As a general rule, silence alone does not constitute fraud.

KEY TERMS - MATCHING EXERCISE: Select the term which best completes each statement below and write the corresponding number in the ANSWERS column.

Column I	Column II	Answers
1. Conduct in which a parent through unfair persuasion induces a child to enter a contract.	1. Materiality	1. _____
	2. Rescission	2. _____
2. A statement by a seller that a car is the best "deal" in town.	3. Mistake of existence	3. _____
		4. _____
3. An element of fraud of sufficient substance to induce reliance in another to enter a contract.	4. Concealment	5. _____
	5. Undue influence	
		6. _____
4. The kind of mistake in which neither party is aware that the goods contracted to sell have been destroyed.	6. Defrauded person	7. _____
	7. Opinion	
		8. _____
5. A defense for failure to read a contract.	8. Mistake of law	9. _____
	9. Fiduciary	
6. The kind of mistake for which courts will not generally grant relief.	10. Duress	10. _____
		11. _____
7. The remedy that returns the parties to the status quo by cancelling the contract.	11. Scienter	12. _____
	12. Fraud	
		13. _____
8. The person who is often unduly influenced by a guardian.	13. Voidable	14. _____
	14. Void	
9. One who is in a relationship of trust and confidence with another.	15. Ward	15. _____
10. The classification of a contract induced by improper threats or undue influence.	16. Damages	
	17. Unilateral mistake	
11. The classification of a contract induced by actual physical force.	18. Valid	
	19. Fraudulent person	
12. The element of fraud that consists of knowledge of the falsity of the intentional misrepresentation.	20. Silence	

13.   The innocent person upon whom
        fraud is committed.

14.   The use of improper physical or
        mental coercion to create a
        contract.

15.   The person who commits fraud.

MULTIPLE CHOICE: Select the alternative which best completes each statement below and write the
corresponding letter in the ANSWERS column.
                                                                    Answers

1.   When the courts decide that one should not be held to a contract that was
        not entered into voluntarily, they are speaking of (a) a mistake of the facts
        (b) a mistake of the law (c) duress (d) none of the above.
                                                          1. _____

2.   A creditor could threaten to (a) sue a debtor in civil court (b) criminally
        prosecute the debtor (c) do both of the above (d) do both but be guilty of
        duress in each instance.
                                                          2. _____

3.   A contract obtained by fraud in the inducement is generally (a) void (b)
        voidable (c) enforceable (d) none of the above.
                                                          3. _____

4.   A contract obtained by fraud in the execution is generally (a) void (b)
        voidable (c) mutually enforceable (d) none of the above.
                                                          4. _____

5.   A necessary element for fraud is a false representation concerning (a) a
        material fact (b) an opinion (c) a prediction (d) none of the above.
                                                          5. _____

6.   Generally, when a person gives an opinion that later proves to be
        erroneous, the person is liable for (a) fraud (b) duress (c) undue influence
        (d) none of the above.
                                                          6. _____

7.   A seller is obligated to disclose to a buyer (a) all defects concerning the
        subject matter (b) latent defects concerning the subject matter (c) defects
        that would be discovered by an ordinary examination (d) none of the
        above.
                                                          7. _____

8.   The denial of knowledge of a fact which one knows to exist can form the
        basis for (a) concealment (b) fraud (c) conversion (d) all of the above.
                                                          8. _____

9.   The required elements for fraud in the inducement are (a) a false
        representation of a material fact (b) a false representation made with
        knowledge of its falsity and intent to deceive (c) a false misrepresentation
        which is justifiably relied upon (d) all of the above.
                                                          9. _____

10.   An erroneous understanding or an inaccurate belief which if acted upon
        may produce an unfortunate result for the acting party is (a) fraud (b)
        duress (c) undue influence (d) a mistake.
                                                          10. _____

11. Courts will not grant relief from (a) duress (b) fraud (c) a mistake of law
(d) undue influence.   11. _____

12. An example of a confidential relationship in which one party could
unfairly persuade another to create a contract is (a) an attorney and client
(b) a physician and patient (c) a trustee and beneficiary (d) all of the
above.   12. _____

13. A voidable contract is created when (a) one person unduly influences
another (b) an agent breaches her fiduciary duty to her principal (c) there
has been a mutual mistake of a material fact (d) all of the above.   13. _____

CASE PROBLEMS - SHORT ESSAY ANSWERS: Read each case problem carefully.   When
appropriate, answer by stating a Decision for the case and by explaining the rationale - Rule of Law -
relied upon to support your decision.

1. Abner, who is negotiating the sale of his business to Betty, informs Betty that his business made a
$10,000 profit during the last year. Betty tells Abner she will let him know of her decision to buy
in one week. During this week, but before Betty gives her decision, Abner finds a mistake in the
books which shows that he made only $5,000 profit last year. Betty accepts Abner's offer. Betty
now wants to rescind for misrepresentation concerning last year's profit. Can Betty rescind?
Explain.

Decision: _____
_____
Rule of Law: _____
_____

2. X points a gun at Y and orders Y to sign a written contract or be shot. X knows the gun is not
loaded; Y does not. Later, Y repudiates the contract, and X claims the contract exists because the
gun was empty. Does a contract exist? Explain.

Decision: _____
_____
Rule of Law: _____
_____

3. Barney signs a document without reading it.   Later he discovers the document is a written
contract. Since no fraud was involved, Barney claims he had no knowledge that he was signing a
contract and therefore lacked contractual intent. Does a contract exist? Explain.

Decision: _____
_____
Rule of Law: _____
_____

4. Seller, in good faith, informs buyer that the stock of a certain corporation will probably be listed
on the New York Stock Exchange within two weeks. Buyer, relying on this statement, buys the
stock. Can buyer rescind when it is discovered the statement was incorrect? Can buyer sue for

damages?

Decision: _____

_____

Rule of Law: _____

_____

5.   Seller offers to sell buyer 1,000 bushels of potatoes growing on seller's farm. Buyer accepts the offer. The potatoes were destroyed by a flood three hours before the contract was signed. Neither buyer nor seller knew of the flood. Can the buyer recover from the seller, if the seller fails to deliver the potatoes? Explain.

Decision: _____

_____

Rule of Law: _____

_____

CHAPTER 10
Consideration

SCOPE NOTE

Parties bargaining for an exchange of items of value is a central factor in the creation of a contract. Understanding the function and purpose of consideration in the formation of valid, enforceable agreements is crucial. What is legally sufficient consideration? How do courts address the issue of adequacy of consideration? How do "moral consideration" and legal consideration differ? These and other issues associated with consideration are developed in this Chapter.

EDUCATIONAL OBJECTIVES

1. Define and explain the central position occupied by consideration in the formation of a contract.

2. Enumerate the types of acts/promises that constitute legally sufficient consideration.

3. Distinguish between the various tests used to determine legally sufficient consideration.

4. Discuss the meaning and importance of forbearance in the context of consideration.

5. Clarify the doctrine of consideration in debtor-creditor agreements.

6. Point out situations and related rationale where binding agreements exist even without consideration.

CHAPTER OUTLINE

A. Legal Sufficiency
    1. Definition - consideration exchanged for a promise must be either a legal detriment to the promisee or a legal benefit to the promisor.
    2. Unilateral contracts - a promise for an act or forbearance to act.
    3. Bilateral contracts - a promise for a promise.
    4. Adequacy - legal sufficiency has nothing to do with adequacy of consideration.
    5. Mutuality of obligation - both parties to a contract must give consideration for it to be

legally binding.
- a. Illusory promises - the literal terms of a promise impose no obligation on the promisor.
- b. Output and requirement contracts - an agreement to sell the entire production of a seller or to purchase all the materials of a particular kind.
- c. Exclusive dealing contracts - a manufacturer grants an exclusive franchise to a distributor to sell its goods in a designated area.
- d. Conditional contracts - a contract does not exist until a specific event occurs.
6. Pre-existing public obligation - such a duty is not consideration.
7. Pre-existing contractual obligation - also is not consideration.
- a. Modification of a pre-existing contract - must be supported by mutual consideration.
- b. Settlement of an undisputed debt - is not legally sufficient and thus is not consideration.
- c. Settlement of a disputed debt - acceptance of the lesser amount discharges the debt.
- d. Substituted contracts distinguished - such contracts are valid and discharge the original contract.
B. Bargained for Exchange
1. Past consideration - is no consideration and unenforceable.
2. Moral obligation - is no consideration and unenforceable.
3. Third parties - may be consideration if the promisor requests the benefit be given to a third person.
C. Contracts Without Consideration
1. Promise to pay debt barred by the Statute of Limitations - an action to enforce a debt must be initiated within a set time period after the debt was due.
2. Promise to pay debt discharged in bankruptcy - another exception to the requirement of consideration if allowed by the Bankruptcy Act.
3. Promissory estoppel - if reliance on a promise occurs, the promisor is prohibited from denying the promise.
4. Contracts under seal - a formal contract.
- a. Renunciation - a written and signed waiver that can discharge a contract without consideration.
- b. Firm offer - a written offer signed by a merchant to buy or sell goods is not revocable for lack of consideration during the time stated that it is open, not to exceed three months.

TRUE-FALSE: Circle true or false.

Answers

T   F   1. Consideration is basically whatever is given in exchange for something else.

T   F   2. The central idea behind consideration is that the contracting parties have entered into a bargained exchange with one another.

T   F   3. Valid consideration may exist even though the promises of both parties to a contract are not legally sufficient.

T   F   4. Legal sufficiency is equivalent to adequacy of consideration.

T   F   5.   A legal detriment to you may be nothing more than attending a college, at the request of another, that you might not have attended otherwise.

T   F   6.   Past consideration is not valid consideration, therefore, no contract exists.

T   F   7.   An exchange of the offeror's promise for the offeree's forbearance is consideration.

T   F   8.   A new promise of an obligor to perform a pre-existing contractual duty is a legal detriment.

T   F   9.   Promises to purchase as much of an item as one may want or desire are generally upheld.

T   F   10.   If, before maturity of a debt, the creditor accepts from the debtor a lesser sum offered in full satisfaction, the entire debt will be cancelled.

T   F   11.   Under the Uniform Commercial Code, a contract for the sale of goods can be effectively modified by the parties without new consideration so long as the modification was intended and in good faith.

T   F   12.   A promise made to satisfy a pre-existing moral obligation does constitute valid consideration.

KEY TERMS - MATCHING EXERCISE: Select the term which best completes each statement below and write the corresponding number in the ANSWERS column.

Column I	Column II	Answers
1. A debt that is certain as to the monetary amount.	1. Disputed debt	1. _____
	2. New promise	2. _____
2. One way in which the Statute of Limitations time period may be extended.	3. Charitable subscriptions	3. _____
		4. _____
3. Although technically a gift, courts generally rule such promises are binding.	4. Legal sufficiency	
	5. Illusory promise	5. _____
4. The result when a promisee takes definite and substantial action in reliance on the promisor's promise.	6. Requirements contract	6. _____
		7. _____
	7. Legal detriment	8. _____
5. Doing something you are under no prior legal obligation to do.	8. Legal benefit	9. _____
		10. _____

6. The test for consideration which
    is not dependent on the adequacy
    of the consideration.

7. A promise that is so indefinite
    no obligation is imposed on the
    promisor.

8. An agreement that affords sellers
    an assured market for all their
    goods.

9. An agreement to purchase all the
    materials of a particular kind
    that the purchaser needs.

10. A promise to pay the previous
    debts of an elderly parent is an
    example of this unenforceable
    promise.

11. A contested obligation to pay
    a sum certain in money.

12. An unenforceable promise made
    on account of something that
    the promisee has already done.

13. Laws that provide a prescribed
    period of time in which actions
    to enforce payment of debts
    must be initiated after the debts
    become due.

14. An example of a formal contract.

15. A claim in a breach of contract
    case that can be discharged
    without consideration by a written
    waiver signed and delivered by the
    aggrieved party.

9. Firm offer

10. A promise to
    satisfy a moral
    obligation

11. Output contract

12. Promissory estoppel

13. Undisputed debt

14. Contract under seal

15. Consideration

16. Statute of Limitations

17. Bankruptcy

18. Renunciation

19. Statute of Frauds

20. Past consideration

11. _____

12. _____

13. _____

14. _____

15. _____

MULTIPLE CHOICE: Select the alternative which best completes each statement below and write the corresponding letter in the ANSWERS section.

Answers

1. Consideration for a promise may be defined as (a) an act other than a
    promise (b) a forbearance (c) the creation, modification or destruction of a
    legal relation (d) all of the above.

                                                                        1. _____

2.   The receipt by the promisor of that which the promisor had no prior legal
     right to receive is a (a) legal benefit (b) legal detriment (c) contract (d) gift.   2.   _____

3.   An event, the happening of which qualifies the duty of performance of a
     promise, is called a (a) consideration (b) condition (c) gratuitous promise (d)
     none of the above.   3.   _____

4.   The contract created when a promise is exchanged for an act or a
     forbearance to act is a (a) bilateral contract (b) void contract (c) gratuitous
     contract (d) unilateral contract.   4.   _____

5.   The person to whom a promise is made is called the (a) offeree (b)
     promisor (c) promisee (d) donee.   5.   _____

6.   Where the amount of the debt to be paid has not been agreed upon by the
     parties, there is (a) an exclusive dealing (b) an undisputed debt (c) a
     disputed debt (d) none of the above.   6.   _____

7.   A promise made to perform a pre-existing public or contractual obligation
     is generally (a) binding (b) a contract (c) unenforceable (d) none of the
     above.   7.   _____

8.   According to the U.C.C., a binding promise which requires no
     consideration is (a) an agreement made in good faith modifying a contract
     for the sale of goods (b) a written offer to buy or sell goods by a merchant
     during the time the offer is open (c) a written waiver, signed and delivered
     by the aggrieved party, of a claim due to an alleged breach of contract (d)
     all of the above.   8.   _____

9.   A promise which the promisor should reasonably expect to induce action or
     forbearance by the promisee may be binding under the doctrine of (a)
     gratuitous contracts (b) waiver (c) promissory estoppel (d) none of the
     above.   9.   _____

10. An exception to the requirement of consideration is (a) a new promise by a
     debtor to pay a debt dismissed by the Statute of Limitations (b) a promise
     to pay a debt discharged in bankruptcy (c) a promise under seal in some
     States (d) all of the above.   10. _____

11. Which of the following facts operates as a sufficient promise to renew the
     running of the Statute of Limitations?   (a) a voluntary, unqualified
     admission that the debt is owed (b) a partial payment of the debt (c) a
     statement that that Statute will not be used as a defense (d) all of the
     above.   11. _____

12. Contracts under seal (a) are informal contracts (b) require an impression on
     wax to be binding today (c) are required by the Uniform Commercial Code
     to contain seals in all contracts for the sale of goods (d) none of the above.   12. _____

13.   A promise to give a person a present on the person's birthday (a) is a
        contract (b) is a condition (c) lacks consideration (d) none of the above.   13.   _____

CASE PROBLEMS - SHORT ESSAY ANSWERS: Read each case problem carefully.   When
appropriate, answer by stating a Decision for the case and by explaining the rationale - Rule of Law -
relied upon to support your decision.

1.   In early 1984, Mrs. Good signed a pledge to the All Heart Fund for the sum of $25,000. Later,
        she was hardpressed for money and wished to rescind. As attorney for the fund, what could you
        argue?

        Decision: _____

        _____
        Rule of Law: _____

        _____

2.   Samantha fixed Ray's car and tendered a bill of $75.00. Ray, in good faith, disputed the debt and
        returned $60.00 by check to Samantha stating on the check, "payment in full." Samantha cashed
        the check and months later sued for the $15.00. What result?

        Decision: _____

        _____
        Rule of Law: _____

        _____

3.   Amy sells a piano to Betty for $1,000. The next day, Betty asks Amy to guarantee (warrant) the
        condition of the piano, and Amy agrees. How would this case be decided by the U.C.C.?
        Explain.

        Decision: _____

        _____
        Rule of Law: _____

        _____

4.   If Mary saves the life of Bill's son, and Bill, in a moment of gratitude, tells Mary he will pay her
        $5,000 for her heroism, can Mary demand the $5,000 in a court of law? Explain.

        Decision: _____

        _____
        Rule of Law: _____

        _____

5.   William's uncle, Ben, promises William that if he does not drink or smoke until he is 30, Ben will
        pay William $10,000. William fulfills his part of the agreement. Ben refuses to pay. What right
        does William have?

        Decision: _____

        _____
        Rule of Law: _____

        _____

CHAPTER 11

Illegal Bargains

SCOPE NOTE

A valid, binding agreement must contain acts and promises which are legal. Illegal acts and promises generally make an agreement void. Validity of subject matter, as an essential element of a contract, is discussed in this Chapter in terms of the types of restricted/unlawful acts and promises that invalidate an agreement as well as the remedial consequences of such illegality.

EDUCATIONAL OBJECTIVES

1. Define and give examples of "invalid subject matter."

2. Enumerate different classes of illegal agreements.

3. Discuss the relationship between illegality and divisible contracts.

4. Describe how types of illegality influence the availability of remedies.

5. Give examples of how illegality of bargain varies among states.

CHAPTER OUTLINE

A. Violations of Statutes
    1. Licensing statutes - may be regulatory to protect the public from unqualified persons or merely for the purpose of raising revenue.
    2. Gambling statutes - are generally not enforceable with some exceptions.
    3. Sunday statutes - Blue laws which prohibit certain types of commercial activity on Sundays.
    4. Usury statutes - laws that establish a maximum rate of permissible interest on contract loans.
B. Violations of Public Policy
    1. Tortious conduct - a promise to commit a tort is unenforceable on public policy grounds.
    2. Common law restraint of trade - made such contracts illegal.
        a. Sale of a business - today if restraints covering territory and time are reasonable, they are allowed.

        b.   Employment contracts - not to compete may be allowed if reasonable and necessary.
    3.   Obstructing the administration of justice - such agreements are illegal.
    4.   Corrupting public officials - also illegal and unenforceable.
    5.   Exculpatory clauses - a clause that excuses one party from liability for her tortious conduct is usually unenforceable.
    6.   Unconscionable contracts - the Code and Restatement deny enforcement to such contracts.

C.   Effect of Illegality
    1.   Unenforceability - if an agreement is illegal neither party can successfully sue and recover.
    2.   Exceptions
        a.   Party withdrawing before performance - can recover.
        b.   Party protected by statute - can recover.
        c.   Party not equally at fault - can recover.
        d.   Party ignorant of facts making bargain illegal - can recover.
        e.   Partial illegality - provides two possibilities: either the contract is wholly unenforceable or only the illegal part of the contract will be unenforceable.

TRUE-FALSE: Circle true or false.

Answers

T   F   1.   The term "illegal bargain" is directly equivalent to "illegal contract."

T   F   2.   A bargain is "illegal" when its formation or performance is criminal or tortious or opposed to public policy.

T   F   3.   One who has practiced a trade in violation of a regulatory statute will normally be able to collect a fee for services.

T   F   4.   A revenue measure seeks to protect the public against the incompetent or unqualified practitioner.

T   F   5.   Normally, the courts have refused to recognize the enforcement of a gambling contract.

T   F   6.   At common law, a valid contract could be made on Sunday.

T   F   7.   A "usury law" will protect the borrower by providing for a minimum interest rate.

T   F   8.   At common law, any restraint upon an individual's right to exercise a trade was illegal and void.

T   F   9.   An agreement by a candidate for public office to make a certain appointment after winning an election is legal.

T   F   10.   In all cases, the entire agreement is void if any part of the promise (agreement) is illegal.

T   F   11.   A promise by an employer not to press criminal charges against an embezzling employee who restores the stolen funds is enforceable.

T   F   12.   A seller's "time-price differential" is not subject to usury statute regulation in the absence of specific legislation.

KEY TERMS - MATCHING EXERCISE: Select the term which best completes each statement below and write the corresponding number in the ANSWERS column.

	Column I		Column II		Answers
1.	A contract term that excuses one party from liability for that person's own negligence.	1.	Revenue measure	1.	_____
		2.	Lotteries	2.	_____
2.	A typical restraint which usually accompanies the sale of a business.	3.	Injunction	3.	_____
		4.	Time-price differential	4.	_____
3.	A decision by courts that upholds the reasonable restrictions in a contract but deletes the un-reasonable ones.			5.	_____
		5.	"Public policy"		
		6.	Usury law	6.	_____
4.	A statute that historically pro-tected a borrower of money from excessive interest charges on the loan.	7.	"Blue-pencil" rule	7.	_____
		8.	"Blue Sky Law"	8.	_____
		9.	Exculpatory clause	9.	_____
5.	A statute that prohibits the sale of unregistered securities.	10.	An agreement not to compete	10.	_____
6.	A law commonly applied to the professions of law, medicine, and dentistry.	11.	Regulatory measure	11.	_____
		12.	Licensing statute	12.	_____
7.	A form of gambling that, if permitted at all, is usually state regulated and operated.	13.	Unenforceable	13.	_____
				14.	_____
8.	Statutes that prohibit certain types of commercial activity on Sunday.	14.	Blue laws	15.	_____
		15.	Unconscionable		
9.	The rationale used by a court that may allow a statute to reach beyond its stated bounds.	16.	Reasonable		
		17.	Forbearance		
10.	A contract of sale, the terms of which are too harsh, unfair or unjust.	18.	Criminal conduct		
		19.	Employment contracts		
		20.	Garnishment		

11. A measure designed for the pro-
    tection of the public against
    unqualified persons.

12. The type of restraint of trade
    that is enforceable.

13. A court order prohibiting an
    employee from competing with her
    former employer in a described
    area for a given time.

14. The agreement managers are often
    required to sign restraining them
    from competing with their employers
    during the time of their employment.

15. A measure regarded as a taxing
    measure.

MULTIPLE CHOICE: Select the alternative which best completes each statement below and write the corresponding letter in the ANSWERS column.

Answers

1. "Blue Laws" are State statutes which (a) follow the common law rule that a valid contract can be made on Sunday (b) prohibit certain types of commercial activity on Sunday (c) prohibit acts of "necessity" or "charity" from being performed on Sunday (d) none of the above.

    1. _____

2. A common example of a licensing statute would be one (a) prohibiting larceny (b) prohibiting forgery (c) requiring professional people to register (d) all of the above.

    2. _____

3. A statute that requires the licensing of plumbers but does not establish standards of competence would be a (a) revenue statute (b) criminal statute (c) regulatory statute (d) usury statute.

    3. _____

4. A scheme for the distribution of property by chance among persons who have paid or agreed to pay a valuable consideration for the chance is a (a) usury loan (b) gambling statute (c) lottery (d) all of the above.

    4. _____

5.   A statute establishing a maximum rate of permissable interest is a (a) Sunday statute (b) gambling statute (c) usury law (d) revenue statute.   5. _____

6.   To find a transaction usurious, the courts have traditionally required the following factor(s) (a) a loan or forbearance (b) money which is repayable absolutely (c) an interest charge exacted in excess of the interest rate allowed by law (d) all of the above.   6. _____

7.   In a loan situation, ordinary expenses by the lender which are permissible and therefore are not considered in determining the issue of usury include (a) costs of examining title (b) investigating the credit rating of the borrower (c) drawing necessary documents and inspecting the property (d) all of the above.   7. _____

8.   The usual method by which an employer seeks to enforce a convenant not to compete by a former employee is (a) specific performance (b) rescission of the employment contract (c) an injunction (d) none of the above.   8. _____

9.   If a seller takes unfair advantage of a buyer in an unequal bargaining position and extorts an exorbitant price for the purchased goods, the contract is a(an) (a) gambling contract (b) usury contract (c) exculpatory contract (d) unconscionable contract.   9. _____

10.   The typical restraint of trade could occur in a situation such as a (a) sale of a business, including the good will (b) sale of merchandise (c) sale of a covenant (d) none of the above.   10. _____

11.   The classification of an agreement to commit a tort or a crime is (a) valid (b) voidable (c) unenforceable (d) none of the above.   11. _____

12.   Generally, when an agreement is illegal (a) neither party can win a lawsuit against the other for breach (b) neither party can recover damages for any services rendered (c) the court will leave the parties where it finds them (d) all of the above.   12. _____

13.   The type of reasonable restraint on the seller of a business that a court will enforce is a restraint that covers (a) time (b) territory (c) both time and territory (d) none of the above.   13. _____

CASE PROBLEMS - SHORT ESSAY ANSWERS: Read each case problem carefully. When appropriate, answer by stating a Decision for the case and by explaining the rationale - Rule of Law - relied upon to support your decision.

1.   The maximum rate of interest in state Z is 8%. The legal rate is 6%. If A loans B $1,000 and the parties agree that B is to pay $72.00 as interest each year ($6.00 per month), is the contract usurious? Explain.

         Decision: _____

         _____

Rule of Law: _____
_____

2.   Adam had Barbara, a plumber, install a shower in Adam's home. When Adam learned Barbara
     wasn't licensed, he declined to pay. The pertinent statute has the payment of $10.00 as its only
     requirement for a plumber's license. Barbara sues. Decide and discuss.

     Decision: _____
     _____
     Rule of Law: _____
     _____

3.   After searching three weeks for an apartment to rent, Abby finds one suitable for her family.
     Daniel, the landlord, adds to the lease agreement Abby must sign if she wants the apartment, a
     clause stating that he will not be liable for any negligence he might cause while the apartment is
     rented. Is this clause enforceable? Explain.

     Decision: _____
     Rule of Law: _____
     _____

4.   A sold a barber shop to C. The contract called for A not to enter the barber business in the
     county for a period of five years. Two years later, A opened a barber shop across town from C,
     and C sued. Decide and discuss.

     Decision: _____
     Rule of Law: _____
     _____

5.   A contracts with B whereby B is to kill C for $50,000. Although B could be criminally prosecuted
     for this act, B wanted the contract with A enforced. What result?

     Decision: _____
     Rule of Law: _____
     _____

CHAPTER 12

Contractual Capacity

SCOPE NOTE

Another basic requirement of a valid, enforceable contract is capacity -- the ability of a party to make a binding agreement. Various groups of people are deemed to lack such ability, either completely or partially. Who are these persons and what tests are applied to determine when someone possesses or lacks contractual capacity? This is the focus of Chapter Twelve.

EDUCATIONAL OBJECTIVES

1.   Distinguish between classes of persons considered totally incompetent and those who are only partially limited relevant to contractual capacity.

2.   Discuss the rationale underlying excusing certain persons from contractual obligations which they have entered.

3.   Identify minimal obligations ("necessaries") to which incapacitated parties are held.

4.   Understand the significance of and restrictions on affirmance/disaffirmance.

5.   Clarify the consequences of false representations of capacity as they relate to disaffirmance.

CHAPTER OUTLINE

A.   Minors - a person who is not of legal age.
   1.   Liability for necessaries - is liable for the reasonable value of necessaries actually delivered to the minor.
   2.   Liability on contracts - general rule: minor's contracts are voidable at the minor's option.
      a.   Ratification - is binding on the minor but only if it occurs after the minor reaches legal age.
      b.   Disaffirmance - the right of a minor to avoid a contract.
   3.   Liability for misrepresentation of age - majority of States still allow the minor to disaffirm the contract.

4. Liability for tort connected with contract - generally minors are liable for their torts but if the tort is so connected to a contract that a court must enforce both the contract and the tort, the minor in such cases is not liable for the tort.

B. Incompetent Persons - persons who lack mental capacity.
   1. Mental illness or defect - allows the person to make voidable contracts.
   2. Person under guardianship - such a person's contracts are void not voidable.

C. Intoxicated Persons - as a general rule, an inebriated person makes voidable conracts.

TRUE-FALSE: Circle true or false.

Answers

T   F   1. All persons have the capacity to make a valid contract.

T   F   2. Today, almost without exception, a minor's contract is valid once made.

T   F   3. It is conceivable that a court would rule school instruction, such as a college education, a necessary.

T   F   4. A minor has no power to ratify a contract while still a minor.

T   F   5. A minor may not disaffirm a contract after becoming an adult.

T   F   6. Under the U.C.C., personal property conveyed by a minor to a buyer and subsequently reconveyed by that buyer to a third person, e.g., a bona fide purchaser for value, can be recovered by the minor.

T   F   7. In contract law in the majority of the States, when age is misrepresented by a minor, the minor will be bound to the contract.

T   F   8. A mentally incompetent person cannot avoid a contract for necessaries.

T   F   9. As a general rule, if intoxication is voluntary, the intoxicated party may not avoid a contract.

T   F   10. An incompetent person's voidable contracts may not be ratified or disaffirmed even if the person becomes competent.

T   F   11. Ratification of a contract by a minor must be express to be legally binding.

T   F   12. Generally, minors are not liable for their torts.

KEY TERMS - MATCHING EXERCISE: Select the term which best completes each statement below and write the corresponding number in the ANSWERS column.

Column I	Column II	Answers
1. Persons whose property is supervised by court order and whose contracts are void.	1. Torts	1. _____
	2. Disaffirmance	2. _____

2.   Persons who are unable to under-
      stand the nature and effect of
      their acts or unable to act
      reasonably.

3.   The return of property or the
      equivalent of what has been
      received.

4.   The theory under which incompe-
      tent persons and minors are held
      contractually liable.

5.   Acts for which minors have always
      been held liable as a general rule.

6.   An act by a minor that is not
      allowed until majority age when
      a contract involves the conveyance
      of land.

7.   An act that binds the minor to
      the contract only upon reaching
      majority age.

8.   Minors who are basically on their
      own, free from parental control.

9.   The kind of fraud today for which
      some courts are denying dis-
      affirmance by minors.

10.   Those things regarded as necessary
      to maintain oneself in a parti-
      cular station of life.

11.   Items of personal property such
      as boats and T.V. sets that are
      not considered necessities of life.

12.   The classification of most con-
      tracts made by minors.

13.   An infant who has not attained
      legal age.

14.   A person appointed by a court to
      manage the property of an
      incompetent individual.

---

3.   Ratification

4.   "Emancipated"
      minors

5.   Luxury items

6.   Case law

7.   Necessaries

8.   Intoxicated persons

9.   Misrepresentation
      of age

10.   Persons under
      guardianship

11.   Minor

12.   Quasi contract

13.   Convicts

14.   Incompetent
      persons

15.   Restitution

16.   Void

17.   Adult

18.   Ward

19.   Voidable

20.   Guardian

---

3.   _____

4.   _____

5.   _____

6.   _____

7.   _____

8.   _____

9.   _____

10.   _____

11.   _____

12.   _____

13.   _____

14.   _____

15.   _____

15. The classification of a contract
     made by a person who is under
     guardianship by court order.

MULTIPLE CHOICE: Select the alternative which best completes each statement below and write the
corresponding letter in the ANSWERS column.   Answers

1. An item considered a necessity is (a) lodging (b) medicine (c) a textbook
    (d) all of the above.   1. _____

2. Cameras, tape recorders, and the like are usually classified as (a) luxury
    items (b) necessaries (c) professional items (d) none of the above.   2. _____

3. A minor may choose to approve a contract after becoming an adult by (a)
    the payment of money (b) ratification (c) a loan (d) none of the above. 3. _____

4. Under proper circumstances, which of the following would most likely be a
    necessary? (a) new boat (b) T.V. set (c) class ring (d) new suit.   4. _____

5. Which of the following persons does not have limited contractual capacity?
    (a) minors (b) eccentric persons (c) insane persons (d) intoxicated persons. 5. _____

6. Ratification (a) makes the contract valid and binding from the beginning
    (b) is final and cannot be withdrawn (c) must validate the entire contract
    (d) all of the above.   6. _____

7. By the majority view, a minor who wishes to disaffirm an executed
    contract for the sale of a chattel must (a) pay for it (b) simply return it (c)
    return and pay for the use of it (d) return it in the same condtion as it was
    received.   7. _____

8. Based upon the principle of quasi contract, which of the following persons
    is liable for necessaries? (a) minors (b) incompetent persons (c) intoxicated
    persons (d) all of the above.   8. _____

9. Generally, minors are liable for the tort of (a) libel (b) negligence (c)
    assault and battery (d) all of the above.   9. _____

10. Ratification of a contract by an incompetent person can (a) be done at any
    time (b) be done when sane (c) be done only while insane (d) never be
    done.   10. _____

11. An incompetent person may (a) be a person who is mentally ill (b) be a
    person who has a mental defect (c) ratify or disaffirm contracts when the
    person becomes competent (d) all of the above.   11. _____

12. An intoxicated person (a) has contractual capacity (b) makes void contracts
    like a minor (c) makes voidable contracts like an incompetent person (d)
    none of the above.   12. _____

13.   Ratification of a minor's contract may be (a) implied (b) express (c) created
       by continued use of the property (d) all of the above.   13. _____

CASE PROBLEMS - SHORT ESSAY ANSWERS: Read each case problem carefully.   When
appropriate, answer by stating a Decision for the case and by explaining the rationale - Rule of Law -
relied upon to support your decision.

1.   Mary is a minor.   Mary looks like she is over eighteen (majority age) and tells Bob that she is
       twenty years old.   Mary buys a motorcycle from Bob for $300.   After using the motorcycle in a
       race over the weekend, Mary returns it to Bob and demands he return her money on the basis that
       she is, in fact, a minor.   What result?   Explain.

       Decision: _____

       _____

       Rule of Law: _____

       _____

2.   Your friend's brother is unstable and in fact has been judged insane by a court.   He goes out and
       orders $2,000 worth of blue jeans.   The merchant wants to complete the sale.   How would you
       advise your friend?   Explain.

       Decision: _____

       _____

       Rule of Law: _____

       _____

3.   Charlie, at age 20, in a State where one is still a minor at 20, signs a contract to buy a new
       Corvette.   He keeps it until he is 24, when it finally falls apart.   Charlie wishes to disaffirm the
       contract.   Can he?   Explain.

       Decision: _____

       _____

       Rule of Law: _____

       _____

4.   A is intoxicated.   For months B has tried to buy A's Picasso painting, but each time A has refused
       to sell.   B again makes the offer, and A, in his inebriated condition, accepts.   When A becomes
       sober and learns of the contract, A refuses to sell.   B sues.   What result?

       Decision: _____

       _____

       Rule of Law: _____

       _____

5.   Howard, a minor, has just moved into an apartment and is preparing to enter the freshman class at the University. A sales person convinces Howard to sign a contract for the purchase of cooking utensils, e.g., pots and pans. The contract reads that the purchaser (Howard) agrees the utensils are necessaries. Howard wants to disaffirm the contract. How would you advise him? Explain.

Decision: _____

_____

Rule of Law: _____

_____

CHAPTER 13

Contracts in Writing

SCOPE NOTE

Most oral contracts are fully enforceable regardless of their form. Some agreements, however, because of the perceived importance of their subject matter, must be written and signed to be enforceable. This Chapter focuses on the Statute of Frauds and specific provisions of the U.C.C. which dictate those agreements that must be in writing and signed for enforcement. Parties to an otherwise valid, oral agreement that "falls within the Statute of Frauds" will most likely encounter a court refusal to enforce it. Parties entering oral agreements that fall "outside the Statute of Frauds" need not worry about lack of enforcement due to the absence of writing yet they should recognize the advisability of reducing their agreement to a written form to avoid conflict and confusion over the terms, conditions, and interpretations of their contract.

EDUCATIONAL OBJECTIVES

1. Enumerate classes of contracts which must be written and signed to be enforced.

2. Describe the type and extent of writing required to comply with the provisions of the Statute of Frauds.

3. Identify exceptions to the general rule that contracts "within the Statute of Frauds" must be in writing and signed to be enforced.

4. Discuss those agreements that, although not required, should nevertheless be in writing.

5. Define and discuss the Parol Evidence Rule.

6. Distinguish the terms parol, parol evidence, and the Parol Evidence Rule.

7. Enumerate exceptions to the Parol Evidence Rule.

8. Explain the significance and effect of primary and secondary rules of contract interpretation.

CHAPTER OUTLINE

I.   Statute of Frauds
     A.   Contracts Within the Statute of Frauds - include certain oral contracts only.
          1.   Suretyship provision - a promise to a creditor to perform the duties of the debtor.
               a.   Promise must be collateral - a promise that say "I'll pay if the debtor doesn't."
               b.   Main purpose doctrine - an exception to the suretyship provision.
               c.   Promise made to debtor - is not within the statute.
          2.   Executor-administrator provision - a promise to pay personally the debts of the decedent is within the statute.
          3.   Marriage provision - a promise made in consideration of marriage is within the statute.
          4.   Land contract provision - a promise to transfer any interest in land is within the statute.
          5.   One year provision - all contracts that cannot possibly be performed within one year are within the statute.
               a.   The possibility test - can the contract possibly be performed within one year.
               b.   Computation of time - the year runs from the time the agreement is made.
               c.   Full performance by one party - makes the promise of the other party enforceable.
          6.   Sales of goods - the Code provides that a contract for the sale of goods over $500 is not enforceable unless in writing.
          7.   Modification or rescission of contracts within the Statute of Frauds - oral contracts modifying existing contracts are unenforceable but an oral rescission of a written contract may be effective.
     B.   Methods of Compliance
          1.   Writing or memorandum - must comply with the requirements of the Statute of Frauds.
               a.   General contract provisions - the writing must specify the parties, the subject matter, the terms, and it must be signed.
               b.   U.C.C. provisions - are more liberal.
          2.   Other methods of compliance under the U.C.C. - cover the sale of goods.
               a.   Written confirmation - the Code sets requirements for contracts between merchants.
               b.   Admission - the Code permits an oral contract for the sale of goods to be enforced if a party admits a contract was made.
               c.   Specially manufactured goods - may be enforceable according to the Code.
               d.   Delivery or payment and acceptance - partial performance may validate a contract for those goods which have been accepted.
     C.   Effect of Noncompliance - the oral contracts are unenforceable.
II. Parol Evidence Rule
     A.   The Rule - a written contract that contains the complete agreement of the parties may not be modified in any way with the use of parol (oral or written) evidence.
     B.   Situations to Which the Rule Does Not Apply - eight exceptions are listed.
     C.   Supplemental Evidence - may be used to explain a written contract.
III. Interpretation of Contracts - the determination of the meaning to be given to the written language of a contract is outside the scope of the Parol Evidence Rule.

TRUE-FALSE: Circle true or false.

Answers

T   F   1.   Except as provided by statute, an oral contract is just as valid and enforceable as a written one.

T   F   2.   Contracts of a type or class governed by the Statute of Frauds are said to be "within" the Statute.

T   F   3.   The Statute of Frauds is rendered inapplicable when the "main purpose doctrine" is available.

T   F   4.   If an executor promises to pay the decedent's debt out of the executor's own pocket, it is unenforceable unless in writing and signed.

T   F   5.   Only the "party to be charged" must have signed the written contract or memo in order to make it legally binding.

T   F   6.   If they are to be enforced, all oral contracts must be in writing according to the Statute of Frauds.

T   F   7.   Courts do not regard promises made by a surety to a debtor as being within the Statute of Frauds.

T   F   8.   Mutual promises to marry do not have to be in writing according to the Statute of Frauds.

T   F   9.   An oral contract to care for a handicapped person while that person attends college for the next four years is not enforceable.

T   F   10.   Parol evidence consists of oral evidence only.

T   F   11.   An executed (completely performed) oral contract is no longer within the Statute of Frauds.

T   F   12.   The theory of the Parol Evidence Rule is the parties will voluntarily and intentionally state in a written contract all terms to which they have agreed.

KEY TERMS - MATCHING EXERCISE: Select the term which best completes each statement below and write the corresponding number in the ANSWERS column.

Column I	Column II	Answers
1. The name given a promise to pay the debt of another if the debtor fails to pay.	1. Unenforceable	1. _____
	2. Parol evidence	2. _____

2.   Another name for the defendant, i.e., the person who must sign a written contract according to the Statute of Frauds.

3.   Another name for stocks and bonds.

4.   The term that means speech or words.

5.   Any evidence consisting of words, spoken or written, that are not contained in a written contract.

6.   The classification of an oral contract that is to last the lifetime of another.

7.   The doctrine that is an exception to the Statute of Frauds section that deals with promises to answer for the debt of another.

8.   Oral or written words of any prior agreement will not be permitted to vary, change, alter, or modify the terms of a written contract.

9.   Another name for tangible (movable) personal property as defined by the U.C.C.

10.   The classification of an oral contract that is in noncompliance with the Statute of Frauds.

11.   The source of law that governs the enforceability of contracts for the sale of goods.

12.   The law the requires certain types of contracts to be in a particular form to be enforceable.

13.   The name for a person who promises a creditor to perform the obligations of a third person.

3.   "Main purpose"   3. _____

4.   Goods   4. _____

5.   "Original promise"   5. _____

6.   Voidable   6. _____

7.   Parol   7. _____

8.   Void   8. _____

9.   "Collateral promise"   9. _____

10.   Statute of Frauds   10. _____

11.   "Party to be charged"   11. _____

12.   Securities   12. _____

13.   Parol Evidence Rule   13. _____

14.   Estoppel   14. _____

15.   Enforceable   15. _____

16.   Promisee

17.   Executor

18.   Administrator

19.   Surety

20.   Uniform Commercial Code

14.   The kind of promise made by a promisor
        who agrees to become primarily
        liable for its performance.

15.   The person named in a valid will to
        administer the estate of the
        decedent.

MULTIPLE CHOICE: Select the alternative which best completes each statement below and write the corresponding letter in the ANSWERS column.

Answers

1.   The Statute of Frauds requires all contracts that cannot be performed within one year to be in writing. The year runs from the time the (a) performance is to begin (b) contract is made (c) contract is breached (d) none of the above.

1. _____

2.   The signature of the "party to be charged" (a) must be handwritten (b) must be at the bottom of the last page of the contract (c) may be typewritten or printed (d) none of the above.

2. _____

3.   The U.C.C. allows an oral contract for the sale of goods to be enforced if (a) the party defending against the contract admits it (b) the goods are to be specially manufactured (c) payment has been made and accepted (d) all of the above.

3. _____

4.   The basic difference between the "main purpose doctrine" and the "leading object rule" is (a) one of fundamental law (b) a slight variance in technique (c) nothing -- they are the same (d) none of the above.

4. _____

5.   Which of the following are within the Statute of Frauds? A man promises a woman (a) an allowance to marry him (b) to convey land to her if they marry (c) to share his estate with her brother if she will marry him (d) all of the above.

5. _____

6.   Which of the following is personal propety? (a) growing crops (b) land (c) buildings (d) easements.

6. _____

7.   The parol evidence rule does not apply to a contract (a) that is partly oral and partly written (b) with a typographical error (c) that has ambiguous terms (d) all of the above.

7. _____

8.   If you orally contracted for the sale of goods, at what price would you become concerned with the requirements of the Statute of Frauds? (a) $5,000 (b) $500 (c) $50,000 (d) $450.

8. _____

9.   The person appointed by the court to administer the estate of a decedent who died without a will is the (a) administrator (b) executor (c) executrix (d) none of the above.

9. _____

10.   The parol evidence rule does not apply to a defense to a contract of (a) fraud (b) duress (c) undue influence (d) all of the above.   10. _____

11.   The kind of promise in which the promisor is not the person who is primarily liable is (a) an original promise (b) a collateral promise (c) an objective promise (d) none of the above.   11. _____

12.   The reason a court may deem it inequitable for the Statute of Frauds to apply after reliance by the purchaser in a land sales contract is (a) hardship (b) the "part performance doctrine" (c) the "main purpose doctrine" (d) none of the above.   12. _____

13.   The parol evidence rule does not apply if the written contract (a) is illegal (b) contains a clerical error (c) is subsequently and mutually rescinded (d) all of the above.   13. _____

CASE PROBLEMS - SHORT ESSAY ANSWERS: Read each case problem carefully. When appropriate, answer by stating a Decision for the case and by explaining the rationale - Rule of Law - relied upon to support your decision.

1.   A and B have a valid written contract. A telephones B, and they mutually agree to rescind the contract. In a lawsuit between A and B, can B prevent A from introducing this oral evidence? Explain.

       Decision: _____

       _____

       Rule of Law: _____

       _____

2.   A and B agree in a written memo to the sale of "some things." The writing doesn't specify the quantity of the items to be sold. Could this writing be enforced in court? Explain.

       Decision: _____

       _____

       Rule of Law: _____

       _____

3.   A, a carpenter, and B, a homeowner, make an oral contract whereby B is to give A a certain tract of land in return for A's building an addition to B's house. Is this contract enforceable by A upon completion of the construction? Explain.

       Decision: _____

       _____

       Rule of Law: _____

       _____

4.   A is the only person who can use widgets. A places an oral order with XYZ Company to make 10,000 widgets at $2.00 each. Later, A refuses to accept the widgets and alleges the Uniform Commercial Code Statute of Frauds as a defense to the suit for breach of contract. Who prevails?

Explain.

Decision: _____

_____

Rule of Law: _____

_____

5.   After an oral contract for the sale of a tract of land has been made, Allen writes a letter to
      Bernard, repeating that he will sell the land to Bernard, and Allen signs the letter. Bernard refuses
      to buy, and Allen sues. Bernard asserts the Statute of Frauds. Decide.

Decision: _____

_____

Rule of Law: _____

_____

CHAPTER 14

Rights of Third Parties

SCOPE NOTE

As a general rule, only the original contracting parties have rights to enforce an agreement or seek damages for its breach. In some cases, however, persons not original parties to an agreement may have enforceable rights under it. Additionally, original parties to a contract might wish to transfer to others the right to receive performance or the duty to perform contained in the original agreement. Chapter Fourteen addresses the type of contractual relations that create non-original-party enforceable rights and duties under a contract from the perspective of third party beneficiary contracts as well as assignment and delegation.

EDUCATIONAL OBJECTIVES

1. Define and discuss the significance of assignment/delegation.

2. Identify classes of rights and duties that cannot be assigned or delegated.

3. Explain rules of priority controlling multiple assignment situations.

4. Differentiate important characteristics and relative advantages/disadvantages among assignment, delegation and novation.

5. Distinguish assignment/delegation from third party beneficiary contracts.

6. Discuss differences between creditor, donee and incidental beneficiaries.

CHAPTER OUTLINE

I.   Assignments and Delegations
    A.   Assignment of Rights
        1.   Requirements of an assignment - no special words are necessary to create an assignment and consideration is not required for an effective assignment.
           a.   Revocability of assignments - if a contract exists between the assignor and the

assignee, the assignor cannot revoke the assignment without the assent of the assignee.

    b.   Partial assignments - a transfer of part of the contractual rights to one or more assignees.

  2.   Rights that are assignable - as a general rule most contract rights are assignable.

  3.   Rights that are not assignable - are those to protect the obligor or the public.

    a.   Assignments which materially increase the risk or burden - are not assignable.

    b.   Assignments of personal rights - or of a highly personal nature are not assignable.

    c.   Express prohibition against assignment - is handled differently by the Code than by common law.

    d.   Assignments prohibited by law - and public policy regulate the assignment of certain contract rights.

  4.   Rights of the assignee

    a.   Obtains rights of assignor - but no new rights.

    b.   Notice - to the obligor of an assignment is not required.

  5.   Implied warranties of assignor - to the assignee are listed.

  6.   Successive assignments of the same right - the majority rule is that the first assignee in point of time prevails over subsequent assignees.

  B.   Delegation of Duties - of a contract to a third person is allowed in some cases.

II.   Third Party Beneficiary Contrcts

  A.   Intended Beneficiary - as part of the original contract a third party obtains a benefit that is enforceable.

  1.   Gift promise - is the case in which the third party is a donee beneficiary.

  2.   Creditor beneficiary - is the case in which the third party is a creditor beneficiary.

  3.   Rights of intended beneficiary - are those that can be enforced.

  B.   Incidental Beneficiary - is not an intended beneficiary and she has no enforceable rights under the contract.

TRUE-FALSE: Circle true or false.

Answers

T   F   1.   At early common law, an assignment of a contractual right was wholly ineffective.

T   F   2.   A delegation of duties is the voluntary transfer of contract rights to a third party.

T   F   3.   To be valid, an assignment must be in writing.

T   F   4.   Just as rights are assignable, so are duties.

T   F   5.   Rights and duties of a highly personal nature cannot be assigned nor delegated.

T   F   6.   A valid assignment requires that notice be given to the obligor.

T   F   7.   Assignments of future wages are governed by statutes which sometimes prohibit them.

T   F   8.   The assignee of a contract claim has rights superior to those of the assignor.

T   F   9.   An assignee will lose the rights against the debtor if the latter pays the assignor without notice of the assignment.

T   F   10.   Unlike an assignment or a novation, a delegation of duties leaves the delegator and the delegatee liable for proper performance of the original contractual duties.

T   F   11.   In a third party beneficiary life insurance contract, the donee beneficiary has the right to sue and recover from the promisor (insurance company) but not from the promisee (insured).

T   F   12.   In a third party beneficiary contract, the creditor beneficiary may sue either or both the original promisor and the promisee.

KEY TERMS - MATCHING EXERCISE: Select the term which best completes each statement below and write the corresponding number in the ANSWERS column.

Column I	Column II	Answers
1. A method of discharging a contract in which a third party becomes bound upon a promise to the obligee.	1. Creditor beneficiary	1. _____
2. An assignment of parts of a claim to different assignees.	2. Incidental beneficiary	2. _____
3. A third party designated by the two parties of a contract to receive benefits and rights from the performance of the contract.	3. Personal services	3. _____
	4. Delegation	4. _____
4. An assignment of the same right to different persons.	5. Delectus personae	5. _____
5. A second assignee who may collect an account before the first assignee in time and keep it.	6. Partial assignment	6. _____
	7. Subsequent assignee	7. _____
6. An intended beneficiary of a contract who receives the benefit of the contract as a gift.	8. Assignor	8. _____
7. The guarantee the assignor, who receives value, makes to the assignee.	9. Donee beneficiary	9. _____
	10. Third party beneficiary contract	10. _____
8. A contract in which a party promises to render a performance to a third person.	11. Novation	11. _____
	12. An assignee in good faith who gives value	12. _____
	13. Intended beneficiary	13. _____
	14. Implied warranty	14. _____
		15. _____

9. A third party who obtains possible benefits but no rights under the contract.

10. The transfer of contract duties to a third person.

11. The person who makes an assignment.

12. A requirement for a valid contract but not for an effective assignment.

13. The most common contract right that may be assigned.

14. An example of a contract right that is not assignable.

15. The person to whom a contract duty is transferred.

15. Successive assignments

16. Obligor

17. Payment of money

18. Delegatee

19. Consideration

20. Assignee

MULTIPLE CHOICE: Select the alternative which best completes each statement below and write the corresponding letter in the ANSWERS column.

Answers

1. Contract rights are not assignable that (a) materially increase the risk upon the obligor (b) transfer personal contract rights (c) are prohibited by law (d) all of the above.

1. _____

2. The following is not assignable (a) an option contract (b) a wage assignment (c) a partial assignment (d) an automobile liability policy.

2. _____

3. Which of the following could be considered a personal service contract? A contract involving (a) highly skilled work (b) professional work (c) manual labor (d) all of the above.

3. _____

4. If the delegator desires to be discharged from a duty, the delegator will have to seek which of the following from the obligee? (a) payment (b) a novation (c) another obligee (d) none of the above.

4. _____

5. In a suit by the assignee against a debtor (obligor), the debtor may plead (a) fraud (b) failure of consideration (c) duress (d) all of the above.

5. _____

6. A third party who benefits from the performance of a contract which was not the intention of the parties to the contract is (a) a creditor beneficiary (b) a donee beneficiary (c) an incidental beneficiary (d) none of the above.

6. _____

7. An example of a third party donee beneficiary contract is (a) a life insurance policy (b) a fire insurance policy (c) an assumption of a mortgage in a real estate purchase (d) none of the above.

7. _____

8.   Courts enforce contracts for the benefit of all of the following except (a) incidental beneficiaries (b) donee beneficiaries (c) creditor beneficiaries (d) none of the above.

8. _____

9.   According to the majority rule in the United States involving successive assignments of the same rights, which of the following prevails? The first assignee (a) to give notice (b) in point of time (c) to reassign (d) none of the above.

9. _____

10. A subsequent assignee in good faith who gives value may prevail over the prior assignee when the subsequent assignee obtains (a) payment or satisfaction of the obligor's duty (b) a judgment against the obligor (c) a new contract with the obligor (d) all of the above.

10. _____

11. The person to whom an assignment is made is (a) an assignor (b) an assignee (c) an obligor (d) a delegatee.

11. _____

12. When a valid delegation has been made (a) only the delegator is liable for performance of the contractual duty (b) only the delegatee is liable for performance of the duty (c) both delegator and delegatee are liable (d) none of the above.

12. _____

13. A delegation will not be permitted if (a) it is prohibited by statute (b) it is prohibited by public policy (c) the duties delegated are personal (d) all of the above.

13. _____

CASE PROBLEMS – SHORT ESSAY ANSWERS: Read each case problem carefully. When appropriate, answer by stating a Decision for the case and by explaining the rationale – Rule of Law – relied upon to support your decision.

1.   Unknown to Y, X took out a life insurance policy naming Y, her best friend, as the beneficiary. X died, and the company attempted to deny Y recovery. What result?

Decision: _____

_____

Rule of Law: _____

_____

2.   For service to be done by A, B promises to purchase and deliver a new motorcycle to A. A completes the work. B refuses to buy and deliver the motorcycle. C, the exclusive motorcycle dealer (who would obviously benefit), brings suit against B. What result?

Decision: _____

_____

Rule of Law: _____

_____

3. A buys an appliance from company X on credit. A then assigns the right to the credit purchase to B. The company says that it will not honor the assignment. B sues. What result?

    Decision: _____

    _____

    Rule of Law: _____

    _____

4. E agrees to construct a swimming pool for X. E then delegates the duties to Y Swimming Pool Company. X refuses to allow Y Company to do the work. Y and E bring suit against X. What result?

    Decision: _____

    _____

    Rule of Law: _____

    _____

5. X, being an unscrupulous fellow, assigns the right to future wages first to Y and then to T. T gives notice to the employer first. Both T and Y seek to obtain the wages. Who prevails?

    Decision: _____

    _____

    Rule of Law: _____

    _____

CHAPTER 15

Performance, Breach, and Discharge

SCOPE NOTE

The cycle of the existence of a contract -- formation, operation, termination -- is completed in this Chapter. The events, developments, and conduct that relieve parties of their contractual obligations are discussed. Also addressed is the impact the presence of conditions has on performance under the terms of the agreement.

EDUCATIONAL OBJECTIVES

1. Identify the requirements for adequate performance through payment of money.

2. Differentiate between "substantial performance" and "partial performance" both in terms of definitional elements and remedial options.

3. Discuss the methods and significance of termination through agreement of the parties.

4. Explain the circumstances under which termination occurs through operation of law.

5. Develop the doctrinal importance of Frustration of Purpose and Commercial Impracticability.

6. Define and discuss the significance of anticipatory repudiation.

7. Outline the problems associated with personal satisfaction as a performance evaluator.

8. Discuss the effect of impossibility of performance on contractual obligations.

9. Enumerate types of contractual conditions and their influence on the duties of parties under the agreement.

CHAPTER OUTLINE

A. Conditions - a condition is an event whose happening or non-happening affects a duty of performance under a contract.

    1.   Express conditions - are explicitly set forth in language.

    2.   Implied-in-fact conditions - are understood by the parties to be part of the agreement even though they are not stated in express language.

    3.   Implied-in-law conditions - are imposed by law in order to accomplish a just and fair result.

    4.   Concurrent conditions - are performances by two promisors that are to take place at the same time.

    5.   Conditions precedent - an event that must occur before performance under a contract is due.

    6.   Conditions subsequent - is an operative event which terminates an existing duty.

B.   Discharge by Performance - the most frequent method of discharging a contract duty.

C.   Discharge by Breach - which is the failure of a party to perform his promise.

    1.   Breach by one party as a discharge of the other

        a.   Material breach - is an unjustifiable failure to perform substantially the duties promised in a contract.

        b.   Substantial performance - essential but not complete performance.

    2.   Prevention of performance - one party interferes with the performance of another constituting a breach.

    3.   Anticipatory repudiation - a party repudiates the contract in advance.

    4.   Material alteration of written contract - to operate as a discharge, a party must intentionally and materially alter the written contract.

D.   Discharge by Agreement of the Parties

    1.   Mutual rescission - an agreement between the parties to terminate their contract duties.

    2.   Substituted contracts - the parties agree to rescind their original contract and enter into a new one.

    3.   Novation - a substituted contract involving three parties.

    4.   Accord and satisfaction - an agreement of a promisee in a contract to accept a substituted performance in satisfaction of an existing contractual duty.

    5.   Release and covenant not to sue - a release is a discharge under seal but a covenant not to sue does not discharge the contract duty.

E.   Discharge by Operation of Law

    1.   Subsequent illegality - due to a new law may discharge the duty of performance.

    2.   Impossibility - subjective impossibility does not discharge the contractual duty but objective impossibility may.

    3.   Bankruptcy - does discharge a contractual duty.

    4.   Statute of Limitations - does not discharge the duty but does bar the creditor's remedy.

    5.   Merger - causes the contract to be discharged.

TRUE-FALSE: Circle true or false.

Answers

T   F   1.   Discharge of a contract refers to the termination of the duties created upon the formation of the contract.

T   F   2.   A condition is an operative event that may limit the obligation to perform a contract.

T   F   3.   There is no difference between the breach of a promise and the failure, or non-happening, of a condition: they are the same.

T   F   4.   "Provided that" is a phrase connoting an implied condition often found in a contract.

T   F   5.   The standard of satisfaction in matters involving personal taste is that of the reasonable man.

T   F   6.   A condition precedent is an event that precedes the creation of a duty of immediate performance under a contract.

T   F   7.   Once the parties to a contract agree to an accord, the contract is discharged.

T   F   8.   An oral agreement to rescind a written contract is never valid.

T   F   9.   Less than exact performance does not fully discharge a party to a contract.

T   F   10.   Bankruptcy and the Statute of Limitations are methods of discharging a contract by operation of law.

T   F   11.   A material breach of a contract discharges the aggrieved party from any further duty under the contract.

T   F   12.   Breach of contract is the failure of a party to perform her promises.

KEY TERMS - MATCHING EXERCISE: Select the term which best completes each statement below and write the corresponding number in the ANSWERS column.

Column I	Column II	Answers
1. The position of the Code that any deviation from the promised performance in a sales contract constitutes a material breach of the contract.	1. Novation	1. _____
	2. Material alteration	2. _____
		3. _____
2. An announcement prior to the date performance is due that a party will not perform.	3. Merger	4. _____
	4. Concurrent conditions	5. _____
3. The act that is technically a discharge under seal of an existing duty.	5. Nonmaterial breach	6. _____
	6. Condition precedent	7. _____
4. An agreement between the parties to terminate their respective duties under the contract.	7. Perfect tender rule	8. _____
	8. Prevention of performance	9. _____

5.   An acceptable substituted per-
     formance that replaces the
     original contractual obligation.

6.   An agreement that involves three
     parties whereby one is a substi-
     tute obligee or obligor.

7.   An act that may result in a dis-
     charge of the entire contract
     because of the unauthorized
     relevant changes by a party to
     the contract.

8.   The embodiment of terms of one
     contract into another that is
     of a different and higher degree.

9.   The kind of conditions in which
     the contract promisors' proposed
     reciprocal and agreed performances
     are to take place at the same time.

10. A procedure in which one party
     substantially interferes with the
     other's performance of a contract
     and that acts as a discharge.

11. A name for the injured party who
     has a right to sue for breach of
     contract.

12. One example of a supervening
     illegality.

13. The kind of breach that does not
     discharge a contract but allows a
     plaintiff to recover damages.

14. An executory accord does not dis-
     charge a contract until this
     performance is completed.

15. The term for an attempted per-
     formance.

9.   Anticipatory breach   10. _____

10. Retraction   11. _____

11. Release   12. _____

12. Illegality   13. _____

13. Mutual rescission   14. _____

14. Satisfaction   15. _____

15. Accord

16. Aggrieved person

17. Material breach

18. War

19. Frustration of
     purpose doctrine

20. Tender

MULTIPLE CHOICE: Select the alternative which best completes each statement below and write the corresponding letter in the ANSWERS column.

Answers

1. An agreement between the parties to a contract to cancel their original contract and enter a new contract is a (a) substitution (b) novation (c) release (d) none of the above.

    1. _____

2. Where no one is able to perform the contract for reasons beyond the control of the parties, the contract is discharged due to (a) a mistake (b) impossibility (c) fraud (d) a concurrent obligation.

    2. _____

3. A material breach of contract (a) always gives the aggrieved party a cause of action (b) excuses non-performance by the other party (c) discharges the other party from any further duty to perform (d) all of the above.

    3. _____

4. The running of the Statute of Limitations on a contract between a creditor and debtor (a) discharges the debt (b) acts as an accord (c) bars the creditor's remedy (d) all of the above.

    4. _____

5. Which of the following may cause a binding promise to cease to be binding? (a) performance of the parties (b) a discharge by operation of law (c) an excuse for non-performance (d) all of the above.

    5. _____

6. A condition may be (a) express (b) implied-in-fact (c) implied-in-law (d) all of the above.

    6. _____

7. The expressions "on condition that" and "as soon as" are often part of (a) implied conditions (b) subsequent statements (c) express conditions (d) concurrent conditions.

    7. _____

8. An operative event that terminates the existing contractual duty of immediate performance is a (a) condition subsequent (b) condition precedent (c) concurrent condition (d) none of the above.

    8. _____

9. Tender of payment of a debt past due (a) discharges the debt (b) does not discharge the debt if the creditor refuses to accept the tender (c) makes the debt unconditional (d) none of the above.

    9. _____

10. An agreement between the parties to a contract to terminate their respective contractual duties is a (a) rescission (b) material alteration (c) novation (d) none of the above.

    10. _____

11. The most frequent method of discharging a contractual duty is a discharge by (a) breach (b) performance (c) operation of law (d) impossibility.

    11. _____

12. Which of the following is not a method of discharging contractual duties by agreement of the parties? (a) novation (b) substitution (c) bankruptcy (d) rescission.

    12. _____

13.   A war between two nations that discharges contracts between citizens of
        the nations is an example of a discharge by (a) breach (b) operation of law
        (c) agreement (d) none of the above.   13.   _____

CASE PROBLEMS - SHORT ESSAY ANSWERS: Read each case problem carefully.   When
appropriate, answer by stating a Decision for the case and by explaining the rationale - Rule of Law -
relied upon to support your decision.

1.   A rents a room from B to watch the Duke of Earle ride by in a parade. B knows this is the
        reason. The Duke is assassinated by revolutionaries before the parade. B sues for the rent. What
        result?

        Decision: _____

        _____

        Rule of Law: _____

2.   X from Russia and Y from Red China contract for the sale of vodka. War breaks out between the
        two countries. How does this affect the contract?
        Decision: _____

        Rule of Law: _____

        _____

3.   X has purchased a bicycle from Y and now owes Y $150. X, Y, and Z agree that Z will pay the
        debt and X will be discharged. If Z refuses to pay the money, can Y sue Z? Explain.
        Decision: _____

        Rule of Law: _____

        _____

4.   X employs Y to work for one year beginning March 1, and on February 28, Y refuses to begin
        the job. X doesn't really care and agrees. Then X hires Z. X decides in May to sue Y for
        damages. What result?

        Decision: _____

        Rule of Law: _____

        _____

5.   B contracts in writing to sell a car to A for $1,500. Nothing is written about time of delivery or
        payment. A demands the delivery before payment as A needs the car now but won't be able to
        pay for it until later. B refuses, and A sues for specific performance. What result?

        Decision: _____

        Rule of Law: _____

        _____

Remedies

SCOPE NOTE

Adequate performance by both parties to a contract discharges their duties. In cases where performance is inadequate -- "defective" -- a breach has occurred. What forms of relief both at law and in equity are available to injured parties when they are faced with performance falling short of the terms of the agreement? How do these remedies differ? When will the non-breaching party be forced to make an election between mutually exclusive remedies?

EDUCATIONAL OBJECTIVES

1. Distinguish the various types of damages.

2. Discuss the importance of liquidated damages.

3. Enumerate the types of relief available from a court of equity and when they apply.

4. Identify the various formulas used to compute damages.

5. Explain the role and meaning of the Mitigation of Damages Doctrine.

CHAPTER OUTLINE

A. Monetary Damages
   1. Compensatory damages – the right to these damages for breach of contract is always available to the injured party.
   2. Nominal damages - a small amount of damages fixed without regard to the amount of loss.
   3. Reliance damages - loss caused by reliance upon the contract.
   4. Foreseeability of damages - the breaching party is liable for loss he had reason to foresee as a probable result of his breach.
   5. Damages for misrepresentation
      a. Fraud - a party induced by fraud to enter a contract may recover damages in a tort action.

   b. Non-fraudulent misrepresentation - out-of-pocket damages are allowed.
  6. Punitive damages - damages awarded in cases involving willful, wanton, or malicious conduct.
  7. Liquidated damages - a provision in a contract by which the parties agree to the damages to be paid in event of breach.
  8. Mitigation of damages - the injured party must lessen the damages he may sustain.

B. Remedies in Equity
  1. Specific performance - an equity court degree that the defaulting party perform her contractual duties.
  2. Injunctions - formal court order commanding a person to refrain from doing something.

C. Restitution
  1. Party injured by breach - is entitled to restitution (a return of the consideration that was given).
  2. Party in default - is entitled to restitution for any benefit she has given in excess of the loss she has caused.
  3. Statute of Frauds - if the statute applies, each party is entitled to restitution to benefits conferred on the other party.
  4. Voidable contracts - in such contracts, the party who rescinds is entitled to restitution.

D. Limitations on Remedies
  1. Election of remedies - a choice does not necessarily prevent a person from seeking a second remedy.
  2. Loss of power of avoidance
   a. Affirmance - of a contract will not allow the party who affirms to later avoid the contract.
   b. Delay - may cause the loss of the power of avoidance.
   c. Rights of third parties - the intervening rights of third parties may limit the power of avoidance and the accompanying right to restitution.

TRUE-FALSE: Circle true or false.

Answers

T F 1. A breach of contract means a failure to perform a contract promise.

T F 2. The injured party can always seek and obtain money damages from the wrongdoer for breach of contract.

T F 3. The purpose of allowing damages for breach of contract is to put the injured party in as good a position as the wrongdoer.

T F 4. A party with the power of avoidance has no time limit for rescinding a contract.

T F 5. After learning that the goods sold to the buyer are unfit, the buyer may continue to use the goods and thereby sue the seller for greater damages.

T F 6. An example of nominal damages would be a $100,000 recovery for personal injury which one suffers as a result of a traffic mishap.

T   F   7.   The remedy of specific performance will generally be granted for breach of a contract for personal services.

T   F   8.   Punitive damages are always recoverble for breach of contract.

T   F   9.   For breach of contract, the injured party may recover consequential damages for lost profits.

T   F   10. Liquidated damages must bear a reasonable relationship to the actual or probable damage suffered for breach of a contract.

T   F   11. The purpose of restitution is to restore the injured party to the position she was in before the contract was made.

T   F   12. An injunction is the equitable remedy that compels the performance of a contract according to its terms.

KEY TERMS – MATCHING EXERCISE: Select the term which best completes each statement below and write the corresponding number in the ANSWERS column.

Column I	Column II	Answers
1. The usual judgment for breach of contract.	1. Common law	1. _____
2. A recovery of $1.00 and costs.	2. Penalty	2. _____
3. A remedy looking to deter future conduct.	3. Uniform Commercial Code	3. _____
4. A provision in the contract calling for payment of money in the event of breach of the contract.	4. Money damages	4. _____
5. When breach occurs, the plaintiff is required to lessen damages if possible.	5. Fraud	5. _____
6. A return of the consideration, or its value, to the aggrieved party.	6. Uniqueness	6. _____
7. The source of law that allows a defrauded party the right to rescind the contract and recover damages for breach of a contract for the sale of goods.	7. Specific performance	7. _____
	8. Special damages	8. _____
	9. Nominal damages	9. _____
	10. Injunction	10. _____
	11. Punitive damages	11. _____
	12. Contempt of court	12. _____

8.   A remedy for non-compliance with an injunction.

9.   The characteristic of real property that allows the equity court to always grant the remedy of specific performance for breach of a sales contract.

10. The method the court uses to enforce a contract for an employee's exclusive personal services where damages for a breach are inadequate.

11. The kind of damages that protect the injured party's expectation interest.

12. A remedy that results in placing the injured party in as good a position as she would have been in had the contract not been made.

13. The damages the injured party may recover that are equal to the difference between the value of what she has received and the value of what she was given for it.

14. An unreasonable sum of money included as a provision of a contract that is to be paid in the event of a breach of the contract.

15. An equitable remedy whereby the court corrects a written contract to make it conform to the true agreement of the parties.

13. Mitigation   13. _____

14. Restitution   14. _____

15. Liquidated damages   15. _____

16. Out-of-pocket damages

17. Reliance damages

18. Reformation

19. Benefit-of-the-bargain rule

20. Compensatory damages

MULTIPLE CHOICE: Select the alternative which best completes each statement below and write the corresponding letter in the ANSWERS column.

Answers

1.   A remedy for breach of contract that represents the actual dollar loss to the plaintiff is (a) specific performance (b) compensatory damages (c) restitution (d) punitive damages.   1. _____

2. A court order conveying the title to a parcel of land from the seller to the buyer in compliance with their contractual agreement is (a) restitution (b) punitive damages (c) specific performance (d) none of the above.

2. _____

3. Ordering a reconveyance of land would be (a) restitution (b) specific performance (c) punitive damages (d) compensatory damages.

3. _____

4. Hadley v. Baxendale involved an issue of (a) nominal damages (b) foreseeability of injury (loss) (c) an intentional tort (d) punitive damages.

4. _____

5. Unreasonable payment for non-performance as expressed in the contract is deemed (a) a penalty (b) liquidated damages (c) punitive damages (d) all of the above.

5. _____

6. A reasonable payment for non-performance as expressed in a contract is deemed (a) a penalty (b) liquidated damages (c) punitive damages (d) all of the above.

6. _____

7. Damages that arise directly out of the breach of contract are called (a) nominal damages (b) consequential damages (c) incidental damages (d) reliance damages.

7. _____

8. A liquidated damages clause that becomes a penalty because it is excessive is (a) enforceable at a reasonable rate (b) unenforceable (c) enforceable (d) reasonable.

8. _____

9. Specific performance will be granted by an equity court when the case involves (a) a contract for personal services (b) a performance by a concert pianist (c) a unique item of property (d) none of the above.

9. _____

10. Remedies that are mutually exclusive or inconsistent require an election of remedies. Which of the following would require the election? (a) specific performance and restitution (b) restitution and total damages (c) specific performance and compensation for incidental damages (d) only a and b above.

10. _____

11. A contract can be avoided due to (a) lack of capacity (b) fraud (c) duress (d) all of the above.

11. _____

12. A party who has the right and power to avoid a contract may lose that power because (a) she affirms the contract (b) she unreasonably delays in disaffirming the contract (c) rights of third parties intervene (d) all of the above.

12. _____

13. The remedies of specific performance and injunction (a) will not be granted where there is an adequate remedy at law (b) are remedies at law (c) will be granted if the contract is created by fraud or duress (d) none of the above.

13. _____

CASE PROBLEMS - SHORT ESSAY ANSWERS: Read each case problem carefully. When appropriate, answer by stating a Decision for the case and by explaining the rationale - Rule of Law - relied upon to support your decision.

1. Suppose that you own a legal gambling hall and the roulette wheel breaks down. You desperately need this machine in operation to continue business. In order to have the wheel fixed, you deliver it to Ace Repairs, hoping that they will rush it back to you. Ace takes weeks to repair the wheel. Is there any legal remedy you might pursue?

Decision: _____

Rule of Law: _____

_____

2. Suppose X, a lawyer, tells A, the trusting client, that the deal X has been working on for A is all set and that all A need do is give X $5,000. As it turns out, X knowingly defrauded A. Can A get more than $5,000 damages? Explain.

Decision: _____

Rule of Law: _____

_____

3. A and B have a contract whereby if one party breachs the contract, the other is entitled ot $2,000. B breaches in the most minor of ways. Can A enforce the clause for the $2,000? Explain.

Decision: _____

Rule of Law: _____

_____

4. A and B have a contract whereby A is to manufacture 5,000 lawnmowers for B. After 500 are built, B repudiates the contract. A pays no attention and continues to build. A then sues B. What result?

Decision: _____

Rule of Law: _____

_____

5.   A offers to sell B an antique car, a one-of-a-kind rare gem. After the written contract is made, A decides not to sell. Can B force A to part with the car? Explain.

Decision: _____

_____

Rule of Law: _____

_____

Relationship with Principal and Agent

SCOPE NOTE

If it were required that all commercial transactions be conducted directly between primary parties only, business would progress at a snail's pace and the marketplace process would be cumbersome. To facilitate the flow of commerce, representatives are appointed to act on behalf of others within a defined scope of authority in negotiating and finalizing business agreements covering a broad range of substantive areas. In Chapter 17, the law of agency, which regulates the relationship of one person (agent) acting on behalf of another (principal), its basic concepts and terminology, is introduced. The nature of the agency relationship itself, how it is created, the legal identities of its originating parties and how their rights and duties differ from other legal relationships are focused upon.

EDUCATIONAL OBJECTIVES

1. Define and discuss the benefits derived from an agency relationship.

2. Enumerate the methods for creating a valid agency relationship.

3. Explain the qualifications necessary for a principal or agent.

4. Know the source and significance of the duties and liabilities owed by agents and principals to one another.

5. Outline the tort liability of principals and agents.

6. List and explain the various ways in which an agency relationship comes to an end.

CHAPTER OUTLINE

I. Nature of Agency - contractual relationship usually involving fiduciary duties.
    A. Definition - one party (principal) engages another (agent) to act on their behalf
    B. Scope of Agency Purposes - defined by contract; facilitate conducting multiple businesses
    C. Other Legal Relations

        1.   Independent contractor
        2.   Broker
        3.   Bailee
        4.   Trustee

II.   Creation of Agency - to accomplish any legal purpose; contractually based
    A.   Formalities - generally none required unless Statute of Frauds applies
    B.   Capacity
        1.   Capacity to be a principal - general legal (contractual)
        2.   Capacity to be an agent - generally not required but lack of makes contract voidable

III.   Duties of Agent to Principal - defined by contract; generally one of proper performance
    A.   Duty of Obedience - relevant, lawful instructions unless an emergency
    B.   Duty of Diligence - use reasonable care
    C.   Duty to Inform - relevant, accurate, important information
    D.   Duty to Account - for all monies relevant to agency relationship
    E.   Fiduciary Duty

IV.   Duties of Principal to Agent
    A.   Contractual Duties - primary determiner; standard of proper performance
        1.   Compensation - reasonable amount for services
        2.   Reimbursement - reasonable expenses in carrying out proper objectives
        3.   Indemnification - for losses incurred in carrying out proper objectives
    B.   Tort duties - reasonable cooperation; reasonable safety

V.   Termination of Agency - relationship comes to an end
    A.   Acts of the Parties - based on conduct of parties
        1.   Lapse of time - specified or reasonable length of time
        2.   Mutual agreement of the parties - recission
        3.   Fulfillment of purpose - proper performance
        4.   Revocation of authority - principal unilaterally ends
        5.   Renunciation by the agent - agent unilaterally ends
    B.   Operation of Law - based on changed circumstances
        1.   Bankruptcy
        2.   Death
        3.   Incapacity
        4.   Change in business conditions
        5.   Loss or destruction of the subject matter
        6.   Loss of qualification of principal or agent
        7.   Disloyalty of agent
        8.   Change of law
        9.   Outbreak of war
    C.   Irrevocable Agencies - authority of agent combined with special interest or obligation

TRUE-FALSE: Circle true or false.

Answers

T   F   1.   Most forms of business associations, including partnership, sole proprietorships, and corporations, are based on the general principles of agency law.

T   F   2.   An agent who is a minor can only make voidable contracts on behalf of an adult, capacitated principal.

T   F   3.   A person having interests adverse to that of another is generally not permitted to act as an agent for that other person.

T   F   4.   Employers are generally not responsible for the torts of independent contractors committed during the course of employment.

T   F   5.   The law of agency is mainly controlled by the U.C.C.

T   F   6.   A fiduciary duty is one which arises out of a position of trust and confidence between persons.

T   F   7.   Agents employed to sell may not become purchasers for themselves.

T   F   8.   When a principal wrongfully revokes an agent's authority, the agent may recover money damages for breach of contract.

T   F   9.   When an agency agreement does not mention an amount of compensation for the agent, the principal is under no obligation to pay for the agent's services.

T   F   10.   The power of the principal to terminate an agency is unlimited.

T   F   11.   When conducting business on behalf of a principal, an agent is usually a party to the contract entered into with the third person.

T   F   12.   Agency relationships terminate when the subject of the agency (goods to be sold by an agent) are destroyed through no one's fault.

KEY TERMS - MATCHING EXERICSE: Select the term which best completes each statement below and write the corresponding number in the ANSWERS column.

Column I	Column II	Answers
1. A legal relationship under which an individual acts as the business representative of another person.	1. Diligence	1. _____
	2. Master	2. _____
2. Persons who authorize others to act on their behalf.	3. Disloyalty	3. _____
3. One acting on behalf of another under an agency relationship created without consideration.	4. Recission	4. _____
	5. Renunciation	5. _____
4. An agent's duty to perform work with reasonable care and skill.	6. Principal	6. _____
	7. Agency	7. _____

5.   Agent's duty to keep accurate records regarding conduct on behalf of the principal and supply such records to the principal.

6.   A person who contracts to act for another but is not controlled by that other person in the performance of authorized acts.

7.   Termination of agency that does not trigger liability for losses suffered as a result of the termination.

8.   Acts by an agent that are adverse to the principal's interest.

9.   The withdrawal of the agent's authority by the principal to act on the latter's behalf.

10.   Notice to the principal given by the agent that the agent wishes to discontinue the agency.

11.   Principal's duty to pay an agent for authorized expenses paid out of the agent's own pocket.

12.   Principal's duty to pay an agent for losses suffered by the latter while acting in an authorized manner.

13.   A form of agency under which the agent acts as an attorney for the principal.

14.   A scholarly treatise on agency law.

15.   Federal court proceedings granting judicial relief to financially troubled debtors.

8.   Infants

9.   Gratuitous agent

10.   Independent contractor

11.   Servant

12.   Revocation

13.   Operation of law

14.   Fiduciary

15.   Account

16.   Indemnification

17.   Restatement of agency law

18.   Bankruptcy

19.   Power of attorney

20.   Reimbursement

8. _____

9. _____

10. _____

11. _____

12. _____

13. _____

14. _____

15. _____

MULTIPLE CHOICE: Select the alternative which best completes each statement below and write the corresponding letter in the ANSWERS column.

Answers

1. Agency relationships are generally created by (a) operation of law (b) statute (c) contract (d) equitable estopple.

    1. _____

2. Examples of information that agents are duty bound to communicate to their principals include (a) insolvency of debtors and customers of the principal (b) change of marital status of a creditor of the principal (c) change in credit rating of independent contractors (d) pending tax increases on property owned by the agent.

    2. _____

3. In most situations (a) agency contracts must be sealed and notarized to be valid (b) no specific formalities are required for valid agency contracts (c) agency contracts must be written to be enforceable (d) agency contracts must be witnessed to be valid.

    3. _____

4. All contracts made by an agent appointed by a minor principal are (a) voidable (b) valid (c) void (d) nullity.

    4. _____

5. The person who employs another, having control over the physical details of that other's performance is the (a) agent (b) employer (c) independent contractor (d) none of the above.

    5. _____

6. An agency is terminated by (a) mutual agreement of the parties (b) fulfillment of the agency's purpose (c) insanity, death or bankruptcy of either principal or agent (d) all of the above.

    6. _____

7. Which of the following are duties owed a principal by the agent? (a) to act with reasonable care (b) to act only as authorized (c) to inform the principal of all relevant information (d) all of the above.

    7. _____

8. Which of the following is not a duty an agent owes to the principal? (a) ratification (b) diligence (c) loyalty (d) accounting.

    8. _____

9. Under the Restatement, the two main elements to an agency relationship are _____ by the principal and _____ by the agent. (a) accord/satisfaction (b) authorization/consent (c) indemnification/compensation (d) receivership/allocation.

    9. _____

10. When the parties to an agency or the agency contract do not specify how long the agency relationship is to last, it expires (a) automatically at the end of 90 days (b) no later than 2 weeks after the contract is signed (c) at the end of a reasonable length of time (d) none of the above.

    10. _____

11. Tort duties owed by an employer-principal to an employee-agent include (a) insuring that work settings are hazard free (b) liability for intentional torts of employees (c) warning employees of any risk associated with the job (d) none of the above.

    11. _____

12. Upon revocation of an agency, the agent's authority to bind the principal to contracts with third parties (a) ends immediately (b) continues for a three week period when all parties are merchants under the U.C.C. definition of that term (c) lasts until the third party has notice or knowledge of the revocation (d) none of the above.

12. _____

13. Principal Paul and Agent Abel enter an agreement whereby Abel agrees to sell, for a fee, Paul's pickle packing plants. Shortly after reaching their agreement, Paul, having inhaled excessive amounts of pickling vapor, is adjudicated mentally incompetent and Abel is confined to a hospital with a severe case of shingles. Their relationship (a) ceases through subsequent incapacity (b) continues unaffected by these tragedies (c) terminates through changed business conditions (d) ends due to changes in law.

13. _____

CASE PROBLEMS - SHORT ESSAY ANSWERS: Read each case problem carefully. When appropriate, answer by stating a Decision for the case and by explaining the rationale - Rule of Law - relied upon to support your decision.

1. A promises to personally try a lawsuit for B but instead asks a fellow attorney and friend to do it because A doesn't have enough time. May A do this? Explain.

Decision: _____
_____
Rule of Law: _____
_____

2. P instructs A to buy stock in two corporations. A, instead, sells A's own stock to P at the market price without disclosing this fact to P. Can P rescind this transaction? Explain.

Decision: _____
Rule of Law: _____
_____

3. A hires B to sell A's home. The market price is $50,000. B finds a buyer for $51,500 and tells A the house sold for $50,000. Can B keep the $1,500 profit on the sale? Explain.

Decision: _____
_____
Rule of Law: _____
_____

4. P authorizes A to sell one of P's valuable paintings. A sells the painting to C at a price exceptionally favorable to P. C wants another of P's paintings and is willing to pay "any price." Can A sell it to C?

Decision: _____
_____

Rule of Law: _____

_____

5.   English businessperson Throckmorton contracts with Argentine businessperson Dominequez to
      represent Throckmorton in various business dealings in Argentina. What affect on this contract
      would a flare-up of British-Argentine hostilities over the Balkin Islands have? Explain.

Decision: _____

_____

Rule of Law: _____

_____

CHAPTER 18

Relationship with Third Parties

SCOPE NOTE

Our discussion of agency law concludes by addressing the rights/duties of the originating parties to the agency relationship vis-a-vis third persons. Both contract and tort foundations for liability are focused upon. Attention is given to those situations where the agent is acting with and without the principal's authority. Also discussed are circumstances which trigger third-party liability to the originating parties.

EDUCATIONAL OBJECTIVES

1. Define and explain the nature of the principal's contractual liability to third persons.

2. Distinguish among the various types of authority bases for agent conduct.

3. Discuss when an agent may delegate authority to another and the effect of such delegation.

4. Explain the effects of termination of agency and ratification on the principal's contractual liability.

5. Develop the principal's direct and vicarious tort liability to third persons based on the authorized or unauthorized acts of the agent.

6. Know the basis for criminal liability of principals to third persons.

7. Enumerate the situations when the agent is personally liable to third persons in terms of warranty of authority, competency and existence of the principal, and disclosure of representative status.

8. Explain the breadth of agent liability for the torts committed during the agency.

CHAPTER OUTLINE

I. Relationship of Principal and Third Parties
    A. Contract Liability of the Principal - party to conract made by agent within scope of authority

1. Types of authority - scope of agent's authority
    a. Actual express authority - written or spoken
    b. Actual implied authority - reasonable inferences (incidental and customary)
    c. Apparent authority - stems from expectations of others based on principal's words or conduct
2. Fundamental rules of contractual liability
3. Delegation of authority - sub-agents; ministerial acts contrasted with personalized acts
4. Effect of termination of agency upon authority - notice requirement
5. Ratification - retroactive approval of unauthorized acts

B. Tort Liability of the Principal
   1. Direct liability of the principal - agent acting under specific direction of principal
   2. Vicarious liability of principal for authorized acts of agent - misconduct within scope of authority
   3. Vicarious liability of principal for unauthorized acts of agent - misconduct beyond scope of authority
       a. The doctrine of respondeat superior - carrying out objectives or under principal's control
       b. Torts of independent contractor - generally no liability

C. Criminal Liability of the Principal - generally none without participation, direction, approval

II. Relationship of Agent and Third Persons

A. Contract Liability of Agent
   1. Disclosed principal - none since not a party
   2. Unauthorized contracts - generally not liable as a party
       a. Agent's implied warranty of authority - liable for breach of contract
       b. Misrepresentation - liable for how authority misrepresented
       c. Agent assumes liability - personal liability of agent
   3. Partially disclosed principal
       a. Liability of the parties
       b. Rights of partially disclosed principal
   4. Undisclosed principal - both agent and principal liable
   5. Non-existent or incompetent principal - agent personally liable

B. Tort Liability of Agent - outside scope of authority
C. Rights of Agent Against Third Person - usually no contract breach recovery

TRUE-FALSE: Circle true or false.

Answers

T   F   1.   An agent can bind the principal to a contract with apparent authority.

T   F   2.   Apparent authority is the same as express authority.

T   F   3.   A principal may never be held criminally accountable for the acts of an agent.

T   F   4.   Authority to make contracts for a principal is usually inferred from the agent's authority to conduct business for the principal.

T   F   5.   Subagents, appointed with authority from the principal, are agents of both the principal and the agent.

T   F   6.   An agent for a disclosed principal is a party to the contract made on behalf of the
                    principal and is liable to the third person with whom the contract is made.

T   F   7.   For the doctrine of respondeat superior to take effect, the agent must be acting within
                    the normal scope of employment.

T   F   8.   The principal may be liable for an agent's contracts but not for the agent's torts.

T   F   9.   Ratification by a principal of an agent's unauthorized acts may occur only through
                    express language of the principal.

T   F   10.   When conduct of the parties terminates an agency, the agent's apparent authority
                    continues with respect to some third persons until actual notice of the termination is
                    given to them.

T   F   11.   Situations of apparent authority apply to cases of both disclosed and undisclosed
                    principals.

T   F   12.   Ratification cannot occur in settings where the principal is undisclosed.

KEY TERMS - MATCHING EXERCISE: Select the term which best completes each statement below
and write the corresponding number in the ANSWERS column.

Column I	Column II	Answers
1. Persons who are not employees of the parties for whom services are performed.	1. Apparent authority	1. _____
	2. Vicarious	2. _____
2. Spoken or written authority communicated by the principal to the agent.	3. Privity of contract	3. _____
	4. Actual	4. _____
3. Transferring to another the right or power to perform some act.	5. Authority	5. _____
	6. Allocation	6. _____
4. An agency in which a third party deals with the agent knowing only the existence but not the identity of the principal.	7. Express	7. _____
	8. Ratification	8. _____
5. The type of liability a principal incurs when an agent commits an unauthorized negligent act while in the scope of employment.	9. Delegation	9. _____
	10. Contract liability	10. _____
		11. _____
6. The doctrine that makes a principal liable for the agent's torts.	11. Respondeat superior	

7.   The principal's confirmation or adoption of an agent's unauthorized act.

8.   The kind of agency in which a third person believes there is no agency relationship.

9.   A basic type of authority which is based on the consent shown by the principal to the agent.

10.   The power of an agent to change the legal status of a principal.

11.   Type of authority arising out of the principal's behavior which creates in another's mind the reasonable, justified belief that the agent has actual authority.

12.   Authority arising from the statements or behavior the principal demonstrates to the agent.

13.   A principal whose existence and identity are known by the the party.

14.   Persons acting on behalf of an agent.

15.   Express statement ot a third party of the termination of an agency relationship.

12.   Frolic of his/ her own

13.   Undisclosed

14.   Independent contractors

15.   Partially disclosed

16.   Disclosed

17.   Actual notice

18.   Constructive notice

19.   Implied

20.   Subagent

12. _____

13. _____

14. _____

15. _____

MULTIPLE CHOICE: Select the alternative which best completes each statement below and write the corresponding letter in the ANSWERS column.

Answers

1.   A valid ratification (a) may stem from unauthorized acts of an agent regardless of whether the principal existed at the time of the acts (b) cannot be revoked once made (c) relates back only to the time of disclosure of the principal (d) none of the above.

1. _____

2.   Normally the principal is not liable for contracts created by an agent's acts which are (a) unauthorized (b) expressly authorized (c) actually authorized (d) implicitly authorized.

2. _____

3. Principals adjudged liable for their agents' torts have rights of (a) equitable contribution (b) injunctive relief (c) indemnification (d) condemnation against the agents.

3. _____

4. An agent is liable to the third person if the agent (a) acts for an undisclosed principal (b) exceeds the authority granted by the principal (c) commits a tortious act (d) all of the above.

4. _____

5. When a third party discovers the identity of an undisclosed principal, the third party (a) may hold either the principal or agent to performance of the contract (b) may hold both liable for the contract (c) may sue and get a judgment against both principal and agent (d) none of the above.

5. _____

6. A ratification must be (a) communicated to the agent (b) communicated to the third person (c) manifested by words (d) none of the above.

6. _____

7. When agents falsely represent to third persons that they are authorized by the principals to make contracts for them the agents are (a) ultimately not liable (b) liable in tort (c) liable in contract (d) none of the above to the third party.

7. _____

8. Under the Restatement, employee conduct within scope of employment includes actions (a) motivated to serve the employer (b) within set time and space limits (c) of the kind for which employees have been hired (d) all of the above.

8. _____

9. When agents guarantee third persons that principals will carry out the terms of contracts (a) the agents are liable for nonperformance by the principals (b) only principals are liable for their nonperformance (c) no suretyship exists between the agents and third persons (d) the principals have rights of reimbursement against the agent.

9. _____

10. Actions by an agent which make the agent liable on the contract entered into between the principal and the third party include (a) making the contract in the principal's name only (b) committing any crime (c) making the contract in the agent's name only (d) all of the above.

10. _____

11. When a third party obtains a judgment against an agent who represents an undisclosed principal whose identity and existence have become known to the third party (a) the principal's liability remains intact (b) a right of reimbursement against the principal arises in the agent's favor (c) constructive ratification cuts off any rights the principal might have against the agent (d) none of the above.

11. _____

12. Conditions which indicate a principal's intent to allow an agent to delegate authority to another include (a) prior dealings among the parties (b) presumption per se (c) constructive notice (d) all of the above.

12. _____

13.   Effective constructive notice is achieved through (a) radio announcements (b) statements in geographically proper newspapers of general circulation (c) billboard ads (d) handbills.

13. _____

CASE PROBLEMS - SHORT ESSAY ANSWERS: Read each case problem carefully. When appropriate, answer by stating a Decision for the case and by explaining the rationale - Rule of Law - relied upon to support your decision.

1.   For the past five years, Agent A, acting on behalf of Principal P, has purchased new model year cars from Cardealership C for P's company fleet. Each year, A trades in the previous year's cars. The past year has been quite financially difficult for P's company so to reduce expenditures, P directs A not to purchase new model year cars but to retain last year's models for at least another year. C is not aware of P's changed plans nor does A inform C of this fact when, disregarding P's instructions, A trades in the last year's models and purchases new ones. When A refuses to pay for them and C seeks payment from P, may P validly avoid payment based on the express refusal to A for the authority to make the purchases? Explain.

Decision: _____

_____

Rule of Law: _____

_____

2.   A, agent for P, is told by P to deliver an important paper to X immediately. Time is essential. Hoping to please P, A drove the company car at a high rate of speed and unfortunately struck T. Can T sue A? Explain.

Decision: _____

_____

Rule of Law: _____

_____

3.   A, an agent for disclosed principal P, makes a contract with third party T on behalf of P for the purchase of property insurance from which A will be paid $500 by P. If T breaches the contract, can A sue T? Explain.

Decision: _____

_____

Rule of Law: _____

_____

4.   In a case involving an undisclosed principal, an agent buys goods on credit but does not pay for them. Later the seller of the goods discovers the fact of the agency and the identity of the principal. The seller obtains a judgment against the principal, but the principal is insolvent. Can the seller recover from the agent? Explain.

Decision: _____

_____

Rule of Law: _____

_____

5.   P, the owner of Blackacre, hires X an independent contractor, to build a hotel on P's land. When X begins to break the ground, X uses dynamite to loosen the earth. T, who lives three blocks away, has five windows broken due to the concussion from the explosions. Can T sue P even though X was an independent contractor? Explain.

Decision: _____

_____

Rule of Law: _____

_____

AGENCY UNIT RESEARCH QUESTIONS: Drawing upon information contained in the text, as well as outside sources, discuss the following questions:

1.   In what areas of our business and personal lives are we likely to encounter principles of agency law?

2.   How has legislative and administrative law pre-empted certain common law agency principles? What rationale underlies these changes?

CHAPTER 19

Introduction to Sales

SCOPE NOTE

We have already studied contract law. That area of the law, in addition to Article 2 of the U.C.C., controls transactions for the sale of goods. The following Chapter introduces the legal intricacies associated with the law of sales. Knowing basic terminology, the requirements for a valid sales contract and fundamental legal doctrines which control this area of law provide a useful, essential foundation for understanding the specific fields of legal inquiry which comprise the body of the law of sales.

EDUCATIONAL OBJECTIVES

1.   Distinguish between the approaches to sales contracts under common law and U.C.C. Article 2.

2.   List the various Article 2 doctrines controlling sales contracts.

3.   Develop the various requirements for a valid sales contract, including mutual agreement, consideration and various formality restrictions.

4.   Discuss how sales contracts differ from other non-goods contracts and transactions.

5.   Describe the U.C.C. provisions exclusively applicable to sales between merchants.

6.   Discuss the significance of the doctrine of unconscionability in the law of sales.

CHAPTER OUTLINE

I.   Nature of Sales Contracts - buyer and seller rights/duties
    A.   Definition - transfer of title to goods for a price
        1.   Governing law - U.C.C. Article 2
        2.   Nonsales transactions in goods - bailments, leases, gifts, security interests
    B.   Fundamental Principles of Article 2

1.   Good faith - honesty in fact; commercial reasonableness
2.   Unconscionability - fairness and decency
3.   Expansion of commercial practices - course of dealing, usage of trade
4.   Sales by and between merchants - separate rules under the Code
5.   Liberal administration of remedies - place nonbreaching party in as good a position as if proper performance had occured
6.   Freedom of contract - parties can vary Code provisions
7.   Validation and preservation of sales contracts - Code reduces commercial law requirements

II.   Formation of a Sales Contract - requirements for valid, enforceable agreement
  A.   Manifestation of Mutual Assent - meeting of the minds
    1.   Definiteness of an offer - Code allows for reasonable indefiniteness
      a.   Open price - reasonable price at delivery
      b.   Open delivery - reasonable time at seller's place of business
      c.   Open quantity - output and requirement contracts
      d.   Other open terms - Code provides various rules
    2.   Irrevocable offers - three month maximum for written assurance to keep offer open
    3.   Variant acceptances - Code modifies common law mirror image rule
    4.   Manner of acceptance - any manner, any medium that is reasonable
    5.   Auctions - without or with reserve compared
  B.   Consideration
    1.   Contractual modifications - Code discards common law requirement of separate consideration
    2.   Discharge of claim after breach - written, signed, delivered waiver, enforceable without separate consideration.
    3.   Firm offers - no consideration required
  C.   Form of the Contract
    1.   Statute of Frauds - sale of goods for $500 or more
      a.   Modification of contracts within the Statute of Frauds - must be written if resulting contract is within the Statute
      b.   Written compliance - more liberal than common law
      c.   Alternative methods of compliance - sworn admittance to contract existence; oral contract for specially manufactured goods; delivered and accepted goods
    2.   Parol evidence - modified by course of dealing, trade usage, course of performance
    3.   Seal - Code makes inoperative for sale of goods

TRUE-FALSE: Circle true or false.

Answers

T   F   1.   Employment contracts, service contracts and insurance contracts are not covered by Article 2 of the U.C.C.

T   F   2.   Contracts for the sale of goods costing $300 or more must be in writing to be enforceable.

T   F   3.   Under the Code, sales contracts containing omitted terms are unenforceable due to their lack of definiteness.

T   F   4.   Under the Code, merchants are held to a higher standard of commercial reasonableness than are non-merchants.

T   F   5.   A written memorandum, signed by a merchant seller, confirming an earlier oral contract falling within the Statute of Frauds, binds a merchant buyer unless the latter effectively objects.

T   F   6.   Retracted bids at auctions automatically revive the previously submitted bid.

T   F   7.   A contract for the sale of timber to be cut and removed by purchaser is a sale of goods under the U.C.C.

T   F   8.   A lease of goods is similar to a bailment.

T   F   9.   Unless the parties provide otherwise, place of delivery of goods is seller's place of business.

T   F   10. According to U.C.C. provisions, sales contracts valued at $15,000 or more must be under Department of Commerce seal to be valid.

T   F   11. An exchange of goods for services is a sale.

T   F   12. As a general rule, the remedial provisions of the Code are narrowly interpreted and applied to prevent unjust enrichment to the party injured by another's breach of contract.

KEY TERMS – MATCHING EXERCISE: Select the term which best completes each statement below and write the corresponding number in the ANSWERS column.

	Column I		Column II	Answers
1.	A present transfer of title to goods in exchange for a price.	1.	Option	1. _____
2.	Movable, tangible personal property.	2.	Mirror image rule	2. _____
3.	The performance standard controlling parties to sales contracts on their contractual duties.	3.	Seller	3. _____
		4.	Sale	4. _____
4.	A transfer of title and possession without return consideration.	5.	Possession	5. _____
5.	A transfer of possession to goods without a transfer of title.	6.	Security agreement	6. _____
		7.	Goods	7. _____
				8. _____

6. A common method of doing business prevalent in a particular area of commerce.

7. An auction at which the auctioneer may not withdraw items put up for sale unless no bids are made.

8. The common law doctrine that required acceptances of offers to comply exactly with the terms of the offer.

9. Sales contracts which are harsh and unfair because of the unequal bargaining positions of the parties.

10. A contractual agreement granting a creditor the right to obtain possession of goods upon a debtor's default.

11. A contract binding the offeror to keep the offer open for a specific time period.

12. Written statement signed by non-breaching party discharging breaching party for liability for non-performance.

13. Transfer of possession to another for a specific time for return payment.

14. Irrevocable offer made by a merchant.

15. Auctions at which auctioneer may withdraw goods at anytime until completion of the sale.

8. Without reserve

9. Gift

10. Trade usage

11. Good faith

12. Implied warranty

13. Unconscionable

14. Merchants

15. Bailment

16. Waiver

17. Firm offer

18. With reserve

19. Lease

20. Trust

9. _____

10. _____

11. _____

12. _____

13. _____

14. _____

15. _____

MULTIPLE CHOICE: Select the alternative which best completes each statement below and write the corresponding letter in the ANSWERS column.   Answers

1. Property included under the U.C.C.'s definition of goods includes (a) real property (b) negotiable instruments (c) growing crops (d) all of the above.

1. _____

2. The area of law once conrolling sales of goods was (a) Restatement of Sales (b) Trade Mercantilism (c) Uniform Sales Act (d) Law Merchant.

2. _____

3. Modifications of sales contracts must be (a) supported by consideration (b) made in good faith (c) witnessed in writing (d) all of the above to be valid under the terms of the U.C.C.

3. _____

4. Acceptance of the terms of a sales offer may be indicated by (a) conduct (b) words (c) presumed intention (d) all of the above.

4. _____

5. Under the Code, merchants are persons who (a) deal in certain goods (b) hold themselves out to have special knowledge peculiar to certain goods (c) employ an agent who professes to have special knowledge peculiar to goods (d) all of the above.

5. _____

6. A pattern of business relations existing between parties often doing business with one another is called a/n (a) trade pattern (b) course of dealing (c) usage of trade (d) none of the above.

6. _____

7. Written contractual terms intended as the final, complete agreement of the parties may not be altered, contradicted or supplemented by prior or contemporaneous agreement evidence under the (a) Parol Evidence Rule (b) Fair Interpretation Doctrine (c) last in First Controlling Rule (d) none of the above.

7. _____

8. Consideration which the buyer promises the seller in exchange for the goods is referred to as the (a) cost minus depreciation (b) price (c) appreciation (d) pledge.

8. _____

9. The Code expressly defines unconscionability as (a) criminal dishonesty (b) fraud in execution (c) deceit (d) none of the above.

9. _____

10. An "open-price" term in a sales contract may be filled in by (a) later agreement between the parties (b) a bailment (c) an auction (d) a conditional sale.

10. _____

11. The Code's sales provisions (a) are mandatory and must be strictly followed by contracting parties (b) are monitored and enforced by the F.T.C. (c) may be changed by contracting parties (d) none of the above.

11. _____

12. The Code has changed general contract law regarding the formation of sales contracts (a) to bring more formality to this process (b) by allowing States greater freedom to apply their own rules of law (c) by favoring commercial over consumer interests (d) to modernize and promote fairness in contract law.

12. _____

13. Under the Code, an oral contract for the sale of $850 worth of pencils is enforceable (a) if a party admits that negotiations for such a sale occurred (b) only to the extent of delivered and accepted units (c)

totally as long as partial performance has occurred (d) only upon
complete performance by both parties.   13. _____

CASE PROBLEMS - SHORT ESSAY ANSWERS: Read each case problem carefully. Answer by
stating a Decision for the case and by explaining the rationale - Rule of Law - relied upon to support
your decision.

1.   S, a nail wholesaler, offers to sell to B, a hardware dealer, 2 tons of nails for $600.00. S sends B a
     signed memo stating the offer will remain open for five business days. Two days later, S sends a
     telegram to B revoking the offer. B ignores the attempted revocation and transmits an acceptance
     which S refuses to honor. Do the parties have a contract? Explain.

     Decision: _____
     _____

     Rule of Law: _____
     _____

2.   B enters a contract with S for the purchase of the entire production output of S's mobile home
     manufacturing facility from March through June. Since the exact quantity of homes to be
     purchased is not stated, is this contract invalid due to indefiniteness?

     Decision: _____
     _____

     Rule of Law: _____
     _____

3.   A financially strapped elderly retired couple, H and W, enter an installment purchase contract with
     S, a door-to-door salesperson, for a dishwasher, retail value of $180, calling for forty payments of
     $220 each. After making two installment payments, H and W become dissatisfied, not with the
     dishwasher, but its price. Can they withdraw from this contract with S? Why or why not?

     Decision: _____
     _____

     Rule of Law: _____
     _____

4.   Penny, pet store operator, receives an offer mailed from Yummy Pet Supplies, Inc., for the sale of
     6 months supply of Yummy pet food products to be sold in Penny's store. Penny, knowing
     Yummy's reputation for quality, reasonably priced products, believes this pet food line will
     increase her business and quickly accepts Yummy's offer, adding in her acceptance letter that she'd
     like samples of Yummy's grooming products to examine for possible sale in her store. A few days
     after Penny sends her acceptance letter, she receives a call from Yale Yummy, C.E.O. of Yummy,
     Inc., saying he considers Penny's letter a rejection and a counter offer which he finds unpalatable
     and refuses to do business with her. Penny thinks she has a contract. Who wins this dispute?

     Decision: _____
     _____

     Rule of Law: _____
     _____

5.   Wally Widget is the only person who would want or could use wadgets. Wally places an oral order with the Wadget Company to make 10,000 wadgets at $2.00 each. Later, Wally refuses to accept the completed wadgets and alleges the Uniform Commercial Code Statute of Frauds as a defense to the suit for breach of contract. Decide.

Decision: _____
_____

Rule of Law: _____
_____

CHAPTER 20

Transfer of Title and Risk of Loss

SCOPE NOTE

Studying the legal doctrines associated with title to personal property and sales of goods is vital to understanding the law of sales. Title passage in various types of sales transactions and the factors used to determine passing of title are discussed in Chapter Nineteen. In addition to ownership considerations, parties to sales transactions must know their rights and duties at the various stages of their business dealings. In the event of damage or destruction to goods sold, who bears the risk of loss? When may the parties to a sales transaction protect their interest in goods through insurance? The factors used in deciding risk-of-loss issues as well as the various U.C.C. provisions controlling this area are also examined in this Chapter.

Another important aspect of the legal identities of parties to a sales transaction is knowing under what circumstances someone with less than full ownership may transfer title to purchasers of goods. What difficulties are created when an innocent buyer purchases another person's goods believing that the sale was authorized by and is made with the permission of the true owner? These issues are also addressed in Chapter Twenty which develops the rules used to determine the rights of adversary parties (usually the purchaser and the original owner) in cases of attempted title transfer by a non-owner of goods. The situations in which the innocent buyer prevails are discussed as well as those cases where the original owner's title to the sold goods is protected. The Chapter closes with a discussion of the rights that creditors of the goods seller have in the goods sold. Guidelines to purchasers from and creditors of the seller are presented which aid in determining priority of interest in these confusing transactions.

EDUCATIONAL OBJECTIVES

1.   Enumerate the types of issues directly related to title location concerns.

2.   Identify the rules used in determining title passage and how they are influenced by type of goods, shipment terms, the use of documents of title and other related circumstances.

3.   Explain the importance of identifying goods to the contract.

4.   Define and point out the significance of a buyer's "special property interest."

5.   Delineate the various rules associated with determining risk of loss when no breach of contract has occurred.

6.   Distinguish sale on approval from sale or return.

7.   Describe how shipment terms, possession of the goods byaa bailee and breach of contract affect risk-of-loss issues.

8.   Explain the legal policies in competition with one another in non-owner sales of goods.

9.   Distinguish between void and voidable title transfers both at common law and under the U.C.C.

10.   Define and describe the significance of a bona-fide purchaser for value.

11.   Discuss the treatment of an innocent buyer under the U.C.C.

12.   Describe the importance of the doctrine of entrusting as developed in the U.C.C.

13.   Define "bulk transfer" and list Code requirements applicable to such transactions.

14.   List the type of transactions exempted from Article 6 control.

15.   Discuss the effect of not complying with Article 6.

CHAPTER OUTLINE

I.   Transfer of Title and Other Property Rights
      A.   Passage of Title - from seller to buyer
            1.   Physical movement of goods - delivery made by moving goods; title passes at time and place seller delivers
                  a.   Shipment contracts - require authorized seller to send goods to buyer; do not require delivery at particular destination; title passes at time and place of delivery to carrier
                  b.   Destination contracts - require seller to deliver goods to particular destination; title passes upon tender at destination
            2.   No movement of goods - delivery made without moving the goods; title passes upon delivery of title document (where contract calls for delivery) or at time and place of contracting (goods identified to contract and no documents are to be delivered)
      B.   Other Property Rights
            1.   Special property interest - buyer obtains special rights to goods when goods are identified to the contract by seller
            2.   Insurable interest - Code provides buyer's insurable interest exists upon identification of goods to the contract
            3.   Security interest - secures payment or performance of an obligation
      C.   Power to Transfer Title - problem cases: seller not rightful owner of goods or authorized to sell goods; seller possesses goods of another; may have power to transfer good title to certain buyers (good faith purchaser, buyer in ordinary course)
            1.   Void and voidable title to goods
            -     a.   Void title - no title to goods; original owner can regain goods; bona fide

purchaser does not cut off such right

      b.   Voidable title - circumstances which may cut off former owner's right to regain goods; bona fide purchaser retains title

    2.   Entrusting goods to merchant - repair contracts; purchaser of goods during ordinary course of business cuts off original owner's rights to regain goods

II.   Risk of Loss - placement of loss between seller and buyer where goods have been damaged, destroyed, or lost without fault of either

    A.   Risk of Loss in Absence of a Breach

        1.   Agreement of the parties - contract divides, shifts risk

        2.   Trial sales

           a.   Sale on approval - possession, not title transferred to buyer for stated period of time; title and risk of loss remain with seller until buyer's approval or acceptance.

           b.   Sale or return - goods sold and delivered to buyer with option to return; risk of loss on buyer until title revested by return

           c.   Consignment - delivery of possession to an agent for sale by agent; Code treats as a sale or return

        3.   Contracts involving carriers

           a.   Shipment contracts - seller not required to deliver goods to a particular destination; risk of loss passes to buyer upon delivery of goods to carrier

           b.   Destination contracts - seller required to deliver goods to particular destination; risk of loss passes to buyer at destination upon tender

        4.   Goods in possession of bailee - risk of loss influenced by presence of third party; goods held by bailee (storage, transit) for delivery without being moved; risk of loss passes to buyer upon receipt of title documents or other documents

        5.   All other sales - goods in possession of buyer, or not in posssession; risk of loss passes to buyer at time of receipt, tender or otherwise

    B.   Risk of Loss Where there is a Breach

        1.   Breach by seller - risk of loss remains on seller until buyer accepts goods or seller has remedied the defect

        2.   Breach by buyer - seller may treat risk of loss as resting on the buyer "for a commercially reasonable time"

III.   Sales of Goods in Bulk - transfer of goods, not in ordinary course of the transferor's business, of a major part of the materials, supplies, merchandise, or other inventory; fear that debtor may fraudulently liquidate assets by a bulk sale and conceal or divert the proceeds without paying creditors

    A.   Requirements of Article 6 - Code provisions must be met for a bulk transfer to be effective against creditors

    B.   Exempted Bulk Transfers - bulk transfers which need not comply with Article 6 to be valid transfers

    C.   Effect of Failure to Comply with Article 6 - goods still subject to claims of unpaid creditors

    D.   Application of the Proceeds - question of what obligation transferee (purchaser) owes to transferor's (seller's) creditors

    E.   Auction Sales - Code requirements for valid sales

        1.   Transferor furnishes auctioneer sworn list of creditors and assists in preparation of a schedule of property to be sold

        2.   Auctioneer receives and retains the list of creditors and schedule of property for six months and permits inspection by creditors

3. Auctioneer gives notice by registered or certified mail at least 10 days before auction to all creditors named in list and to all other persons known to have claims against the transferor

TRUE-FALSE: Circle true or false.

Answers

T   F   1.   Parties to a sales contract may, by agreement, define who will assume risk of loss for damage or destruction of the goods.

T   F   2.   Under the Code, buyers must own goods before they are insurable.

T   F   3.   The U.C.C. does not use title location as the primary means to determine the rights of parties to a sales contract when goods are damaged.

T   F   4.   The power and right to transfer title are one and the same.

T   F   5.   In sales of goods by non-owners, the policies of ownership protection and marketplace stability come into conflict.

T   F   6.   When a seller ships non-conforming goods to a buyer, risk of loss remains on the seller until the buyer accepts the goods.

T   F   7.   Under "no arrival, no sale" contracts, title and risk of loss pass to the buyer upon arrival of the goods at destination.

T   F   8.   A bulk sale is a transfer not in the ordinary course of business.

T   F   9.   Under modern law, a minor seller may avoid a sale of goods and recover them from a third party bona fide purchaser for value.

T   F   10.   A risk faced by creditors of a debtor-seller of goods in bulk is that the latter may use the bulk sale to liquidate assets and keep the sale proceeds from the creditors.

T   F   11.   The bulk sales provisions of the Code are designed to protect creditors of a merchant debtor from the latter's fraud.

T   F   12.   A shipment contract requires a seller to deliver goods at a specified location.

KEY TERMS - MATCHING EXERCISE: Select the term which best completes each statement below and write the corresponding number in the ANSWERS column.

Column I		Column II		Answers
1. Steps taken by the seller to choose goods which meet contractual specifications.	1.	Bulk sale	1.	_____
	2.	Freight forwarder	2.	_____

2.   A transfer of goods to a merchant dealing in the type of goods transferred.

3.   An interest in personal property which protects performance of a promised, future obligation.

4.   A good faith purchaser for value who purchased from a merchant during normal business hours.

5.   The interest acquired under circumstances which allow former owner-vendors to revoke a sale and recapture their prior ownership.

6.   Burden assumed by either party to a sales contract for destruction or damage to the goods.

7.   Transfer of title to goods under which buyer retains an option to revest title in the seller.

8.   Shipment method by which the seller retains possession of the goods, preventing their delivery, until the purchase price is paid.

9.   Transfer of goods for a period of time during which buyer determines whether or not to purchase them.

10.   A transfer for value not in the ordinary course of business, of a substantial portion of the equipment, materials, inventory, supplies or merchandise of the business.

11.   Someone lacking both the power and right to sell goods.

3.   Sale or return

4.   Initial carrier

5.   Voidable title

6.   Bailee

7.   Security interest

8.   Identification

9.   Entrusting

10.   F.A.S.

11.   Buyer in the ordinary course

12.   Risk of loss

13.   C.O.D.

14.   Sale on approval

15.   Sale

16.   C.I.F.

17.   Good faith purchaser for value

18.   Tender

19.   Destination

20.   Thief

3.   _____

4.   _____

5.   _____

6.   _____

7.   _____

8.   _____

9.   _____

10.   _____

11.   _____

12.   _____

13.   _____

14.   _____

15.   _____

12. One buying goods honestly without
     knowledge of any title problems.

13. Shipment contract calling for
     seller to pay insurance and
     freight costs.

14. Contract requiring seller to ship
     goods to a specific location.

15. Duty of seller to make conforming
     goods available to the buyer for a
     reasonable time and notify the
     buyer of this fact.

MULTIPLE CHOICE: Select the alternative which best completes each statement below and write the corresponding letter in the ANSWERS column.

Answers

1.   A reason for the legal policy to protect existing ownership of goods is to
     (a) make transfers easier (b) protect involuntary bailees (c) ensure that
     people are not required to retain possession or control of goods at all
     times to maintain their ownership in them (d) none of the above.   1. _____

2.   The controversy which commonly follows a non-owner's sale of goods
     pits a (a) non-owner against an owner (b) non-owner against a good
     faith purchaser for value (c) good faith purchaser for value against an
     owner (d) none of the above.   2. _____

3.   Bulk transfers exempted from U.C.C. Article 6 coverage include (a)
     general assignments in favor of the bulk seller's creditors (b) sales of
     exempt   property   (c)   sales   by   personal   representatives
     (executor/executrix) (d) all of the above.   3. _____

4.   Code requirements making bulk transfers valid against creditors of the
     bulk transferor include (a) central filing by the transferee (b) notice of
     the transfer by the transferee to all listed creditors of the transferor (c) a
     conditional pledge signed by the transferor (d) a recorded factor's lien. 4. _____

5.   When the seller alone has identified goods to the contract, other goods
     may be substituted by the seller until the seller (a) defaults (b) becomes
     insolvent (c) notifies the buyer of final identification (d) all of the
     above.   5. _____

6.   Persons holding void and therefore no title include (a) finders (b) bailors
     (c) people acquiring goods through undue influence (d) all of the above.   6. _____

7.   Examples of voidable title include acquisition through (a) mistake (b)
     fraud in the execution (c) sale or gift from someone under guardianship
     (d) all of the above.   7. _____

8.   A/n _____ is delivering personal property to an agent for sale
        by that person. (a) allocation (b) approval transfer (c) consignment (d)
        none of the above.

8.   _____

9.   Under a sale on approval, the buyer's failure to reasonably notify the
        seller of an election to return the goods is (a) identification (b)
        acceptance (c) ratification (d) consignment of the goods.

9.   _____

10.   Under the U.C.C., risk of loss is determined by who (a) holds title to
        the goods (b) has greater control over the goods (c) occupies the position
        of equitable receiver (d) all of the above.

10.   _____

11.   The Code's approach to risk of loss is (a) a transactional approach (b)
        based on State secured credit laws (c) generally outmoded and antiquated
        (d) none of the above.

11.   _____

12.   The Code treats a consignment sale as (a) one on approval (b) a bailment
        (c) a sale or return (d) a lease.

12.   _____

13.   Generally, in cases of breach of contract, the Code places the risk of
        loss (a) on both parties equally (b) on the offeror (c) on the party
        financing the transaction (d) on the non-performing party.

13.   _____

CASE PROBLEMS - SHORT ESSAY ANSWERS: Read each case problem carefully. Answer by
stating a Decision for the case and by explaining the rationale - Rule of Law - relied upon to support
your decision.

1.   A, an auctioneer, makes an auction-sale bulk transfer of B's goods. A failed to comply with the
        provisions of the U.C.C. regulating bulk sales by an auctioneer. A turns over the net proceeds of
        the sale to B's creditors but the amount covers only 10% of the total debt. The creditors seek to
        avoid the transfers to the purchasers at the auction and have the goods returned. The auction
        purchasers vigorously oppose the creditor's action. Who wins this dispute?

        Decision: _____

        Rule of Law: _____
        _____

2.   B pays cash for goods purchased from S. Unable to take immediate delivery, B arranges for the
        goods to remain with S for a week and a half. Three days following the sale to B, S sells the same
        goods to C, who takes delivery. B, upon returning for delivery, learns of the sale to C and seeks
        to replevin the goods from C. C resists. Who has title to the goods?

        Decision: _____

        Rule of Law: _____
        _____

3.   A transfers a fur coat to retail furrier B for repair and storage. During B's regular business hours,

C purchases the coat from B. What are A's rights against purchaser C? Explain.

Decision: _____

_____

Rule of Law: _____

_____

4.   Owner of grain stored in E's elevator sells the grain to B. Every bushel of grain in the elevator is covered by an outstanding negotiable document of title evidencing ownership. Upon selling the grain in the elevator, owner delivers the title document to the buyer. Shortly thereafter, the elevator burns with all contents lost. Who bears the loss for the sold grain, elevator owner, grain owner or buyer? Explain.

Decision: _____

_____

Rule of Law: _____

_____

5.   S ships goods to B using a carriage contract providing for delivery "ex ship" at a specific dock. While the boat carrying the goods is maneuvering into position, it strikes the dock and sinks with total loss of its cargo. Who absorbs the loss of the goods? Explain.

Decision: _____

Rule of Law: _____

_____

CHAPTER 21

Products Liability: Warranties and Strict Liability in Tort

SCOPE NOTE

The purchaser of goods expects that they will conform to certain quality and title standards. When a seller's performance falls below such standards, when goods are defective, a breach of warranty usually exists making the seller liable for resulting damages. What protection is given the buyer against title/quality defects? What guarantees run to the innocent purchaser providing protection against unfair/dishonest business practices? In the following Chapter, these issues are focused upon in terms of basic terminology and principles of warranty law contained in the U.C.C.

EDUCATIONAL OBJECTIVES

1.   Identify the types of transactions to which warranty law applies.

2.   Enumerate the various categories of express and implied warranties and how they are created.

3.   Discuss how the "Puffing Doctrine" and the Parol Evidence Rule affect warranty protection.

4.   Analyze how Caveat Emptor interacts with warranty liability.

5.   Explain the various U.C.C. requirements for validity excluding/limiting warranty protection, both express and implied.

6.   Identify the roles played by the doctrine of privity, the trade usage doctrine and the buyer's examination duty in warranty considerations.

7.   Discuss the Code's application of warranty protection to third parties.

8.   Identify significant changes brought to warranty law by the enactment of federal warranty legislation.

9.   Explain the influence of contributory negligence and assumption of the risk on warranty liability.

10.   Explain strict liability and its relevance to products liability cases.

11.   Outline burden of proof requirements under strict liability and demonstrate how they apply to cases of personal injury caused by defective goods.

12.   Review the impact of contributory negligence and assumption of the risk in product liability cases.

CHAPER OUTLINE

I.   Warranties - seller's obligation regarding satisfactory performance (quality, title, quantity, etc.) in sales of goods
      A.   Types of Warranties - created by agreement or by operation of law
           1.   Warranty of title - good title; valid transfer; no encumberances
           2.   Express warranties - created by parties; statements of fact; basis of bargain
           3.   Implied warranties - created by law
                a.   Merchantability - merchant seller; ordinary, average quality
                b.   Fitness for particular purpose - any seller; seller's knowledge and buyer's reliance
      B.   Obstacles to Warranty Actions - difficulties, problems associated with claims based on warranty breach
           1.   Disclaimer or modification of warranties - clauses in a contract; Code dictates validity requirements
                a.   Express exclusions
                b.   Buyer's examination or refusal to examine
                c.   Conflict of warranties - intent of parties controls
                d.   Federal legislation relating to warranties of consumer products - Magnusson-Moss provisions; role of F.T.C.
           2.   Privity of contract - business relationship giving use to rights of recovery
                a.   Horizontal privity - non-contracting parties (users, bystanders)
                b.   Vertical privity - remote sellers on distribution chain
           3.   Notice of breach - buyer's duty to notify seller of defects
           4.   Plaintiff's conduct - as a defense to warranty based recovery
                a.   Contributory negligence - not a defense
                b.   Voluntary assumption of risk - recognized as a valid defense
II.   Strict Liability in Tort - merchant seller liability for defective products that are ultra-hazardous
      A.   Nature - sellers, manufacturers, sailors, leasors
           1.   Defective condition - plaintiff must prove existence; cause of is not material
                a.   Manufacturing defect
                b.   Design defect
                c.   Inadequate warning or instructions
           2.   Unreasonably dangerous - ultra-hazardous defective condition
      B.   Obstacles to Recovery - problems recovering under strict liability
           1.   Disclaimers and notice - contractual defenses not valid in consumer transactions; courts allow in commercial dealings
           2.   Privity - standing to sue based on business relationship
                a.   Horizontal privity - recovery rights in buyers, users, bystanders
                b.   Vertical privity - any merchant seller in distribution chain
           3.   Plaintiff's conduct - as a defense to strict liability based recovery
                a.   Contributory negligence - generally no defense

    b.   Comparative negligence - recovery amount reduction
    c.   Voluntary assumption of the risk - generally a valid defense
    d.   Misuse or abuse of the product - does it create danger; is it foreseeable by seller
4.   Subsequent alteration - substantial change in product's condition may be a defense
5.   Statute of Repose - State legislation limiting the time for which manufacturers are liable for defective products

TRUE-FALSE: Circle true or false.

Answers

T   F   1.   A recent and important development in the area of products liability is the theory of strict liability in tort.

T   F   2.   Sellers are always required to warrant goods they sell.

T   F   3.   Extending products liability to manufacturers of goods has not reduced the liability of sellers to purchasers of defective goods.

T   F   4.   All sellers impliedly warrant the merchantability of the goods they sell.

T   F   5.   For the implied warranty of fitness for a particular purpose to apply, the buyer must specifically inform the seller of the express purpose for which the goods are purchased.

T   F   6.   The U.C.C. reduces the controlling influence that contractual privity has in breach of warranty disputes.

T   F   7.   Under the theory of strict liability in tort, a plaintiff must show how and why a product became defective to establish a recovery right.

T   F   8.   Strict liability may not be disclaimed, excluded or modified by contract.

T   F   9.   Manufacturers or sellers must warn purchasers of all possible hazards associated with any use of products sold.

T   F   10.   Contributory negligence is not an effective defense in a suit against a seller of goods for breach of warranty.

T   F   11.   Implied warranties arise by acts of parties and not through operation of law.

T   F   12.   Liability for personal injuries caused by unreasonably dangerous defective goods extends to lease transactions.

KEY TERMS – MATCHING EXERCISE: Select the term which best completes each statement below and write the corresponding number in the ANSWERS column.

Column I	Column II	Answers

Column I

1. Early rule of common law which placed on buyers total assumption of loss due to defective goods.

2. Action on the part of a buyer which nullifies the seller's implied warranty liability for obvious defects.

3. Statements of opinion or value made by a seller which are not a basis for warranty liability.

4. A seller's statement amounting to a definite assurance regarding the description, quality or condition of goods sold.

5. Liability without fault imposed by law as a matter of public policy in sales of defective products posing unreasonably dangerous hazards.

6. Voluntarily using a known defective product in the face of danger.

7. The contractual relationship which early common law required between a plaintiff and defendant before recovery based upon breach of warranty could be obtained.

8. The common law tort defense which completely bars plaintiffs from any recovery due to self-carelessness.

9. An act of Congress seeking to prevent deception and protect consumer purchasers by providing for competent product warranty information.

Column II

1. Sales Act
2. Contributory negligence
3. Comparative negligence
4. Expert
5. Disclaimer
6. Strict liability
7. Puffing
8. Caveat emptor
9. Express warranty
10. Assumption of risk
11. Consumer products
12. Inspection of goods
13. By sample
14. Privity
15. Magnuson-Moss Act
16. Trade usage
17. Sale on approval
18. Merchantable
19. Waiver
20. Statutes of repose

Answers

1. _____
2. _____
3. _____
4. _____
5. _____
6. _____
7. _____
8. _____
9. _____
10. _____
11. _____
12. _____
13. _____
14. _____
15. _____

10.   The tort doctrine applicable to
        reduce a plaintiff's damages
        recovery by the degree of the
        plaintiff's contributory fault.

11.   One whose statements of opinion
        may create warranty liability.

12.   Of fair, average and medium
        quality.

13.   Regular industry customs that may
        create warranty liability.

14.   Positive, explicit, unequivocal
        statements eliminating warranty
        liability.

15.   Legislation limiting the time
        during which manufacturers are
        liable for injuries caused by
        products.

MULTIPLE CHOICE: Select the alternative which best completes each statement below and write the corresponding letter in the ANSWERS column.   Answers

1.   The duty to warn of dangers or hazards associated with the use of
        products arises from (a) the duty of due care (b) specific statutory
        provisions (c) the spreading of the risk theory (d) none of the above.   1.   _____

2.   Of the following, who is normally not subject to strict liability in tort?
        (a) supplier of component parts (b) manufacturer of finished goods (c)
        purchaser (d) retailer.   2.   _____

3.   Under the Code, liability of the seller for express warranty is made
        dependent on whether the statement in question was (a) the basis for the
        bargain (b) a repudiation of the contract (c) the basis for damages (d)
        made with the necessary intent.   3.   _____

4.   The Code's extension of seller warranty applies to (a) employees of the
        buyer (b) household guests of the buyer (c) guest passengers in the
        buyer's car (d) all of the above.   4.   _____

5.   A defense in tort which may be successfully used by the seller against
        an injured buyer of defective goods in a breach of warranty suit is (a)
        assumption of the risk (b) res ipsa loquitur (c) contributory negligence
        (d) equitable cloture.   5.   _____

6.   Sellers of products are liable for injuries that result from (a) any misuse
       of a product (b) unanticipatable product abuse (c) foreseeable misuse of
       a product (d) all of the above.   6. _____

7.   Which of the following is not a required element of proof for strict
       liability under Section 402A, Restatement of Torts, Second Edition? (a)
       merchant seller (b) life expectancy of product (c) defective condition (d)
       unchanged condition of the product.   7. _____

8.   Implied warranties are excludable by (a) the words "as is" (b) usage of
       trade (c) course of dealing (d) all of the above.   8. _____

9.   The implied warranty of merchantability speaks to goods being (a) safe
       from any defect (b) suitable for any purpose (c) adequately labeled,
       packaged and contained (d) all of the above.   9. _____

10.   Warranties of quality under the Code generally do not apply to sales of
       (a) land (b) services (c) stocks (d) all of the above.   10. _____

11.   Situations where title warranties do not run with the transaction include
       (a) sheriff's sales (b) foreclosure sales (c) judicial sales (d) all of the
       above.   11. _____

12.   At early common law, implied title warranties (a) were not recognized
       under the doctrine of caveat emptor (b) ran with most commercial
       transactions (c) existed only in sales between merchants (d) were
       recognized only in sales involving secured credit.   12. _____

13.   _____ privity concerns sellers in the product distribution
       chain with whom the buyer did not deal. (a) equitable (b) vertical (c)
       horizontal (d) constructive   13. _____

CASE PROBLEMS - SHORT ESSAY ANSWERS: Read each case problem carefully. Answer by
stating a Decision for the case and by explaining the rationale - Rule of Law - relied upon to support
your decision.

1.   B, a sportsperson, purchases a handwarmer from a non-merchant neighbor, M. B carries the
       handwarmer in a coat pocket while hunting and suffers burns when the handwarmer explodes.
       May B bring suit against M using a strict liability theory for the injuries caused by the defective
       handwarmer? Explain.

       Decision: _____

       _____

       Rule of Law: _____

       _____

2.   B buys a used car from S, a used car dealer. B drives the car for two days when suddenly, all
       four wheels fall off and the steering mechanism collapses. What rights has B against S? Discuss.

Decision: _____

Rule of Law: _____

_____

3.   B purchases a bottle of hair coloring. The label contains a conspicuously typed and displayed
      caution: "WARNING. Always make a patch test before using this product." B applies the
      coloring, according to its directions, to a table top in an attempt to remove a water stain. The
      next day, the table is ruined. B sues the manufacturer for the damages to the table. Who prevails
      and why?

      Decision: _____

      Rule of Law: _____

      _____

4.   B purchased 40 lbs. of 1/8" steel rods cut to six-foot lengths. The contract price was $800. When
      the rods arrived, B accepted them. Sometime later, B discovers that some of the rods are not 1/8"
      and others are more than six feet. B sues S for breach of warranty. The value of the rods
      accepted was $700. Their value, had they conformed to the contract, would have been $1000.
      What is the level of B's damages? Explain.

      Decision: _____

      Rule of Law: _____

      _____

5.   While eating pieces of fried chicken at Chuck's Chicken Coup, customer C chokes on a chicken
      bone which becomes stuck in her throat. C sues restaurant owner B for her injuries, arguing that
      the presence of the inedible bone was a breach of the implied warranties of fitness and
      merchantability. Evaluate C's argument.

      Decision: _____

      Rule of Law: _____

      _____

CHAPTER 22
Performance

SCOPE NOTE

The terms of the sales contract as well as various provisions of the U.C.C. control the nature and interpretation of the rights/duties of the parties in performing on their sales agreement. It is the seller's obvious duty to deliver conforming goods at the proper time and location. Conversely, the buyer's self-evident duty is to accept properly tendered conforming goods and offer proper payment. The U.C.C. provisions controlling interpretation of contractual terms vis-a-vis performance give direction to how issues in this area are to be resolved. Besides outlining the broad performance rights/obligations of the parties, this Chapter introduces the complex issues and resolution guidelines associated with improper performance.

EDUCATIONAL OBJECTIVES

1. Describe the "perfect tender" rule as it applies to both parties of a sales contract.

2. Discuss the seller's proper delivery obligation in terms of method, location and time.

3. Identify situations under which the seller's duties under the "perfect tender" rule are altered.

4. Explain the buyer's performance duties under the "perfect tender" rule in terms of payment and inspection.

5. Enumerate the buyer's rights upon improper delivery.

6. Define and discuss the significance of acceptance.

7. Differentiate between the buyer's right to reject and to revoke acceptance.

8. Explain the doctrine of "cure" in the context of improper performance.

9. Describe the significance of substituted performance.

144

10. Outline circumstances which excuse non-performance in the context of failure of conditions and damage to goods.

CHAPTER OUTLINE

I. Performance by the Seller - buyer's expectations are met and contract duties are discharged; tender of delivery
    A. Time and Manner of Delivery - reasonableness; enable buyer to take possession
    B. Place of Tender - seller's place of business or where goods are located unless otherwise specified
        1. Shipment contracts - no destination specified; point of shipment
        2. Destination contracts - specified destination; at that point
        3. Goods held by bailee - tender title document
        4. Goods held by seller - seller's place of business
    C. Quality of Tender - degree of performance that is acceptable
        1. Perfect tender rule - conforming exactly to contract requirements
        2. Agreement by the parties - contractual modifications of perfect tender
        3. Cure by the seller - for non-conforming goods; early tender or acceptance by buyer
        4. Installment contracts - substantial value; impairment of specific installment or whole contract
II. Performance by the Buyer - duty to accept and pay for conforming goods
    A. Inspection - prior to payment or acceptance
    B. Rejection - refusal to accept non-conforming goods
    C. Acceptance - willingness to become owner (payment duty)
    D. Revocation of Acceptance - value impairing non-conformity; notice and cure
    E. Obligation of Payment - at time and place of receipt
III. Excuses for Non-Performance - Code provisions for risk allocation when parties fail to mention in their agreement
    A. Casualty to Identified Goods - prior to acceptance (offer terminated) or after acceptance (risk of loss provisions govern)
    B. Non-happening of Presupposed Conditions - discharge due to impossibility where condition is basic assumption of contract
    C. Substituted Performance - commercial impracticability triggers duty for commercially reasonable alternative

TRUE-FALSE: Circle true or false.

Answers

T   F   1. A sales contract may call for the seller to deliver goods prior to receiving payment.

T   F   2. Delivery may be tendered at any hour and conducted in any manner as the seller chooses.

T   F   3. Both parties to a sales contract are automatically excused from performance when the expressly provided for manner of delivery becomes impossible.

T   F   4. The buyer's acceptance of goods cuts off any right to reject them.

T   F   5.   Parties to a sales contract may not alter the application of the perfect tender rule to their transaction through contractual provisions.

T   F   6.   Unless the contract provides otherwise, payment is due at the time and place where the buyer is to receive the goods.

T   F   7.   A C.O.D. shipment contract requires buyer payment for the goods prior to inspection.

T   F   8.   Under the Code, acceptance of goods must always be in writing, signed by the buyer.

T   F   9.   When the sales contract does not specify the location for delivery, the place for delivery is deemed the buyer's place of business.

T   F   10.   When a buyer has rejected goods due to their nonconformity, the seller bears the burden of establishing that the goods conform to the contract.

T   F   11.   Usually fires, strikes or lock-outs are sufficient to excuse contractual performance on the grounds of performance impossibility.

T   F   12.   For a buyer to revoke acceptance, the seller's defective performance must substantially impair the value of the goods.

KEY TERMS – MATCHING EXERCISE: Select the term which best completes each statement below and write the corresponding number in the ANSWERS column.

	Column I		Column II	Answers
1.	The act which fulfills the expectations of the parties to their contract and discharges their contractual duties.	1.	Shipment contract	1. _____
		2.	Seller	2. _____
2.	A sales agreement calling for delivery and payment of goods in separate lots.	3.	Installment contract	3. _____
				4. _____
		4.	Possession	5. _____
3.	A unit of goods that is a single whole for the purposes of sale, a division of which substantially impairs its identity, value or use.	5.	Cure	6. _____
		6.	Commercial unit	7. _____
4.	The buyer's refusal to accept and make payment on non-conforming goods.	7.	Performance	8. _____
		8.	Revoke	9. _____
5.	A transaction under which the buyer is not required to make payment for the goods at the time they are received.	9.	Substituted performance	10. _____
		10.	Perfect Tender Rule	11. _____

6. Sellers prompt, timely delivery of conforming goods, following buyer's rightful rejection of non-conforming goods.

7. The obligation facing the parties to a sales contract when the agreed manner of performance has become commercially untenable without fault of either party.

8. A sales contract containing C.O.D., C.I.F., and C.F. delivery terms.

9. Duty imposed on the seller under the Code requiring tender of delivery exactly conforming to contractual terms.

10. Buyer's expression of willingness to become owner of goods.

11. Consideration buyer must give seller upon accepting commercial unit of nonconforming goods.

12. Buyer's pre-acceptance right to examine goods to insure that they conform to the contract.

13. Seller's duty to make available to the buyer conforming goods.

14. U.C.C. doctrine that discharges peformance when unforeseen events not anticipatable by the parties make performance on extreme hardship.

15. Buyer's duty upon accepting conforming goods.

11. Acceptance

12. Credit sale

13. Cancellation

14. Money damages

15. Rejection

16. Inspection

17. Commercial Impracticability

18. Payment

19. Tender

20. Contract rate

12. _____

13. _____

14. _____

15. _____

MULTIPLE CHOICE: Select the alternative which best completes each statement below and write the corresponding letter in the ANSWERS column.

Answers

1. When the sales contract does not mention time for delivery, the seller (a) has a reasonable time following the contractual execution to deliver the goods (b) must deliver the goods on buyer's demand (c) has no more than 60 days to deliver the goods (d) none of the above.

1. _____

2.   Following a buyer's rejection of non-conforming goods, a seller may rightfully (a) hold the buyer in breach (b) sell the goods elsewhere and thus avoid all liability to the buyer (c) rightfully refuse to reimburse the buyer for inspection expenses (d) undo the defective tender by promptly delivering conforming goods within the allowed performance time.

2.   _____

3.   Under a shipment contract, the seller must (a) deliver the goods to a carrier (b) issue a document of title for the goods to the buyer (c) make a reasonable contract of cartage (d) all of the above.

3.   _____

4.   To be effective, revocation of acceptance must be made (a) within a year after the goods are delivered (b) within a reasonable time after the non-conformity of the goods is discovered (c) in writing only (d) by a receiver in equity.

4.   _____

5.   Merchant buyers possessing rightfully rejected goods must (a) reship them (b) resell them (c) follow the reasonable instructions of the seller concerning their disposal (d) place them in trust.

5.   _____

6.   Factors relevant to the materiality of a breach of a sales contract include (a) U.C.C. definitions (b) contract subject matter (c) provisions in the constitution (d) res judicata.

6.   _____

7.   Upon delivery of conforming goods, the buyer must (a) tender payment (b) issue a document of title in favor of the seller (c) warehouse the goods until the seller is paid (d) all of the above.

7.   _____

8.   A buyer's right of inspection (a) can be exercised anytime (b) may not be eliminated by a clause in the contract (c) requires the buyer to bear inspection expenses (d) is usually nonexistent.

8.   _____

9.   Acceptance takes place when the buyer (a) fails to reject the goods (b) informs the seller that the goods are conforming (c) tells the seller that, despite nonconformities, the goods are adequate (d) all of the above.

9.   _____

10.   A sales contract containing the delivery terms "exship," "F.O.B. city of buyer," "no arrival, no sale," is a (a) substituted contract (a) destination contract (c) tendered contract (d) none of the above.

10.   _____

11.   Upon delivery of non-conforming goods a buyer may (a) reject all of the goods (b) accept all of the goods (c) accept any commercial unit or units and reject the rest (d) all of the above.

11.   _____

12.   Under an installment contract, when the seller has tendered non-conforming goods, the buyer (a) may reject the installment if its value is substantially impaired and the seller cannot cure the non-conformity (b) can immediately cancel the contract and hold the seller in total breach (c) has an absolute right of rejection (d) none of the above.

12.   _____

13.   A sales contract is performable in installments (a) in all cases (b) only in commercial transactions between merchants (c) only if the parties so agree (d) none of the above.

13.   _____

CASE PROBLEMS - SHORT ESSAY ANSWERS: Read each case problem carefully. When appropriate, answer by stating a Decision for the case and by explaining the rationale - Rule of Law - relied upon to support your decision.

1.   B orders two dozen personalized Halloween masks from Costume Supplies, Inc., delivery and payment at B's residence. While seller's truck is making the delivery, a flash flood strikes and sweeps the truck away. A few hours later, the truck and its driver are found, but the delivery items are a total loss. S informs B of the near tragedy and tells B, regrettably, that their contract is cancelled. B, needing the masks for an upcoming party, demands that S provide substitute masks or a lawsuit will follow. Is S required to provide replacement masks as B asserts? Discuss.

Decision: _____

Rule of Law: _____

_____

2.   B ordered 20,000 1/2-inch bolts from S, delivery in installments of 1,000 bolts per month in 20 different shipments. Payment was to occur on the first day of each month. On the third shipment, B is a day late in making payment. S gives immediate notice of cancellation of the entire contract. Decision for whom and why?

Decision: _____

Rule of Law: _____

_____

3.   Henrietta Hunter purchases a new hunting rifle from Barney's sporting goods store. An avid sportswoman, Henrietta is ready to pay top dollar for top quality. Upon unpacking the rifle and readying it for use, she notices tiny scratches on the lever and nicks in the handle. A perfectionist, Henrietta is furious and storms back to Barney's demanding a full refund. Barney refuses her request, arguing that the gun is still suitable for hunting purposes and Henrietta's dissatisfaction is over mere cosmetic blemishes. Who wins this dispute and why?

Decision: _____

Rule of Law: _____

_____

4.   B, a merchant, receives a shipment of non-conforming bananas from S. B rejects them and notifies S to come and get them. S remains silent. B does nothing and the bananas spoil. In a suit by S against B for the loss of the bananas, who wins and why?

Decision: _____

Rule of Law: _____

_____

5.   B and S, American business executives, enter a sales contract for 5,000 Australian widgees at 50
        cents apiece, delivery at B's place of business, no later than August 14. Diplomatic relations
        between America and Australia become strained. By July 21, the countries cut off diplomatic
        relations, call home their respective ambassadors and place an embargo on all mutual trade. When
        S is unable to deliver the specified widgees at the appointed time and place, B sues for breach.
        Who wins and why?

        Decision: _____
        _____

        Rule of Law: _____
        _____

Remedies

SCOPE NOTE

Chapter 23 brings our study of the law of sales and its related fields of inquiry to a close by addressing the problems and issues related to inadequate performance under the sales contract. The breadth of remedies made available under the U.C.C. to a non-breaching party are outlined. It is vitally important to note the key factors associated with a breach that dictate which particular choice of remedies will be available and efficacious to the innocent, non-breaching party.

EDUCATIONAL OBJECTIVES

1. Describe the pre-acceptance remedies made available to both non-breaching buyer and seller.

2. Outline the pre-acceptance breaching party's rights and duties.

3. Explain the non-breaching party's choice of remedies following acceptance.

4. Define and discuss the implications of anticipatory repudiation.

5. Identify how insolvency of the breaching party affects the choice-of-remedies question.

6. Discuss choice-of-remedy issues in the context of installment contract.

7. Define liquidated damages vis-a-vis the ability of the parties to limit or expand their choice of remedies in the agreement.

8. Evaluate the role of equity in enforcing sales contracts.

CHAPTER OUTLINE

I. Remedies of the Seller - triggered by buyer's default (wrongful reaction, wrongful revocation of acceptance, refusal to make payment)

    A. To Withhold Delivery of the Goods - goods in seller's or warehouser's possession

    B.   To Stop Delivery of the Goods - goods in carrier's possession

    C.   To Identify Goods to the Contract - buyer's anticipatory repudiation

    D.   To Resell the Goods and Recover Damages - good faith, commercial reasonableness duties

    E.   To Recover Damages for Non-acceptance or Repudiation - market price/contract price difference

    F.   To Recover the Price - no ready resale market

    G.   To Recover Incidental Damages - commercially reasonable charges

    H.   To Cancel the Contract - terminate agreement

    I.   To Reclaim the Goods Upon Buyer's Insolvency - within 10 days after receipt of goods

II.   Remedies of the Buyer - triggered by seller's wrongful default (failure to deliver conforming goods)

    A.   To Cancel the Contract - notice requirement

    B.   To Recover Payments Made

    C.   To Cover - difference between cover costs and original contract price

    D.   To Recover Damages for Non-delivery or Repudiation - difference between market price and contract price

    E.   To Recover Identified Goods upon the Seller's Insolvency - based on buyer's special property interest

    F.   To Sue for Replevin

    G.   To Sue for Specific Performance - goods are unique; money damages not effective

    H.   To Enforce a Security Interest in the Goods – to extent of payment

    I.   To Recover Damages for Breach in Regard to Accepted Goods - difference between value in defective condition and value as warranted

    J.   To Recover Incidental Damages - any reasonable expenses in undoing loss from breach

    K.   To Recover Consequential Damages - resulting losses of which seller had notice

III.   Contractual Provisions Affecting Remedies - parties agree to remedies

    A.   Liquidation or Limitation of Damages - reasonable approximation of actual loss

    B.   Modification or Limitation of Remedy by Agreement - parties may expand or restrict U.C.C. designated remedies

TRUE-FALSE: Circle true or false.

Answers

T   F   1.   An unpaid seller, faced with a buyer's material breach of the contract or insolvency, may properly withhold or stop delivery of the goods.

T   F   2.   When a buyer has breached the sales contract, the seller may resell the goods at either a public or private sale.

T   F   3.   A bona fide purchaser at a resale takes title to the goods subject to the superior interests of the original buyer when the seller fails to properly notify the breaching original buyer of the time, date and location of the resale.

T   F   4.   Failure of a buyer to "cover" upon the seller's breach will bar the buyer from seeking other remedies.

T   F   5.   A buyer acquires a special property interest in existing goods when they are identified to the contract.

T F 6. A provision in a sales contract providing for liquidated damages is void per se.

T F 7. A sales contract may validly limit consequential damages for commercial loss.

T F 8. A contract for the sale of consumer goods may validly limit consequential damages for commercial loss.

T F 9. An unpaid seller may reclaim goods delivered to a buyer anytime after the seller has learned of the buyer's insolvency.

T F 10. The Code has adopted the common law approach to specific performance.

T F 11. The goal of Code remedy provisions is to place the non-breaching party in as good a position as if the breaching party had properly performed.

T F 12. The Code uses both equity and bankruptcy definitions of insolvency.

KEY TERMS – MATCHING EXERCISE: Select the term which best completes each statement below and write the corresponding number in the ANSWERS column.

Column I	Column II	Answers
1. Inability to meet debts as they come due.	1. Equitable insolvency	1. _____
2. Resale of goods at which a non-breaching, unpaid seller may be a purchaser.	2. "Cover"	2. _____
3. The buyer's remedy to purchase substitute goods elsewhere following the seller's failure to perform properly.	3. Bankruptcy insolvency	3. _____
4. Injury resulting to a person or property caused by breach of warranty.	4. Specific performance	4. _____
5. An action to recover goods in the possession of and wrongfully withheld by another.	5. Consequential damages	5. _____
6. A provision in a sales contract calling for liquidated damages at an unacceptably high level.	6. Replevin	6. _____
	7. Penalty	7. _____
	8. Liquidated damages	8. _____
	9. Cancellation	9. _____
		10. _____
		11. _____
		12. _____

7. The non-breaching party's termination of the contract in response to the breaching party's failure of performance.

8. Unpaid seller's right to retake goods from an insolvent buyer.

9. Commercially reasonable expenses incurred by a seller in connection with the remedies available following a buyer's breach.

10. Buyer's equitable remedy compelling seller to deliver conforming goods as described in the sales contract.

11. Failure of a contracting party to properly perform contractual duties.

12. Seller's remedy when the market price-contract price difference fails to place seller in as good a position as if buyer had performed properly.

13. Notice prior to performance date that one intends not to carry out their contractual duties.

14. Standard merchants must follow when deciding whether to finish manufacturing goods or cease manufacturing or sell the partially finished goods for scrap value.

15. Common law doctrine requiring non-breaching party to choose a single remedy to the exclusion of all others.

10. Reclamation

11. Highest standard of care

12. Incidental damages

13. Public sale

14. Speculative damages

15. Dilatory

16. Anticipatory repudiation

17. Breach

18. Election of remedies

19. Commercial reasonableness

20. Breach

13. _____

14. _____

15. _____

MULTIPLE CHOICE: Select the alternative which best completes each statement below and write the corresponding letter in the ANSWERS column.

Answers

1. A seller's right to stop delivery ceases when (a) a carrier acknowledges that goods are held for the seller (b) a bailee acknowledges that goods are held for the buyer (c) goods are rejected by the buyer (d) all of the above.

1. _____

2.   A seller may recover as damages against a breaching buyer (a) the
        difference between the market price and the contract price plus
        incidental damages (b) the profit that would have been received had the
        deal gone through plus incidental damages (c) liquidated damages as
        provided for in the contract (d) any of the above.   2. _____

3.   A buyer may exercise a right of cover when (a) conforming goods have
        been wrongfully rejected (b) the seller has made proper delivery of
        conforming goods (c) the seller has repudiated the sales contract (d) the
        buyer has improperly revoked acceptance.   3. _____

4.   Identification of goods to the contract may be made by (a) the seller
        only (b) the buyer only (c) either the seller or buyer (d) the court after
        an action at law has been brought.   4. _____

5.   A sales contract between buyer and seller may (a) not limit a remedy
        provided for by the Code (b) provide for fewer remedies than those
        specified in the Code (c) allow for penalties in lieu of stipulated
        damages (d) none of the above.   5. _____

6.   A decree of specific performance may (a) include provisions regarding
        payment of the purchase price (b) never be given to a seller (c) only be
        awarded in real estate transactions (d) be awarded in an action at law.   6. _____

7.   Upon cancellation of a sales contract, (a) the cancelling party's duty of
        future performance is discharged (b) all security interests in the goods
        are voided (c) a trustee in bankruptcy is treated as an assignee of the
        contract (d) none of the above.   7. _____

8.   A seller's reclamation right is always subject to (a) the buyer's business
        partners (b) an equitable receiver (c) a buyer in the ordinary course of
        business from the non-performing purchaser (d) a bank.   8. _____

9.   Following buyer's breach, an unpaid seller may recover the contract
        price when the (a) buyer has rejected the goods (b) goods are damaged
        and the risk of loss remains with the seller (c) goods are identified to
        the contract and they have no resale market value (d) none of the above.   9. _____

10.   Insolvency for the purposes of federal bankruptcy law occurs when (a) a
        receiver is appointed to take control of the debtor's assets (b) the
        debtor's total liabilities exceed total assets (c) the debtor has stopped
        making payments on debts during the normal course of business (d) a
        fraudulent conveyance has been made.   10. _____

11.   When the buyer has breached the sales contract, the seller
        _____ unfinished goods. (a) may cease manufacture and
        resell them for scrap (b) may finish their manufacture and identify them
        to the contract (c) must use reasonable judgment to minimize losses (d)
        all of the above.   11. _____

12.   When liquidated damages are provided for they must be (a) provable
        through appraisal (b) commensurate with the anticipated or actual losses
        (c) no more than $500 (d) supported by affidavits of value.   12. _____

13.   A buyer who has "covered" the seller's breach may recover (a) all losses
        (b) the difference between the cost of "cover" and the contract price
        plus incidental or consequential damages (c) "B" above minus expenses
        saved as a result of the seller's breach (d) none of the above.   13. _____

CASE PROBLEMS - SHORT ESSAY ANSWERS: Read each case problem carefully.   When
appropriate, answer by stating a Decision for the case and by explaining the rationale - Rule of Law -
relied upon to support your decision.

1.   B breaches a sales contract and S elects to resell the goods. The contract price called for a $10,000
        payment from B. The resale realized $18,000 for S. In a suit by B against S for the excess above
        the contract price, what might B recover and why?

        Decision: _____
        _____
        Rule of Law: _____
        _____

2.   B ordered $10,000 worth of grade A grotaberries from S. On May 1, S shipped grade A
        wingaberries which were rightfully rejected by B. The following day, B bought grade A
        grotaberries on the open market from another supplier for $9,000. In a suit against S for the
        breach, what are the damages recoverable by B? Explain

        Decision: _____
        _____
        Rule of Law: _____
        _____

3.   B enters a contract with S for the sale of $10,000 worth of feather dusters. The dusters were
        labeled with B's name at S's warehouse. On July 10, B makes a $2,500 advance to S. A day later,
        B learns that S is insolvent. Fearing a loss of both the money and the goods, B seeks your advice.
        What should be done to protect B's interests?

        Decision: _____
        _____
        Rule of Law: _____
        _____

4.   B receives a shipment of nails from a building materials supplier that are non-conforming to the
        contract. B had made a down payment of $200 on the contract. B writes to S and notifies S of
        an intent to reject the nails. Three months pass without B receiving any reply from S. What may
        B do? Discuss.

        Decision: _____
        _____

Rule of Law: _____

_____

5.   Art dealer A contracts with art collector C to purchase one of C's Rembrandt paintings. Later, because of the painting's sentimental value, C repudiates the contract. In a suit by A against C, what remedy will A most likely seek? Explain.

Decision: _____

Rule of Law: _____

_____

SALES UNIT
RESEARCH QUESTIONS: Drawing upon information contained in the text, as well as outside sources, discuss the following questions.

1. In response to performance breakdowns in new cars, some States have adopted what is popularly known as New Car Lemon Laws. Explain the rationale for these laws and identify their significant provisions. What are the advantages and disadvantages of these laws? Does your State have such a law? Explain why you support or oppose your State's position on this issue.

2. In the past two decades, the incidence of product liability lawsuits has grown dramatically. What factors have contributed to this litigation "explosion?" What beneficial and negative consequences flow from this development? What changes in the law, as well as management policies and practices, have been/should be made to meet financial burdens created by the increased incidence of product liability lawsuits?

Form and Content

SCOPE NOTE

Commercial paper occupies a crucial position in today's marketplace. Commerce moves on written contracts to pay sums of money which pass for and are accepted as money in most marketplace transactions. This Chapter introduces the law regulating the issuance and use of commercial paper. The development of the law of commercial paper is traced and the most commonly used forms of commercial paper are explained. Also discussed is the key concept of negotiability. The terminology and rules addressed in Chapter 24 form a useful basis for understanding the subsequent chapters on commercial paper law.

EDUCATIONAL OBJECTIVES

1. Explain the importance and function of commercial paper in today's business.

2. Compare creating commercial paper performance duties to contractual performance duties.

3. Define and discuss the significance of negotiability.

4. Identify the essential elements of a negotiable instrument.

5. Differentiate contract assignment from negotiating commercial paper.

6. Discuss the effect on negotiability of various provisions/omissions in a written promise to pay.

7. Distinguish the essential characteristics of the various forms of negotiable commercial paper.

8. Identify the rights/duties of parties under the various types of commercial paper.

CHAPTER OUTLINE

I.   Negotiability - makes commercial paper pass for money: convenience and safety; facilitates credit extension

II.   Types of Commercial Paper - number, status of parties; statements made
   A.   Order to Pay - three party instrument: drawer; drawee; payee
        1.   Drafts - time; sight; bank; trade acceptance
        2.   Checks - drawer has funds deposited in drawee
   B.   Promises to Pay - two party instrument: maker, payee
        1.   Notes - collateral, installment, mortgage
        2.   Certificates of deposit - bank acknowledges money received

III.   Form of Commercial Paper - requirements for validity and negotiability
   A.   Writing - form or type of not important
   B.   Signed - any authorized means; by maker or drawer
   C.   Promise or Order to Pay - more than request or authorization
   D.   Unconditional - payment right clear from face of document
        1.   Reference to other agreements - make payment conditional and instrument non-negotiable
        2.   The particular fund doctrine - make payment conditional and instrument non-negotiable
   E.   Sum Certain in Money
        1.   Money - official medium of exchange
        2.   Sum certain - present value known from face of document
   F.   No Other Promise or Order - acts additional to payment; makes document non-negotiable
   G.   Payable on Demand or at a Definite Time - no time designated for demand paper
        1.   "On or before" clauses - time paper
        2.   At a fixed period after a stated date - time paper
        3.   At a fixed period after sight - time paper
        4.   At a definite time subject to acceleration - time paper
        5.   At a definite time subject to extension - time paper
   H.   Payable to Order or to Bearer - words of negotiability
        1.   Payable to order - named person
        2.   Payable to bearer - no payee designated
   I.   Terms and Omissions and Their Effect on Negotiability
        1.   Absence of statement of consideration - no effect
        2.   Absence of statement of where the instrument is drawn or payable - no effect
        3.   Sealed instruments - no effect
        4.   Dating of the instrument - undated; incorrectly dated; post or antedated
        5.   Incomplete instruments - awaits authorized completion
        6.   Ambiguous instruments - construed to favor negotiability

TRUE-FALSE: Circle true or false.

Answers

T   F   1.   A promise to pay out of a specific fund is conditional and renders commercial paper non-negotiable.

T   F   2.   An acceleration clause in commercial paper destroys negotiability because of the uncertainty of the due date.

T   F   3.   A certificate of deposit is a written receipt for deposited money with a financial institution which the latter promises to pay out at some future date.

T   F   4.   The location of a maker's signature on a promissory note affects its enforceability and negotiability.

T   F   5.   The U.C.C. requires that for commercial paper to be negotiable, it must be payable on demand or at a definite time.

T   F   6.   Antedating or postdating commercial paper destroys its negotiability.

T   F   7.   Failure to state on commercial paper its place for payment does not automatically destroy negotiability.

T   F   8.   Omitting the words "order," "bearer" or their equivalent makes a note non-negotiable.

T   F   9.   A note payable, "Sixty days after Maker's death," is negotiable under the U.C.C.

T   F   10.   Commercial paper made payable "to order of cash" is a bearer instrument.

T   F   11.   The negotiability of an instrument must be determined on its face without further inspection, inquiry or reference to another source.

T   F   12.   A bank draft is a form of promissory note.

KEY TERMS - MATCHING EXERCISE: Select the term which best completes each statement below and write the corresponding number in the ANSWERS column.

Column I	Column II	Answers
1. Instruments payable immediately upon presentation to the drawee.	1. Trade acceptance	1. _____
	2. Money	2. _____
2. A medium of exchange adopted by a government as its currency.	3. Acceleration	3. _____
3. An instrument payable only upon the occurrence of a future, uncertain event or act.	4. Time draft	4. _____
	5. Sight drafts	5. _____
4. A check drawn by a bank on itself payable to the order of a named payee.	6. Installment	6. _____
	7. Bearer	7. _____
	8. Negotiability	8. _____

5.   A three party instrument payable on a specific future date.

6.   A legal concept which gives commercial paper its high degree of usefulness and marketability in commercial transactions.

7.   The determinable minimum payment to be made on commercial paper.

8.   The person ordered to pay a draft.

9.   A clause that gives a payee the right to demand payment before a note is mature.

10. An instrument drawn by the seller of goods on their purchaser made payable to the seller.

11. A use for negotiable instruments other than as substitute for money.

12. A two party negotiable instrument.

13. Instruments payable at a definite time.

14. Another name for commercial paper.

15. The most common form of commercial paper.

9.   Credit device   9.   _____

10. Assignment   10. _____

11. Sum certain   11. _____

12. Cashier's check   12. _____

13. Collateral note   13. _____

14. Non-negotiable   14. _____

15. Drawee   15. _____

16. Instruments

17. Promissory note

18. Check

19. Time paper

20. Barter

MULTIPLE CHOICE: Select the alternative which best completes each statement below and write the corresponding letter in the ANSWERS column.

Answers

1.   An order to pay a sum certain is conditional if an instrument (a) states its consideration (b) specifies it is subject to another agreement (c) indicates it is secured by a mortgage (d) refers to the transaction which created it.   1.   _____

2.   The signature of the maker of a note may be (a) under an assumed name (b) a thumb print (c) made by an authorized agent (d) all of the above.   2.   _____

3.   The primary obligor on a promissory note is the (a) acceptor (b) cosignor (c) payee (d) none of the above.   3.   _____

4.   An instrument that is an order by one party upon another party to pay a third party is a (a) promissory note (b) draft (c) bond (d) collateral note.

4. _____

5.   Negotiability of an instrument is adversely affected by (a) not dating the instrument (b) a clause authorizing payment in goods (c) a clause providing for extension of the maturity date (d) its being under seal.

5. _____

6.   To be negotiable, commercial paper must be (a) signed by its maker (b) an unconditional promise to pay a sum certain (c) payable on demand or at a definite time (d) all of the above.

6. _____

7.   Negotiability applies to (a) warehouse receipts (b) investment securities (c) bills of lading (d) all of the above.

7. _____

8.   The various types of commercial paper are generally called (a) instruments (b) documents of title (c) payment contracts (d) none of the above.

8. _____

9.   An undated instrument made payable "two days after the date" (a) is negotiable (b) lacks consideration (c) is not negotiable (d) is complete on its face.

9. _____

10. Commercial paper which does not specify a payment date is (a) demand paper (b) non-negotiable (c) fatally incomplete (d) all of the above.

10. _____

11. Which of the following is not a type of commercial paper?   (a) certificate of deposit (b) bill of lading (c) draft (d) promissory note

11. _____

12. The bank upon which a check is drawn is the (a) drawer (b) drawee (c) payee (d) accommodation party.

12. _____

13. An instrument payable to "John Doe, County Collector of Cook County" is payable (a) to order (b) to bearer (c) on condition (d) to accommodation.

13. _____

CASE PROBLEMS - SHORT ESSAY ANSWERS: Read each case problem carefully.   When appropriate, answer by stating a Decision for the case and by explaining the rationale - Rule of Law - relied upon to support your decision.

1.   B purchases a television set from S and executes a 30 day note which reads, "nine hundred ($90) dollar purchase price." S accepts the note and is later faced with B asserting the $90 is the cost of the transaction. B steadfastly refuses to pay $900. S sues B for the $810 difference. Who wins the dispute?

Decision: _____

_____

Rule of Law: _____

_____

2.   M executes a promissory note payable to P in twenty-five days. The note contains a provision allowing M to extend the maturity date for an additional fifteen days. What effect does the extension option have on the note's negotiability? Explain.

Decision: _____

_____

Rule of Law: _____

_____

3.   M's 90 day $100 note at 6% interest, payable to P, provides for the addition of collection costs to the amount due if the holder has to resort to legal procedures for collection. Is this a negotiable instrument? Explain.

Decision: _____

_____

Rule of Law: _____

_____

4.   M executes a promissory note by typing the necessary information on a sheet of paper and signing it with a rubber stamp. Has the note been properly signed? Discuss.

Decision: _____

_____

Rule of Law: _____

_____

5.   M writes out in longhand, with an affixed signature, "I owe C $150," and dates the instrument. C transfers the memorandum to D to discharge a debt C owed D. Does D have an enforceable right of payment against M? Explain.

Decision: _____

_____

Rule of Law: _____

_____

Transfer

SCOPE NOTE

Usually, a negotiable instrument will have a useful life extending beyond the transaction which created it. The first taker of commercial paper most likely will transfer it to another person. The process followed in effectively transferring the rights/duties contained in negotiable instruments to other parties is discussed in the following Chapter. Requirements for a valid transfer, negotiation, are explained in Chapter 25 in relation to the different types of commercial paper.

EDUCATIONAL OBJECTIVES

1. Distinguish the definitional elements and effects of transfer by assignment from those of negotiation.

2. Identify the various types of indorsement and their respective uses.

3. Summarize the rights/duties of the parties to an indorsement.

CHAPER OUTLINE

I. Transfer and Negotiation - assignment (non-negotiable paper) contrasted to negotiation (negotiable paper, makes transferee a holder; by delivery, or delivery and indorsement)
II. Indorsements - transferor's signature; type of determines right and duties of parties
    A. Blank Indorsements - bearer paper; negotiable by delivery
    B. Special Indorsements - order paper; negotiable by delivery and indorsement
    C. Restrictive Indorsements - restrictions on indorsee's payment rights
        1. Conditional indorsements - payment subject to an event
        2. Indorsements prohibiting further transfer - unrestricted
        3. Indorsements for deposit or collection - in banking process
        4. Indorsements in trust - first taker must comply with
    D. Qualified Indorsements - "without recourse"; limits liability
    E. Negotiations Subject to Recission - negotiation valid even though transaction is void or voidable

165

TRUE-FALSE: Circle true or false.

Answers

T   F   1.   A finder of lost bearer commercial paper can become a holder.

T   F   2.   An indorsement "pay to the order of Mary" is a blank indorsement.

T   F   3.   The usual way to disclaim indorser's liability is to add the words "without recourse" along with the indorser's signature.

T   F   4.   The transferee of an instrument can be a holder either by negotiation or by assignment.

T   F   5.   Trust indorsements make the indorser a fiduciary.

T   F   6.   Under the U.C.C., a properly worded restrictive indorsement may prevent further transfer or negotiation of the instrument.

T   F   7.   A conditional indorsement is a type of restrictive indorsement.

T   F   8.   A blank indorsement transforms a bearer instrument into an order instrument.

T   F   9.   An indorsement "for collection" places the instrument within the banking system for deposit or collection.

T   F   10.   A qualified indorsement terminates negotiability and stops further negotiation of the paper.

T   F   11.   Absent any agreement of assignment, it is presumed that in transfers for value, the parties intend for a negotiation to occur.

T   F   12.   It is preferable from the transferee's standpoint to take an instrument by assignment and not by negotiation.

KEY TERMS – MATCHING EXERCISE: Select the term which best completes each statement below and write the corresponding number in the ANSWERS column.

	Column I		Column II		Answers
1.	An indorsement bearing only the indorser's signature, designating no indorsee.	1.	Holder	1.	_____
		2.	Shelter Rule	2.	_____
2.	A separate document, containing an indorsement, firmly affixed to commercial paper.	3.	Transfer	3.	_____
		4.	Blank	4.	_____

3.   An indorsement not in the chain
     of title to assist in obtaining
     money.

4.   One possessing commercial paper
     drawn, issued or indorsed to the
     possessor, the possessor's order,
     or in blank.

5.   Transferring commercial paper that
     makes the transferee a holder.

6.   An act specifying the person to
     whom or to whose order an
     instrument is payable.

7.   An act which makes the rights of
     an indorsee subject to the
     ocurrence of a certain event.

8.   The legal doctrine granting a
     non-holder transferee the rights
     of a holder if the transferee
     takes the instrument from a
     holder in due course.

9.   Indorsing an instrument with the
     words "payment to a for B."

10. Commercial paper transferred by
     possession alone, making it
     equivalent to cash.

11. Transferring commercial paper by
     which the transferee does not
     become a holder.

12. A "for deposit only" indorsement.

13. Commercial paper that must be
     indorsed for proper transfer.

14. Transferee of commercial paper
     who is not a holder.

15. Liability of the indorser that
     is not affected by a qualified
     indorsement.

5.   Accommodation
     indorsement

6.   Assignee

7.   Bearer paper

8.   Payor

9.   Qualified

10. Conditional
     indorsement

11. Collection
     indorsement

12. Trust indorsement

13. Special
     indorsement

14. Allonge

15. Negotiation

16. Order paper

17. Equitable

18. Assignment

19. Warranty

20. Restrictive

5. _____
6. _____
7. _____
8. _____
9. _____
10. _____
11. _____
12. _____
13. _____
14. _____
15. _____

MULTIPLE CHOICE: Select the alternative which best completes each statement below and write the corresponding letter in the ANSWERS column.   Answers

1. Transferring non-negotiable commercial paper operates as a/n
    (a) negotiation (b) indorsement (c) accommodation (d) assignment.   1. _____

2. An indorsement reading "Pay Sue only" is treated as a(n) (a) conditional
    indorsement (b) assignment (c) unrestricted indorsement (d) subsequent
    cancellation by the Code.   2. _____

3. All indorsements disclose the (a) type of interest transferred (b) liability
    of the indorser (c) method of subsequent negotiation (d) all of the
    above.   3. _____

4. Fraud (a) has no effect on a properly negotiated instrument (b)
    invalidates negotiation (c) prevents the transferee from becoming a
    holder (d) makes an instrument void.   4. _____

5. An indorsement must always be (a) in ink (b) witnessed by at least two
    other people (c) either written on the instrument or on an allonge (d)
    written twice wherever used.   5. _____

6. When the payee of a check simply signs a name on the back of the
    check without more, the indorsement is (a) special, qualified and non-
    restrictive (b) blank, unqualified and non-restrictive (c) conditional,
    special and in trust (d) none of the above.   6. _____

7. When an instrument has been made payable to the order of its holder
    and the holder's name is misspelled, the holder may (a) do nothing since
    all rights have ceased (b) bring suit and recover against the indorsee (c)
    legally and equitably change their name for the purpose of securing the
    instrument (d) indorse the instrument in the misspelled name, in their
    own name or both.   7. _____

8. Indorsements may be (a) equitable or civil (b) restrictive or non-
    restrictive (c) logical or sequential (d) chronological or baited.   8. _____

9. An indorsement containing the words "without recourse" is a/n (a) blank
    (b) qualified (c) Drach (d) unqualified.   9. _____

10. An unqualified indorser guarantees (a) payment only if specific
    conditions have been met (b) that value has been given for the
    instrument (c) payment on the instrument (d) that all persons named on
    the instrument had good title.   10. _____

11. Generally, subject to specified exception, the transfer of an instrument
    vests in the transferee (a) only those rights as the transferor has (b) no
    new rights (c) fifty percent of the transferor's rights (d) none of the
    above.   11. _____

12.   An order instrument (a) may never be changed to bearer paper (b) may
        be changed to bearer paper by a blank indorsement (c) may be changed
        to bearer paper only if done within twenty-four hours after receipt (d)
        none of the above.   12. _____

13.   The words "Pay Alex" (a) are sufficient to make an instrument
        negotiable (b) fail the specificity test for valid indorsement (c) make an
        instrument bearer paper (d) are sufficient to make an order indorsement.   13. _____

CASE PROBLEMS - SHORT ESSAY ANSWERS: Read each case problem carefully.   When
appropriate, answer by stating a Decision for the case and by explaining the rationale - Rule of Law -
relied upon to support your decision.

1.   X issued a note "payable to the order of Y."   Y indorses the note "Pay to Z only if Safe-Way
        Airlines Flight 602 arrives at Hollman Field by 2:30 p.m., August 23, 1980."   On August 20, 1980,
        Z presents the note to X for payment.   X refuses to honor the note, arguing the controlling
        influence of Y's indorsement.   Z sues X for wrongful dishonor of the note.   What result?

        Decision: _____

        _____

        Rule of Law: _____

        _____

2.   X indorses a $1,000 note, "pay Y $650 of this note."   What is the effect of this indorsement?
        Explain.

        Decision: _____

        _____

        Rule of Law: _____

        _____

3.   M executes a $500 note "payable to bearer" and delivers it to P.   P indorses the note "pay to the
        order of X."   Sometime later, P loses the note and F finds it.   F presents the note to M for
        payment. Must M honor F's presentment?   Explain.

        Decision: _____

        _____

        Rule of Law: _____

        _____

4.   T steals a $250 bearer note from P.   T sells the note to B who presents it for payment.   Is B
        rightfully entitled to payment?

        Decision: _____

        _____

        Rule of Law: _____

        _____

5.   A indorses an instrument to B in blank. Assuming B is the holder, what can B do to prevent the instrument from being treated as cash? Discuss.

Decision: _____

Rule of Law: _____

_____

Holder in Due Course

SCOPE NOTE

As a general rule of contract law, assigning rights under a contract not only creates in the assignee the same rights held by the assignor but also exposes the assignee to liability on the defenses to performance which could have been validly asserted against the assignor. This latter fact, in the marketplace of commercial paper, would constitute a substantial cloud on the marketability and usefulness of these instruments. Chapter 26 addresses the circumstances under which this vulnerability of the taker of a negotiable instrument is removed, thus enchancing the transferability of the instrument. The Holder in Due Course Doctrine is focused upon. How must a taker of a negotiable instrument acquire it to achieve Holder in Due Course status? What are the benefits of such status? Under what circumstances may a Holder in Due Course still face non-payment vulnerability? These are the type of issues which are the focus of discussion in the following Chapter.

EDUCATIONAL OBJECTIVES

1. Identify and discuss the significance of the requirements which must be met to acquire Holder in Due Course status.

2. Explain situations where even though Holder in Due Course requisites have been met, the status will be denied the holder.

3. Define and discuss the significance of the "Shelter Rule."

4. Distinguish the definitional elements of the two major classes of payment defenses.

5. Enumerate the payment defenses effective only against "ordinary" holders.

6. List and understand the importance of payment defenses assertable against all holders of commercial paper.

7. Know the types of contracts which make a Holder in Due Course vulnerable to personal defenses.

CHAPTER OUTLINE

I. Requirements of a Holder in Due Course - created by due negotiation of commercial paper; transferee's rights greater than transferor's
    A. Holder - transferee with payment rights
    B. Value - consideration actually given
    C. Good Faith - honesty in fact; no actual knowledge of a defense
    D. Lack of Notice - actual knowledge; implied knowledge
        1. Notice an instrument is overdue - time paper or demand paper
        2. Notice an instrument has been dishonored - payment refusal
        3. Notice of a claim or defense - defect knowable from paper or surrounding circumstances
II. Holder in Due Course Status - protected rights to payment
    A. A Payee May Be a Holder in Due Course - payee not a party to the issuance of note
    B. The Shelter Rule - holder not qualifying as an HDC acquires such rights through a prior HDC
    C. Special Circumstances Denying Holder in Due Course Status - HDC status denied due to misconduct (fraud, theft, other illegality)
III. The Preferred Position of a Holder in Due Course - party obligated to make payment seeks to avoid payment obligation
    A. Real Defenses - effective against any holder including HDC; usually stems from a void transaction
        1. Minority - as a simple contract defense
        2. Void obligations - stemming from illegal transaction or insanity
        3. Fraud in the execution - deception regarding nature of the document
        4. Discharge in insolvency proceedings - bankruptcy
        5. Discharge of which the holder has notice
        6. Forgery and unauthorized signature
        7. Material alteration - changes obligations of parties
    B. Personal Defenses - not effective against an HDC
IV. Procedure in Recovering on Instrument
V. Limitations Upon Holder in Due Course Rights - State and Federal law restricting availability of HDC status in consumer credit transactions

TRUE-FALE: Circle true or false.

Answers

T   F   1.   The U.C.C.'s definition of good faith stresses honesty-in-fact under a transaction.

T   F   2.   An example of failure to give value for the purposes of determining holder in due course status occurs when a holder of an instrument gives it to another person.

T   F   3.   Value for the purposes of negotiable instrument law is the same as consideration in the law of contracts.

T   F   4.   According to the U.C.C., one who takes a post-dated check has notice of a claim or defense and therefore can never become a holder in due course.

T   F   5.   The Code does not specify what is reasonable time for the purposes of determining whether a note is overdue.

T   F   6.   The U.C.C. specifically states when minority is available as a defense on an instrument and under what circumstances it may be claimed.

T   F   7.   One who claims holder in due course status bears the burden of establishing the validity of that claim.

T   F   8.   A person whose signature has been forged on an instrument is usually liable for payment to holders in due course.

T   F   9.   Under the Code, a reasonable time for presentment on a check is 30 days.

T   F   10.   The F.T.C. has changed the effect of the holder in due course doctrine in consumer credit transactions.

T   F   11.   One who takes an instrument knowing that all previous parties have been discharged may still acquire the status of holder in due course.

T   F   12.   A transferee of stolen commercial paper who takes from the person who stole the instrument cannot become a holder in due course.

KEY TERMS – MATCHING EXERCISE: Select the term which best completes each statement below and write the corresponding number in the ANSWERS column.

Column I	Column II	Answers
1. The possessor of a negotiable note who, by its terms, is entitled to payment.	1. Shelter rule	1. _____
	2. Subjective	2. _____
2. The test for good faith adopted by the Code.	3. Forgery	3. _____
	4. Holder	4. _____
3. An irrevocable commitment made by a bank for payment on its depositor's check.	5. Objective	5. _____
	6. Fraud in the execution	6. _____
4. The act of affixing another person's signature to an instrument without actual, apparent or implied authority.		7. _____
	7. Certification	8. _____
	8. Acceleration	
5. Factual misrepresentation inducing a party to sign a note without knowing or having an opportunity to know its nature or material terms.	9. Void	9. _____
	10. Ratification	10. _____

6. Defenses effective against all
    holders except those in due course.

7. Process by which an unauthorized
    signature is transformed into a
    valid one.

8. Defenses available against any
    holder, including one in due course.

9. Doctrine which transforms a non-due-
    course holder into a holder in due
    course if they have taken the
    instrument from a holder in due course.

10. Insolvency proceedings which can
    operate to discharge a party from any
    liability on a note to all holders,
    including those in due course.

11. Transferee of negotiable commercial
    paper who takes instrument for value
    in good faith and without notice of
    dishonor, outdatedness or defenses
    to payment.

12. Changing the rights and responsibilities
    of parties to commercial paper.

13. Concept that facilitates free flow of
    commercial paper.

14. Refusal to pay or accept a negotiable
    instrument.

15. Type of contractual obligation which
    has given use to commercial paper that
    triggers valid defenses to payment
    against a holder in due course.

11. Real   11. _____

12. Bankruptcy   12. _____

13. Personal   13. _____

14. Valid   14. _____

15. Cancellation   15. _____

16. Material alteration

17. Dishonor

18. Negotiability

19. Holder in
    Due Course

20. Estoppel

MULTIPLE CHOICE: Select the alternative which best completes each statement below and write the corresponding letter in the ANSWERS column.

Answers

1. Methods of acquiring commercial paper which preclude the transferee
    from becoming a holder in due course include (a) purchase at a judicial
    sale (b) acquisition through legal process (c) purchase at a non-regular
    bulk transaction (d) all of the above.   1. _____

2.   Personal defenses include (a) fraud in the inducement (b) forgery (c) bankruptcy discharge (d) all of the above.

2. _____

3.   According to the U.C.C., notice of an event is (a) actual (b) notification of it (c) reason to know of it (d) all of the above.

3. _____

4.   The purpose of the shelter rule is to (a) provide marketability of commercial paper to holders in due course (b) guarantee rights of cloture to holders of commercial paper (c) protect interests of all transferees of commercial paper (d) guard against the hardships associated with equitable discharge.

4. _____

5.   Real defenses include (a) duress making the transaction void (b) minority (c) fraud in the execution (d) all of the above.

5. _____

6.   Material alteration discharges a party on the note when (a) it is made for any purpose (b) done with intent to defraud (c) it specifies payment more than 25 days after the initial payment date (d) done for no value.

6. _____

7.   To quality as a holder in due course, a transferee must acquire an instrument (a) for no value (b) and hold possession of it for at least ninety days (c) without notice of certain specified matters (d) for the purpose of subsequent transfer to an heir.

7. _____

8.   Signing a negotiable instrument by carbon copy in the induced belief that only an autograph is being given is an example of (a) failure of consideration (b) fraud in the execution (c) non-delivery (d) fraud in the inducement.

8. _____

9.   The effect of the F.T.C. rule applying to consumer credit transactions is to make transferees of negotiable paper associated with the transaction (a) holders in due course (b) trustees (c) receivers (d) assignees.

9. _____

10.   Shortening the time for payment on a note by operation of a provision in the note is (a) ademption (b) abatement (c) acceleration (d) none of the above.

10. _____

11.   Which of the following does not constitute value given? (a) a check for future services (b) a check as security for a debt (c) a check as payment for a debt (d) exchanging negotiable instruments.

11. _____

12.   A _____ is protection against liability. (a) claim (b) defense (c) allonge (d) privilege

12. _____

13.   The doctrine that prevents someone from asserting a defense to liability because their conduct caused another person to change their position to their own loss or hardship is (a) negligence (b) lackes (c) estoppel (d) trust.

13. _____

CASE PROBLEMS - SHORT ESSAY ANSWERS: Read each case problem carefully. When appropriate, answer by stating a Decision for the case and by explaining the rationale - Rule of Law - relied upon to support your decision.

1.   M issues a $1,000 note payable to P and delivers it. P negotiates the note to H who promises to pay $850 for it by the end of the month which H does. On payment of the $850, what rights to payment has H acquired, the original value of $1,000 or the $850 that was paid? Explain.

Decision: _____

Rule of Law: _____

_____

2.   P fraudulently induces M to execute a $1,000 note payable to P. Following delivery of the instrument, P negotiates the note to holder in due course H who in turn re-negotiates the note back to P. Has P acquired the status of a holder in due course? Discuss.

Decision: _____

Rule of Law: _____

_____

3.   M buys a new car with a note payable to seller S reading "thirty-five hundred dollars ($350)." S changes the figure to $3,500 and negotiates the note to H, who attempts to collect from M. M refuses to make payment asserting material alteration by S. Who wins this dispute and why?

Decision: _____

Rule of Law: _____

_____

4.   M draws a check on bank B payable to P. P presents the check to B for payment. Shortly before a teller at bank B cashes the check, B learns that M has issued a stop payment notice due to fraud. Has B acquired notice sufficient to preclude it from becoming a holder in due course?

Decision: _____

Rule of Law: _____

_____

5.   B purchases for home use, on an $850 installment contract, a riding mower from S. As part of the transaction, B issues a $750 note payable to S for the balance remaining after B's $100 down payment. S negotiates the note to holder in due course H. After three weeks of frustrating, breakdown-ridden use of the new mower, marred by B's refusal to service the defects, B revokes acceptance of the mower and notifies H that the note is being cancelled. H refuses to accept B's cancellation, asserting that as a holder in due course, the defense of defective goods is not valid against him. Is H correct?

Decision: _____

Rule of Law: _____

_____

Liability of Parties

SCOPE NOTE

Payment on commercial paper is the eventual goal of the parties utilizing it. A basic rule regarding payment liability is that no one faces a duty of payment unless their signature appears on the instrument. But, with all names that might appear on an instrument after a number of negotiations, how is the order of payment obligation determined? In Chapter 27, the rules controlling liability for payment are developed. Special attention must be given to the type of intrument used and the relation of the parties to that instrument.

EDUCATIONAL OBJECTIVES

1. Differentiate primary from secondary parties.

2. Identify the types of commercial paper in which the payment obligation is triggered by acceptance.

3. Outline the procedure for acceptance.

4. List the various conditions which must be met, and their respective procedures, before secondary parties are liable on the instrument.

5. Discuss when the conditions precedent for secondary party liability are waived or excused.

6. Explain the meaning and significance of accommodation parties.

7. Distinguish transfer and presentment warranties and explain party liability for breach of those warranties.

8. Explain the effect on payment liability of such problems as conversion, imposters and fictitious payees.

9. Enumerate the various circumstances which terminate a party's payment obligations on the instrument.

177

CHAPTER OUTLINE

I.   Contractual Liability - based on agreement of parties
  A.   Signature - on commercial paper required for liability
    1. Authorized signatures - agent, maker, indorser, drawer
    2. Unauthorized signatures - forger has liability
  B.   Liability of Primary Parties - based on authorized signatures, contractual liability
    1. Makers - notes
    2. Acceptors - drafts
  C.   Liability of Secondary Parties - conditional liability based on certain preconditions
    1. Indorsers and drawers
    2. Conditions precedent to liability
      a. Presentment - demand for payment or acceptance
      b. Dishonor - refusal to pay or accept
      c. Notice of dishonor - refusal to pay or accept
      d. Protest - certified dishonor in cases of foreign drafts
      e. Delay in presentment, notice, or protest excused
      f. Presentment, notice, or protest excused
      g. Presentment excused
      h. Waiver of presentment, notice, or protest
    3. Disclaimer by secondary parties - qualified indorsement
  D.   Liability of Accommodation Parties - status of accommodating party
  E.   Special Situations Affecting Liability
    1. The imposter rule - maker or drawer bears loss when paper issued in name of impersonated party
    2. The fictitious payee rule - maker or drawer bears loss
  F.   Liability for Conversion - wrongful payment (on forgery); refusal to pay or return
II.   Liability Based on Warranty
  A.   Warranties on Transfer - made by transferor for value; liability depends on type of transfer (delivery alone or delivery with indorsement)
    1. Good title
    2. Signatures genuine
    3. No material alteration
    4. No defenses
    5. No knowledge of insolvency
  B.   Warranties on Presentment - made by presenter
    1. Good title
    2. Genuineness of signature of maker and drawer
    3. No material alteration
III.   Termination of Liability - discharge of payment obligation
  A.   Payment or Satisfaction
  B.   Tender of Payment - discharges interest, court costs, attorneys fees
  C.   Cancellation and Renunciation - acts against paper, separate writing, surrender of paper
  D.   Impairment of Recourse or Collateral - acts by holder
  E.   Other Methods of Discharge
    1. Fraudulent, material alteration
    2. Re-acquisition by prior holder

3. Unexcused delay, presentment, notice or protest
4. Contractual discharge
5. Certification by holder

TRUE-FALSE: Circle true or false.

Answers

T   F   1.   Generally a person is not contractually liable on commercial paper unless the person's signature appears on the instrument.

T   F   2.   The two recognized types of payment liability for commercial paper are contractual and warranty based.

T   F   3.   When a check is certified at the request of the holder, the drawer is discharged but not indorsers.

T   F   4.   Presentment for payment is prerequisite for a primary party to be liable on a negotiable instrument.

T   F   5.   Presentment of an uncertified check should be made within thirty days after its date of issuance in order to hold the drawer of the check liable.

T   F   6.   Presentment of an uncertified check should be made within seven days after an indorsement in order to hold the indorser liable.

T   F   7.   Notice of dishonor of an instrument must be given in writing.

T   F   8.   The law of suretyship applies to accomodation parties and gives rise to contribution rights among the parties.

T   F   9.   Transfer warranties run to any subsequent good faith holder of the instrument when transfer is by delivery alone without indorsement.

T   F   10. Transferors of negotiable instruments warrant that they have no knowledge of insolvency proceedings pending against the maker, acceptor or drawer of an instrument.

T   F   11. Under the Code, a waiver of protest is also a waiver of presentment and of notice of dishonor.

T   F   12. When a forged instrument has been paid by the drawee, the loss can be shifted to the drawer by charging the latter's account..

KEY TERMS – MATCHING EXERCISE: Select the term which best completes each statement below and write the corresponding number in the ANSWERS column.

Column I	Column II	Answers

Column I

1. The promise of a bank to honor a check when it is subsequently presented for payment.

2. The drawee bank's refusal to pay the amount stated on a check.

3. A doctrine holding the maker or drawer of paper liable for payment notwithstanding the wrongful indorsement of someone impersonating the named payee.

4. The act which makes the drawee of a draft primarily liable.

5. Notice of dishonor made under the hand and seal of a notary public.

6. Persons who sign a negotiable instrument for the purpose of lending their credit to another party on the note.

7. The tort of wrongfully exercising dominion over another's personal property.

8. The demand made by a holder on the maker or drawee for acceptance or payment of the instrument.

9. The most obvious way for a party to discharge liability on an instrument.

10. Doctrine holding a drawer liable for payment notwithstanding fraud by the drawer's agent in inducing issuance of the instrument.

Column II

1. Drawer
2. Conversion
3. Drawee
4. Certification
5. Acceptor
6. Presentment
7. Accommodation parties
8. Acceptance
9. Protest
10. Signature
11. Dishonor
12. Fictitious Payee Rule
13. Payment
14. Imposter Rule
15. Secondary
16. Primary
17. Renunciation
18. Warranty
19. Disclosure
20. Reimbursement

Answers

1. _____
2. _____
3. _____
4. _____
5. _____
6. _____
7. _____
8. _____
9. _____
10. _____
11. _____
12. _____
13. _____
14. _____
15. _____

11. Liability imposed on signers and non-
    signers of commercial paper as a
    result of the transfer, payment or
    acceptance of the instrument.

12. The type of payment obligation
    assumed by makers of promissory
    notes and acceptors of drafts.

13. Someone secondarily liable for
    payment on a check.

14. General duty of a drawer following
    a drawee's proper payment of an
    instrument.

15. Written statement by a holder
    giving up right of payment.

MULTIPLE CHOICE: Select the alternative which best completes each statement below and write the corresponding letter in the ANSWERS column.   Answers

1. Indorsers and drawers of checks have _____ liability for
   payment (a) primary (b) no (c) secondary (d) tertiary.   1. _____

2. Acceptance of an instrument is effective only when (a) it is in the
   drawee's own handwriting (b) it is oral (c) it is made within 14 days
   after issuance (d) none of the above.   2. _____

3. The conditions precedent to the liability of secondary parties do not
   include (a) protest (b) default (c) notice of dishonor (d) presentment.   3. _____

4. The proper person to make a protest is (a) a bank cashier (b) a United
   States consul (c) any police officer (d) an equitable receiver.   4. _____

5. Notice of dishonor must be given by a bank on or before midnight (a)
   on the day of dishonor (b) three days after dishonor (c) on the next
   banking day following receipt of a dishonor notice (d) within twenty-
   four hours after certification.   5. _____

6. To assure that acceptance will be proper, the drawee may require (a)
   reasonable identification of the person making presentment (b) proof of
   mature indorsement (c) notice of dishonor (d) certification of protest. 6. _____

7. Examples of conversion include (a) waiver of presentment (b) adoption
   by protest (c) payment on an instrument bearing a forged indorsement
   (d) none of the above.   7. _____

8.   Check drawers and indorsers may avoid their usual secondary
      contractual payment obligation by making or indorsing the paper (a)
      without recourse (b) as accommodation parties (c) without certification
      (d) none of the above.   8.   _____

9.   Any mark, made in any manner which indicates a present intent to
      validate commercial paper is a (a) protest (b) signature (c) contribution
      (d) payment.   9.   _____

10.   Methods by which a party's liability on an instrument may be
      discharged include (a) material alteration (b) unexcused delay in
      presentment (c) notice of dishonor (d) all of the above.   10.   _____

11.   Examples of unauthorized signatures include (a) using rubberized stamps
      (b) mechanized signatures (c) an agent exceeding authority (d) all of the
      above.   11.   _____

12.   Code warranties running with the sale of commercial paper include (a)
      drawee and payee warranties (b) presenter and transferor warranties (c)
      statutory and judicial warranties (d) none of the above.   12.   _____

13.   When bearer paper is transferred by delivery alone, the transferor
      warrants to all subsequent holders (a) nothing since warranties in the
      case run only to an immediate transferee (b) good title (c) no defense
      (d) no dishonor.   13.   _____

CASE PROBLEMS – SHORT ESSAY ANSWERS: Read each case problem carefully.   When
appropriate, answer by stating a Decision for the case and by explaining the rationale - Rule of Law -
relied upon to support your decision .

1.   A maintains a checking account at XYZ Bank, having $1,000 on deposit. A draws a check for
      $500 in favor of M. A has the check certified by the bank and gives it to M. Before M presents
      the check for payment, XYZ Bank ceases operations due to insolvency. When M makes
      presentment for payment, the bank refuses to pay. What can M do? Explain.

      Decision: _____

      Rule of Law: _____

      _____

2.   A makes a promissory note in favor of B payable at State Bank in 60 days at 10% interest per
      month. After 60 days, A is willing and able to pay the note at the bank. B takes a round-the-
      world tour for a year while the interest builds on the note. A asks your advice about liability on
      the note and interest. Explain.

      Decision: _____

      Rule of Law: _____

      _____

3. H holds a draft payable at the Trust Bank main office. H meets an official of the drawee on the street and requests payment. The official refuses and says it must be paid at the specified location. Is this a dishonor? Explain.

Decision: _____

Rule of Law: _____

_____

4. M, executing an instrument on behalf of P, signs it "M, as agent" without naming P. The instrument is negotiated to H who seeks payment from M. Who is liable on this document? Explain.

Decision: _____

Rule of Law: _____

_____

5. M executes a note payable to P for $800. P raises the amount to $1,800 and negotiates it to holder in due course H. H presents the note for payment to M who pays the $1,800. Discovering the error a short time later, M seeks reimbursement of the $1,000 overpayment from H. H refuses to pay. Who wins? Explain.

Decision: _____

Rule of Law: _____

_____

Bank Deposits and Collections

SCOPE NOTE

In the past four chapters, we have looked at the life cycle of commercial paper. From drafting the instrument, through its transfer, to discharge of its parties, hopefully through payment, the legal principles regulating this area of commerce have been developed. The following Chapter completes the cycle by addressing the procedures attendant to lodging one type of commercial paper, a check, within its payment process, the banking system. Attention is given to the rights and obligations of the various banks along the chain of payment as well as to the parties to the instrument as controlled by Article 4 of the U.C.C. The discussion closes with an examination of the emerging importance of electronic fund transfers.

EDUCATIONAL OBJECTIVES

1. Discuss the collection process and the relationship of payor and collecting banks.

2. Describe the contractual relationship between a bank and its customers.

3. Explain bank liability for wrongfully dishonoring a check.

4. Identify the methods for and effect of stopping payment.

5. Develop the meaning and importance of a customer's duty to inspect monthly statements.

6. Outline bank alternatives upon the death or incompetence of a customer.

7. Enumerate the requisites for and effect of final payment.

8. Explain the importance of electronic fund transfers.

9. Outline the major provisions of the Electronic Fund Transfer Act.

CHAPTER OUTLINE

I.   Collection of Items – check clearing, payment procedure
        A.   Collecting Banks – non-payor bank handling check
                1.   Duty of care – handle check properly
                2.   Duty to act seasonably – midnight deadline rule
                3.   Indorsements
                4.   Warranties
                5.   Final payment
        B.   Payor Banks – drawee bank obligated to make payment
II.   Payor Bank and its Customer
        A.   Payment of an Item – insufficient funds, stale checks, wrongful dishonor problems
        B.   Stop Payment Orders – reasonable time to comply and wrongful payment problems
        C.   Bank's Subrogation Rights on Improper Payment – forged signatures, material alterations, forged indorsements
        D.   Customer's Death or Incompetence – notice and reasonable opportunity to act upon; 10 days after death rule
        E.   Customer's Duties – reasonable care: examine statements; discover and report errors, forgeries, etc.
III.   Electronic Fund Transfer
        A.   Types of Transfers
                1.   Automated teller machines
                2.   Point of sale systems
                3.   Direct deposits and withdrawals
                4.   Pay by phone systems
        B.   Electronic Fund Transfer Act
                1.   Disclosure
                2.   Documentation and periodic statements
                3.   Preauthorized transfers
                4.   Error resolution
                5.   Consumer liability
                6.   Liability of financial institution

TRUE–FALSE: Circle true or false.

Answers

T   F   1.   Most business transactions involve checks as the method of payment.

T   F   2.   Under the Code, deposits made by check are available for immediate drawing by the depositing customer.

T   F   3.   Holders of checks have no right to force drawee banks to pay them even when sufficient funds are in the drawer's account to cover the checks.

T   F   4.   Any day a bank is open constitutes a banking day.

T   F   5.   A stop payment order is never renewable.

T   F   6.   A bank may continue to certify or pay checks drawn by a deceased customer for up to ten days after the customer's death, regardless of the bank knowing of the death.

T   F   7.   The customer bears a duty of reasonably prompt and careful examination of both the account statements and the paid items made available by the bank.

T   F   8.   There are no exceptions to the "midnight deadline" rule in determining whether a bank has acted seasonably.

T   F   9.   When an item received by a depository bank has no indorsement, the only recourse open to the bank is to return the item to its customer.

T   F   10.   Projections are that electronic fund transfers will replace checks as primary vehicles of payment in commerce.

T   F   11.   Collecting banks must use extraordinary care in handling items transferred to it for collection.

T   F   12.   A collecting bank has the duty to act seasonably.

KEY TERMS - MATCHING EXERCISE: Select the term which best completes each statement below and write the corresponding number in the ANSWER column.

Column I	Column II	Answers
1. The bank at which an item is presented for credit to the payee's account.	1. Depository	1. _____
2. The bank on which an item is drawn.	2. Float	2. _____
	3. Payor	3. _____
3. The type of initial credit given to a bank's customer before an item is finally paid.	4. Banking day	4. _____
4. The concept underlying the determination of whether a bank has met its duty to act seasonably.	5. Intermediate	5. _____
	6. Posting	6. _____
	7. Midnight deadline	7. _____
		8. _____
5. Terminal point in the collection process constituting the turn-around point from which the proceeds of the item begin their return flow.	8. Point of sale transfer	9. _____
	9. Two years	10. _____

6. A statement countermanding the drawer's order to the bank authorizing it to pay a certain sum of money and charge the amount to the drawer's account.

7. An automatic transfer of funds from a bank to a merchant completed through machines at the merchant's place of business.

8. The normal indorsement made when a bank forwards an item for collection.

9. The term describing a check drawer's use of funds between time of issuance of and final payment on the check.

10. The procedure followed by the payor bank in deciding to pay an item and making a record of the payment.

11. A group of banks cooperating together to settle accounts with one another on a daily basis.

12. Time period in which customer must report alterations or unauthorized signatures after statements or items are made available to preserve rights against a bank.

13. The exclusive focus of E.F.T.A.

14. Relationship between collecting banks and owner of an instrument pending final settlement.

15. General duties of bank customers regarding their own accounts.

10. Check

11. Pay any bank

12. Collection guaranteed

13. Provisional

14. Final payment

15. Stop payment order

16. Agency

17. Clearing house

18. Consumer protection

19. Examination and notice

20. One year

11. _____

12. _____

13. _____

14. _____

15. _____

MULTIPLE CHOICE: Select the alternative which best completes each statement below and write the corresponding letter in the ANSWERS column.

Answers

1. Customers or collecting banks transferring items in return for settlement or consideration warrant that (a) signatures on the instrument are genuine and authorized (b) no parties in the collection chain have filed

1. _____

for bankruptcy (c) no restrictive endorsements have been made (d) all of the above.

2. Reasons why a bank would dishonor a check and return the item include (a) the drawer not holding an account at the bank (b) a forged signature on the item (c) insufficient funds in the drawer's account (d) all of the above.

2. _____

3. Electronic fund transfers are preferred over checks because they (a) eliminate the check drawer's float of funds (b) reduce the time and expense of processing checks (c) both a and b (d) neither a nor b.

3. _____

4. Items received after the cutoff hour fixed by the bank for receipt of such items may be treated as having been received at (a) the beginning of the day of actual receipt (b) the opening of the day after the next banking day (c) the opening of the next banking day (d) none of the above.

4. _____

5. A payor bank is under no obligation to pay an uncertified check which is over (a) six weeks old (b) six months old (c) sixty days old (d) none of the above.

5. _____

6. Steps involved in posting an item include (a) appointing a receiver (b) freezing the drawer's assets (c) verifying a signature (d) all of the above.

6. _____

7. Where the customer's account is not sufficient to pay all items presented, the bank must charge them against the account (a) in the order of their arrival (b) in any order deemed reasonable by the bank (c) in reverse order of their arrival (d) according to their date of issuance.

7. _____

8. When a customer believes that a monthly statement from their bank contains errors, the customer must notify the bank within _____ days of the error (a) 60 (b) 30 (c) 45 (d) 14.

8. _____

9. The steps taken by a bank in presenting an item for collection include (a) choosing a reasonable method of forwarding the item (b) acting within a reasonable time after receipt of the item (c) careful routing of the item (d) all of the above.

9. _____

10. When a bank mistakenly pays a check over a customer's valid stop order, it is liable to the customer for the (a) customer's losses resulting from the payment (b) amount of the payment (c) incidental loss to the bank (d) none of the above.

10. _____

11. Electronic transfers not regulated by E.F.T.A. include transactions between (a) businesses (b) financial institutions (c) businesses and financial institutions (d) all of the above.

11. _____

12.   Situations in which a financial institution is not liable for E.F.T. errors include (a) employee negligence (b) equipment failure (c) customer account subject to legal process (d) all of the above.

12.   _____

13.   The type of relationship between collecting banks and an owner of an item after final settlement is (a) agency (b) debtor-creditor (c) conservatorship (d) none of the above.

13.   _____

CASE PROBLEMS - SHORT ESSAY ANSWERS: Read each case problem carefully. When appropriate, answer by stating a Decision for the case and by explaining the rationale - Rule of Law - relied upon to support your decision.

1.   A issues a $750 check to B drawn on A's $600 account with bank C. C honors the item when presented for payment and charges A's account. The bank then seeks the $150 difference from A plus service charges for the overdraft created. A refuses to pay, maintaining that it was the bank's obligation to dishonor the check since it knew sufficient funds were lacking to cover it. Who wins this dispute? Explain.

Decision: _____

_____

Rule of Law: _____

_____

2.   Cathy Consumer, short of cash, decides to withdraw money from her bank account by using her bank card at an automated teller. She discovers, however, that both the bank card and her PIN card are missing from her purse. Searching at home, in her car, at friends' houses and at work leads to nothing. She cannot find the card anywhere. Meanwhile, Frank Fraud, having found Cathy's cards, has made $200 in withdrawals from her account. To what extent, if at all, is Cathy liable for these withdrawals?

Decision: _____

_____

Rule of Law: _____

_____

3.   B purchases $20,000 worth of lumber from S, for use in homes B is constructing, with a check drawn on B's $40,000 checking account at PQR Bank. S negotiates the check to holder in due course, H. Much of the lumber B received from S is rotten so B notifies PQR Bank to stop payment. H presents B's $20,000 check for payment, and the bank honors the stop payment notice. What may H do to realize payment on the item? Explain.

Decision: _____

_____

Rule of Law: _____

_____

4.   A presents an item to bank R for collection at 2:30 on Friday afternoon. The bank has a 2:00 p.m. cut-off time. On the following Wednesday, bank R forwards the item for collection. The person who was ultimately liable for the item files a bankruptcy petition one day before the item

is presented to the person for payment. A claims the bank did not act seasonably. Decide.

Decision: _____

_____

Rule of Law: _____

_____

5. Millionaire spendthrift D issues a check drawn on an account with bank P payable to R for $10,000. Two days earlier, D's relatives had instituted an incompetency proceeding against D seeking to remove his financial responsibility. The court declares D incompetent a day before R presents the $10,000 check to the bank P for payment. Unaware of D's adjudication of incompetence, bank P honors the check and charges D's account. The relatives learn of this fact and bring suit against the bank for wrongful payment. Who wins? Explain.

Decision: _____

_____

Rule of Law: _____

_____

COMMERCIAL PAPER UNIT

RESEARCH QUESTIONS:

1.   What effects have advancements in computer technology had on the principles and practice of negotiable instruments law?   What changes have occurred/need to occur in the law to accommodate further developments in computer technology and vice versa?

2.   Over the past several years, Congress has enacted major changes in banking law.   What developments were these new laws intended to meet?   Discuss the major provisions of these laws and the rationale underlying them.

CHAPTER 29
Nature and Formation

SCOPE NOTE

Businesses are usually organized in one of three different forms: a sole proprietorship; a partnership; or a corporation. Chapters 29 through 32 develop the law of partnerships and limited partnerships and Chapters 33 through 36 discuss corporation law.

The basis for the discussion of the law of partnership is the Uniform Partnership Act. In Chapter 29, the legal principles associated with the nature and formation of a partnership are discussed. Also focused upon is the character of property interest related to a partnership as well as the comparative advantages and disadvantages associated with this form of business organization.

EDUCATIONAL OBJECTIVES

1. Define and discuss the criteria for determining partnership existence.

2. Contrast the types of partnerships and partners.

3. Explain the substantive and procedural requirements for establishing a partnership.

4. Discuss the nature of the property interest held by a partnership.

5. Understand the theories and principles of partnership law included in the Articles of Partnership.

6. Develop the importance of contract law in the formation of a partnership.

CHAPTER OUTLINE

A. Nature of Partnership
    1. Definition - a partnership is an association of two or more persons to carry on, as co-owners, a business for profit.
    2. Entity theory - a legal entity is a unit with the capacity of possessing legal rights and being

subject to legal duties.
   a.   Partnership as a legal entity - the UPA recognizes a partnership as a legal entity distinct from its members for some purposes.
   b.   Partnership as a legal aggregate - a partnership is an aggregate for some purposes and thus it cannot sue nor be sued in the firm name unless a statute allows it.
3.   Types of partners - numerous types are listed.
B.   Formation of a Partnership
   1.   Articles of partnership - a written agreement creating a partnership.
      a.   Statute of Frauds - does not usually apply to a contract for the formation of a partnership and thus no writing is required to create one.
      b.   Firm name - there are some restrictions on the choice of a name for the partnership.
   2.   Tests of partnership existence
      a.   Association - the partnership must have two or more persons who agree to be partners.
      b.   Business for profit - for a partnership to exist, there must be a business for profit in addition to the co-ownership of property.
      c.   Co-ownership - of a business is essential for the existence of a partnership.
   3.   Partnership capital and property - total money and property contributed by the partners is the partnership capital while the sum of all of the partnership assets including capital is the partnership property.
   4.   Rights in specific partnership property - of a partner is in the form of ownership called a tenancy in partnership.
   5.   Partner's interest in the partnership.
      a.   Assignability - a partner may sell or assign her interest in the partnership, but this does not cause dissolution.
      b.   Creditor's rights - a partner's interest is subject to the claims of that partner's creditors who may obtain a charging order (a type of judicial lien) against the partner's interest.

TRUE-FALSE: Circle true or false.

Answers

T   F   1.   Partnerships pay Federal income tax on the profits they acquire.

T   F   2.   Generally, a partnership cannot sue or be sued in its own name in the absence of a permissive statute.

T   F   3.   A judgment creditor of a partnership can demand payment of the entire amount of the debt from any one of the partners.

T   F   4.   A partnership cannot acquire title to real property in its own name.

T   F   5.   A partnership must be organized as a business for profit.

T   F   6.   The fact that two or more persons own property jointly in itself establishes a partnership.

T   F   7.   Unless each partner takes an active part in the management of the firm, a partnership does not exist.

T   F   8.   The Statute of Frauds does not specifically cover contracts for the establishment of a partnership.

T   F   9.   Under common law, a partnership was considered an entity.

T   F   10. The Uniform Partnership Act (U.P.A.) is a primary source of partnership law in all states except Louisiana.

T   F   11. When a partner sells or assigns her interest in the partnership, the partnership is dissolved.

T   F   12. A partner's interest in the partnership is subject to the claims of that partner's individual creditors.

KEY TERMS - MATCHING EXERCISE: Select the term which best completes each statement below and write the corresponding number in the ANSWERS column.

Column I	Column II	Answers
1. The written agreement that creates a partnership.	1. Partnership	1. _____
2. A person who is not a partner but who is entitled to share profits of a partnership.	2. Capital	2. _____
3. A group of persons acting as co-owners to carry on a business for profit.	3. Sole proprietorship	3. _____
	4. Ostensible partner	4. _____
4. Another name for a partner by estoppel.	5. General partner	5. _____
5. Partners who are liable for a firm's debt only to the extent of their own capital contributions.	6. Nominal partner	6. _____
	7. Limited partner	7. _____
6. A unit that has the acknowledged capacity to possess legal rights and to be subject to legal duties.	8. Capacity	8. _____
	9. Secret partner	9. _____
	10. Legal entity	10. _____
7. A real partner who plays no part in the management of the business.	11. Joint stock company	11. _____
	12. Sub-partner	12. _____

8. A key factor determining whether a natural person may become part of a partnership.

9. Form of business organization in which one person operates the enterprise alone.

10. Aggregate total of money and property committed to the operation of a business enterprise.

11. A form of business association, not a partnership, organized to accomplish a single business transaction.

12. Another name for the articles of partnership that creates the partnership.

13. The penalties provided by statute for not disclosing to the public the real names of partners conducting the partnership under a fictitious name.

14. A partner who has unlimited liability for partnership debts, full management powers, and who shares in the profits.

15. A partner whose membership in the partnership is not disclosed to the public.

13. Articles of partnership

14. Silent partner

15. Equitable partner

16. Partnership agreement

17. Surplus

18. Fine or imprisonment

19. Statute of Frauds

20. Joint venture

13. _____

14. _____

15. _____

MULTIPLE CHOICE: Select the alternative which best completes each statement below and write the corresponding letter in the ANSWERS column.   Answers

1. Title to real property that becomes a partnership asset may be conveyed (a) in the name of the partnership according to the U.P.A. (b) only to an individual partner (c) only in the names of all the partners (d) none of the above.

1. _____

2. Which of the following is not a test for determining the existence of a partnership? (a) co-ownership (b) conducting a business (c) profit sharing (d) business experience.

2. _____

3. One of the following could be a partnership: a (a) medical clinic (b) political organization (c) literary society (d) charitable foundation.

3. _____

4. A real partner, who is both a silent and a secret partner, is called (a) dormant patner (b) special partner (c) sub-partner (d) nominal partner.

4. _____

5. Sharing of profits, sharing of losses, and the right to manage and control the business are specific tests for determining (a) proprietorship (b) co-ownership (c) corporate existence (d) all of the above.

5. _____

6. The capacity in which partners hold themselves out to the world is as an (a) equitable shareholder (b) investor (c) agent (d) irrevocable donee.

6. _____

7. The partnership name (a) must include the name of all the partners (b) may be a fictitious name (c) must include the name of at least one of the partners (d) may be the same name as an existing corporation.

7. _____

8. The Uniform Partnership Act holds that no inference that a partnership exists can be made where profits are received in payment of (a) a debt (b) wages (c) an interest on a loan (d) all of the above.

8. _____

9. Contributions by a partner to the partnership may include (a) services (b) property (c) money (d) all of the above.

9. _____

10. The capacity in which the Internal Revenue Service views a partnership is as (a) an entity (b) a non-taxable proprietorship (c) an aggregate (d) none of the above.

10. _____

11. The Uniform Partnership Act broadly defines "person" to include (a) individuals (b) partnerships (c) corporations (d) all of the above.

11. _____

12. The formation of a partnership may result from (a) an oral or written agreement between the parties (b) an informal arrangement (c) the conduct of the parties (d) all of the above.

12. _____

13. An enforceable agreement can provide for all of the following except (a) any conceivable arrangement of capital investment and profit distribution (b) continuity of the partnership in the event of one member's death or retirement (c) the oral formation of a partnership that is to last for five years (d) none of the above.

13. _____

CASE PROBLEMS - SHORT ESSAY ANSWERS: Read each case problem carefully. When appropriate, answer by stating a Decision for the case and by explaining the rationale - Rule of Law - relied upon to support your decision.

1. A and B are nieces of X. X dies and under a will leaves apartment buildings to A and B as tenants in common. A and B continue to manage and lease the apartments cooperatively. At the end of each year, A and B split the profits from the rents collected. Do A and B have a partnership? Explain.

Decision: _____

Rule of Law: _____

_____

2.   A and B are partners. C, with A and B's knowledge, agrees to represent himself as another
       member of the partnership to X. On the basis of C's representation, X loans a large sum of
       money to the partnership of A and B. Can X force C to contribute to the repayment of the loan?
       Explain.

Decision: _____

Rule of Law: _____

_____

3.   A has been declared a mentally incompetent person by a court's decision, and the judge has
       appointed a guardian for A. If A enters into a partnership agreement with B, does a partnership
       exist? Explain.

Decision: _____

Rule of Law: _____

_____

4.   A, B, and C are partners. All three share in the profits and losses of the business, but only A and
       B manage the business. In addition, C's membership in the business is not disclosed to the public.
       What type of partner is C? Explain.

Decision: _____

Rule of Law: _____

_____

5.   A, B, and C are members of a partnership. They have orally contracted to form their partnership
       and to continue its business for five years. Is their contract to form a partnership enforceable?
       Explain.

Decision: _____

Rule of Law: _____

_____

Duties, Rights, and Liabilities

SCOPE NOTE

Chapter 30 continues our discussion of partnership law. The Chapter examines the legal doctrines and principles which control the operations of a partnership. What are the rights/duties existing among the members of the partnership? What are the rights/duties of people doing business with the enterprise? These and other topics are the primary themes of Chapter 30.

EDUCATIONAL OBJECTIVES

1. Trace the various categories of partnership authority and discuss the extent of responsibilities associated with each.

2. Explain the liability of partners in terms of contract, tort and agency theories.

3. Define and discuss the significance of a partnership by estoppel.

4. Understand the nature and substance of duties partners owe one another.

5. Outline the specific rights partners have with one another.

CHAPTER OUTLINE

I. Relationship of Partners to One Another
   A. Duties Among Partners - the legal duties imposed upon partners are listed below.
      1. Fiduciary duty - each partner owes a duty of absolute and utmost good faith and loyalty to his partners.
      2. Duty of obedience - each partner must act in obedience to the partnership agreement.
      3. Duty of care - each partner owes a duty of faithful service to the best of her ability to the partnership.
   B. Rights Among Partners - provided by law are listed below.
      1. Right to share in distributions - which are transfers of partnership property from the partnership to the partners.

      a.   Right to share in profits - each partner is entitled to a share of the profits.

      b.   Right to return of capital - after all partnership creditors are paid, each partner is repaid her capital contribution.

      c.   Right to return of advances - if a partner makes loans to the firm, she is entitled to repayment plus interest.

      d.   Right to compensation - generally, no partner is entitled to payment for acting in the partnership business.

    2.   Right to participate in management - each partner has an equal voice in management.

    3.   Right to choose associates - no person can become a partner without the consent of all the partners.

    4.   Enforcement rights - the law provides partners with the means to enforce rights and duties.

      a.   Right to information and inspection of the books - is a right of each partner.

      b.   Right to an accounting - which is an equitable proceeding for a comprehensive and effective settlement of all partnership affairs and a partner is entitled to this proceeding.

II.   Relationship Between Partners and Third Parties

    A.   Contracts of Partnership - the act of every partner binds the partnership to transactions within the scope of partnership business unless the partner does not have actual or apparent authority.

      1.   Authority to bind partnership - a partner may bind the firm by her act if she has any of the kinds of authority listed below.

        a.   Actual express authority - may be oral or written and it is usually included in the partnershp agreement.

        b.   Actual implied authority - is authority that is reasonably deduced from the nature or terms of the partnership agreement.

        c.   Apparent authority - is authority that may be reasonably considered to exist by a third person.

      2.   Partnership by estoppel - imposes partnership duties and liabilities upon a person who is not a partner but who has either represented herself or consented to be represented as a partner.

    B.   Torts of Partnership - a partnership is liable for any loss or injury caused by a wrongful act or omission of any partner while acting within the ordinary course of the business or with authority.

    C.   Admissions of and Notice to a Partner - admissions by a partner may be used as evidence against the partnership and notice to any partner of any matter relating to the firm's affairs binds the partnership.

    D.   Liability of Incoming Partner - a person admitted as a partner into an existing partnership is liable for all of the obligations of the partnership arising before her admission, but this liability may be satisfied only out of partnership property.

TRUE-FALSE: Circle true or false.

Answers

T   F   1.   Each partner owes a duty of good faith and loyalty to the other partners.

T   F   2.   Upon termination of the partnership, partners are entitled to the return of their capital contributions after all debts have been paid.

T   F   3.   Generally, when partners are repaid their capital contributions, they also receive interest on the contribution.

T   F   4.   In most cases, the proportion in which partners bear business losses depends on their relative capital contributions.

T   F   5.   An incoming partner has unlimited liability for all obligations arising after the partner's admission.

T   F   6.   Partners who loan money to the partnership beyond their capital contribution become creditors of the firm.

T   F   7.   Generally, a partner is entitled to compensation for services performed for the firm.

T   F   8.   In an action on tort liability, the plaintiff must sue all the partners jointly.

T   F   9.   A partnership is not bound by notice to a partner of a matter relating to partnership affairs since such notice must be given to all partners.

T   F   10.   Much of the law of partnership is based on the law of agency.

T   F   11.   If a partner has neither actual authority nor apparent authority, the partnership is bound only if it ratifies the act of the partner.

T   F   12.   Any lawsuit based upon breach of contract brought against the partners must name all the partners as defendants.

KEY TERMS - MATCHING: Select the term which best completes each statement below and write the corresponding number in the ANSWERS column.

Column I	Column II	Answers
1. A principle that establishes the right persons have to select their own partners.	1. Indemnification	1. _____
	2. Unlimited personal liability	2. _____
2. The right one partner who pays all the partnership debts has against the other non-paying partners.		3. _____
	3. Agency law	
	4. Express authority	4. _____
3. The liability of a general partner.	5. Limited personal liability	5. _____
4. A major basis for partnership law and liability.		6. _____
	6. Distribution	7. _____
5. Actual partnership authority that is oral or written.	7. Accounting	8. _____

6.   The court in which a partner sues for an accounting.

7.   The partnership created when persons not partners hold themselves out as partners.

8.   Partnership authority reasonably deducible from the partnership and the relations of the partners.

9.   The relationship of trust and confidence existing between partners.

10.   A transfer of partnership property from the partnershp to a partner.

11.   A type of negligence somewhat les than gross negligence.

12.   Another name for loans a partner makes to the partnership.

13.   A detailed statement of financial transactions.

14.   An act that requires the consent of all of the partners.

15.   The duty violated by a partner who extends credit to her relatives using partnership funds.

8.   Delectus personae

9.   Court of equity

10.   Change in membership

11.   Fiduciary

12.   Apparent authority

13.   Court of law

14.   Implied authority

15.   Partnership by estoppel

16.   **Contributory** negligence

17.   Advances

18.   Ratification

19.   Duty of obedience

20.   Culpable negligence

9.   _____

10.   _____

11.   _____

12.   _____

13.   _____

14.   _____

15.   _____

MULTIPLE CHOICE: Select the alternative which best completes each statement below and write the corresponding letter in the ANSWERS column.   Answers

1.   Upon termination of a solvent partnership, partners are entitled to the (a) return of their capital contributions (b) interest on their capital contributions by right of implication (c) repayment of their loans to the partnership without interest (d) none of the above.

1.   _____

2.   Decisions that require unanimous agreement of the partners include (a) changing the enterprise's place (city) of business (b) adding a new partner (c) submitting a dispute to arbitration (d) all of the above.

2.   _____

3.   The duties of a partner include the duty of (a) care (b) loyalty (c) obedience (d) all of the above.

3.   _____

4.   Authority of a partner to act that is specifically provided for in the partnership agreement is (a) apparent (b) equitable (c) express (d) apportioned.

4. _____

5.   A partner does not have implied authority to (a) assign partnership property for the benefit of partnership creditors (b) hire employees (c) fire employees (d) purchase property for the business.

5. _____

6.   A partner does not have apparent authority to (a) pay individual debts out of partnership assets (b) endorse checks (c) give warranties in selling goods (d) enter into contracts for advertising.

6. _____

7.   The rights of a partner do not include the right to (a) compensation for performing partnership business (b) sue the partnership for damages (c) add a friend or relative to the partnership without consent of all the partners (d) all of the above.

7. _____

8.   Liability of general partners for valid partnership contracts is (a) limited personal liability (b) joint liability (c) joint and several liability (d) none of the above.

8. _____

9.   Liability of general partners for torts of a partner or an employee doing company business is (a) limited personal liability (b) joint liability (c) joint and several liability (d) none of the above.

9. _____

10.   The rights of a partner include the right to (a) share profits (b) participate in managing the business (c) a repayment of capital contributions (d) all of the above.

10. _____

11.   A partner may not (a) compete with the partnership business (b) acquire for himself a partnership asset (c) make a profit from the partnership business other than his agreed compensation (d) all of the above.

11. _____

12.   A partner must manage the partnership business without (a) any negligence (b) culpable negligence (c) ordinary negligence (d) all of the above.

12. _____

13.   A partner's form of ownership of specific partnership property is a (a) joint tenancy (b) tenancy in common (c) tenancy in partnership (d) none of the above.

13. _____

CASE PROBLEMS - SHORT ESSAY ANSWERS: Read each case problem carefully.   When appropriate, answer by stating a Decision for the case and by explaining the rationale - Rule of Law - relied upon to support your decision.

1.   Floral Designs is a partnership among A, B, and C.   A sells his partnership interest to P, who alleges that as a result of the purchase, she is now a co-partner with B and C. Accordingly, she demands a voice in managing the firm, and B and C refuse.   P threatens suit.   Who wins? Explain.

Decision: _____

_____

Rule of Law: _____

_____

2.   Futuristic Concepts is a partnership owned by P, B, and Q who have provided in the Articles of
      Partnership that profits should be shared equally. P and B decide to change the method of sharing
      profits. Q finds the change in method unacceptable and demands that the original equal-share
      method be retained. P and B resist asserting "majority rules." What result? Explain.

      Decision: _____

      _____

      Rule of Law: _____

      _____

3.   While acting for the partnership, A completes a business transaction that nets the firm over
      $50,000. A demands payment for the work or an increase in the partnership profits. The other
      partners refuse. What result? Explain.

      Decision: _____

      _____

      Rule of Law: _____

      _____

4.   Without authority from her co-partners B and C, A assigns a truck owned by the firm to Z, a
      creditor of the partnership. Z demands the truck. The partners refuse to relinquish it. Who
      prevails? Explain.

      Decision: _____

      _____

      Rule of Law: _____

      _____

5.   A, B, and C are partners. B is wrongfully excluded from the management of the partnership
      business. B commences a lawsuit against the partnership seeking damages. Is B entitled to this
      remedy? Explain.

      Decision: _____

      _____

      Rule of Law: _____

      _____

Dissolution, Winding Up, and Termination

SCOPE NOTE

Chapter 31 continues our discussion of partnership law. The Chapter examines the legal doctrines and principles which control the operations and termination of a partnership. What happens when the partnership ends its existence? These and other topics dealing with the management and dissolution of the partnership are the primary themes of Chapter 31.

EDUCATIONAL OBJECTIVES

1. Trace the various categories of partnership authority and discuss the extent of responsibilities associated with each upon dissolution and termination of the partnership.

2. Define and discuss dissolution and its causes.

3. Explain and discuss the rights of partnership creditors.

4. Outline the specific rights partners have during and after dissolution.

5. Contrast partnership dissolutions harmonious with and contravening to the partnership contract.

6. Discuss procedures associated with "winding up" a partnership in the context of an insolvent and solvent enterprise.

7. Develop the significance of continuing a partnership as opposed to termination.

CHAPTER OUTLINE

A. Dissolution
    1. Causes of dissolution
        a. Dissolution by act of the partners - a partner always has the power but not always the right to dissolve the partnership by her own acts.
        b. Dissolution by operation of law - death, bankruptcy, or subsequent illegality dissolve

the partnership.

    c.   Dissolution by court order - four ways are listed that cause dissolution by a court order.

  2.   Effects of dissolution

    a.   Authority - dissolution causes actual authority of a partner to act for the partnership to terminate, but apparent authority persists.

    b.   Existing liability - dissolution does not itself discharge the existing liability of any partner.

B.   Winding Up

  1.   The right to wind up - belongs to any partner upon dissolution.

  2.   Distribution of assets - assets are reduced to cash and distributed to creditors and then to partners.

    a.   Solvent partnership - assets of the partnership are greater than its liabilities.

    b.   Insolvent partnership - liabilities to creditors are greater than the assets of the partnership.

    c.   Contribution of partner upon insolvency - generally, partners contribute equally to the losses of the partnership.

  3.   Marshaling of assets - segregating partnership assets and liabilities from those of the individual partners.

C.   Continuation after Dissolution

  1.   Right to continue partnership - three rights are listed.

    a.   Continuation after wrongful dissolution - a partner who wrongfully withdraws cannot force liquidation.

    b.   Continuation after expulsion - an expelled partner cannot force liquidation.

    c.   Continuation agreement of the partners - is the best and most reliable way of preserving a partnership after dissolution.

  2.   Rights of creditors - are listed whenever a change in the membership of the partnership occurs.

TRUE-FALSE: Circle true or false.

Answers

T   F   1.   Partners owe one another fiduciary duties of good faith and loyalty.

T   F   2.   Upon termination of the partnership, partners are entitled to the return of their capital contributions after all debts have been paid.

T   F   3.   Upon dissolution, the partnership is terminated.

T   F   4.   The proportion in which partners bear business losses depends on their relative capital contributions.

T   F   5.   Dissolution may occur by acts of the partners or by operation of law.

T   F   6.   Partners who loan money to the partnership beyond their capital contribution become creditors of the firm but their claims are secondary to the claims of other creditors of the partnership.

T   F   7.   A partnership is dissolved any time its membership changes, and a new partnership is formed.

T   F   8.   Upon dissolution, the liability of all partners to creditors and other third parties ends.

T   F   9.   Courts generally will grant a decree of specific performance of a partnership contract.

T   F   10.   A partner expelled from the partnership pursuant to the terms of the partnership contract cannot force the liquidation of the enterprise.

T   F   11.   Termination of a partnership occurs when the process of winding up has been completed.

T   F   12.   A partner always has the power and the right to dissolve the partnership by his own actions.

KEY TERMS - MATCHING EXERCISE: Select the term which best completes each statement below and write the corresponding number in the ANSWERS section.

Column I	Column II	Answers
1. The process of liquidating a partnership.	1. Contribution	1. _____
2. The right one partner who pays all the partnership debts has against the other non-paying partners.	2. Bankruptcy	2. _____
	3. Novation	3. _____
3. The change in the relationship of partners resulting when one partner withdraws from the operation of the business.	4. Marshaling	4. _____
	5. Dissolution by operation of law	5. _____
	6. Termination	6. _____
4. An agreement among a retiring partner, continuing partners, and creditors whereby the retiring partner may be discharged from existing liabilities.	7. Dissolution by act of the partners	7. _____
	8. Winding up	8. _____
5. Segregating and separating assets and liabilities of a partnership from those of the respective partners.	9. Continuation	9. _____
	10. Change in membership	10. _____
	11. Fiduciary	11. _____
6. An agreement used to guarantee the ongoing operations of a partnership following the death, disability, or retirement of a partner.	12. Dissolution by court order	12. _____
		13. _____
		14. _____
		15. _____

7. Dissolution caused by death of a partner.

8. Partnership authority which terminates upon dissolution.

9. The relationship of trust and confidence existing between partners.

10. The final state in ending the existence of a partnership.

11. The type of notice a withdrawing partner makes by newspaper publication that may protect her from further liability of the firm.

12. The type of notice a withdrawing partner must give to creditors of the partnership prior to dissolution.

13. Dissolution caused by the incompetence of a partner.

14. Partnership authority that continues upon dissolution unless proper notice of the dissolution is given to third parties.

15. A partnership in which the partnership assets exceed the partnership liabilities (debts) to creditors.

13. Apparent authority

14. Actual authority

15. Partnership by estoppel

16. Actual notice

17. Solvent partnership

18. Trustee

19. Insolvent partnership

20. Constructive notice

MULTIPLE CHOICE: Select the alternative which best completes each statement below and write the corresponding letter in the ANSWERS column.   Answers

1. Upon termination of a solvent partnership, partners are entitled to the (a) return of their capital contributions (b) interest on their capital contributions by right of implication (c) repayment of their loans before payment to creditors (d) none of the above.   1. _____

2. Dissolution occurs by (a) court order (b) an act of the partners (c) operation of law (d) all of the above.   2. _____

3. An act which dissolves a partnership by operation of law is (a) an agreement of the parties (b) the bankruptcy of a partner (c) the proper expulsion of a partner (d) all of the above.   3. _____

4.   Upon dissolution, authority of a partner that binds the partnership for acts for the business unless notice of the dissolution is given third parties is (a) apparent (b) equitable (c) actual (d) apportioned.

4.   _____

5.   Which of the following does not occur during the winding up period of a partnership? (a) the termination of the partners' liability (b) the payment of creditors (c) the distribution of assets (d) the collection of debts.

5.   _____

6.   Dissolution by act of the partners occurs when a (a) partner withdraws (b) partner dies (c) judge dissolves the partnership (d) partner becomes insane.

6.   _____

7.   Under the UPA, a partner has the right to liquidate the partnership except when (a) contrary to the partnership contract (b) that partner has been properly expelled (c) there is unanimous agreement for continuation (d) all of the above.

7.   _____

8.   When membership of a partnership changes, (a) default occurs (b) the partnership is dissolved (c) estoppel bars further withdrawal of other partners (d) none of the above.

8.   _____

9.   A court will order the dissolution of a partnership if (a) a partner is incompetent (b) a partner is guilty of conduct prejudicial to the business (c) the business cannot operate profitably (d) all of the above.

9.   _____

10.   Placing an advertisement in a newspaper of general circulation calling attention to the dissolution of a named partnership is called (a) actual notice (b) equitable notice (c) notice by attention (d) constructive notice.

10.   _____

11.   Continuation agreements that allow partnerships to continue business after dissolution are (a) the best and most reliable way to preserve a partnership (b) used to insure continuity after a partner's death (c) used to insure continuity after a partner's retirement (d) all of the above.

11.   _____

12.   Under Federal bankruptcy law, the person who is appointed to administer the assets of the partnership is the (a) general partner (b) marshal (c) trustee (d) none of the above.

12.   _____

13.   Which of the following is not a stage that leads to the extinction of a partnership? (a) dissolution (b) distribution (c) liquidation (d) termination.

13.   _____

CASE PROBLEMS - SHORT ESSAY ANSWERS: Read each case problem carefully. When appropriate, answer by stating a Decision for the case and by explaining the rationale - Rule of Law - relied upon to support your decision.

1.   X, Y, and Z are partners. Z wants to retire from the firm (partnership) and terminate her liability to existing creditors of the partnership. X and Y want to continue the partnership business. Are

these desires possible? Explain.

Decision: _____

Rule of Law: _____

_____

2.   In question 1 above, how can Z, the retiring partner, protect herself against liability on contracts
      that are entered into by the partnership between the time of her resignation and actual
      withdrawal? Explain.

Decision: _____

Rule of Law: _____

_____

3.   A, B, and C are partners.   Each originally contributed $5,000 to the partnership.   If, after
      dissolution and liquidation, the firm's assets are $100,000 and its debts owed to creditors are
      $40,000, how much will be C's share of the assets if according to the partnership contract they are
      to be divided equally among the partners? Explain.

Decision: _____

Rule of Law: _____

_____

4.   Without authority from his co-partners, B and C, and in breach of their partnership agreement, A
      assigns a truck owned by the firm to Z, an individual creditor of A. Z demands the truck. The
      partners, B and C, refuse to relinquish it. Can the partnership be dissolved? Explain.

Decision: _____

Rule of Law: _____

_____

5.   A, B, and C are partners. With A's and B's consent, C retires. Pursuant to their agreement, A
      and B agree to assume all the old debts and obligations of the firm and proceed with the
      accounting and dissolution. X, a creditor of the firm before dissolution, has a debt which A and
      B cannot satisfy, so X sues C. C refuses to pay X arguing the controlling influence of C's
      agreement with A and B. Who prevails? Explain.

Decision: _____

Rule of Law: _____

_____

CHAPTER 32

Limited Partnerships

SCOPE NOTE

Chapter 32 ends our discussion of partnership law with a review of one of the fastest growing forms of partnership: the limited partnership. This Chapter identifies the rights/duties that exist among the members of the limited partnership, explains the procedures for the formation and dissolution of the limited partnership, and discusses the advantages/disadvantages of this partnership as well as other forms of business associations, e.g., the business trust, mining partnerships, and joint ventures.

EDUCATIONAL OBJECTIVES

1. Discuss the criteria for the formation and dissolution of a limited partnership.

2. Explain the liability of limited partners concerning torts or contracts of the partnership.

3. Discuss the rights and duties of limited partners.

4. Identify the advantages and disadvantages of other forms of business associations, e.g., mining partnerships, joint ventures, business trusts, etc.

CHAPTER OUTLINE

A. Limited Partnerships
    1. Definition - a partnership formed by two or more persons under the laws of a State and having at least one general partner and one limited partner.
    2. Formation - requires substantial compliance with the limited partnership statute.
        a. Filing of certificate - of the limited partnership with the Secretary of State is required.
        b. Name - of the limited partnership may not contain the surname of the limited partner in most cases.
        c. Contributions - may be in the form of cash, property or services.
        d. Defective formation - the limited partnership is formed when the certificate is filed; if improperly or not done, liability of the limited partners may be in jeopardy.

        e.   Foreign limited partnerships - are considered foreign in any State in which it has not been formed.

    3.   Rights

        a.   Control - is in the hands of the general partners.

        b.   Choice of associates - no partner can be added without the consent of all partners.

        c.   Withdrawal - the certificate determines the right and method of withdrawal although generally a general partner may withdraw at any time by giving written notice to the other partners.

        d.   Assignment of interest - is the partner's share in the profits and her right to distribution of partnership assets.

        e.   Profit and loss sharing - is allocated among the partners except limited partners are not generally liable for losses beyond their contribution of capital.

        f.   Distributions - of assets are shared by partners as provided in their partnership agreement.

        g.   Loans - all partners may be secured or unsecured creditors of the partnership.

        h.   Information - all records must be kept at the partnership office and each partner has the right to inspect the records.

        i.   Derivative actions - limited partners may sue on behalf of the partnership if general partners refuse to bring the action.

    4.   Duties and liabilities

        a.   Duties - general partners have a fiduciary duty to limited partners.

        b.   Liabilities - limited partners have limited personal liability.

    5.   Dissolution

        a.   Causes - limited partners do not have the right to dissolve the partnership, but four causes are listed.

        b.   Winding up - generally this is done by the general partners.

        c.   Distribution of assets - the priorities in distributing the assets of a limited partnership are listed.

B.   Other Types of Unincorporated Business Associations

    1.   Joint venture - a form of temporary partnership to carry out a particular business enterprise for profit.

    2.   Joint stock company - a form of general partnership which is a cross between a corporation and a partnership.

    3.   Mining partnerships - an association of owners of the mineral rights in land.

    4.   Limited partnership associations - a legal hybrid but called a partnership association.

    5.   Business trusts - a transfer of the legal title to specific property to one person for the use and benefit of another.

TRUE-FALSE: Circle true or false.

Answers

T   F   1.   The amount of capital invested in limited partnerships has declined substantially since 1916.

T   F   2.   The major advantage of limited partnerships is that the sale of such partnerships is not subject to governmental regulations.

T   F   3.   Members of a limited partnership association are not personally liable for the debts of the association.

T   F   4.   One difference between a mining partnership and a general partnership is that death of a mining partner does not dissolve the mining partnership.

T   F   5.   The causes of dissolution and the priorities in the distribution of the assets are the same for the limited partnership as they are for the general partnership.

T   F   6.   A general partner has a fiduciary duty to the limited partners, but it is unclear whether the limited partners have a fiduciary duty to the general partners.

T   F   7.   A general partnership and a limited partnership have the same formal requirements for their formation.

T   F   8.   The personal liability of a limited partner for partnership debts is limited to the amount of capital the limited partner has contributed.

T   F   9.   A limited partner has no right to participate in the management of the limited partnership.

T   F   10.   Limited partners always share the profits of the limited partnership equally.

T   F   11.   Today, a promise by a limited partner to contribute to the limited partnership is not enforceable unless it is written and signed.

T   F   12.   Unlike a corporation, a joint stock company is formed by contract and not by State authority.

KEY TERMS – MATCHING EXERCISE: Select the term which best completes each statement below and write the corresponding number in the ANSWERS column.

Column I	Column II	Answers
1. A partnership composed of one or more general partners and one or more limited partners.	1. General partnership	1. _____
	2. Joint venture	2. _____
2. A kind of limited partnership that cannot enforce actions in a State's courts for business transactions until it registers.	3. Limited personal liability	3. _____
		4. _____
	4. Fiduciary duty	
3. The first step in the extinguishment of a general or limited partnership.	5. Limited partnership	5. _____
		6. _____
4. Another name for a business trust that has the power to own and sell real estate.	6. Dissolution	7. _____
	7. Capital contribution	8. _____

5.   The document that is filed in the Secretary of State's office in the State in which the limited partnership has its principal office.

6.   Another name for a joint stock association that is formed by contract and not by State authority.

7.   The type of partnership in which death or insanity of a partner causes dissolution of the partnership.

8.   A form of temporary partnership organized to carry out a single business operation for profit.

9.   The extent or the amount of liability of a limited partner for losses of the partnership.

10. An association of several owners of the mineral rights in land for the purpose of extracting the minerals for profit.

11. A method a partner can use to transfer her partnership interest.

12. The kind of obligation a general partner owes a limited partner.

13. The person to whom a limited partner may transfer her partnership interest.

14. The person who contributes to the capital of a business in a good faith but erroneous effort to become a limited partner.

15. The office or person with whom a foreign limited partnership must register before transacting any business in the State.

8.   Foreign limited partnership

9.   Massachusetts trust

10. Certificate

11. Constructive trust

12. Assignee

13. Joint stock company

14. Limited partnership associations

15. Mining partnership

16. Assignor

17. Equity participant

18. Attorney General

19. Secretary of State

20. Assignment

9.   _____

10. _____

11. _____

12. _____

13. _____

14. _____

15. _____

MULTIPLE CHOICE: Select the alternative which best completes each statement below and write the corresponding letter in the ANSWERS column.   Answers

1.   Generally, death of a partner dissolves the following (a) a mining partnership (b) a limited partnership (c) a joint venture (d) none of the above.

1. _____

2.   Which of the following uniform laws governs the creation and operation of limited partnerships? (a) U.P.A. (b) U.L.P.A. (c) R.U.L.P.A. (d) all of the above.

2. _____

3.   Both general and limited partners (a) have limited personal liability (b) have the right to manage the partnership (c) must unanimously consent to add a partner to the partnership (d) all of the above.

3. _____

4.   A basic difference between a general partnership and a limited partnership is (a) a statute must exist that provides for the formation of the limited partnership (b) the limited partnership must comply with statutory requirements (c) the limited partners' liability is limited to their capital contributions (d) all of the above.

4. _____

5.   The uniform laws provide that a limited partner shall have the same rights as a general partner to (a) inspect the partnership books (b) copy records of the firm's business (c) obtain tax returns of the limited partnership (d) all of the above.

5. _____

6.   Failure of a limited partnership to comply with the statutory requirements for its formation may result in (a) a name change of the firm (b) the loss of limited liability for the limited partners (c) the loss of the limited partner's right to manage the partnership (d) all of the above.

6. _____

7.   Which of the following is a legal entity that resembles a corporation but whose members are not personally liable for its debts? (a) mining partnership (b) joint stock company (c) limited partnership association (d) business trust.

7. _____

8.   In a business trust, the person who has the responsibility of managing the trust is the (a) trustee (b) beneficiary (c) limited partner (d) joint venturer.

8. _____

9.   Death or bankruptcy (a) of a limited partner dissolves the partnership (b) of a general partner dissolves the partnership (c) never have any effect on the limited partnership (d) none of the above.

9. _____

10.   Limited partners (a) must share the profits of the partnership equally (b) must receive the return of their capital contributions at the same time (c) may contribute cash, property, or services under the revised act (d) all of the above.

10. _____

11.   A limited partnership requires that (a) all partners must be limited
        partners (b) the number of limited and general partners must be equal
        (c) the partnership be created according to statutory law (d) none of the
        above.   11. _____

12.   If the surname of a limited partner is used in the partnership name, the
        limited partner (a) is entitled to a higher percentage of the partnership
        profits (b) may participate in the management of the partnership (c) is
        liable to creditors who are unaware of the limited partnership (d) all of
        the above.   12. _____

13.   A joint venturer (a) generally lacks authority to bind other members of
        this business venture (b) is not the agent of other co-venturers (c) who
        dies does not necessarily cause the dissolution of the joint venture (d) all
        of the above.   13. _____

CASE PROBLEMS - SHORT ESSAY ANSWERS: Read each case problem carefully.   When
appropriate, answer by stating a Decision for the case and by explaining the rationale - Rule of Law -
relied upon to support your decision.

1.   For 1987, XYZ Limited Partnership has a $50,000 loss.   Carol is a limited partner of the firm.
        Must Carol pay for a share of this loss from her personal assets?   Explain.

        Decision: _____
        _____
        Rule of Law: _____
        _____

2.   A and B form a limited partnership.   A is the general partner; B is the limited partner.   The name
        of their company is A and B Partnership.   C agrees to make a loan to the partnership.   If the
        partnership defaults on this loan, whom can C sue?   Explain.

        Decision: _____
        _____
        Rule of Law: _____
        _____

3.   A, B, and C are members of a joint venture.   They buy a large tract of land surrounding a lake,
        subdivide it, and begin selling the lots at a generous profit.   If A dies, is the joint venture
        dissolved?   Explain.

        Decision: _____
        _____
        Rule of Law: _____
        _____

4.   A, B, and C form a limited partnership.   A and B want to add D to the partnership as a new
        general partner.   Under the uniform act, can this be done?   Explain.

Decision: _____

_____

Rule of Law: _____

_____

5.   Bob, Carol, Ted, and Alice agree to form a limited partnership. They are prepared to execute and sign a certificate but are unsure what is required by the uniform act. Explain to them what the certificate of limited partnership contains.

Decision: _____

_____

Rule of Law: _____

_____

CHAPTER 33

Nature, Formation, and Power

SCOPE NOTE

The most common form of business organization among modern industrial businesses is the corporation. It is a major institution of the private sector. In today's economy, corporations occupy a significant position as employers, taxpayers, and primary participants in the flow of goods and services constituting G.N.P. How did this form of business organization evolve? Why is it so popular in certain sectors of the marketplace? These and other related concerns are the subject of Chapters 33-36. In these Chapters, the law of corporations is discussed including its basic doctrines, principles and terminology.

Chapter 33 focuses upon what a corporation is, the functions it performs, how corporations are created, and the type of powers they can hold. This Chapter serves as a general introduction to corporation law that can help in understanding the subsequent chapters that address particular aspects of a corporation's operational identity.

EDUCATIONAL OBJECTIVES

1. Define and explain the basic characteristics of a corporation.

2. Trace the historical development of corporations.

3. Compare the advantages/disadvantages of the corporate form of business organization.

4. Outline the various rights/duties associated with a corporate legal identity.

5. Differentiate among the various kinds of corporations.

6. Enumerate the substantive and procedural formalities associated with effectively establishing a corporation.

7. Understand the consequences of ineffective formation of a corporation.

8. Identify the meaning and importance of the phrase "piercing the corporate veil."

9.   Discuss the sources, nature, and kinds of operation powers a corporation holds.

10.   Define and develop the importance of "ultra vires."

11.   Know the tort and criminal liability of a corporation.

CHAPTER OUTLINE

I.   Nature of Corporations
    A.   Corporate Attributes
        1.   Legal entity - makes the corporation separate and apart from its shareholders with rights and liabilities entirely distinct from theirs and it allows the corporation to sue or be sued.
        2.   Creature of the State - a corporation must be formed by compliance with a State incorporation statute.
        3.   Limited liability - means the shareholders are not personally liable for corporate debts.
        4.   Free transferability of corporate shares - may be done by sale, gift, or pledge.
        5.   Perpetual existence - is common and included in the articles of incorporation.
        6.   Centralized management - the shareholders elect the board of directors which manages the business.
        7.   As a person - a corporation is considered a person under the Federal Constitution Amendments.
        8.   As a citizen - a corporation is considered a citizen of the State of its incorporation and of the State of its principal place of business.
    B.   Classification of Corporations
        1.   Public or private - a corporation is formed for both purposes.
        2.   Profit or non-profit - a corporation is formed for profit or for charitable, educational, or scientific (non-profit) purposes.
        3.   Domestic or foreign - it is domestic in the State in which it is incorporated and foreign in all others.
        4.   Closely held - a corporation owned by a small number of persons.
        5.   Professional corporations - a corporation formed by duly licensed professionals.
II. Formation of a Corporation
    A.   Organizing the Corporation
        1.   Promoters - a person who originates and organizes the corporation.
            a.   Promoters' contracts - contracts created by the promoter before the corporation is formed.
            b.   Promoters' fiduciary duty - is due to the fiduciary relationship among themselves as well as to the corporation, its subscribers, and its initial shareholders.
        2.   Subscribers - the persons who offer to purchase capital stock in a corporation yet to be formed.
        3.   Selection of State for incorporation - generally is the State in which the corporation intends to be located and do business.
    B.   Formalities of Incorporation
        1.   Selection of name - it must contain a word or words that indicate it is a corporation.
        2.   Incorporators - persons who sign and file the articles of incorporation.
        3.   Articles of incorporation - the charter or basic governing document of the corporation.

4.   Organization meeting - the first meeting to adopt corporate bylaws and elect officers.

5.   Bylaws - the rules that govern the internal management of the corporation.

III.   Recognition or Disregard of Corporateness

A.   Defective Incorporation

1.   Common-law approach - a defectively formed corporation was accorded corporate attributes.

a.   Corporation de Jure - is a corporation formed in substantial compliance with the statute.

b.   Corporation de Facto - is a corporation not formed in compliance with the statute but is recognized as a corporation.

c.   Corporation by Estoppel - estoppel does not create a corporation.

d.   Defective corporation - the courts deny the associates the benefits of incorporation.

2.   Statutory approach - if the articles are filed, that is generally conclusive proof of proper incorporation under the statute.

B.   Piercing the Corporate Veil

1.   Closely held corporations - its shareholders may relax the traditional corporate formalities without courts piercing the veil.

2.   Parent-subsidiary - courts will pierce the corporate veil and hold the parent liable for the debts of its subsidiary under certain circumstances.

IV.   Corporate Powers

A.   Sources of Corporate Powers

1.   Statutory powers - provided by the Model Act are listed.

2.   Express charter powers - are stated in the articles of incorporation.

3.   Implied powers - exist by reasonable inference of the statute or the charter.

B.   Ultra Vires Acts

1.   Effect of Ultra Vires Acts - most statutes abolish the defense of ultra vires in an action by or against a corporation.

2.   Remedies for Ultra Vires Acts - three remedies are possible under the Model Act.

C.   Liability for Torts and Crimes - a corporation is liable for the torts committed by its agents in the course of their employment, and it may be convicted of a criminal offense for the conduct of its employees (officers or directors).

TRUE-FALSE: Circle true or false.

Answers

T   F   1.   A corporation incorporated under the laws of one State is known as a foreign corporation in other States.

T   F   2.   If the sole shareholder of a corporation willfully destroys corporate property by fire, the doctrine of "piercing the corporate veil" will protect the fire insurance company.

T   F   3.   A corporation can have its principal place of business in one State and be incorporated under the laws of another State.

T   F   4.   A corporation is "de jure" if it has failed to meet some of the technical requirements for incorporation.

T   F   5.   The powers of a corporation are limited to the express powers granted either in its charter or by the statutes of its State of incorporation.

T   F   6.   A corporation is liable for the torts of its agents and employees while they are engaged in company business.

T   F   7.   A corporation may be formed only by compliance with a State incorporation statute.

T   F   8.   A corporation is a legal entity, and therefore it is liable for its debts.

T   F   9.   A shareholder of a corporation is the owner and an agent of the corporation.

T   F   10. Title to corporate property belongs to the shareholders.

T   F   11. A transfer of corporate stock by gift or sale from one shareholder to another causes dissolution of the corporation.

T   F   12. A corporation may be incorporated in one State and conduct all or most of its operations in another State.

KEY TERMS – MATCHING EXERCISE: Select the term which best completes each statement below and write the corresponding number in the ANSWERS column.

Column I	Column II	Answers
1. The kind of liability shareholders usually have.	1. Perpetual	1. _____
2. A corporation organized substantially in compliance with the statutes.	2. De jure	2. _____
	3. Limited liability	3. _____
3. Another name for the certificate of incorporation which authorizes a corporation to do business.	4. De facto	4. _____
	5. Charter	5. _____
4. The procedure a court uses to disregard the corporate entity when it is wrongfully used to avoid personal accountability.	6. Pierce the corporate veil	6. _____
	7. Promoter	7. _____
		8. _____
5. The person who signs and files the articles of incorporation.	8. Incorporator	9. _____
	9. Respondeat superior	
6. The person who may be individually liable for contracts made prior to the corporation's existence.	10. Subscriber	10. _____
		11. _____
7. Corporate acts that are beyond the scope of its powers.	11. Diversity of citizenship	12. _____

8. The rules and regulations that govern a corporaton's internal management.

9. The doctrine that imposes liability on a corporation for the torts committed by its agents and employees during their employment.

10. The term that signifies that the parties to a lawsuit are from different States.

11. Payments made to shareholders from profits of the corporation.

12. A corporation owned by a small number of persons such as a family or friends.

13. The potential lifetime of a corporation.

14. Another name for a public corporation.

15. The individuals appointed to run the operations of a corporation on a day-to-day basis.

12. Bylaws   13. _____

13. Unlimited liability   14. _____

14. Ultra Vires   15. _____

15. "Inc." or "Ltd."

16. Officers

17. Dividends

18. Closely held corporation

19. Municipal corporation

20. Board of directors

MULTIPLE CHOICE: Select the alternative which best completes each statement below and write the corresponding letter in the ANSWERS column.   Answers

1. The person who offers to buy stock in a non-existing corporation is a (a) promoter (b) incorporator (c) subscriber (d) none of the above.   1. _____

2. The debts of a corporation are satisfied from (a) assets of the corporation (b) a shareholder's personal assets (c) an incorporator's personal assets (d) all of the above.   2. _____

3. A shareholder is (a) a principal of the corporation (b) an agent of the corporation (c) liable only for corporation torts (d) none of the above.   3. _____

4. Most incorporation statutes require that a corporation name (a) not be the same as the name of an existing corporation doing business within the State (b) contain wording that indicates it is a corporation (c) both A and B (d) none of the above.   4. _____

5.   A promoter's profits may be allowed if they are (a) disclosed to the
     corporation (b) relatively small (c) secret (d) none of the above.   5. _____

6.   A corporation whose existence cannot be challenged by the State is a (a)
     corporation de facto (b) corporation by estoppel (c) corporation de jure
     (d) none of the above.   6. _____

7.   A corporation derives all of its power and its existence from (a) its
     charter (b) the State (c) the articles of incorporation (d) the bylaws.   7. _____

8.   A corporation cannot be guilty of a crime (a) because it is impossible
     for it to have a guilty mind (b) because it is impossible to imprison a
     corporation (c) because it is an artificial "person" (d) the statement is
     false.   8. _____

9.   An ultra vires act by the corporation may be remedied by (a) an
     injunction brought by a shareholder (b) a representative suit by
     shareholders for the corporation against the officers (c) a proceeding to
     dissolve or enjoin the corporation brought by the Attorney General of
     the State (d) all of the above.   9. _____

10. Generally, all of the following are proper names for a corporation
     except (a) Johnson and Son, Inc. (b) Merry Widow Corporation (c) A. B.
     Lincoln and Company (d) T. F. Elliot, Ltd.   10. _____

11. The existence of a corporation is terminated by the (a) death of a
     shareholder (b) withdrawal or retirement of a director (c) addition of a
     new officer (d) none of the above.   11. _____

12. Corporations may be classified as (a) public or private (b) profit or
     nonprofit (c) domestic or foreign (d) all of the above.   12. _____

13. The following individuals need not be shareholders of the corporation
     (a) officers of the corporation (b) creditors of the corporation (c)
     members of the corporation's board of directors (d) all of the above.   13. _____

CASE PROBLEMS - SHORT ESSAY ANSWERS: Read each case problem carefully.   When
appropriate, answer by stating a Decision for the case and by explaining the rationale - Rule of Law -
relied upon to support your decision.

1.   A, B, and C plan to go into business together. A and B have limited assets. C is very wealthy.
     Would it be advantageous for C to insist upon a corporation? Explain.

     Decision: _____

     _____

     Rule of Law: _____

     _____

2.   A bartender of an incorporated tavern illegally sells liquor to a minor. The act is a crime under
     the State law. If the bartender is a non-owner, can the tavern be criminally prosecuted for the

illegal sale? Explain.

Decision: _____
_____

Rule of Law: _____
_____

3.   A promoter contracts with B to engage B to manage ABC Corporation upon its incorporation. The
      directors of ABC Corporation refuse to accept the terms of the contract, and B refuses to be
      employed by ABC Corporation except on the terms of the contract with the promoter. What are
      B's rights? Explain.

Decision: _____
_____

Rule of Law: _____
_____

4.   X, a promoter of a corporation created to do business as a shopping center, collects a 20%
      commission on the sale of land to the corporation. X does not inform the directors of the
      corporation. Can X keep the commission? Explain.

Decision: _____
_____

Rule of Law: _____
_____

5.   A, B, and C hire attorney Y to incorporate their dry cleaning partnership. All formal steps for
      incorporation are taken except publication of the articles in a legal newspaper and filing of the
      articles with the register of deeds in the county of the corporation's principal place of business.
      A, B, and C rely on Y to take all necessary steps and believe the procedures have been completed.
      Thereafter, a customer is seriously injured by dry cleaning fumes. Can the customer sue A, B, and
      C personally on the theory that the corporation is not validly formed and A, B, and C are still
      operating as partners? Explain.

Decision: _____
_____

Rule of Law: _____
_____

Financial Structure

SCOPE NOTE

In Chapter 34, the financial structure of a corporation is discussed. The legal concepts and rules relating to corporate funding, stocks and bonds, payment of dividends, and transfer of ownership of shares are focused upon.

EDUCATIONAL OBJECTIVES

1. Distinguish among the various classes of stock commonly used in corporate financing.

2. Develop the difference between "par" and "no par" value.

3. Discuss the procedures related to issuing, redeeming, cancelling and acquiring stock.

4. Explain the nature of the shareholder's dividend rights and liabilities.

5. Differentiate among the several types of dividends.

6. Understand the dividend declaration and payment process.

7. Identify what is meant by wrongful and illegal dividends.

8. Contrast the methods of marketing shares of stock.

9. List the warranties that run with a transfer of shares.

10. Develop the consequences of wrongful indorsement of lost or stolen securities.

11. Explain the securities registration process.

CHAPTER OUTLINE

I. Debt Securities
    A. Authority to Issue Debt Securities - also called bonds, is a sole responsibility of the board of directors.
    B. Types of Debt Securities

1.   Unsecured bonds - or debentures, have only the obligation of the corporation backing them.
2.   Secured bonds - are creditor claims enforceable against general corporate assets and also a lien on specific corporate property.
3.   Income bonds - are debt securities that condition the payment of interest on corporate earnings.
4.   Convertible bonds - may be exchanged for other securities at a specified ratio.
5.   Callable bonds - are bonds that are subject to redemption.

II.   Equity Securities
   A.   Issuance of Shares
      1.   Authority to issue - is within the articles of incorporation.
      2.   Qualification of stock - all States have statutes regulating the issuance and sale of corporate shares and securities.
      3.   Pre-emptive rights - a shareholder's right to purchase a proportionate part of a new share issue.
      4.   Amount of consideration for shares - depends on the type of shares being issued.
         a.   Par value stock - may be issued for any amount set by the directors or shareholders.
         b.   No par value stock - also may be issued for any amount.
         c.   Treasury stock - are shares that have been issued and then reacquired by the corporation, and they also may be sold for any amount.
      5.   Payment for newly issued shares - depends on two issues discussed below.
         a.   Type of consideration - may include cash, property, or services but not promissory notes or future services.
         b.   Valuation of consideration - exchanged for shares is determined by the directors.
      6.   Liability for shares - a shareholder's only liability is to pay to the corporation the full consideration for the shares issued.
   B.   Classes of Shares
      1.   Common stock - frequently the only class of stock issued and it has no special rights or preferences.
      2.   Preferred stock - has superior rights to common stock over dividends and assets upon liquidation.
         a.   Dividend preferences - means that preferred shareholders will receive full dividends before any are paid to common holders.
         b.   Liquidation preferences - after creditors are paid, preferred holders usually receive assets ahead of common holders.
         c.   Additional rights and limitations - preferred stock may have these.
      3.   Stock rights and options - rights of existing shareholders to purchase corporate shares of a specific class or classes.

III.   Dividends and Other Distributions
   A.   Types of Dividends and Other Distributions
      1.   Cash dividends - most common type of dividend.
      2.   Property dividends - a dividend of property.
      3.   Stock dividends - a ratable distribution of additional shares to the shareholders.
      4.   Stock splits - each of the issued and outstanding shares is split into a greater number of shares.
      5.   Liquidating dividends - a distribution of capital assets to shareholders upon termination.
      6.   Redemption of shares - is the option by the corporation to repurchase its own shares.
      7.   Acquisition of shares - may be by purchase, gift or otherwise.
   B.   Legal Restrictions on Dividends and Other Distributions
      1.   Definitions - legal concepts and finance terms concerning corporation assets are

defined.
2. Legal restrictions on cash dividends
   a. Earned surplus test - some States permit dividends to be paid only from earned surplus.
   b. Surplus test - a number of States permit dividends out of earned or capital surplus.
   c. Net asset test - the MBCA as amended in 1980 and the Revised Act use this test.
   d. Nimble dividends - dividends permitted by timely action of the directors in a year in which the corporation had no earnings.
3. Legal restrictions on liquidating distributions - States usually permit distributions, or dividends, in partial liquidation from capital surplus.
4. Legal restrictions on redemptions and acquisition of shares - redemption and the purchase of its own shares may not be made at a time when the corporation is insolvent or when the purchase would make it insolvent.

C. Declaration and Payment of Dividends - is accomplished at the direction of the board of directors.

D. Liability for Improper Dividends and Distributions - the Model Act imposes joint and several liability upon the directors to the corporation or to its creditors.

IV. Transfer of Investment Securities
   A. Ownership of Securities
      1. Record of ownership - shares represented by certificates or uncertificated shares are registered on books (records) kept for that purpose.
      2. Duty of issuer to register transfer of security - the issuing corporation has this duty and to then issue new certificates to the new owner under certain conditions.
      3. Lost, destroyed, or stolen certificated securities - under any of these conditions, the owner is entitled to a new certificate if other requirements are met.
   B. Transfer of Securities
      1. Restrictions on transfer - are seldom made, but if they exist, they are included in the articles or bylaws.
      2. Statute of Frauds - a contract for the sale of securities is not enforceable unless it satisfies the Statute of Frauds.
      3. Manner of transfer - includes methods of transfering certificated and uncertificated securities.
      4. Bona fide purchasers - are good faith purchasers for value and their transfer rights are included.
      5. Transfer warranties - given to a purchaser for value are listed.
      6. Forged or unauthorized indorsement - the owner of certificated securities is not deprived of title by a transfer bearing a forged or unauthorized indorsement.

TRUE-FALSE: Circle true or false.

Answers

T   F   1. Common and preferred stock are examples of debt investment securities.

T   F   2. Common stock shareholders generally bear the heaviest loss if a corporation fails.

T   F   3. A corporation's board of directors and shareholders share the responsibility for declaring dividends.

T   F   4. The current profits or net earnings of a corporation are the only lawful source of corporate dividends.

T   F   5.   Generally, a stock dividend increases the shareholder's relative interest in the net worth of the corporation.

T   F   6.   The purchaser of a bond issued by a corporation becomes an owner of the corporation like a shareholder.

T   F   7.   Preferred shareholders have priority to the assets of the corporation over creditors of the corporation.

T   F   8.   A shareholder has no right to transfer shares of stock by sale or gift.

T   F   9.   The buyer of a security bearing a forged indorsement does not acquire title to the security (stock).

T   F   10.   A corporation that issues stock is under a duty to register transfers of its certificated stock and to issue new stock certificates to the new owner.

T   F   11.   Modern statutes expressly authorize the articles of incorporation to deny or limit a shareholder's preemptive rights.

T   F   12.   A stock split is a ratable distribution of additional shares of the capital stock of the corporation to its shareholders.

KEY TERMS – MATCHING EXERCISE: Select the term which best completes each statement below and write the corresponding number in the ANSWERS column.

Column I	Column II	Answers
1. The evidence of a shareholder's interest in a corporation.	1. Indorsement	1. _____
	2. Negotiation	2. _____
2. The statute containing the rules applicable to stock transfer.	3. Model Act	3. _____
3. The procedure which enables the bona fide purchaser (transferee) of stock to take title free of adverse claims not noted on the stock certificate.	4. "An appropriate person"	4. _____
	5. Bona fide purchaser	5. _____
	6. U.C.C. Article 8	6. _____
4. The person specified in the stock certificate or entitled to it by special indorsement who may transfer the registered stock by indorsing and delivering it.	7. Stock certificate	7. _____
	8. Blue Sky laws	8. _____
	9. Preemptive rights	9. _____
5. The State statute that regulates the issuance and sale of corporate securities.	10. Equity securities	10. _____
	11. No par stock	11. _____
	12. Par value stock	12. _____

6. A transferee of stock who is a purchaser for value in good faith.

7. Stock in which the stated value is found in the articles of incorporation.

8. A shareholder's right to purchase a pro rata share of every new offering of stock by the corporation.

9. A source for financing corporations that includes common stock.

10. The dividend paid to preferred shareholders for all arrearages on their stock before any dividends are paid on the common stock.

11. Stock of a corporation that have been issued and subsequently reacquired by the corporation.

12. Another name for unsecured bonds.

13. A written offer made by corporations to interest people in buying stock.

14. A direct or indirect transfer of money or other property by a corporation to its shareholders in respect of any of its shares.

15. The breakup of outstanding shares of corporate stock into a greater number of shares, each representing a smaller interest in the corporation.

13. Nimble dividend

14. Cumulative dividend

15. Liquidating dividend

16. Debentures

17. Prospectus

18. Distribution

19. Stock split

20. Treasury stock

13. _____

14. _____

15. _____

MULTIPLE CHOICE: Select the alternative which best completes each statement below and write the corresponding letter in the ANSWERS column.

Answers

1. The duty to register a transfer of securities and issue new certificates to the new owner is performed by the (a) shareholders (b) promoters (c) incorporators (d) corporation.

1. _____

2. Valid consideration for the issuance of shares of a corporation generally includes (a) cash (b) property (c) services to the corporation (d) all of the above.

2. _____

3. In all States, cash dividends may be paid from (a) stated capital (b) earned surplus (c) capital surplus (d) any surplus.

3. _____

4.   Preferred shareholders may be entitled to (a) liens on corporate assets (b) cumulative dividends (c) rights superior to creditors (d) none of the above.

4. _____

5.   The board of directors who vote for or assent to the distribution of an illegal dividend are (a) not liable to the corporation (b) jointly liable (c) severally liable (d) both jointly and severally liable to the corporation or to its creditors.

5. _____

6.   When an unsuspecting shareholder receives an illegal dividend from a solvent corporation, the majority rule is the shareholder (a) may keep the dividend (b) must refund the dividend (c) may be sued by creditors of the corporation (d) none of the above.

6. _____

7.   The transferee of stock is a bona fide purchaser if (a) the transferee pays value in good faith (b) the transferee has no notice of any adverse claim (c) the certificate is properly indorsed (d) all of the above.

7. _____

8.   The shareholder is entitled to a new stock certificate if the original is (a) lost (b) destroyed (c) stolen (d) all of the above.

8. _____

9.   If an innocent purchaser of a stock certificate bearing a forged indorsement resells the certificate to a bona fide purchaser, legal right to the shares belongs to the (a) innocent purchaser (b) bona fide purchaser (c) original owner whose signature was forged (d) none of the above.

9. _____

10.   Only shareholders on the corporate record books can (a) vote (b) receive dividends (c) receive reports of corporate assets and finances (d) all of the above.

10. _____

11.   The term that constitutes the entire surplus of a corporation other than its earned surplus is (a) stated capital (b) net assets (c) capital surplus (d) none of the above.

11. _____

12.   Dividends are (a) prohibited from being paid if the corporation is insolvent (b) declared and distributed by the officers of the corporation (c) in the form of cash or stock but not other kinds of property (d) none of the above.

12. _____

13.   A contract for the sale of stock is enforceable if (a) it is written and signed by the parties (b) it satisfies the requirements of the Statute of Frauds (c) an admission is made in court that a contract exists (d) all of the above.

13. _____

CASE PROBLEMS - SHORT ESSAY ANSWERS: Read each case problem carefully. When appropriate, answer by stating a Decision for the case and by explaining the rationale - Rule of Law - relied upon to support your decision.

1.   The XYZ Corporation issues 100 shares of no par stock valued at $10,000 to A and B in exchange for land valued in good faith by all parties to be worth $10,000. XYZ goes bankrupt, and the land is sold for $6,000. Can A and B be held liable for the balance of $4,000 by the corporation's creditors? Explain.

Decision: _____

_____

Rule of Law: _____

_____

2. The XYZ Corporation intends to redeem its preferred stock. The company has only $10,000 in cash, and it intends to use it all to redeem part of its outstanding $100 par stock. Several creditors of XYZ seek to enjoin the redemption alleging that XYZ will have no money with which to pay its debts. Can the corporation redeem the stock? Explain.

Decision: _____

_____

Rule of Law: _____

_____

3. XYZ Corporation declared a cash dividend on common stock. Before the dividend was paid, the board of directors voted to revoke the dividend on grounds that, due to changed circumstances, the corporation needed the funds. Can holders of the common stock force the company to pay the dividend? Explain.

Decision: _____

_____

Rule of Law: _____

_____

4. A was an innocent purchaser of a stock certificate bearing a forged indorsement. A sells the certificate to B, a bona fide purchaser. B discovers the forgery and sues A for the value B paid A. What result? Explain.

Decision: _____

_____

Rule of Law: _____

_____

5. A, the bona fide purchaser of an unauthorized indorsed stock certificate, receives from B Corporation a newly reregistered certificate. B Corporation discovers the improper indorsement and wishes to cancel A's ownership. What result? Explain.

Decision: _____

_____

Rule of Law: _____

_____

Management Structure

SCOPE NOTE

This Chapter develops the nature of the relationship between a corporation, its directors, officers, and shareholders. What role do shareholders play in setting corporate policy? Particular attention is paid to the management functions of corporations. Who peforms these functions? What is the source and nature of their authority? What limitations are placed on such authority? How is corporate policy established and executed? These and related issues are the focus of attention in Chapter 35 in its development of the rules and doctrines which control the management area of corporate law.

EDUCATIONAL OBJECTIVES

1.   Identify and explain the rights and liabilities of shareholders.

2.   Discuss proxy, cumulative, and trust voting.

3.   Understand the nature and function of a board of directors.

4.   Identify the qualifications for service on and the process of appointment to a board of directors.

5.   Discuss the scope of powers/responsibilities held by corporate directors and explain the purpose of board meetings.

6.   Know what management powers are delegated to corporate officers and outline the process of delegation.

7.   List corporate officers and explain their responsibilities and basis for authority.

8.   Outline the selection/removal procedure for corporate officers as well as how they are compensated.

9.   Enumerate the kinds of duties and standard of care to which corporate officers are held.

CHAPTER OUTLINE

I.   Corporate Governance
II.   Role of Shareholders
     A.   Voting Rights of Shareholders
          1.   Election and removal of directors - is the voting right of the shareholders, usually one vote per share.
          2.   Approval of fundamental changes - like amendments to the articles of incorporation require shareholder approval.
          3.   Concentrations of voting power
               a.   Proxies - a shareholder may vote either in person or by written proxy.
               b.   Voting trusts - are devices designed to concentrate corporate control in one or more persons.
               c.   Shareholder agreements - shareholders may agree in advance to vote in a specific manner for the election or removal of directors or other matters.
     B.   Enforcement Rights of Shareholders
          1.   Right to inspect books and records - is a right of shareholders if for a proper purpose.
          2.   Shareholder suits - the ultimate recourse is a shareholder's suit against or on behalf of the corporation.
               a.   Direct suits - are brought to enforce a shareholder's claim against the corporation.
               b.   Derivative suits - are brought by one or more shareholders on behalf of the corporation.
          3.   Shareholder's right to dissent - concerns certain corporate actions such as mergers.
III.   Role of Directors and Officers
     A.   Function of the Board of Directors
          1.   Selection and removal of officers - the directors hire and can fire the officers.
          2.   Capital structure - and the financial policy of the corporation are determined by the directors.
          3.   Fundamental changes - such as making, amending, and repealing bylaws are decided by the directors.
          4.   Dividends - are declared by the directors including the amount and type of dividends.
          5.   Management compensation - for both officers and directors is determined by the directors.
     B.   Election and Tenure of Directors
          1.   Election, number, and tenure of directors - directors are elected at annual meetings of the shareholders and hold office for one year. State statutes usually set the number.
          2.   Vacancies and removal of directors - a vacancy may be filled by a majority vote of the remaining directors while removal is done by the shareholders' vote.
          3.   Compensation of directors - Model Act authorizes the board to fix the compensation for directors.
     C.   Exercise of Directors' Functions
          1.   Quorum and voting - a majority of the directors is a quorum, and it is necessary for a vote.
          2.   Action taken without a meeting - can be done only if consent in writing is signed by all of the directors.
          3.   Delegation of board powers - may be done by a majority vote of the directors.
          4.   Directors' inspection rights - include the right to inspect corporate books and records.
     D.   Officers

1.   Selection and removal of officers - is done by the directors.
2.   Role of officers
      a.   President - the principal executive officer.
      b.   Vice-President - serves in the absence of the President.
      c.   Secretary - keeps minutes, is custodian of the corporate records and stock transfer books.
      d.   Treasurer - has custody and is responsible for all funds and securities of the corporation.
3.   Authority of officers
      a.   Actual express authority - arises from the incorporation statute, the articles, the bylaws, and resolutions of the directors.
      b.   Actual implied authority - officers have this authority to do what is reasonably necessary.
      c.   Apparent authority - arises when a third party relies on the fact that an officer has exercised the same authority in the past.
      d.   Ratification - a corporation may ratify the unauthorized acts of its officers.
E.   Duties of Directors and Officers
      1.   Duty of obedience - directors and officers must act within their authority.
      2.   Duty of diligence - they must exercise ordinary care and prudence.
            a.   Reliance upon others - they are permitted to entrust important work to others.
            b.   Business judgment rule - precludes imposing liability upon the directors for honest mistakes of judgment.
      3.   Duty of loyalty - they owe to the corporation and its shareholders.
            a.   Conflict of interests - a contract between officers or directors and the corporation is voidable.
            b.   Loans to directors - by the corporation are not permitted without shareholder authorization.
            c.   Corporate opportunity - directors and officers may not usurp any corporation opportunity.
            d.   Transactions in shares - the issue of shares at favorable prices to management could constitute a breach of the fiduciary duty.
            e.   Duty not to compete - directors and officers may not compete with the corporation.
F.   Indemnification of Directors and Officers - a corporation may indemnify a director of officer for liability incurred if he acted in good faith and he was not adjudged negligent or liable for misconduct.

TRUE-FALSE: Circle true or false.

Answers

T   F   1.   Bylaws may require a number greater than a simple majority of the directors for a quorum in order to transact corporate business.

T   F   2.   Shareholders elect the corporation's board of directors who manage the business of the corporation.

T   F   3.   Because they are so important to a publicly held corporation, directors are usually full-time employees who owe a fiduciary duty to the shareholders.

T   F   4.   The bylaws of a corporation set forth the duties of each officer of the corporation.

T   F   5.   Under the Revised Act of 1984, one person may be both the president and secretary of a corporation.

T   F   6.   Each corporation must comply with rigid common law requirements establishing the qualifications of directors.

T   F   7.   Although officers and directors are generally free from personal liability on contracts of the corporation, they are personally liable for breaching any duty they owe to the corporation and shareholders.

T   F   8.   According to the Model Act, a vacancy on the board of directors may be filled by a majority vote of the remaining directors.

T   F   9.   Shareholders and directors generally do not have the right to inspect the books of the corporation.

T   F   10.   Cumulative voting works to the advantage of the majority shareholders.

T   F   11.   The vast majority of corporations are closely held corporations.

T   F   12.   Directors and officers of a corporation may not engage in their own private business interests during their tenure with the corporation.

KEY TERMS - MATCHING EXERCISE: Select the term which best completes each statement below and write the corresponding number in the ANSWERS column.

Column I	Column II	Answers
1. An action taken by a shareholder to enforce the right to inspect corporate books.	1. Liability of directors	1. _____
	2. Voting trust	2. _____
2. The small fee paid a director for attendance at meetings.	3. Short-swing	3. _____
3. The essence of this obligation is the subordination of self-interest to the interest of the corporation.	4. Honorarium	4. _____
	5. Bylaws	5. _____
4. The shareholder's remedy for breach of fiduciary duty by a director.	6. Insider	6. _____
	7. Quorum	7. _____
5. The classification of a contract made between a director and the corporation.	8. Fiduciary duty	8. _____
	9. Majority	9. _____

6.   The term that describes two corpora-
       tions having common directors.

7.   The number of directors usually
       necessary for a quorum.

8.   An officer or director who has
       advance information not available
       to the public which may affect the
       future market value of stock.

9.   An agreement created when all or
       part of a corporation's stock is
       transferred to trustees who vote
       the stock.

10.   The voting procedure that may
       allow a minority shareholder to
       obtain minority representation on
       the board of directors.

11.   The principle that courts will not
       substitute their judgment for a
       good faith decision by the
       directors or officers of a
       corporation.

12.   The principal executive officer of
       the corporation.

13.   The minimum number of members
       necessary to be present at a meeting
       in order to transact business.

14.   A shareholder's authorization to an
       agent to vote her shares at a
       particular meeting.

15.   Rules adopted by a corporation to
       manage its internal affairs.

10.   Derivative suit

11.   Voidable

12.   Interlocking
       directorate

13.   Void

14.   Cumulative voting

15.   Direct suit

16.   **Best judgment rule**

17.   Secretary

18.   Proxy

19.   Treasurer

20.   President

10.   _____

11.   _____

12.   _____

13.   _____

14.   _____

15.   _____

MULTIPLE CHOICE: Select the alternative which best completes each statement below and write the corresponding letter in the ANSWERS column.   Answers

1.   Because of their positions of trust and loyalty, directors can best be
       described as (a) fiduciaries (b) trustees (c) salespersons (d) none of the
       above.

                                                                                          1.   _____

2.   Generally, a corporation has the following officers, a (a) president (b) secretary (c) treasurer (d) all of the above.

    2. _____

3.   Typically, bylaws include (a) the time and place of shareholders' meetings (b) the qualifications of directors (c) the number of directors needed for a quorum (d) all of the above.

    3. _____

4.   Directors are most often elected for a term of (a) 3 years (b) 6 years (c) 5 years (d) 1 year.

    4. _____

5.   A method of ridding the corporation of a poor director is (a) firing the director (b) removal by vote of the shareholders (c) removal by a quorum of the other directors (d) none of the above.

    5. _____

6.   Officers of a corporation are (a) appointed by the shareholders (b) removed by the shareholders (c) agents of the corporation (d) all of the above.

    6. _____

7.   The majority of the members of the board of directors constitutes a (a) quorum (b) bylaw directorate (c) proxy (d) all of the above.

    7. _____

8.   Director power might include (a) fixing the selling price of newly issued shares (b) amending the bylaws (c) initiating merger proceedings (d) all of the above.

    8. _____

9.   In an election of directors of a corporation, cumulative voting allows a (a) shareholder to distribute votes among many candidates (b) shareholder to give all votes to one candidate (c) minority shareholder to obtain minority representation on the board if a certain minimum number of shares are owned (d) all of the above.

    9. _____

10.   In relation to other contracts, courts subject contracts between corporations with interlocking directorates with (a) more scrutiny (b) less scrutiny (c) the same scrutiny as other corporations' contracts (d) no scrutiny since such contracts are void.

    10. _____

11.   A closely held corporation has (a) a small number of shareholders (b) no ready market for its shares (c) shareholders who are often also the corporation's directors and officers (d) all of the above.

    11. _____

12.   The only potential personal liability a shareholder may have would be liability for (a) defective incorporation (b) disregard of corporateness (c) receipt of improper distributions (d) all of the above.

    12. _____

13.   The duties the directors and officers of a corporation are required to perform include the duties of (a) obedience (b) diligence (c) loyalty (d) all of the above.

    13. _____

CASE PROBLEMS - SHORT ESSAY ANSWERS: Read each case problem carefully.   When appropriate, answer by stating a Decision for the case and by explaining the rationale - Rule of Law - relied upon to support your decision.

1.   In a corporation with cumulative voting, X has only ten shares. Each share has one vote. There are three directors to be elected. Explain the possible voting methods X can follow.

Decision: _____

_____

Rule of Law: _____

_____

2.   If A, as president of B Corporation, learns of a good buy in land that the corporation expected to buy and would use profitably, can A buy the land personally without informing the corporation? Explain.

Decision: _____

_____

Rule of Law: _____

_____

3.   All the directors of X Corporation vote to convey by deed corporate land to Z. Each of the directors votes separately on the matter without a board meeting. Is such a vote binding on the corporation? Explain.

Decision: _____

_____

Rule of Law: _____

_____

4.   X, director of Y Corporation, using X's best judgment, convinces the corporation to enter into a contract with Z Corporation.   Y Corporation loses a lot of money on the contract.   The shareholders bring suit against X for the loss. What result?

Decision: _____

_____

Rule of Law: _____

_____

5.   X, an out-of-state director of Y Corporation, has not attended a directors' meeting for five years. The corporation suffers serious losses, and the shareholders seek to hold X liable. What result?

Decision: _____

_____

Rule of Law: _____

_____

Fundamental Changes

SCOPE NOTE

Chapter 36 brings our discussion of corporation law to a close. The Chapter focuses on laws regulating the amending of the corporation's charter, the termination of the corporation's existence, and cases where independent business enterprises seek to join forces. Why would individual corporate enterprises wish to combine operations? What forms of combination are recognized by the law? How and why would a corporation terminate its existence? How are corporations regulated by the respective States in which they operate? These and other pertinent concerns complete our study of corporate law.

EDUCATIONAL OBJECTIVES

1.   Discuss the methods and procedures for amending a corporation's charter.

2.   Distinguish between the processes related to, the reasons for, and the effect of consolidation and merger.

3.   Discuss shareholder rights/remedies related to opposing corporate combinations.

4.   Contrast voluntary and involuntary dissolution procedures and their related effects.

CHAPTER OUTLINE

A.   Charter Amendments
   1.   Authority to amend – statutes permit the articles of incorporation to be amended.
   2.   Procedure – the board of directors adopts a resolution setting forth the proposed amendment which then must be approved by a majority vote of the shareholders.
B.   Combinations
   1.   Purchase or lease of all or substantially all of the assets – of another corporation results in no change in the legal personality of either corporation.
      a.   Regular course of business – if sale or lease is in this manner, approval of the directors is required but not of the shareholders.
      b.   Other than in regular course of business – then the sale or lease also requires approval

of the shareholders.
2. Purchase of shares - an alternative to the purchase of the assets of another corporation.
    a. Sale of control - the courts require that such sales be made with due care.
    b. Tender offer - another method of purchasing shares of another corporation.
3. Compulsory share exchange - a method of share acquisition that is compulsory on all owners of the acquired shares.
4. Merger - of two or more corporations is the combination of all of their assets.
5. Consolidation - combines the assets of two or more corporations in which title is taken by a newly created corporation.
6. Going private transactions - a corporate combination that makes a publicly held corporation a private one.
    a. Cash-out combinations - are used to eliminate minority shareholders by forcing them to accept cash or property for their shares.
    b. Management buy-out - is a transaction by which existing management increases its ownership of a corporation and eliminates its public shareholders.
7. Dissenting shareholders - a shareholder's statutory right to dissent and receive payment for her shares when she objects to fundamental changes in the corporation.
C. Dissolution
    1. Nonjudicial dissolution - dissolution without judicial proceedings are listed.
    2. Judicial dissolution - disolution with judicial proceedings are listed.
    3. Liquidation - the winding up of the corporation's affairs and liquidation of its assets.
    4. Protection of creditors - the statutory safeguards for creditors after dissolution of the corporation.

TRUE-FALSE: Circle true or false.

Answers

T   F   1.   It is illegal for one corporation to acquire all the assets including the good will of another corporation.

T   F   2.   The purchase of all the assets of one corporation by another completely alters the legal existence of both.

T   F   3.   Unlike a sale, mergers require one corporation to cease existence.

T   F   4.   The surviving corporation in a merger assumes the merged corporation's debts and liabilities.

T   F   5.   The dissenting shareholders in a merger have no recourse.

T   F   6.   Dissolution terminates the corporation's existence and requires the corporation to liquidate its assets.

T   F   7.   Shareholders of each corporation in a consolidation must receive new stock of the same class from the newly formed corporation.

T   F   8.   Fundamental changes such as amendments to the articles of incorporation generally require the approval of the corporation's shareholders.

T   F   9.   Dissenting shareholders in a merger or consolidation must notify the corporation in writing of their objections and of their demand for payment for their stock.

T   F   10.   Involuntary liquidation of a corporation is usually conducted by the corporation's board of directors.

T   F   11.   According to the Revised Act, all amendments to a corporation's articles of incorporation require shareholders' approval.

T   F   12.   If acts of the directors are illegal or fraudulent, the shareholders may bring a court action for dissolution of the corporation.

KEY TERMS – MATCHING EXERCISE: Select the term which best completes each statement below and write the corresponding number in the ANSWERS column.

Column I	Column II	Answers
1. A combination of corporations leaving one survivor.	1. Parent corporation	1. _____
2. A combination of corporations leaving no survivors but instead a new corporation.	2. Consolidation	2. _____
	3. Merger	3. _____
3. The right of dissenting shareholders to recover the fair value of their shares.	4. Subsidiary corporation	4. _____
	5. Par value	5. _____
4. The name of a corporation owned or acquired by another corporation.	6. Dissolution	6. _____
5. The value of the stock to which a dissenting shareholder is entitled.	7. Creditors	7. _____
	8. Dissenting shareholder	8. _____
6. The method of stopping the continuation of a corporation's business.	9. Fair value	9. _____
7. The persons who have the superior right to the corporate assets upon its dissolution.	10. Preferred shareholder	10. _____
	11. Nonjudicial dissolution	11. _____
8. A shareholder who does not agree with a plan of merger.		12. _____
	12. Short-form merger	13. _____
	13. Liquidation	14. _____
	14. Interstate	15. _____

9. The kind of combination when a corporation owns at least 90% of the outstanding shares of another corporation (called a subsidiary) and combines the subsidiary into itself.

10. The procedure for turning into cash all assets for distribution first to the creditors of a corporation.

11. A general invitation to all the shareholders of a target company to offer their shares for sale at a specified price.

12. Another name for management buy-outs that make extensive use of borrowed funds.

13. The name of a corporation that acquires another corporation.

14. Dissolution of a corporation without court action.

15. Dissolution by a court action brought by a creditor who shows that the corporation is unable to pay its debts as they become due.

15. Appraisal remedy

16. Leveraged buy-outs

17. Judicial dissolution

18. Secretary of State

19. Articles of Incorporation

20. Tender offer

MULTIPLE CHOICE: Select the alternative which best completes each statement below and write the corresponding letter in the ANSWERS column.   Answers

1. Which of the following requires shareholder approval? (a) the amendment of the corporate charter (b) merger (c) consolidation (d) all of the above.

   1. _____

2. The Revised Model Act permits the board of directors to adopt certain amendments without shareholder approval such as (a) making minor name changes (b) extending the duration of the corporation (c) splitting authorized shares if the corporation has only one class of shares (d) all of the above.

   2. _____

3. Dissolution (a) does not terminate the corporation's existence (b) requires the corporation to wind up its affairs (c) requires liquidation of the corporation's assets (d) all of the above.

   3. _____

4. Annual reports of a corporation must be filed with the (a) county recorder (b) board of directors (c) Attorney General (d) Secretary of State.

4. _____

5. Dissolution by court action may be brought by shareholders when acts of the directors are (a) illegal (b) oppressive (c) fraudulent (d) all of the above.

5. _____

6. Nonjudicial dissolution may be accomplished by (a) all shareholders voluntarily (b) expiration of the time for the existence of the corporation (c) an act of the legislature (d) all of the above.

6. _____

7. Involuntary judicial dissolution of a corporation may be commenced by (a) creditors (b) the State (c) shareholders (d) all of the above.

7. _____

8. Statutory provisions governing dissolution (a) do not preserve creditor claims against the corporation (b) require mailing of notice to known creditors (c) do not require notice of any kind (d) none of the above.

8. _____

9. A corporation may be dissolved involuntarily if it failed to (a) pay its franchise taxes (b) file its annual report (c) appoint and maintain a registered agent in the State in the prescribed time (d) all of the above.

9. _____

10. A resolution adopted by the board of directors is required for a (a) merger (b) consolidation (c) compulsory share exchange between corporations (d) all of the above.

10. _____

11. The final procedural act in amending a corporation's charter is the (a) vote of the shareholders (b) vote of the board of directors (c) filing of the articles of amendment (d) issuance of the certificate of amendment by the Secretary of State.

11. _____

12. The directors of a corporation may adopt certain amendments to the articles of incorporation without shareholder approval except an amendment that (a) makes a minor name change (b) changes the voting rights of shareholders (c) extends the duration of the corporation (d) none of the above.

12. _____

13. Shareholder approval is not required for (a) a merger (b) the sale of corporate assets in the usual and regular course of business (c) a consolidation (d) all of the above.

13. _____

CASE PROBLEMS - SHORT ESSAY ANSWERS: Read each case problem carefully. When appropriate, answer by stating a Decision for the case and by explaining the rationale - Rule of Law - relied upon to support your decision.

1.   X Corporation is dissolved by act of the legislature and A, as a creditor, wants to know what A's rights are to the assets. Explain.

Decision: _____

Rule of Law: _____

_____

2.   Abby is a dissenting shareholder to a merger between corporations X and Y. Abby wants nothing to do with the new corporation and wishes to get her money back. The State in which both corporations are located follows the Model Act. Abby does nothing for 45 days, then seeks payment for the shares. Is Abby entitled to payment? Explain.

Decision: _____

Rule of Law: _____

_____

3.   A "short-form merger" takes place between parent Corporation X and subsidiary Corporation Y. Do the dissenting shareholders of each corporation have the right to an appraisal remedy? Explain.

Decision: _____

Rule of Law: _____

_____

4.   A, a director with X Corporation, and B, a director of Y Corporation, believe that their corporations are too much alike and that something ought to be done to eliminate their competition. What possible steps might be taken?

Decision: _____

Rule of Law: _____

_____

5.   X Corporation is a parent corporation to its subsidiary Y after a compulsory share exchange. Y owes A and B large sums of money but refuses to pay them after becoming the subsidiary. Can A and B sue Y Corporation? Explain.

Decision: _____

Rule of Law: _____

_____

CHAPTER 37

Secured Transactions in Personal Property

SCOPE NOTE

Upon entering today's marketplace, purchasers neither expect nor are they expected to pay fully for the goods, services, land or money which they plan to buy. When a seller/lender (creditor) performs completely for a buyer (debtor) who, in return, only partially performs, the unexecuted balance of the buyer's performance is referred to as credit. The importance of such arrangements -- promised future performance in exchange for present full performance -- in today's marketplace is seen in the hundreds of billions of dollars of outstanding commercial and consumer debt. The person who has extended trust (credit) may be either an unsecured or secured creditor. In Chapter 37, the general principles and basic vocabulary of secured credit in personal property transactions are discussed as are the various devices available to creditors to protect their rights and interests.

EDUCATIONAL OBJECTIVES

1. Identify the sources of law which control the issuance and maintenance of secured debt.

2. Explain the requirements for creating a valid security agreement in personal property.

3. Define and discuss the importance of a purchase money security interest.

4. Understand the significance of perfecting personal property security interests.

5. Outline the requirements for validly perfecting a security interest in personal property.

6. Distinguish among the various classifications of personal property in relation to attachment and perfection.

7. Explain the rules for determining priorities among conflicting interests (secured, unsecured creditors; purchasers; bailees; etc.) in common collateral.

8. Discuss the rights/duties of the parties upon debtor default.

CHAPTER OUTLINE

I.   Essentials of Secured Transactions
    A.   Governing law - U.C.C. Article 9
    B.   Contractual base - agreement, value and collateral
II. Classification of Collateral
    A.   Goods - movable tangibles; primary use
        1.   Consumer goods - personal, family, household
        2.   Equipment - business
        3.   Farm products - farming operations
        4.   Inventory - held for sale or manufacturing
        5.   Fixtures - attached to land or building
    B.   Indispensable Paper
        1.   Chattel paper - written document evidencing debt and security interest
        2.   Instruments - commercial paper evidencing debt but no security interest
        3.   Documents - written document evidencing ownership in goods
    C.   Intangibles - not evidenced by indispensable paper
        1.   Accounts - right to payment
        2.   General intangibles - catchall category
III. Attachment - elements necessary to create security interest
    A.   Value - given by secured party; contractual consideration
    B.   Debtor's Rights in Collateral
    C.   Security Agreement - written document; identifies collateral; debtor signature
        1.   Consumer goods - non-purchase money household goods restriction
        2.   After-acquired property - floating lien concept
        3.   Proceeds - sale of collateral
        4.   Future advances
IV. Perfection - protecting security interest against competing interests
    A.   Filing a Financial Statement - document describing collateral, debt and identifying parties
        1.   Where to file - central (Secretary of State) or local (county residence or collateral location) depending on type of collateral
        2.   Improper filing - generally ineffective
        3.   Subsequent change of information - location or use changes; intra or interstate change
    B.   Possession - pledge
    C.   Automatic Perfection - occurs upon attachment
        1.   Purchase money security interest in consumer goods - goods acquired with extended credit
        2.   Temporary perfection - grace period (usually 21 days) for filing; negotiable instruments
V.   Priorities of Secured Creditors - ranking of competing interests in same collateral
    A.   Against Unsecured Creditors - secured prevails
    B.   Against Other Secured Creditors
        1.   Perfected versus unperfected - perfected prevails
        2.   Perfected versus perfected - first perfected prevails
        3.   Unperfected versus unperfected - first to attach prevails
    C.   Against Buyers
        1.   Buyers in the ordinary course of business - cuts off inventory security interest
        2.   Buyers of consumer goods - cuts off unfiled security interest

      3.   Purchasers of intangibles - generally cuts off earlier security interests
           a.   Chattle paper or instruments
           b.   Instruments, documents, securities
      4.   Other buyers
   D.   Against Trustee in Bankruptcy
      1.   Perfected over unperfected security interest
      2.   Preferential transfer avoidance
   E.   Against Lien Creditors - status of holders of judicial and statutory liens
VI.   Default
   A.   Sale of Collateral - public or private sale; debtor notice; deficiency judgment; 60% payment of purchase price in consumer goods cases
   B.   Retention of Collateral - prohibited in certain cases; debtor's right of written objection
   C.   Debtor's Rights - redemption; forced sale

TRUE-FALSE: Circle true or false.

Answers

T   F   1.   An obligation to pay money owed to another must be secured before it is valid and enforceable.

T   F   2.   The Code defines "goods" as movable tangible personal property at the time of attachment.

T   F   3.   A perfected security interest is not valid and enforceable against a trustee of a debtor in bankruptcy.

T   F   4.   A security interest may be perfected by filing a financial statement or taking possession of the collateral.

T   F   5.   Most states require the filing of a financing statement to perfect a security interest in a motor vehicle.

T   F   6.   Perfection of a purchase money security interest in consumer goods occurs without having to file a financing statement.

T   F   7.   Examples of "general intangibles" that meet the Code's classification of collateral are good will, patent rights and contrctual performance rights.

T   F   8.   A debtor has an absolute, unwaivable right of redemption which may be exercised at any time.

T   F   9.   Consumer goods are purchased primarily for personal, family, or household use.

T   F   10.   A goal of Article 9 of the U.C.C. is to reduce the cost associated with and foster the use of secured financing in commercial and consumer transactions.

T   F   11.   For a security interest to attach, the security agreement must refer to and describe the transaction which gave rise to the debt.

T   F   12.   A financing statement that has not been filled in the proper location is always ineffective against competing security interests.

KEY TERMS – MATCHING EXERCISE: Select the term which best completes each statement below and write the corresponding number in the ANSWERS column.

	Column I		Column II		Answers
1.	Goods bought for business or professional use.	1.	Financing statement	1.	_____
2.	Property that is subject to a security interest.	2.	Fixture	2.	_____
3.	The act of making a valid security interest in property enforceable against other creditors of a debtor.	3.	Inventory	3.	_____
		4.	Contract rights	4.	_____
4.	An inventory financing arrangement allowing debtor access to pledged goods that remain under the secured creditor's control.	5.	Equipment	5.	_____
		6.	General intangibles	6.	_____
		7.	Collateral	7.	_____
5.	A document filed to create a public record of the existence of a security interest in identified goods.	8.	Attachment	8.	_____
		9.	Perfection	9.	_____
		10.	Field warehousing	10.	_____
6.	Property not presently owned by a debtor that might be obtained in the future.	11.	Foreclosure	11.	_____
		12.	Account	12.	_____
7.	The act of creating a valid enforceable security interest.	13.	After acquired property	13.	_____
8.	Personal property so firmly attached to a building that it is considered part of it.	14.	Mechanics lien	14.	_____
		15.	Chattel paper	15.	_____
9.	A payment right for sold or leased goods not evidenced by an "instrument."	16.	Secured party		
10.	Property held for sale or lease including raw materials, items used in business or a manufacturer's materials.	17.	Floating lien		
		18.	Redemption		
		19.	Debt		
		20.	Pledge		

11.   Duty to pay money or perform an
       act that is owed to another.

12.   Lender, seller, or other person
       who owns a security interest in
       collateral.

13.   Written document evidencing both
       an obligation to pay money and
       security interest in specific goods.

14.   Delivery of personal property to
       secure payment of a debt.

15.   Debtor's right to pay off a
       default on a debt and regain an
       interest in collateral.

MULTIPLE CHOICE: Select the alternative which best completes each statement below and write the
corresponding letter in the ANSWERS column.

Answers

1.   Priority among competing secured intersts in common collateral is
      governed by (a) State legislation (b) the F.T.C. (c) Article 9 of the
      U.C.C. (d) the equitable doctrine of laches.   1.   _____

2.   One who owes payment or performance on an obligation is the (a)
      secured party (b) debtor (c) attacher (d) perfector.   2.   _____

3.   Under the Code's classification of collateral, goods are divided into (a)
      inventory (b) equipment (c) farm products (d) all of the above.   3.   _____

4.   A security agreement is enforceable between the parties upon (a)
      perfection (b) attachment (c) filing (d) registering.   4.   _____

5.   One who acquires title to property free of either known or unknown
      perfected security interests is a (a) trustee in bankruptcy (b) lien creditor
      (c) buyer in the ordinary course of business (d) all of the above.   5.   _____

6.   A secured transaction involves (a) a money payment obligation (b)
      reditor interest in specific property of the debtor (c) securing payment
      on the debt (d) all of the above.   6.   _____

7.   Priority among competing unperfected security interests in common
      collateral rests on (a) order of attachment (b) location of collateral (c)
      time of filing (d) type of collateral.   7.   _____

8.   A financing statement is automatically effective for a period of (a) 4
      years (b) 8 years (c) 5 years (d) 10 years from the filing date.   8.   _____

9. When two security interests, both perfected by filing, are held by different creditors in the same collateral, priority is determined by (a) time of attachment (b) type of collateral (c) place of filing (d) time of filing.

9. _____

10. The information requried in a financing statement for it to be effective includes (a) the details of the sales transaction creating th debt (b) a description of the collateral (c) co-signature of the debtor's spouse (d) all of the above.

10. _____

11. Examples of value as defined by the Code include (a) an antecedent debt (b) contractual consideration (c) a binding credit extension committment (d) all of the above.

11. _____

12. _____ extends the time period over which a financing statement is effective. (a) continuation statement (b) termination notice (c) release statement (d) filing statement.

12. _____

13. Examples of lien creditors include (a) secured creditors (b) holders of pledges (c) trustees in bankruptcy (d) all of the above.

13. _____

CASE PROBLEMS - SHORT ESSAY ANSWERS: Read each problem carefully. When appropriate, answer by stating a Decision for the case and by explaining the rationale - Rule of Law - relied upon to support your decision.

1. Merchant seller S sold goods to buyer B under a conditional sales contract. Buyer took the goods home but later stopped making payments on the contract. S asserts a right to take possession of the goods. Buyer resists. Who wins this dispute and why?

Decision: _____

Rule of Law: _____

_____

2. Lawyer L receivs a $1,500 loan from bank B. As collateral for the loan, L lists an office library, calling it inventory since the books are continually used. B questions this classification and believes it is improper. Whatj advice can you give?

Decision: _____

Rule of Law: _____

_____

3. Re-read case problem #2. Assume L sells the library to Bev Bookbuyer for $1,000. B seeks to claim the money, but L resists, arguing that B's interest was in the books, not money. Advise B.

Decision: _____

Rule of Law: _____

_____

4.   Borrower B grants lender L a security interst in a sculpture that B owns for $3,500 that L advances to B. A financing statement is executed and filed by L. Sometime later, B pledges the sculpture to C for an additional $1,500. B defaults on both loans. Who has priority to the sculpture? Explain.

Decision: _____

Rule of Law: _____

_____

5.   B, an automobile assembly line worker, purchases from S a $2,500 T.V./stereo entertainment unit under a conditional sales contract. S retains a purchase money security interest in the unit. After properly makign 17 of the 25 $100 monthly payments called for in the contract, B, laid off from the assembly plant, is unable to make any further payments and defaults on the contract. S reposesses the unit with the intent to retain it as full satisfaction on the debt and so informs B. B believes S's actions are improper but S disagrees. Who is right? Explain.

Decision: _____

Rule of Law: _____

_____

CHAPTER 38

Suretyship

SCOPE NOTE

Chapter 38 continues our discussion of security interests in personal property. It focuses on debt enforcement against third party cosigners of the debt payment obligation following debtor default. This area of law, called suretyship, is an alternative to the debt enforcement provisions of U.C.C. Article 9. Suretyship law, as a non-Code method of creating and enforcing security interests, presumes a three party secured transaction: the creditor; the debtor; and one or more parties promising to make payment on the debt if the debtor does not. The terminology, controlling doctrines and enforcement steps of surety law are all examined in Chapter 38.

EDUCATIONAL OBJECTIVES

1. Identify and define the parties involved in a suretyship transaction.

2. Differentiate a strict surety from a guarantor and discuss what significance this difference has under the Statute of Frauds.

3. Explain how surety contracts are created.

4. List various payment defenses available to sureties.

5. Discuss alternative courses of action open to sureties upon making debt payments.

CHAPTER OUTLINE

I. Nature and Formation - contractually based creditor protection (third party agrees to debt payment).
    A. Types of Sureties - surety contrasted with guarantor
    B. Formation - debtor, creditor and third party agreement; Statute of Frauds might apply.
II. Rights of Surety - against creditor or debtor
    A. Exoneration - against debtor to compel payment
    B. Reimbursement - against debtor for payment of debt
    C. Subrogation - takes creditor's rights against debtor

     D.   Contribution - against co-sureties
III.   Defenses of Surety - discharge payment obligation
     A.   Personal defenses of principal debtor - incapacity; bankruptcy; statute of limitations; debtor misconduct
     B.   Personal defenses of surety - fraud; material alteration; general release; contract breach
     C.   Defenses of both surety and principal debtor - forgery; material alteration; debt payment

TRUE-FALSE: Circle true or false.

Answers

T   F   1.   When property covered by an existing mortgage, is sold to a purchaser who acquires the property "subject to" the existing mortgage, the purchaser becomes a surety on the mortgage.

T   F   2.   Suretyships may be created with any contractual wording conveying such intent of the parties.

T   F   3.   Gratuitous surety relationships are binding on the parties involved.

T   F   4.   The surety's obligation to pay the creditor is discharged when the principal debtor is a minor or incapacitated due to a mental condition.

T   F   5.   Failure of the creditor to disclose immaterial facts to the surety is usually not fraud.

T   F   6.   When the debtor's offer of payment is refused by the creditor, both the debtor and the surety are discharged from further obligations under the contract.

T   F   7.   A surety is not obligated to make payment to a creditor when the latter, without the surety's consent, releases the principal debtor from the contract and makes no effort to reserve payment rights against the surety.

T   F   8.   Upon the principal debtor's default, the surety's only recourse is to sue the debtor for the damages caused by the nonpayment.

T   F   9.   In co-suretyships, one of the sureties may be liable for the full debt to the creditor.

T   F   10.   Absent special circumstances or contractual arrangements to the contrary, sureties may not reduce payments to creditors by the amount of the claims debtors might have against the creditors.

T   F   11.   The obligations owed the creditor by the principal debtor and the surety are contractually based.

T   F   12.   The creditor's releasing or impairing the principal debtor's collateral has no effect on the surety's payment duty.

KEY TERMS - MATCHING EXERCISE: Select the term which best completes each statement below and write the corresponding number in the ANSWERS column.

Column I	Column II	Answers

Column I

1. One promising to pay the debts of another.

2. One answering for another's debts only after the creditor has exhausted legal remedies against the debtor.

3. A specialized surety relationship designed to protect employers from the losses caused by dishonest employees.

4. A specialized surety relationship securing compliance with provisions of construction and building contracts.

5. Surety's right against a defaulting debtor upon the former's payment of the debt to the creditor.

6. Non-payment defenses that may be used only by either the principal debtor or the surety but not both.

7. The process under which the surety "steps into the creditor's shoes" following payment by the surety.

8. An exception to the general rule that the Statute of Frauds applies to suretyships.

9. The debt paying surety's right against co-sureties when the former has paid more than their proportionate share of the debt.

10. Money that a public officer must deposit to ensure proper performance of certain duties.

Column II

1. Fidelity bond
2. Reimbursement
3. Uniform Commercial Code
4. Personal
5. Substantive law
6. Surety
7. Injunction
8. Exoneration
9. Money judgment
10. Subrogation
11. Performance bond
12. Main purpose doctrine
13. Contribution
14. Official bond
15. Conditional guarantor
16. Statute of Frauds
17. Payment
18. Bailbond
19. Estoppel
20. Assumption of mortgage

Answers

1. _____
2. _____
3. _____
4. _____
5. _____
6. _____
7. _____
8. _____
9. _____
10. _____
11. _____
12. _____
13. _____
14. _____
15. _____

11.   Purchasing property subject to an outstanding mortgage by which the purchaser becomes the principal debtor and the seller becomes a surety.

12.   Requires surety contracts to be in writing to be enforced.

13.   Right of surety to require principal debtor to make payment to the creditor when the debt is due.

14.   An act that discharges both the surety and principal debtor.

15.   A judicial bond in criminal proceedings.

MULTIPLE CHOICE: Select the alternative which best completes each statement below and write the corresponding letter in the ANSWERS column.   Answers

1.   Situations in which surety relationships are usually created include (a) contract involving minors (b) debts where security interests are readily available (c) pledges (d) all of the above.   1.   _____

2.   A surety relationship does not typically involve a/n (a) creditor (b) investor (c) debtor (d) none of the above.   2.   _____

3.   Surety rights against the principal debtor on the latter's default do not include (a) subrogation (b) contribution (c) partition (d) exoneration.   3.   _____

4.   Suretyships arise from (a) contract law (b) tort law (c) public policy considerations (d) constitutional law.   4.   _____

5.   _____ of the contract is conduct between the principal debtor and the creditor that results in discharge of the surety's contractual duties. (a) execution (b) reimbursement (c) apportionment (d) modification.   5.   _____

6.   Acts by the creditor which discharge payment obligations for both the principal debtor and the surety include (a) forgery (b) fraud (c) coercion (d) all of the above.   6.   _____

7.   Substantial changes in important contractual terms made by one or more parties to the contract is (a) spoilation (b) material alteration (c) substitution (d) none of the above.   7.   _____

8.   Examples of specialized surety relationships include (a) equitable suretyships (b) constructive suretyships (c) judicial bonds (d) all of the above.

8.   _____

9.   Elements required for a valid suretyship include (a) capacity of the parties (b) an incidental third party beneficiary (c) notarization (d) all of the above.

9.   _____

10.   Refusal by the creditor to accept the debtor's offer of payment (a) constitutes a breach of fiduciary duty (b) often leads to criminal indictments (c) is usually grounds for defamation liability (d) terminates interest accruing on the debt.

10.   _____

11.   Defenses discharging both the debtor's and surety's payment obligation include (a) impossibility of performance of debtor's contract (b) mental incompetence of debtor (c) extension of debt maturity (d) all of the above.

11.   _____

12.   Surety relationships are used to (a) obtain credit (b) reduce risk of default (c) all of the above.

12.   _____

13.   Defenses to payment that only the surety can assert include (a) creditor fraud against the surety (b) the surety's incapacity (c) failure of consideration (d) all of the above.

13.   _____

CASE PROBLEMS - SHORT ESSAY ANSWERS: Read each case problem carefully. When appropriate, answer by stating a Decision for the case and by explaining the rationale - Rule of Law - relied upon to support your decision.

1.   Dean Debtor has obtained an $1850 loan from Casper Creditor. Their agreement, cosigned by Samantha Surety, calls for ten $185 monthly payments, final payment to be made no later than December of that year. Falling on financial hard times, Dean approaches Casper to extend the final payment date to March of the following year. Casper agrees. What affect does their action have on Samantha's payment obligations under the contract? Explain.

Decision: _____

_____

Rule of Law: _____

_____

2.   Ben Borrower needs a quick loan for a down payment on a stereo/TV home entertainment center. He obtains a loan from Lenny's Loans, Inc. with the understanding that if Ben defaults, Lenny can seek payment from Ben's buddy Beatrice. Beatrice orally agrees to the arrangement but does not sign the contract. Both Ben and Beatrice assure Lenny not to worry since Beatrice's word is "good as gold." Sometime later, Ben stops making monthly payments on the contract and Lenny seeks payment from Beatrice. Is her promise enforceable? Discuss.

Decision: _____

Rule of Law: _____

_____

3.   Danny Debtor owes Cindy Creditor $18,800 in three separate loans, one for $9,000, another for
     $4,500, and a third for $4,400.   On the $5,400 debt, Cecil Surety has cosigned as a co-debtor.
     Danny makes a $2,700 payment on his account with Cindy including no instructions on how she is
     to apply the money.   Cindy applies the payment to the $9,000 loan and seeks payment of the
     $5,400 from Cecil.   He refuses to make payment arguing that the $2,700 should be applied to the
     $55,400 debt and that he is liable for only $2,700.   Who wins this dispute and why?

     Decision: _____

     Rule of Law: _____

     _____

4.   Charlie Creditor lends $2,100 to Debbie Debtor.   Cosigning the agreement is Salvatore Surety.
     Under the agreement, Debbie has pledged a $2,500 diamond broach to Charlie to secure her
     payment obligation.   The broach is a family heirloom and when other family members learn of
     Debbie's action, they approach Charlie requesting his release of the broach.   Sympathetic to their
     wishes, he agrees.   What effect, if any, does this action have on Sal's suretyship status?   Explain.

     Decision: _____

     Rule of Law: _____

     _____

5.   Ray Ramshackle, president of Ramshackle Construction, Inc., obtains a $425,000 loan from
     Cityville Bank to keep his floundering enterprise afloat.   Cosigning the note is Sally Surety.   Ray's
     business finally sinks and he files bankruptcy.   Cityville seeks payment from Sally, who asserts
     Ray's discharge in bankruptcy as a defense to her payment.   Who prevails and why?

     Decision: _____

     Rule of Law: _____

     _____

Bankruptcy and Relief of Debtors

SCOPE NOTE

Debtors encountering financial problems which prevent timely and proper debt payments have several options to resolve their troubles. Some debt resolution methods involve informal agreements between a debtor and creditors. Others take the shape of formal judicial proceedings under state insolvency and federal bankruptcy laws. When all attempts to reach agreement between debtors and creditors fail, federal bankruptcy is the last option. Chapter 39 focuses on this "last resort" and discusses its historical development as well as the substance and procedure of today's bankruptcy laws. The terminology and the legal principles associated with the three types of bankruptcy proceedings (liquidation, reorganization and wage-earner-debt adjustments) are examined.

EDUCATIONAL OBJECTIVES

1. Differentiate among the various non-bankruptcy forms of debt resolution.

2. Distinguish pre-judgment creditor remedies from post-judgment ones.

3. Explain the commencement procedures for voluntary and involuntary bankruptcy proceedings.

4. Trace the steps in a typical debtor liquidation proceeding.

5. Outline the duties of the parties associated with debtor liquidation proceedings.

6. Contrast the rights of secured and unsecured creditors as well as priority and non-priority claims under federal bankruptcy.

7. Discuss how the debtor's estate may be enlarged or reduced in size and value by the conduct of creditors and the trustee.

8. List non-dischargeable debts and explain the significance of discharge and debtor denial of discharge.

9.   Explain the grounds and procedure for Chapter 11 corporate reorganization plans.

10.   Describe the wage-earner debt-adjustment process and how it benefits the debtor.

CHAPTER OUTLINE

I.   Federal Bankruptcy Law - constitutionally based equitable treatment of creditors; allowing honest debtor a new start
    A.   Case Administration (Chapter 3) - debtor's finances before federal court
        1.   Commencement of the case - debtor/creditor seeks help
            a.   Voluntary petitions - debtor (any person) takes initiative
            b.   Involuntary petitions - creditors take initiative
        2.   Automatic stays - upon petition being filed; of proceeding or enforcement actions
        3.   Trustees - administers debtor's finances
        4.   Meetings of creditors - prove claims; examine debtor; establish committee
    B.   Creditors, the Debtor, and the Estate (Chapter 5)
        1.   Creditors
            a.   Proof of claims - 6 month filing period
            b.   Secured claims - protection of security interest
            c.   Priority of claims - full payment of certain debts in specified order
            d.   Subordination of claims - trustee discretion to promote fair, equitable distribution
        2.   Debtors
            a.   Debtor's duties - cooperation; file proper documents; claim exempt property
            b.   Debtor's exemptions - protected assets not subject to creditor claim
            c.   Discharge - relief from debt enforcement; debtor misconduct denies discharge; certain debts not discharged
        3.   The estate - debtor's assets, legal and equitable; 180 days after acquired property provision
            a.   Trustee as lien creditor - estate enlarging (judicial lien, unperfected security interest)
            b.   Voidable preferences - preferential (unfair) creditor payment
            c.   Fraudulent transfers - intent of debtor and time limitation
            d.   Statutory liens
    C.   Liquidation (Chapter 7) - debtor's finances terminated; new financial life commenced
        1.   Proceedings
        2.   Distribution of the estate
        3.   Discharge
    D.   Reorganization (Chapter 11) - revive a financially distressed business
        1.   Proceedings - voluntary or involuntary
        2.   Plan of reorganization - initiated by debtor, creditor, shareholers or trustee
        3.   Acceptance of plan - by class of claims, class of interests
        4.   Confirmation of plan - court approval based upon
            a.   Good faith
            b.   Feasibility
            c.   Cash payments
            d.   Acceptance by creditors
        5.   Effect of reorganization - binding on creditor and debtor discharged
    E.   Adjustment of Debts of Individuals (Chapter 13) - court supervised restructuring of debt

        1.   Proceedings - regular income requirement
        2.   The plan - 3 year payment plan
        3.   Confirmation - fair, reasonable and feasible; court approval
        4.   Discharge - successful completion of plan
    F.   Adjustment of Debts of Farmers
        1.   Proceeding
        2.   Plan
        3.   Confirmation
        4.   Discharge
II.   Creditor's Rights and Debtor Relief Outside of Bankruptcy - contractually, statutorily based debt payment, restructuring policies and practices
    A.   Creditor's Rights - debt enforcement options
        1.   Pre-judgment remedies - attachment; garnishment
        2.   Post-judgment remedies - levy of execution; supplementary proceedings
    B.   Debtor's Relief - debt restructuring options
        1.   Compositions
        2.   Assignments for benefit of creditors
        3.   Statutory assignments
        4.   Equity receiverships

TRUE-FALSE: Circle true or false.

Answers

T   F   1.   State courts have exclusive jurisdiction over bankrupcty proceedings.

T   F   2.   A debtor need not be insolvent to file for voluntary bankruptcy.

T   F   3.   All creditors of a debtor share equally in the assets of a debtor discharged in bankruptcy.

T   F   4.   A debtor in bankruptcy has a choice of claiming exemptions either under federal bankruptcy law or State law.

T   F   5.   Both intentional and negligent tort claims are non-dischargeable in bankruptcy.

T   F   6.   Creditor claims of equal statutory priority must always be dealt with equally by the bankruptcy court with no claim receiving priority over the others.

T   F   7.   In cases of involuntary bankruptcy, a debtor must owe claims totalling at least $15,000 before a petition may be filed.

T   F   8.   Not all cases of corporate rehabilitation under Chapter 11 will result in the court appointing a trustee to administer the proceedings.

T   F   9.   The only-once-every-six-years limitation for Chapter 7 proceedings does not always apply to cases of wage-earner-debtor-adjustment proceedings.

T   F   10.   A successfully contested involuntary bankruptcy petition resulting in dismissal of the proceedings may lead to creditor liability for the costs, expenses and damages incurred by the debtor in attacking the petition.

T   F   11.   Bankruptcy discharge of a debt does not extinguish any security interest held against the debt.

T   F   12.   Bankruptcy Act provisions for adjusting debts of family farmers specifically exclude corporations from qualifying as a family farmer.

KEY TERMS - MATCHING EXERCISE: Select the term which best completes each statement below and write the corresponding number in the ANSWERS column.

Column I	Column II	Answers
1. A specific sum of money owed to another person.	1. Estate	1. _____
	2. Exemptions	2. _____
2. A contract between a debtor and creditors providing for the pro rata sharing of the creditors in the debtor's assets as satisfaction on the creditors' claims.	3. Composition	3. _____
	4. Receiver	4. _____
3. One who gathers and protects assets of a debtor under an action in equity.	5. Priority claim	5. _____
	6. Preference	6. _____
4. Termination and liquidation of a debtor's financial life.	7. Garnishment	7. _____
	8. Attachment	8. _____
5. Claims which must be fully satisfied before payment may be made to other creditors.	9. Trustee	9. _____
	10. Bank	10. _____
6. Aggregate equitable and legal property interests of the debtor when bankruptcy proceedings are commenced.	11. Straight bankruptcy	11. _____
	12. Debt	12. _____
7. Assets which a bankrupt debtor retains title to that are beyond the reach of creditors.	13. Referee	13. _____
	14. Assignment	14. _____
8. A statutory debt satisfaction proceeding used to seize property of the debtor in the possession of another person.	15. Reorganization	15. _____
	16. Discharge	

9. Bankruptcy proceedings which provide an opportunity for a financially distressed business to preserve its existence by eliminating poor management policies, practices and personnel.

10. A debt enforcement process by which property of the debtor is taken into court custody and applied towards payment.

11. Right to payment enforceable against a bankruptcy debtor.

12. Release from payment obligation through bankruptcy procedure for certain debts.

13. Creditor's interest in debtor's property obtained through judicial process to secure payment on a debt.

14. Court approval of a plan for reorganization.

15. Document obtaind by judgment creditor, served on the debtor by a sheriff ordering payment of the judgment debt.

17. Confirmation

18. Writ of execution

19. Judicial lien

20. Claim

MULTIPLE CHOICE: Select the alternative which best completes each statement below and write the corresponding letter in the ANSWERS column.

Answers

1. The two types of petitions used for commencing bankruptcy proceedings are (a) equitable and legal (b) jurisdictional and stipulatory (c) voluntary and involuntary (d) none of the above.

1. _____

2. Examples of unallowable claims are (a) ones for matured interest (b) those that are not enforceable against the debtor (c) reasonable attorney's fees (d) all of the above.

2. _____

3. Which of the following is not a definitional element of a voidable preference (a) a property transfer made within 90 days of filing a bankruptcy petition (b) intent to defraud creditors (c) insolvency of the debtor (d) payment on a debt owing before the transfer.

3. _____

4.   The party whose duty is to gather, liquidate and distribute the assets of the debtor is the (a) trustee (b) referee (c) creditor (d) none of the above.

4. _____

5.   The purpose of bankruptcy is to (a) make equitable payments to creditors (b) discharge a debtor from unmeetable debts (c) enable a debtor to start a new financial life (d) all of the above.

5. _____

6.   A fraudulent conveyance requires (a) an intent to prefer one creditor over another (b) insolvency of the debtor (c) a transfer of property for little or no return value (d) payment on an antecedent debt.

6. _____

7.   Of the following claims, which are non-dischargeable? (a) alimony payments (b) non-scheduled debts where the creditor had notice of the bankruptcy proceedings (c) payments made subject to a preferential transfer (d) moneys owed to foreign officials.

7. _____

8.   A debtor in bankruptcy must (a) file a joint stipulation with the spouse (b) post a bond with the court amounting to no less than 20% of the aggregate value of all claims owned at time of filing (c) submit a statement of personal preference to the referee (d) file a schedule of assets and liabilities.

8. _____

9.   Requirements for a reorganization plan to be confirmed by the court include (a) filing with the secretaries of state for the residences of the creditors (b) feasibility of the plan (c) the plan providing for a minimal 45% return on a claim for each creditor (d) all of the above.

9. _____

10.   Under a plan of reorganization, creditors with rights of priority to have claims fully satisfied in cash are (a) business partners of the debtor (b) secured creditors (c) employees with wages owing (d) tax officials.

10. _____

11.   _____ occurs when a debtor voluntarily transfers property to a trustee with the understanding that these assets are to be used for payment on all debts then owing. (a) fiduciary trust (b) assignment (c) extension (d) consolidation loan

11. _____

12.   Requirements for the validity of a Chapter 11 reorganization plan include (a) stating how each class of creditor interests/claims will be treated (b) insuring that all claims and interests share assets equally (c) notarized appraisal of the debtor's net worth (d) none of the above

12. _____

13.   Chapter 7 proceedings do not apply to (a) banks (b) railroads (c) insurance companies (d) all of the above.

13. _____

CASE PROBLEMS - SHORT ESSAY ANSWERS: Read each case problem carefully. When appropriate, answer by stating a Decision for the case and by explaining the rationale - Rule of Law - relied upon to support your decision.

1. Sara Student, finishing her last year of medical school, is worried about the $8,500 in student loans she has outstanding. She seeks advice from her first-year-law-school friend, Darence Clarrow, who assures Sarah that if she files for bankruptcy, "all her financial troubles will be over." Is Mr. Clarrow correct? Discuss.

    Decision: _____

    Rule of Law: _____

2. D, recently discharged in bankruptcy, starts receiving calls from Ajax Appliance who urges D to reaffirm the $1,600 debt D had owed Ajax prior to the proceedings. D, worried about the "dire consequences" that Ajax had been referring to in the calls, decides to enter an agreement with Ajax for full payment on the debt. Is this contract with Ajax, who had notice of D's bankruptcy proceedings, enforceable? Explain.

    Decision: _____

    Rule of Law: _____

3. D has fallen upon complete financial disaster. With an estate valued at $45,000, D files a Chapter 7 petition listing the following creditors: a $17,000 debt to Creditor One, $10,000 of which is secured; $8,000 in back due wages to Creditor Two; $6,000 in unpaid income taxes to the Federal government, Creditor Three; a $12,000 unsecured negligence judgment to Creditor Four who has filed this claim with the court; an unsecured $11,000 breach of contract judgment to Creditor Five who has also filed a claim; and a $10,000 unsecured loan from D's in-laws who have not filed their claim although they had notice of the proceedings. List how D's $45,000 will be distributed among these creditors.

    Decision: _____

    Rule of Law: _____

4. Doodles Dingle, his finances in a shambles ($23,000 in liabilities, $4,200 in assets), is spending sleepless nights worrying over the creditor calls that constantly hound him. Having had enough, Doodles files for bankruptcy. At the creditor's meetings it is discovered that eight months prior to Doodles' filing, he had given his sister, Daphne, a $5,200 boat and his brother, Darby, a $7,500 car, both with the understanding that the property would be returned to Doodles when his financial woes were ended. Discuss the significance of Mr. Dingle's transfers.

    Decision: _____

    Rule of Law: _____

5.   Paddywack has over $120,000 tied up in his Knick-Knack Estates realty business. He also has debts of $100,000. With an intent to prefer various creditors over others, Paddywack transfers property worth $15,000 to those creditors. The other creditors ask your advice. Discuss the significance of Paddywack's transfers.

Decision: _____

_____

Rule of Law: _____

_____

DEBTOR AND CREDITOR RELATIONS
RESEARCH QUESTIONS:

1. Research your State's law on exempt property. Compare Federal exemptions with your State's exemptions. If you were to file for bankruptcy, which exemption path would you choose and why?

2. Over the past few years, three major corporate reorganizations, based on similar financial scenarios, have occurred -- Texaco, A.H., Robins and Johns-Mansville/Raybestos-Manhattan cases. What do these cases have in common? Why did these firms choose bankruptcy as a solution to their problems? Is this a proper use of bankruptcy law?

CHAPTER 40
Unfair Competition and Business Torts

SCOPE NOTE

Since the late 19th century, the controlling influence of "laissez-faire" as the philosophy defining the appropriate role of government vis-a-vis business has declined. In response to various private sector developments (anti-competitive practices, deception and fraud, emergence of quasi public interest enterprises), government has undertaken an increasingly active role in regulating the commercial marketplace to prevent certain economic dislocations from occurring that are not considered in the best interest of the nation. Government restraints on business and industry include controls on common carriers, broadcasters, public utilities, banking and investing marketplaces. In Chapter 40, government regulations to prevent abuses that undermine fair, open, and honest competition are discussed. Statutes, administrative regulations, and court rulings defining and proscribing false, deceptive and unfair trade practices are focused upon.

EDUCATIONAL OBJECTIVES

1. Evaluate the policy underlying proscription of false, deceptive and unfair commercial practices.

2. List various types of business torts and their related definitional elements.

3. Identify and define examples of "unfair competition."

4. Explain legislation designed to promote fair, honest competition.

5. Discuss trade-mark, trade-name protection.

6. Describe copyright and patent laws.

CHAPTER OUTLINE

I.   Business Torts - protect, preserve and promote legitimate economic interest.
    A.   Interference with Contractual Relations - intentional wrong doing (bribery, employee coercion, boycotts)

    B.   Defamation - falsehoods damaging business reputation
    C.   Disparagement - falsehoods damaging economic interests
    D.   Appropriation - wrongful economic gain through using another's identity
    E.   Misrepresentation - fraud

II.   Intellectual Property - promote and protect research and innovation
    A.   Trade Secrets - commercially valuable secret information (formula, process, lists, etc.)
    B.   Trade Symbols - Lanham Act
        1.   Types of trade symbols
            a.   Trademark
            b.   Service mark
            c.   Certification mark
            d.   Collective mark
        2.   Registration
        3.   Infringement and remedies
    C.   Trade Names - words and names not within Lanham Act coverage
    D.   Copyrights - original works of art, literature, expression of ideas
        1.   Procedure - federal control
        2.   Rights - compulsory license and fair use rules
        3.   Ownership
        4.   Infringement and remedies
    E.   Patents
        1.   Patentability - useful, new and not obvious
        2.   Procedure - federal registration
        3.   Infringement and remedies

TRUE-FALSE: Circle true or false.

Answers

T   F   1.   Unfair competition concerns business practices that disrupt protected economic and intellectual property interests.

T   F   2.   Employees have a duty not to reveal their employer's secrets to competitors.

T   F   3.   A copyright lasts for a period of 17 years from the date of first publication.

T   F   4.   Patents are issued by State government.

T   F   5.   Descriptive, personal and generic words and names may be protected as trade names.

T   F   6.   An untrue, honest opinion amounts to fraud and is therefore actionable.

T   F   7.   A collective mark identifies or indicates trade union membership.

T   F   8.   The test for malice under the defense of constitutional privilege in a defamation action focuses on the presence of evil intent and ill will underlying the false statement.

T   F   9.   Forces, substances, and conditions of nature are not patentable.

T   F   10.   Copyright protection applies to new ideas or concepts.

T   F   11.   The Pennzoil v. Texaco case illustrates the business tort of intentional interference with contractual relations.

T   F   12.   The torts of defamation and disparagement differ by the former protecting economic interests and the latter practicing reputational interests.

KEY TERMS – MATCHING EXERCISE: Select the term which best completes each statement below and write the corresponding number in the ANSWERS column.

	Column I		Column II		Answers
1.	Unconsented to interference with protected intellectual property interests.	1.	Disparagement	1.	_____
		2.	Palming off	2.	_____
2.	An untrue, derogatory statement about the quality of ownership of another person's property.	3.	Trade secret	3.	_____
		4.	Trademark	4.	_____
3.	Communication of defamatory statements to others.	5.	Trade name	5.	_____
		6.	Fraud	6.	_____
4.	Using a competitor's name or likeness without permission for one's own economic gain.	7.	Copyright	7.	_____
		8.	Sherman Act	8.	_____
5.	Falsely representing one's products as those of another.	9.	Appropriation	9.	_____
		10.	Patent	10.	_____
6.	Protection given authors of original, creative works including music, novels, plays, paintings, and sculptures.	11.	Vertical	11.	_____
		12.	Allonge	12.	_____
7.	A distinguishing symbol identifying tangible goods or products but not services.	13.	Cease & desist order	13.	_____
				14.	_____
8.	Statutorily secured right of monopoly issued to inventors or discoverers of useful new devices or processes.	14.	Infringement	15.	_____
		15.	Publication		
		16.	Compulsory license		
9.	Intentional, knowingly made, false representation of a material fact.	17.	Libel		

10. Confidential information essential to the successful operation of a business.

11. Written, printed or pictoral defamation.

12. A defense to defamation.

13. Damages measure based on the difference between the value of performance received and the value of performance as represented.

14. Symbol identifying and distinguishing one's services from others.

15. Permission to make limited use of copyrighted material usually accompanied by payment of royalties.

18. Benefit of the Bargain

19. Service mark

20. Privilege

MULTIPLE CHOICE: Select the alternative which best completes each statement below and write the corresponding letter in the ANSWERS column.

Answers

1. Which of the following is not considered "intellectual property' (a) trademark (b) trade allocation (c) copyright (d) trade secret.

1. _____

2. Trade secrets include (a) customer lists (b) product formulas (c) production methods (d) all of the above.

2. _____

3. The absolute privilege defense to a defamation cause of action applies to statements made by (a) clergy from the pulpit (b) spouses in the presence of others (c) senators on the floor of the U.S. Senate (d) all of the above.

3. _____

4. _____ is the difference between what was paid for an article and the market value of the article received. (a) benefit of the bargain damages (b) out of pocket damages (c) liquidated damages (d) punitive damages.

4. _____

5. One who actively encourages another to commit a patent infringement is referred to as a/n (a) indirect (b) contributory (c) direct (d) equitable infringer.

5. _____

6. Unfair trade practices include (a) competitive advertising (b) registering trademarks (c) betrayal of trade secrets (d) free competition in the marketplace.

6. _____

7.   Punitive damages are awarded in instances of business torts when (a) compensatory damages are an inadequate remedy (b) negligence is the theory of recovery (c) outrageous or evilly motivated conduct has been engaged in (d) all of the above.

7.   _____

8.   Defamation protects (a) reputational interests (b) economic and property interests (c) contractual relationships (d) all of the above.

8.   _____

9.   To accomplish a valid transfer of copyright ownership, _____ is required. (a) consideration (b) a writing signed by the copyright owner (c) recording (d) all of the above.

9.   _____

10.   _____ is the doctrine that allows reproduction of copyrighted works for the purpose of criticism, news reporting, teaching, comment or research without an infringement occurring. (a) Fair Use (b) Main Purpose (c) Reasonable Decency (d) Good Faith.

10.   _____

11.   "U.L." is an example of a (a) service mark (b) tradename (c) collective mark (d) certification mark.

11.   _____

12.   Patentability depends on the (a) dollar value (b) growth potential (c) newness and usefulness (d) none of the above.

12.   _____

13.   A statement of personal belief or judgment is (a) one of fact (b) an opinion (c) the basis for fraud (d) none of the above.

13.   _____

CASE PROBLEMS - SHORT ESSAY ANSWERS: Read each case problem carefully. When appropriate, answer by stating a Decision for the case and by explaining the rationale - Rule of Law - relied upon to support your decision.

1.   Lanny Lantern comes up with a new design for battery powered portable lamps. Searching for a name to attract and build sales as well as differentiate his product from that of competitors, Lanny coins the phrase, Portalantern. Lanny attempts to register this as a trademark. Will he be successful?

Decision: _____

_____

Rule of Law: _____

_____

2.   A and B have been long time employees of Toys Manufacturing Company. During their employment, they have acquired highly technical skills and knowledge. A competitor of Toys Company, Playthings, Inc., offers A and B higher paying jobs if they leave Toys. Their employment contracts with Toys contain no clause prohibiting employment with a competitor. What, if anything, may Toys Mfg. Co. do to prevent A and B from using the trade secrets of Toys when they go to work for Playthings, Inc.? Explain.

Decision: _____

_____

Rule of Law: _____

_____

3.   Following years of expensive, painstaking research, Dr. Science has discovered a cure for the common cold: a strain of bacteria living in the nodules on the backs of Australian green toads. Excited over potential profits and benefits for humans, Dr. Science is asked whether he intends to patent his discovery. Is his reply, "You bet," legally sound? Explain.

Decision: _____

_____

Rule of Law: _____

_____

4.   The Eskimos of Question 3 fame, enjoy the climatic and cultural wonders of their new home so much that they co-author a book discussing the splendors of Guelph, North Dakota. The Eskimos apply for and receive, but never register, a copyright for their publication. A few years later, another book, Guelph, North Dakota, Paradise Found, is released by Puffer Publishers. The Eskimos, believing the similarities between this book and their earlier work are more than coincidental, sue the authors of the new book for $1,500,000, alleging copyright infringement. Who prevails and why?

Decision: _____

_____

Rule of Law: _____

_____

5.   Cappy Dick, in the market for a new boat for his family of eight, talks to Salesman Hook at Ayhab Boatworks. Telling Hook he is looking for durability, convenience and safety, Cappy is told the Liner model of Crummy Craft is perfectly suited to his needs. Cappy pays $55,000 for the Crummy Craft Liner but soon becomes dissatisfied with it. The boat lacks most of the features Salesman Hook said come with it. In its present state, the boat is worth 442,000. If the boat had the features Salesman Hook told Cappy about, it would be worth $60,000. What remedy should Cappy pursue? Explain.

Decision: _____

_____

Rule of Law: _____

_____

CHAPTER 41

Antitrust

SCOPE NOTE

America's economic philosophy is based on the belief that the public interest (product/service prices, quality, availability and innovation) is best served through free and open competition in the marketplace. Concentration of business power in the hands of merely a few, through combinations and monopolies, is considered an unacceptable threat to the benefits of free, open trade. This Chapter examines the law of trade regulation, designed to prevent activities that constitute unreasonable restraints on trade. The sources of antitrust laws, the types of activities prohibited, and the role of federal courts, administrative agencies, and state laws are all discussed.

EDUCATIONAL OBJECTIVES

1. Evaluate the policy underlying laws proscribing "trusts" and "combinations" which threaten free and open competition.

2. Identify the types of business practices prohibited under Sections 1 and 2 of the Sherman Anti-Trust Act.

3. Define and develop the importance of the "rule of reason" test.

4. Differentiate the types of activities considered inherently anti-competitive under the Sherman Act.

5. Distinguish among the tests used to determine "monopolization" under the Sherman Act.

6. List the types of acts prohibited under the Clayton Act.

7. Explain how the Robinson-Patman Act strengthened government regulation of anti-competitive business practices.

8. Discuss the role of the F.T.C. in promoting fair, open, honest and free competition.

CHAPTER OUTLINE

I.   Sherman Antitrust Act - promote free, open competition; prevent concentrations of economic power
  A.   Restraint of Trade - competition reducing conspiracies, contracts or combinations
      1.   Rule of reason and per se violations
      2.   Price fixing
      3.   Market allocations - vertical, horizontal territory restraints
      4.   Boycotts - refusals to conduct business
      5.   Tying arrangements - coercive reciprocal dealing
  B.   Monopolies - price controls and competition exclusion
      1.   Monopolization - monopoly power and market share
      2.   Attempts to monopolize - intent and chances for success
II.   Clayton Act
  A.   Tying Contracts and Exclusive Dealing - prohibits dealing with a competitor
  B.   Mergers - extent of competition reduction through stock or asset purchases
  C.   Interlocking directorates - same persons on boards of several businesses
III. Robinson-Patman Act - price discrimination prohibited
  A.   Cost Justification - defense to alleged violation
  B.   Meeting Competition - defense to alleged violation
IV.   Federal Trade Commission Act - role and scope of authority of F.T.C.

TRUE-FALSE: Circle true or false.

Answers

T   F   1.   Price fixing is considered the most significant and substantial per se violation of the Sherman Act.

T   F   2.   For business practices to constitute prohibited monopolization attempts, both an intent to monopolize and a probability of success must be shown.

T   F   3.   Violations of the Clayton Act are punished with criminal penalties.

T   F   4.   A major objective of the Sherman Act is to promote free, open competition in the marketplace.

T   F   5.   Price differentials are always Robinson-Patman violations regardless of whether they are based on cost savings or attempts to match competition prices.

T   F   6.   Generally, monopolization by itself is sufficient to constitute a violation of the Sherman Act.

T   F   7.   The F.T.C. is responsible for promoting fair, honest, competitive practices in commerce.

T   F   8.   A victim of a violation of the Sherman Anti-Trust Act is allowed to recover no more than twice the amount of actual loss suffered from the violation.

T   F   9.   Group boycotts are an example of "per se" violations of the Sherman Anti-Trust Act.

T   F   10.   Horticulture, labor and agricultural organizations are specifically subject to antitrust regulation by the Clayton Act.

T   F   11.   The primary goal of antitrust law is to promote and protect free, fair and open competition in the marketplace.

T   F   12.   Unilateral conduct by a single business can constitute an illegal restraint of trade under Section 1 of the Sherman Act.

KEY TERMS - MATCHING EXERCISE: Select the term which best completes each statement below and write the corresponding number in the ANSWERS column.

Column I	Column II	Answers
1. Business arrangements which prevent buyers from doing business with competitors of a seller.	1. Disparagement	1. _____
	2. Conglomerate merger	2. _____
2. Ability of an enterprise to control prices or access to a marketplace.	3. Exclusive dealing contracts	3. _____
		4. _____
3. Business arrangements considered automatic violations of anti-trust laws.	4. Boycott	5. _____
	5. Interlocking directorate	6. _____
4. Doctrine stating that only business arrangements which create unreasonable restraints of trade are violations of the Sherman Anti-Trust Act.	6. Market share	7. _____
	7. Monopoly power	8. _____
	8. Sherman Act	9. _____
5. Business contracts that require a purchaser to buy more than one product from the seller.	9. Rule of reason	10. _____
	10. Horizontal	11. _____
6. Directives calling for an immediate halt to business practices and agreements which violate anti-trust laws.	11. Vertical	12. _____
	12. Market allocations	13. _____
7. Refusal to do business with someone.	13. Cease & desist order	14. _____
8. Anti-trust violations involving restraint of trade agreements among competing retailers.	14. Tying arrangements	15. _____

9. A test to determine whether an enterprise's control of a market is monopolistic based on product and geographic factors.

10. Illegal restraints of trade involving collaboration among competing enterprises to refrain from competition in specified markets.

11. Similar business practices among competing enterprises.

12. Manufacturers setting the prices at which retailers can sell products.

13. Monopoly power gained through superior skill, efficiency and effectiveness and not deliberate misconduct.

14. A company purchasing one of its customers or suppliers.

15. Control over competing enterprises concentrated in a few persons or a small group.

15. Per se violations

16. Fairly acquired

17. Conscious parallelism

18. Robinson-Patman Act

19. Injunction

20. Retail price maintenance

MULTIPLE CHOICE: Select the alternative which best completes each statement below and write the corresponding letter in the ANSWERS column.

Answers

1. The Clayton Act, as amended, prohibits interlocking directorates in corporations which are (a) in direct competition (b) aggregately capitalized to the extent of a million dollars or more (c) engaged in interstate commerce (d) all of the above.

1. _____

2. F.T.C. remedial options include (a) contribution (b) corrective advertising (c) receivership (d) all of the above.

2. _____

3. Which of the following types of business transactions is a "per se" violation of Anti-Trust statutes? (a) floating contracts (b) territorial allocation of markets (c) unilateral boycotts (d) none of the above.

3. _____

4. The Federal Trade Commission was established to (a) enforce state bankruptcy acts (b) draft a model anti-trust code (c) supplement the Sherman and Clayton Anti-Trust Acts (d) enforce Fair Trade Statutes.

4. _____

5. _____ refers to the area in which a firm sells its products or services. (a) geographic market (b) concentrated share (c) product market (d) none of the above.

5. _____

6.   Acquisition of the stock or assets of a competing company is referred to
      as a/n (a) vertical merger (b) conglomerate merger (c) horizontal merger
      (d) none of the above.   6. _____

7.   The F.T.C. investigates (a) false or misleading advertising (b) stock
      swindles (c) fraudulent equitable receiverships (d) all of the above.   7. _____

8.   Which of the following acts prohibits price discrimination: (a) Lanham
      Act (b) Federal Trade Act (c) Robinson-Patman Act (d) Unfair Sales
      Act.   8. _____

9.   Restraints of trade among businesses at different distribution levels are
      labelled (a) triangular (b) vertical (c) multiple (d) equitable anti-trust
      violations.   9. _____

10.   Prior to 1975, retail price maintenance agreements were no anti-trust
      violations under (a) section 1 of the Sherman Act (b) the price
      differential doctrine (c) F.T.C. order (d) State Fair Trade laws.   10. _____

11.   Factors assessed in determining geographic market share include (a)
      transportation costs (b) competitive product quality (c) marketplace
      efficiencies (d) all of the above.   11. _____

12.   Examples of "unfair conduct" under Section 2 of the Sherman Act
      include (a) technological advances (b) research and development
      efficiencies (c) activities intended to exclude competition (d) none of the
      above.   12. _____

13.   Antitrust law examines _____ to determine whether a merger
      violates anti-trust. (a) absolute size of merged entry (b) size of merged
      firm relative to geographic and/or product market share (c) degree of
      unfair conduct (d) none of the above.   13. _____

CASE PROBLEMS - SHORT ESSAY ANSWERS: Read each case problem carefully.   When
appropriate, answer by stating a Decision for the case and by explaining the rationale - Rule of Law -
relied upon to support your decision.

1.   Super Oil Company has contracts with its independent retail stations requiring them to purchase
      and sell only the Super Oil line of tires, batteries and auto accessories. Discuss the validity of this
      business arrangement.

      Decision: _____

      _____

      Rule of Law: _____

      _____

2.   Whiskey, Inc., a liquor distributor, affixes a price tag to every bottle leaving its plant and requires
      all retailers handling its products to sell at the stated price. Discuss the significance of this
      business relationship.

Decision: _____

Rule of Law: _____

_____

3.   Home Furnishing, Inc., a retail furniture store, entered into an agreement with its supplier to sell Home Furnishing's inventory at prices below what the supplier was charging other retail furniture outlets in the same area. Learning of Home Furnishing's contract with the supplier, competitors argued that the agreement violated anti-trust laws. Are they correct? Discuss.

Decision: _____

Rule of Law: _____

_____

4.   Pewtrid Paints, Inc., a manufacturer and retailer of paint products, is conducting a special advertising promotion offering one gallon of paint "free" with every two gallons purchased. The regular price of the paint is $9.99 a gallon. During this advertising campaign, Pewtrid raised its prices to $13.99 a gallon. Is this a violation of the F.T.C. Act? Explain.

Decision: _____

Rule of Law: _____

_____

5.   Metropolis County Bar Association issued a minimum fees schedule to its member attorneys requiring all members to abide by the schedule or face "disciplinary" action. Does this action constitute a violation of the Sherman Act? Discuss.

Decision: _____

Rule of Law: _____

_____

Consumer Protection

SCOPE NOTE

Over the past few decades, law has shown an increased concern for recognizing and protecting the rights of consumer purchasers. At State and Federal levels, legislation, court decisions, and administrative rulings have assumed greater importance in equalizing the relationship between buyers and sellers in the consumer marketplace. Today's consumers are less at the mercy of caveat emptor (let the buyer beware) when they enter the marketplace. They have greater security in knowing that their contractual expectations will be satisfactorily met. Chapter 42 offers an overview of significant Federal legislation designed to advance and protect the rights of purchasers at various stages and in certain types of consumer transactions. The policy underlying the statutes discussed is recognizing and giving legal meaning to the various rights consumers assert under the "Consumer Bill of Rights": right to safety; right to information; right to recovery; right to fairness; and right to satisfactory fulfillment of contractual expectations. Chapter 42 develops the legal doctrines and principles of consumer protection in the context of credit transactions, real estate purchases, warranty coverage, safety, deceptive selling tactics and equality of bargaining positions.

EDUCATIONAL OBJECTIVES

1. Evaluate the policy underlying the emergence and growth of consumer protection laws.

2. Discuss the role of the Federal Trade Commission in controlling and preventing deceptive trade tactics and abusive, unfair warranty coverage practices.

3. Define, discuss the importance of, and identify significant provisions within the Consumer Credit Protection Act.

4. Explain the purpose and effects of the Equal Credit Opportunity Act, the Fair Credit Billing Act, the Fair Credit Reporting Act, the Fair Debt Collection Practices Act, and the Consumer Product Safety Act.

278

CHAPTER OUTLINE

I. Unfair and Deceptive Trade Practices - role of the F.T.C.
   A. Standards - prevent certain business practices resulting in consumer injury
      1. Unfairness - substantial injury; consumer could not avoid
      2. Deception - material misrepresentation likely to mislead reasonable consumer
   B. Remedies - includes fines, injunctions, cease and desist orders
      1. Affirmative disclosure - certain information must be disclosed
      2. Corrective advertising - recant earlier untrue claims
      3. Multiple product orders - cease and desist order for all goods sold by a company
II. Consumer Purchases
   A. Federal Warranty Protection - Magnusson-Moss Act
      1. Clear, meaningful language in written warranties - pre-sale disclosure
      2. "Full" or "limited" designation
      3. Disclaimer of implied warranty - prohibited period
      4. Informal settlement - procedures called for in some cases
   B. Consumer Right of Recission - 3 day cooling off period
      1. Consumer Credit Protection Act
      2. Interstate Land Sales Disclosure Act
      3. Door-to-door sales
III. Consumer Credit
   A. Access to Market - Equal Credit Opportunity Act
   B. Disclosure Requirements
      1. Truth in Lending Act
      2. Fair Credit Billing Act
      3. Real Estate Settlement Procedures Act
   C. Contract Terms
      1. Prepayment issue
      2. Balloon payment clause
      3. Holder in due course rule
   D. Consumer Credit Card Fraud - Credit Card Fraud Act of 1984
      1. Problems of stolen, counterfeited cards
      2. Problems of unauthorized use
   E. Fair Reportage - Fair Credit Reporting Act
   F. Creditors Remedies - Fair Debt Collection Practices Act
IV. Consumer Health and Safety - Consumer Product Safety Act and Commission

TRUE-FALSE: Circle true or false.

Answers

T   F   1.   According to Federal regulation, consumers must be provided access to all facts gathered and contained on them by credit reporting firms without limitations.

T   F   2.   Under Federal warranty law, written warranties may not disclaim implied warranty protection.

T   F   3.   A Sears credit card, a Texaco credit card and an American Express credit card are examples of open-ended credit accounts.

T   F   4.   When a credit card is lost, the card issuer must be notified within 24 hours of the loss otherwise the card owner will be liable for all purchases made by the finder.

T   F   5.   The doctrine of caveat emptor is a long standing, fundamental doctrine of the American free enterprise system which controls today's consumer marketplace.

T   F   6.   The Warner-Lambert case illustrates the FTC's power to order corrective advertising.

T   F   7.   The two basic elements of a credit transaction which must be disclosed to the borrower by the lender are loan repayment terms and the cost of the loan.

T   F   8.   A secured creditor may repossess the goods sold from a defaulting debtor-purchaser and retain them as full satisfaction on the debt under all circumstances.

T   F   9.   Federal warranty regulations require that written warranty protection be given to buyers in all consumer sales over $50 in value.

T   F   10.   Under Federal legislation, advertisements and other promotional communications need not result in actual deception to amount to prohibited misleading or false statements.

T   F   11.   The F.T.C. Act contains provisions which specifically define what constitutes unfair or deceptive practices.

T   F   12.   Because of inadequacies in how the Consumer Credit Protection Act dealt with the problem of credit card fraud, Congress enacted the Credit Card Fraud Act to strengthen federal law regulating this problem.

KEY TERMS - MATCHING EXERCISE: Select the term which best completes each statement below and write the corresponding number in the ANSWERS column.

Column I	Column II	Answers
1. A single transaction issuance of non-revolving credit for a specific period of time.	1. Equal Credit Opportunity Act	1. _____
		2. _____
2. A Federal agency responsible for investigating unfair, deceptive fraudulent and misleading business practices.	2. Foreclosure	3. _____
	3. Waiver of abatement	
		4. _____
3. Federal legislation designed to prevent deception and unfairness in consumer product warranties.	4. Affirmative disclosure	5. _____
		6. _____
	5. Closed-ended	
		7. _____
4. Federal legislation requiring that "statements of record" be filed in certain sales of unimproved land.	6. Rebate	8. _____
	7. Federal Trade Commission	9. _____

5. Federal legislation designed to end abusive, unfair debt enforcement tactics used by collection agencies.

6. One making purchases of goods, services or credit for family, household or personal use.

7. A single payment under a monthly installment credit contract that is disproportionately greater than other monthly payments.

8. Federal legislation enacted to protect purchasers of consumer goods from hazards associated with defective goods.

9. An FTC remedial device requiring advertisers to include in ad copy factual statements that reduce the likelihood of deception or misrepresentation.

10. Federal legislation prohibiting discriminatory extensions of credit.

11. FTC policy requiring advertisers to have a reasonable basis for the claims made in advertisements.

12. Warranty granting purchaser rights of refund or replacement for unrepairable defects as well as no cost repair services.

13. Federal legislation requiring the disclosure of consumer credit costs

14. Federal legislation designed to eliminate various problems associated with credit billing errors.

15. Federal legislation designed to insure accuracy and updatedness of consumer credit information.

8. Magnusson-Moss Act

9. Fair Debt Collection Practices Act

10. Balloon payment

11. Hazardous Product Act

12. Consumer

13. Fair Credit Billing Act

14. Consumer Product Safety Act

15. Interstate Land Sales Full Disclosure Act

16. Full

17. Truth in Lending

18. Fair Credit Reporting Act

19. Substantiation

20. Limited

10. _____

11. _____

12. _____

13. _____

14. _____

15. _____

MULTIPLE CHOICE: Select the alternative which best completes each statement below and write the corresponding letter in the ANSWERS column.

Answers

1.   The total charges payable to the creditor by the debtor in a consumer credit transaction is called a (a) carrying charge (b) lender's fee (c) finance charge (d) credit fee.

1. _____

2.   Purchasers of consumer credit who use their homes as collateral in the consumer transaction may effectively cancel the security interest (a) by telephone (b) in writing if done within three days after the transaction (c) only with the consent of the credit extender (d) none of the above.

2. _____

3.   The goals of Truth in Lending include: (a) promoting competition among credit extenders (b) facilitating comparison shopping for credit terms (c) increasing stability in the consumer credit marketplace (d) all of the above.

3. _____

4.   The cost of consumer credit must be expressed in an (a) annual percentage rate (b) appraisal fee ratio (c) allocated monthly formula (d) appreciated rate schedule.

4. _____

5.   Appeals from F.T.C. orders are taken to (a) Federal District Court (b) U.S. Supreme Court (c) U.S. Court of Appeals (d) Federal Court of Claims.

5. _____

6.   Federal law provides for a three day cooling-off period in (a) purchases of all major appliances (b) door-to-door sales over $25 in value (c) car sales over $6,000 (d) none of the above.

6. _____

7.   Federal warranty law requires that written warranties (a) be written in plain language (b) contain the description label "full" or "limited" (c) explain informal dispute settlement procedures (d) all of the above.

7. _____

8.   Of the following, which is not an example of a consumer transaction? (a) credit card purchase of mechanical repairs to a company delivery truck (b) $600 loan to pay your child's doctor bills (c) $400 loan to pay a balance owing on last year's personal income taxes (d) all of the above.

8. _____

9.   Federal consumer credit protection legislation was designed to (a) restrict access to consumer credit as an anti-inflation measure (b) promote fair and accurate reporting of credit information (c) broaden debt enforcement remedies available to a creditor (d) remove unduly burdensome legal regulation of credit contract terms.

9. _____

10. Information available to a consumer under the Fair Credit Reporting Act includes (a) the actual contents of a credit report file (b) the names of people from whom information was obtained (c) the source of the information (d) all of the above.

10. _____

11.   The Fair Credit Reporting Act applies to (a) security clearance investigations (b) consumer reports used for obtaining insurance (c) reputational reports for entrance into military academies (d) all of the above.

11.   _____

12.   The CPSC does not have regulatory authority over (a) motor vehicles (b) cosmetics (c) food products (d) all of the above.

12.   _____

13.   The Real Estate Settlement Procedures Act (a) seeks to provide residential home purchasers accurate cost information regarding home purchases (b) grants home buyers a three day cooling off period to insure satisfaction with a home purchase (c) places a ceiling on mortgage interest rates (d) all of the above.

13.   _____

CASE PROBLEMS - SHORT ESSAY ANSWERS: Read each case problem carefully.   When appropriate, answer by stating a Decision for the case and by explaining the rationale - Rule of Law - relied upon to support your decision.

1.   Jackson was sent an unrequested credit card from Plakton Petroleum Corporation as part of a promotional campaign. The card was stolen from Jackson's mailbox. The thief made purchases of $250 with the card. When Plakton sends Jackson a monthly statement containing the $250 in charges, what amount will Jackson be responsible for? Explain.

Decision: _____

Rule of Law: _____

2.   P bought $850 worth of furniture from S under an installment vendor credit contract. P is unable to make the fifth $85 monthly payment and S commences garnishment proceedings seeking to have P's employer E apply a percentage of P's wages to the debt. E, greatly upset over being summoned to appear at the garnishment hearing, threatens to discharge P unless the debt to S is quickly paid off. Are E's actions legal?

Decision: _____

Rule of Law: _____

3.   B purchased a new car from car dealer C.D. Under the terms of the credit agreement, B was to make 35 $160 monthly payments. A final, monthly payment of $1,600 was called for to complete the purchase. If B falls on financial hard times and cannot make the final $1,600 payment, does B lose the car? Discuss.

Decision: _____

Rule of Law: _____

4.   B purchases a lawnmower from S for $450. The written contract contains a clause stating that no warranties, express or implied, run with the sale. After two weeks of use, the mower breaks down. Has B any recourse through the Magnusson-Moss Act against S? Explain.

Decision: _____
_____

Rule of Law: _____
_____

5.   New York married couple H and W receives a promotional flyer in the mail from Desert Land Sales Corp. of Arizona. The flyer advertises undeveloped one acre sites as part of a 250 acre residential development in Suntown, Arizona. H and W, deciding the deal and its terms are quite appealing, sign for the purchase of one site. Other than the sales contract itself, H and W were given no other printed materials from Desert Land prior to or following their signing of the contract. Seven months after entering the agreement with Desert Land, H and W are laid off from work. Unable to make payment on their contract with Desert Land, they seek your advice. What will you tell them?

Decision: _____
_____

Rule of Law: _____
_____

Employment Law

SCOPE NOTE

Chapter 43 examines State and Federal laws that direct and control employer-employee relations. Prior to the onset of the industrial revolution, most issues related to working conditions and employment practices were dealt with through contract and tort law doctrines. As American society changed following the industrial revolution, the personal relationship that characterized pre-industrial employer-employee relations was no longer an effective regulatory mechanism. The need arose for a more formal system of intervention to resolve the problems of labor-management relations. This Chapter discusses these laws and their goals to promote employee safety, non-discriminatory employment practices and equality of bargaining power.

EDUCATIONAL OBJECTIVES

1. Evaluate the policies underlying labor relations law.

2. Explain the scope and purpose of Federal regulations on labor-management relations in the context of unionization and collective bargaining.

3. Discuss the breadth of applicability of federal laws prohibiting discriminatory employment practices.

4. Outline State and Federal laws dealing with worker safety issues.

CHAPTER OUTLINE

I. Labor Laws - labor/management relations
    A. Norris-La Guardia Act - labor dispute defined; injunctions limited; yellow dog contracts prohibited
    B. National Labor Relations Act - right to unionize; unfair labor practices and NLRB
    C. Labor-Management Relations Act - employer free speech; ends closed shop; cooling-off period
    D. Labor-Management Reporting and Disclosure Act - corrupt union practices
II. Employment Discrimination Law

     A.   Equal Pay Act - prohibits gender based discrimination
     B.   Civil Rights Act of 1964
          1.   Discrimination
          2.   Reverse discrimination
          3.   Sexual harassment
          4.   Comparable worth
     C.   Age Discrimination in Employment Act
     D.   Rehabilitation Act - prohibits handicap (disability) based discrimination
     E.   Executive Order - affirmative action for Federal contractors

III.   Employee Protection
     A.   Employee Termination at Will
          1.   Statutory limitations
          2.   Judicial limitations
     B.   Occupational Safety and Health Act - workplace safety
     C.   Worker's Compensation - strict liability based; common law defenses ended
     D.   Social Security and Unemployment Insurance
     E.   Fair Labor Standards Act - hours, wages, age and hazard restrictions

TRUE-FALSE: Circle true or false.

Answers

T   F   1.   Common law regulation of employer-employee relations was based on tort and contract doctrines.

T   F   2.   Labor law has traditionally sought to maintain an equitable power balance between employers and employees.

T   F   3.   The Norris-La-Guardia Act specifically authorized Federal courts to employ injunctive relief in all types of labor disputes.

T   F   4.   The Labor-Management Reporting and Disclosure Act outlines a union bill of rights in attempting to bring more democratic practices to unions.

T   F   5.   The Equal Employment Opportunity Act of 1972 is the backbone of the Federal law's position on employment discrimination.

T   F   6.   Federal legislation prohibiting discriminatory employment practices applies only to businesses with gross capitalization over $3,500,000.

T   F   7.   Federal law prohibits mandatory retirement for employees under 70.

T   F   8.   Worker's Compensation Statutes eliminate traditional common law defenses in claims brought by injured employees.

T   F   9.   The Fair Labor Standards Act prohibits employment of 14 to 18 year olds in non-farm hazardous job settings.

T   F   10.   Self employed persons are exempt from coverage under Federal social security legislation.

T   F   11.   Generally, employers are liable for sexual harassment committed by employees only when they know or should have known of the harassment incidents.

T   F   12.   The Occupational Safety and Health Act specifically pre-empts State regulation of work setting safety issues leaving States with little regulatory authority.

KEY TERMS - MATCHING EXERCISE: Select the term which best completes each statement below and write the corresponding number in the ANSWERS column.

Column I	Column II	Answers
1. Controversies over employment terms and conditions or union representation.	1. Estoppel	1. _____
2. Federal legislation intended to protect unionization and collective bargaining efforts of employees.	2. Fair Labor Standards Act	2. _____
3. Federal agency responsible for enforcing employee rights under the Wagner Act.	3. Norris-Laguardia	3. _____
4. Federal legislation designed to prevent various union unfair labor practices.	4. Labor dispute	4. _____
5. Employment programs focused on actively recruiting minority employees.	5. Renunciation	5. _____
6. Federal legislation enacted to promote safe and healthy working conditions.	6. Worker's Compensation laws	6. _____
7. Defense to a common law based injured employee civil court action alleging co-employee negligence as the primary cause of injury.	7. Wagner Act	7. _____
8. Congressional legislation establishing minimum hourly wage schedules.	8. Fellow Servant Rule	8. _____
	9. Taft-Hartley Act	9. _____
	10. OSHA	10. _____
	11. NLRB	11. _____
	12. Reagan Act	12. _____
	13. Social security	13. _____
	14. Fiduciary	14. _____
	15. Affirmative action	15. _____

9.   Federal law providing retirement, death and disability benefits to workers.

10. State statutes creating commissions to administer injured employee damages claims.

11. Employer-employee agreements prohibiting employees from joining or forming a union.

12. Work setting in which non-union members can be hired but must join the union representing other employees to continue on the job.

13. Description of employer affirmative action plans emphasizing racial or gender factors in hiring or promoting to achieve greater balance in formally secured jobs.

14. Concept stressing that wage scales among various jobs should be based on objectively grounded rating systems or performance assessments free of possible sex bias.

15. Common law doctrine allowing employers to hire employees at their own, generally unlimited, discretion.

16. Yellow Dog contract

17. Reverse discrimination

18. Employment at Will

19. Comparable worth

20. Union shop

MULTIPLE CHOICE: Select the alternative which best completes each statement below and write the corresponding letter in the ANSWERS column.

Answers

1.   Present day statutory regulations of employment settings focus on (a) safety and health issues (b) discrimination (c) labor-management relations (d) all of the above.

1. _____

2.   Unfair labor practices by management include (a) mandatory dress codes (b) discrimination against non-union workers (c) refusal to bargain in good faith (d) all of the above.

2. _____

3.   Congressional legislation aimed at ending corrupt labor union practices was the (a) Landrum-Griffin Act (b) Fair Labor Standards Act (c) Norris-La-Guardia Act (d) Fair Dealing Compliance Act.

3. _____

4.   Which of the following is an acceptable pay differential basis under the Equal Pay Act (a) worker's sex (b) worker's age (c) worker's productivity level (d) none of the above.

4.   _____

5.   _____ is responsible for enforcing federal anti-discrimination laws (a) FTC (b) EEOC (c) FAA (d) none of the above.

5.   _____

6.   Federal law allows for discriminatory employment practices based on (a) seniority (b) job qualifications (c) ability tests (d) none of the above.

6.   _____

7.   Employer defenses to common law based injured worker lawsuits do not include (a) promissory estoppel (b) assumption of risk (c) contributory negligence (d) none of the above.

7.   _____

8.   Common law based injured employee actions are found on a/n _____ theory of recovery (a) strict liability (b) nuisance (c) negligence (d) agency.

8.   _____

9.   Federal law requires overtime payment when more than (a) eight hours is worked in a single day (b) 40 hours is worked in a single week (c) 25 hours is worked in a three day period (d) none of the above.

9.   _____

10.   Federal unemployment insurance laws are administered by (a) State programs (b) Federal courts (c) Office of Unemployment Compensation (d) administrative tribunals.

10.   _____

11.   _____ are State statutes prohibiting union shop agreements (a) Closed shop Acts (b) Fair Employment laws (c) Yellow Dog Contract laws (d) Right to Work laws.

11.   _____

12.   Employers can fire employees for (a) trying to form a union (b) missed work days due to jury duty (c) reporting an OSHA violation (d) none of the above.

12.   _____

13.   Union activity amounting to unfair labor practices includes (a) informational leafletting (b) enforcing union shop agreements (c) feather bedding (d) all of the above.

13.   _____

CASE PROBLEMS - SHORT ESSAY ANSWERS: Read each case problem carefully.   When appropriate, answer by stating a Decision for the case and by explaining the rationale - Rule of Law - relied upon to support your decision.

1.   Square Deal Lumber Yard employs male and female workers of all ages in various jobs. The male stock clerks at Square Deal learn that they receive less pay than female yard attendants. The stock clerks argue that this amounts to a violation of the Equal Pay Act. Are they correct? Explain.

Decision: _____

_____

Rule of Law: _____

_____

2.   Aerospace Industries, Inc. puts out a hiring call for trained, experienced retrofitters. Chuck
      Campion, a 25 year old certified retrofitter with 4 years work experience, applies for the job. He
      is turned down, the personnel department explaining that no one under 30 will be hired for the
      jobs. Chuck files a claim against the company arguing violation of federal age discrimination
      laws. Who wins the dispute and why?

      Decision: _____

      _____

      Rule of Law: _____

      _____

3.   Fortisque Thistlemeyer, president and founder of Thistle Theatrical Productions, Inc., is embroiled
      in bitter contract negotiations with the union representing his employees. A bargaining impasse
      has been reached regarding overtime work on national holidays. The union threatens to strike if
      an accommodation cannot be reached. Forty, an outspoken anti-union hardliner, blasts the union
      as a collection of heartless, money-sucking, dishonest ingrates. The union files an unfair labor
      practices charge against him. Who prevails? Discuss.

      Decision: _____

      _____

      Rule of Law: _____

      _____

4.   Charlene Carlisle, a storage drum loader at Petro Processors for the past four years, has just been
      fired. Her employment record is spotless. Petro unloads, stores, and ships hazardous chemical
      wastes generated by chemical manufacturers. OSHA regulations require workers at petro to be
      provided adequate protective goggles, masks, gloves, and outer garments to insure no health
      endangering employee exposure to the toxins Petro handles. A truckload of dioxin contaminated
      wastes arrives at Petro. The manager requests that it be unloaded but Charlene, unable to find a
      proper mask, refused, citing health and safety hazards as her reason. The manager ordered
      Charlene to unload the truck or "face the consequences." She refused and was fired. She alleges
      violation of OSHA and the company denies it. What outcome?

      Decision: _____

      _____

      Rule of Law: _____

      _____

5.   Folsum Meatpacking, Inc. is entering its third month of a particularly bitter labor dispute. Its
      workers are beginning their second month of a strike. In an effort to induce the company to
      settle, the union, which also represents workers at other meatpacking houses in the area, tells those
      members not to handle any meat from shippers or ranchers who do business with Folsum. Folsum
      alleges that the union's activity is an unfair labor practice but the union asserts "just tough business
      tactics." Who is right?

      Decision: _____

      _____

      Rule of Law: _____

      _____

CHAPTER 44
Securities Regulation

SCOPE NOTE

In response to problems of fraud and inaccurate information associated with securities transactions, laws have been passed at State and Federal levels to protect investors from possible loss caused by these abuses. Chapter 44 focuses on securities regulation at the Federal level and traces the Federal government's involvement in controlling the securities marketplace from the early 1930's to the present. The discussion addresses the basic doctrines, principles and terminology that define and control the rights/duties of people engaged in trading investment securities. Also dealt with are the nature and extent of liability for violations of Federal securities laws.

EDUCATIONAL OBJECTIVES

1. Identify the scope, purpose and major provisions of the Securities Act of 1933.

2. Outline the important procedural requirements under the 1933 Act.

3. Distinguish among the various transactions and the types of securities given exemption from coverage under the 1933 Act.

4. Explain the nature and breadth of liability for violations of the 1933 Act.

5. Identify the scope, purpose and major provisions of the Securities Exchange Act of 1934.

6. Discuss the extent or regulatory authority held by the SEC.

7. Develop the purpose and significance of the Foreign Corrupt Practices Act of 1977.

CHAPTER OUTLINE

I.   The Securities Act of 1933 - registration of securities held for public sale
    A.   Definition of a Security - notes, bonds, stocks as investment
    B.   Registration of Securities

            1.   Integrated disclosure
            2.   Shelf registrations
    C.   Exempt Securities
            1.   Regulation A - short form; $1.5 million maximum
            2.   Intrastate issues - parties in one State
            3.   Short-term commercial paper
            4.   Other exempt securities - government issues; bank securities; insurance policies; religious and charity securities
    D.   Exempt Transactions
            1.   Private Placements - less than 35 investors; no publicity
            2.   Limited offers not exceeding $5 million
            3.   Limited offers not exceeding $500,000
            4.   Limited offers solely to accredited investors
            5.   Resales of restricted securities
    E.   Liability - based on statute violations
            1.   Unregistered sales
            2.   False registration statements
            3.   Antifraud provision
            4.   Criminal sanctions

II.   The Securities Exchange Act of 1934 - regulation of public trading
    A.   Registration and Periodic Reporting Requirements
    B.   Anti-fraud Provision
            1.   Requisites of Rule 10b-5
            2.   Insider trading
    C.   Short Swing Profits
    D.   Insider Trading Sanctions Act
    E.   Proxy Solicitations
    F.   Tender Offers
            1.   Defensive tactics
            2.   State regulation
    G.   Misleading Statements in Reports
    H.   Foreign Corrupt Practices Act
            1.   Accounting requirements
            2.   Anti-bribery provisions

TRUE-FALSE: Circle true or false.

Answers

T   F   1.   Federal laws have exclusive jurisdiction over regulating sales of securities.

T   F   2.   The SEC uses registration documents to evaluate the soundness and potential for profit of investment opportunities.

T   F   3.   Intra-state securities transactions are exempt from registration under federal securities regulation laws.

T   F   4.   Liability for selling unregistered securities which were required to be registered under Federal law is absolute, there being no defense for the violation.

T   F   5.   Anti-fraud provisions of the 1933 Securities Act apply only to intra-state sales of securities.

T   F   6.   Securities sales with a value not exceeding a million and a half dollars may be made over any twelve month period and the sales require only notification to the SEC.

T   F   7.   Once an issuer has filed registration documents, no additional filing is required to update the initial registration.

T   F   8.   A major objective of Federal laws focused on preventing fraud in securities transactions is to promote and preserve public confidence in the securities market.

T   F   9.   The Foreign Corrupt Practices Act attempts to prevent bribery of foreign governments and officials by U.S. corporations.

T   F   10. Under Federal laws, the term "security" is limited in its definition to include only stocks and bonds.

T   F   11. The primary goal of the Truth in Securities Act registration requirements is to reveal to potential investors material information that can assist them in assessing the worthiness of an investment opportunity.

T   F   12. A security issue offered and sold only to purchasers residing in a single State by an issuer residing and doing business in the same State is exempt from registration requirements under the 1933 Act.

KEY TERMS - MATCHING EXERCISE: Select the term which best completes each statement below and write the corresponding number in the ANSWERS column.

Column I	Column II	Answers
1. Federal legislation enacted to prevent fraud and promote accessible, truthful information in securities sales.	1. Short-term commercial paper	1. _____
	2. Da Ma Doctrine	2. _____
2. The act required of some securities sellers by which information is disclosed to potential investors.	3. Insider	3. _____
	4. Intra-state	4. _____
3. Documents distributed to potential investors containing required disclosure information.	5. Registration	5. _____
	6. Blue Sky law	6. _____
4. Notes, drafts or other working capital issuances with maturity dates of nine months or less.	7. Tender offer	7. _____
	8. Proxy	8. _____

5. One having knowledge of non-public confidential and material information related to the value of a security.

6. A general invitation to all shareholders of a company to purchase their shares at a specified price.

7. A signed writing, issued by a shareholder, granting authority to another to vote the signer's stock.

8. State laws regulating securities sales.

9. Exempted security transactions by an issuer that do not involve a public offering.

10. Banks, insurance companies and investment firms purchasing securities sold under the private placement provisions of securities regulations.

11. Governmental agency primarily responsible for enforcing Federal securities laws.

12. Descriptor for the three tiered registration system adopted to reduce duplication of effort in complying with requirements under the 1933 and 1934 Acts.

13. Securities sold under such registration exemptions as private placement, accredited investor limited offer, or limited offers under $500,000.

14. Federal legislation imposing civil penalties upon persons conducting securities transactions based on non-public material information.

9. Private placements

10. Accredited investor

11. Exemption

12. Prospectus

13. Constructive disclosure

14. Reasonable diligence

15. Securities Act of 1933

16. Restricted

17. Integrated Disclosure

18. Insider Trading Sanctions Act

19. Porcupine provisions

20. Securities Exchange Commission

9. _____

10. _____

11. _____

12. _____

13. _____

14. _____

15. _____

15.   Restrictive corporate by-laws
       intended to repel hostile takeovers.

MULTIPLE CHOICE: Select the alternative which best completes each statement below and write the corresponding letter in the ANSWERS column.   Answers

1.   The anti-fraud sections of the "Truth in Securities" Act (a) apply to
       securities transactions in interstate commerce (b) impose only criminal
       sanctions for their violations (c) cover only securities sales that are
       exempt from registration (d) none of the above.   1. _____

2.   The date a registration statement becomes effective is _____ after
       filing. (a) 2 months (b) 2 weeks (c) 20 days (d) 1 month.   2. _____

3.   Of the following, which is not information which must be disclosed on
       securities registration forms?   (a) description of the business of the
       registrant (b) certified financial statements (c) management information
       (d) accounting procedures used by registrant.   3. _____

4.   Transactions exempted from registration under the 1933 Act include
       limited offers (a) solely to accredited investors (b) not exceeding $10
       million (c) public displacements (d) all of the above.   4. _____

5.   Security transactions exempt from registration include (a) sales by
       domestic banks (b) sales by domestic governments (c) transactions
       involving short term commitments (d) all of the above.   5. _____

6.   A/n _____ involves an investment for profit derived from the
       management efforts of others (a) debt (b) lease (c) security (d) gift.   6. _____

7.   Enforcement options related to Federal securities laws include (a)
       criminal sanctions (b) administrative remedies (c) civil liability (d) all of
       the above.   7. _____

8.   A defense to an action based on untrue statements contained in a
       registration statement is (a) due diligence (b) innocent mistake (c)
       subjective honesty (d) capitalized equity.   8. _____

9.   Persons who receive non-public material investment information from
       insiders are referred to as (a) co-conspirators (b) accomplices (c) tippers
       (d) none of the above.   9. _____

10.   The Securities Exchange Act of 1934 applies primarily to (a) bankruptcy
       trust securities (b) secondary securities distributions (c) equitable
       receiverships (d) none of the above.   10. _____

11.   Tender offers must be kept open for at least (a) 2 weeks (b) 2 months
       (c) 30 days (d) 20 days.   11. _____

12.   Actions taken by the target company to propose a hostile takeover
        attempt include (a) white knights strategy (b) stock repurchasing by
        insiders (c) reincorporation in States having anti-takeover laws.   12. _____

13.   Recent U.S. Supreme Court rulings have (a) upheld State anti-hostile
        takeover laws (b) ruled that the Williams Act exclusively pre-empts State
        action (c) held golden parachute agreements as unconstitutional (d) none
        of the above.   13. _____

CASE PROBLEMS - SHORT ESSAY ANSWERS: Read each case problem carefully. When
appropriate, answer by stating a Decision for the case and by explaining the rationale - Rule of Law -
relied upon to support your decision.

1.   Ajax, Inc., seeking to raise capital, issued $500,000 in securities during 1978. Regardless of
        whether this issue was subject to State laws, was it entirely exempt from Federal regulation?
        Discuss.

        Decision: _____

        Rule of Law: _____

        _____

2.   Brown, president of Waylay, Inc., owns 25% of that corporation's stock which is registered with
        the SEC. On October 25th, Brown purchases Waylay securities which increases his share of
        ownership to 30%. The following January, Brown sells some of his Waylay shares reducing his
        ownership to 22%. What liability does Brown face for the profits from these transactions?
        Explain.

        Decision: _____

        Rule of Law: _____

        _____

3.   World Food, Inc. is a non-profit organization distributing American crop surpluses to
        underdeveloped nations facing food shortages. To expand its operation, World Food issues
        $250,000 worth of securities. Must this issue be registered with the SEC?

        Decision: _____

        Rule of Law: _____

        _____

4.   Explorations, Inc., to capitalize its development of a natural gas field, registers with the SEC to sell
        $3.5 million in securities. In its registration statement and prospectus, Explorations lists Sammy
        Maudlin and Edith Pringle, famous star from the entertainment world, as members of its board of
        directors. Investor I, reviewing Explorations' registration statement and prospectus, in which the
        working life of the gas field is stated to be at least 25 years, decides to purchase $20,000 of
        Explorations' stock issue. The venture eventually turns sour as Explorations discovers that the
        fields actually have a producing life of just over 10 years. Too short a period to make the

development profitable, Explorations abandons the project. I, remembering the statements made in the prospectus, sues for return of his investment alleging fraud. Named as defendants in the suit are Sammy and Edith who claim no liability since they had no "hands-on" management responsibilities with Explorations. Is I entitled to a return of his $20,000 and are Maudlin and Pringle accountable for it? Discuss.

Decision: _____

_____

Rule of Law: _____

_____

5.   XYZ Corporation, with assets totalling $850,000, needs additional capital to finance an expansion of its operations. The board of directors decides to promote an issue of $300,000 in equity securities to raise the necessary capital. At the time of this issue, XYZ has 230 shareholders owning this class of securities. Must XYZ register the securities it plans to sell if it anticipates trading them over the counter?

Decision: _____

_____

Rule of Law: _____

_____

Accountants' Legal Liability

SCOPE NOTE

Accountants face possible civil and criminal liability stemming from the work they perform for others. Chapter 45 examines common law and statutory bases for such liability.

EDUCATIONAL OBJECTIVES

1. Explain contractually based accountant liability.

2. Distinguish between tort and criminal bases for accountant liability.

3. Discuss controversial issues related to client access to accountant working papers.

4. Develop the importance of client accountant communication privileges.

5. Outline accountant liability under Federal securities and tax laws.

CHAPTER OUTLINE

I. Common Law - liability for improper performance
    A. Contract Liability - agreement defines rights and duties
    B. Tort Liability
        1. Negligence
        2. Fraud
    C. Criminal Liability - fraud; tax and securities laws
    D. Client Information - accountant as independent contractor with non-delegatable duties
        1. Working papers - owned by accountant; confidential
        2. Accountant-client privilege - not generally recognized
II. Federal Securities Law - liability for violations
    A. Securities Act of 1933 - material, false statement in financial statement
    B. Securities Exchange Act of 1934 - false financial statement detrimentally relied on

TRUE-FALSE: Circle true or false.

Answers

T   F   1.   Accountants provide financial information important in economic resource allocation decisions.

T   F   2.   In the relationship with the client, an accountant is responsible for performing only to the level of competence explicitly provided for in the contract.

T   F   3.   Accountants are generally not liable for insuring the absolute accuracy of their reports.

T   F   4.   People whom accountants are held to know as intended recipients and users of their reports include potential investors.

T   F   5.   Accountant criminal liability is mainly based upon Federal securities and tax laws.

T   F   6.   Fines are the only penalties imposed on accountants for violating Federal tax laws.

T   F   7.   The confidentiality of accountant-client communications is not a privilege recognized under either State or Federal law.

T   F   8.   To maintain a civil action against an accountant under Section 11 of the 1933 Security Exchange Act, the plaintiff must establish both privity and reliance.

T   F   9.   Accountants are not civilly liable under Section 18 of the 1934 Securities Exchange Act if their actions are without knowledge of untrue statements and based on good faith motivation.

T   F   10.   Accountants are always liable for releasing information obtained from clients without their consent.

T   F   11.   Accountant liability for services performed is based partly on Federal securities laws.

T   F   12.   The standard of competence applied when an accountant contractually agrees to conduct an audit to find embezzlement is Generally Accepted Auditing Standards.

KEY TERMS - MATCHING EXERCISE: Select the term which best completes each statement below and write the corresponding number in the ANSWERS column.

Column I	Column II	Answers
1. Non-contractual party intended by the contracting parties to receive a direct, primary benefit under the contract.	1. Fraud	1. _____
	2. Due diligence	2. _____
	3. Tort	3. _____

2. Contractual non-performance that terminates an accountant's right to compensation.

3. Failure to use the care of a reasonably competent accountant.

4. Contractual doctrine limiting accountant liability to persons with whom a business relationship (clients) had been established.

5. Accountant's defense to civil liability under Section 11 of the 1933 Securities Exchange Act.

6. Intentional or knowing wrongful conduct.

7. Civil wrong, not a contractual breach, triggering a right of compensatory recovery in the victim.

8. Accountant's records, including data gathering process followed, information obtained and conclusion drawn therefrom.

9. Confidential information which witnesses or others may rightfully refuse to release based on the nature of a relationship existing with the person providing the information.

10. False material statement of fact issued with deceitful intent.

11. Accountant misconduct which triggers criminal liability under federal securities law.

12. One who provides reliable financial information to assist the decision-making of others.

13. Basis for accountant liability under State law.

4. Privileged communication

5. Interpretation

6. Trespass

7. Privity

8. Private interest

9. Third party beneficiary

10. Statute of Limitations

11. Material breach

12. Negligence

13. Working papers

14. Substantial performance

15. Scienter

16. Willful violation

17. Accountant

18. Common law

19. Estoppel

20. Judgment errors

4. _____
5. _____
6. _____
7. _____
8. _____
9. _____
10. _____
11. _____
12. _____
13. _____
14. _____
15. _____

14. Accountant behavior which triggers
a right to compensation for
services less damages for losses
caused by less than complete
performance.

15. Accountant misconduct triggering no
liability so long as professional
duties were performed with care.

MULTIPLE CHOICE: Select the alternative which best completes each statement below and write the corresponding letter in the ANSWERS column.   Answers

1. Which of the following is not a basis for accountant legal liability under State law (a) criminal codes (b) tort law (c) constitutional clauses (d) contract law.   1. _____

2. The basis for tort liability applied to accountants in performing their professional services includes (a) negligence and fraud (b) strict liability and promissory estoppel (c) administrative construction and offsetting partition (d) all of the above.   2. _____

3. Essential elements of a fraud based cause-of-action do not include (a) justifiable reliance (b) false statement of fact (c) knowledge of falsity (d) undue influence.   3. _____

4. Misconduct that is the basis for accountant criminal liability under State law includes (a) breach of fiduciary relationship (b) perjury (c) coercion (d) none of the above.   4. _____

5. Criminal liability for accountants under Federal tax laws includes (a) forgery (b) material alteration of accounting records (c) intentional assistance of a client to prepare false tax returns (d) all of the above.   5. _____

6. Accountant-client confidentiality issues arise in (a) tax disputes (b) civil cases (c) criminal litigation (d) all of the above.   6. _____

7. Accountant liability for false financial information contained in registration statements filed under Section 11 of the 1933 Securities Exchange Act is based on (a) careless audit procedures (b) failure to register working papers (c) confidential meetings with clients (d) all of the above.   7. _____

8. Accountants should not release confidential information drawn from client meetings unless (a) a conflict of interest exists (b) directed to do so by a court order (c) specifically provided for by enabling legislation (d) all of the above.   8. _____

9.   The test for accountant negligence under Section 11 of the 1933 Securities Exchange Act is (a) breach of a fiduciary duty (b) based on trustee duties of care (c) failure to act as prudent people would in managing their own property (d) none of the above.

9. _____

10.   Which of the following is not a valid requirement for an accountant-client contract (a) fiduciary relationship (b) mutual agreement (c) capacity (d) consideration.

10. _____

11.   _____ is accountant misconduct which triggers liability to anyone whom the accountant should have forseen would have relied on the information and would be hurt through such reliance. (a) negligence (b) chemical dependence (c) perjury (d) fraud.

11. _____

12.   An accountant cannot disclose information contained in working papers without (a) payment from the information seeker (b) first filing the papers with the Secretary of State in the client's State of residence (c) client consent or a court order (d) none of the above.

12. _____

13.   _____ is based upon an accountant's reasonable belief that financial statements accompanying a client's SEC registration statement contained accurate, true and complete information at the date the registration became effective. (a) GAAS defense (b) due diligence defense (c) statutory compliance defense (d) none of the above.

13. _____

CASE PROBLEMS - SHORT ESSAY ANSWERS: Read each case problem carefully. When appropriate, answer by stating a Decision for the case and by explaining the rationale - Rule of Law - relied upon to support your decision.

1.   Client contracts with accountant to audit client's business and submit a final annual report by May 15th. Accountant, in accepting the terms of the agreement, assures client that no trouble will be encountered in meeting the completion date. Client is relieved to hear this and repeats the importance of having the audit completed by May 15th since annual reports must be distributed to stockholders by May 20th. During the audit, accountant experiences various unexpected misfortunes: employee illnesses; equipment failure; unavailable records; weather related delays. By May 8th, accountant is less than half through with the audit and May 15th appears an unrealistic goal. What are the rights and liabilities of the parties if May 15th passes with no annual report completed? Explain.

Decision: _____

Rule of Law: _____

2.   In conducting the above audit, accountant discovers various unexplainable discrepancies in client's records. Upon notifying client of this fact, accountant is assured that these are mere "entry oversights" that will "balance out when the audit is completed." Trusting client's word, accountant makes no further inquiries. Sometime later, accountant receives an anonymous tip that client and other company directors are siphoning funds from the company. Accountant does not pursue the

matter, completes the audit and submits the final annual report pointing out the strong financial health of client's company. Relying upon the data, statements and conclusions in the report, various present stockholders in client's company increase their holdings. Shortly thereafter, the S.E.C. files fraud, theft and swindling charges against client and the firm for embezzlement and falsely representing stock value. Client's company collapses, with most stockholders incurring heavy losses. Some stockholders sue accountant for compensatory and punitive damages in an attempt to recapture their losses. Who prevails and why?

Decision: _____

Rule of Law: _____

_____

3. Pursuant to the S.E.C. prosecution mentioned above, client subpoenas accountant working papers to examine for possible evidentiary benefit. Accountant refuses and client sues. Discuss who wins and why.

Decision: _____

Rule of Law: _____

_____

4. Reread Question 1. Assume that instead of a scheduled May 15th completion date that is crucial to client, May 15th is merely referred to as a convenient completion date. By May 16th, accountant has 80% of the final report completed and requires two additional days for finishing. What are the rights and liabilities of the parties at this point?

Decision: _____

Rule of Law: _____

_____

5. In the Federal government's prosecution of client mentioned in Question 2, accountant is called to testify against client. Accountant refuses, alleging that an accountant-client privilege makes all communications between accountant and a client confidential. The judge threatens accountant with contempt unless the information is released. Who wins this dispute and why?

Decision: _____

Rule of Law: _____

_____

REGULATION OF BUSINESS UNIT
RESEARCH QUESTIONS:

1.   Two controversial areas of employment law are AIDS and drug testing of employees. What legal
        issues surround such testing programs? Explain the rationale underlying employer and employee
        perspectives on these tests. How does Federal law deal with such testing programs? How do your
        State laws deal with this controversy?

2.   A recent development in the area of corporate mergers is the hostile takeover phenomenon.
        Identify and explain arguments supporting and opposed to increased legal regulation making this
        type of merger more difficult to achieve. Research your State's laws and explain its approach to
        hostile takeover bids.

CHAPTER 46

Introduction to Real and Personal Property

SCOPE NOTE

Property rights, along with life and liberty, are among the most highly valued elements of our legal identities. English and American law view property rights as a fundamental component of a society governed by a system of laws. In the following chapters, the general principles and basic concepts of the American system of property law are discussed. What is property? What are the various categories of property interests? What limitations are placed on property ownership rights/duties? These and other concerns are the focus of attention in the upcoming readings.

EDUCATIONAL OBJECTIVES

1. Explain what is meant by the term "property."

2. Contrast the basic categories of property.

3. Develop the benefits/burdens of property ownership.

4. Distinguish between acquiring title to personal property by sale and gift.

5. Compare title through accession with title by confusion.

6. Differentiate among taking possession of lost, abandoned and mislaid property.

7. Describe the rules governing the law of fixtures.

CHAPTER OUTLINE

I. Introduction to Property - legally protected rights excluding personal liberty
   A. Kinds of Property - property classified
      1. Tangible and intangible - extent of physical, concrete form
      2. Real and personal - land or freely movable, unattached items
      3. Fixtures - attached (immovable) items

      B.   Incidents of Property Ownership - rights/duties flowing with ownership
           1.   Transfer of property during life - deed required for real property
           2.   Devolution of title on death of owner - probating decedent's estate
           3.   Taxation - sales, property, death, etc., taxes
II.   Personal Property - U.C.C. provisions govern sales of goods, investment securities, commercial paper, secured transactions
      A.   Transfer of Title
           1.   By sale - tangibles and intangibles; title in exchange for price
           2.   By gift - no return consideration
                a.   Delivery - actual v. constructive
                b.   Intent - donor's purpose
                c.   Acceptance - donee's receipt
           3.   By will or descent - follows owner's death
           4.   By accession - owner's rights to value increase; identify changes
           5.   By confusion - fungibles (identical goods) intermixed
           6.   By possession - finder of lost/mislaid property
      B.   Concurrent Ownership - single item owned by more than one person

TRUE-FALSE: Circle true or false.

Answers

T   F   1.   Generally, "property" means those legally protected rights or interests a person holds in physical things and objects.

T   F   2.   Transferring title to property in exchange for return value is referred to as a sale.

T   F   3.   The recipient of a gift is referred to as the donor.

T   F   4.   An innocent converter who changes the identity of another's personal property acquires title thereto if the value of the property has been substantially increased.

T   F   5.   When identical goods of two different owners are accidentally intermixed, all loss falls on the person who caused the "confusion."

T   F   6.   The "finder" of lost property has superior interest in the lost property as against the entire world.

T   F   7.   An owner of land on which lost property is discovered through excavation generally has a superior claim to what is found over the finder.

T   F   8.   Gratuitous promises to make gifts are usually not enforceable.

T   F   9.   When a tenant builds a brick fireplace attached to the living room wall of a leased house, the fireplace can usually be removed by the tenant upon the expiration of the lease.

T   F   10.   Transferring title to personal property is generally less formalized and ritualized than real property title transfers.

T   F   11.   When someone dies without a will, title to personal property passes directly to the decedent's heirs.

T   F   12.   Generally, intention of parties expressed in an agreement is the controlling factor determining whether an article of personal property is a fixture.

KEY TERMS - MATCHING EXERCISE: Select the term which best completes each statement below and write the corresponding number in the ANSWERS column.

Column I	Column II	Answers
1. An act transforming personal property into real property.	1. Accession	1. _____
2. A transfer of property without an exchange for return value.	2. Estoppel	2. _____
3. A category of property which includes land and all items thereon.	3. Attachment	3. _____
4. Property which cannot be reduced to physical possession.	4. Fixture	4. _____
5. Personal property which is attached to land or a building.	5. Consideration	5. _____
6. The basic distinction between a gift and a contract.	6. Conveyance	6. _____
7. Two or more people who hold title to real or personal property concurrently.	7. Gift	7. _____
8. Property that can be reduced to physical possession.	8. Co-tenants	8. _____
9. The doctrine giving an owner of property all that is added to or produced from the property.	9. Real	9. _____
10. Mixing identical goods of various different owners.	10. Deed	10. _____
11. A principal characteristic of personal property.	11. Tangible	11. _____
	12. Intangible	12. _____
	13. Donor	13. _____
	14. Personal property	14. _____
	15. Confusion	15. _____
	16. Constructive	
	17. Personal liberty	
	18. Movability	

12.   Type of delivery where the subject   19.   English Common Law
        of a gift is incapable of annual
        delivery and is accomplished by   20.   Deliberately
        delivering a symbol of ownership.   wrongful

13.   Type of taking that in cases of
        accession gives the original
        owner rights to have improved
        property returned in its value
        enhanced state.

14.   A legally protected interest – a
        right – not falling within the
        definition of property.

15.   Historical source of America's
        property system.

MULTIPLE CHOICE: Select the alternative which best completes each statement below and write the
corresponding letter in the ANSWERS column.   Answers

1.   Of the following, which is not an interest in "property" (a) an easement
        (b) the good will of a business (c) a tenant holding land for five years
        (d) all of the above.   1. _____

2.   Legal consequences related to whether property is personal or real
        include (a) what happens to title at the owner's death (b) how and where
        the property is taxed (c) how title may be effectively transferred during
        the owner's life (d) all of the above.   2. _____

3.   When A gives B the key to A's safe deposit box at Bank Friendly Full
        Service, telling B that the contents of the box are now B's, A has
        _____ delivered the safe deposit box to B. (a) constructively (b)
        actually (c) equitably (d) allocatedly.   3. _____

4.   Requirements for a valid gift include (a) donor's payment (b)
        revocability by a trustee (c) acceptance by the donee (d) all of the
        above.   4. _____

5.   A valid, effective gift must be (a) in writing (b) completed by delivery
        (c) placed in escrow if it is to be made in the future (d) between adults
        only.   5. _____

6.   Forms of concurrent property ownership do not include (a) tenancy in
        severalty (b) joint tenancy (c) community property (d) tenancy in
        common.   6. _____

7. Legal regulations relating to personal property title transfers come primarily from (a) court decisions (b) city ordinances (c) administrative agency rulings (d) none of the above.

7. _____

8. Personal property is a fixture if it (a) has become part of land (b) cannot be removed without material injury (c) is intended to be a fixture by parties (d) all of the above.

8. _____

9. "Trade fixtures" are removable by a tenant (a) provided no material injury will result to the building or land (b) at any time (c) only before the lease has expired (d) only with the consent of the landlord.

9. _____

10. Conflicts over who has superior rights to claim a fixture as theirs commonly arise between (a) Federal and State officials (b) intestate and testate heirs (c) landlords and tenants (d) bailors and bailees.

10. _____

11. Major concepts underlying America's system of property include (a) public ownership (b) constitutional protections of ownership (c) roots in French civil law (d) all of the above.

11. _____

12. Examples of intangible property include (a) patent rights (b) commercial paper (c) mortgages (d) all of the above.

12. _____

13. Where found property is classified _____, the owner of the premises where the property was found prevails over the finder. (a) mislaid (b) abandoned (c) lost (d) none of the above.

13. _____

CASE PROBLEMS - SHORT ESSAY ANSWERS: Read each case problem carefully. When appropriate, answer by stating a Decision for the case and by explaining the rationale - Rule of Law - relied upon to support your decision.

1. While strolling through the park one day, Ragmuffin comes upon a pile of fabric pieces, in assorted sizes and colors. Believing the pieces of cloth discarded junk, Ragmuffin gathers it up, takes it home and sews a beautiful coat of many colors. The fabric actually belonged to Josephine Forgetful who had lost the pieces while picnicking the day before. She lays claim to Ragmuffin's coat and sues to gain possession. Who wins? Explain.

Decision: _____

_____

Rule of Law: _____

_____

2. Generous Gene, desiring to share material wealth with others less fortunate, issues three $250,000 money orders to strangers Sam, Sean and Sallie and delivers them. Gene hears nothing from the three for six months. In the seventh month, Gene receives Sam's returned money order, which had never been deposited, with a note from Sam saying he had taken a vow of poverty and must refuse Gene's generosity. Gene's budget and accounting schedules will be substantially unsettled if the money is refused by Sam. Gene sues Sam to force him to take it. Who prevails and why?

Decision: _____

Rule of Law: _____
_____

3.   While eating lunch at Smith's restaurant, Brown finds a ring on the floor. Brown gives the ring to
       Smith to hold in case the true owner returns. When the true owner cannot be found, Brown
       demands the return of the ring. Smith refuses and Brown sues Smith for the ring. Who prevails?

       Decision: _____

       Rule of Law: _____
       _____

4.   A owns a parcel of land located just off Sunnyside Road. B has leased the land for ten years
       where he has operated a small ice cream store. B's store is made of prefabricated materials. B
       wishes to move and wants to retain the building, claiming it as a "trade fixture." Who has superior
       rights to the store and why?

       Decision: _____

       Rule of Law: _____
       _____

5.   Homeowners H and W sell their home to purchasers M and F. The purchase agreement makes no
       mention of what appliances are to be sold along with the sale of the house. H and W believe that
       no appliances will be sold while M and F believe that most of the household appliances will be
       sold along with the house. Acting on their belief, H and W remove a stereo home entertainment
       center bricked into the fireplace wall of the family room, a combination stove/oven built into the
       center of the kitchen and a lighted, 100 gallon aquarium mounted in the wall of the sunken living
       room. Finding these items absent when they take possession, M and F demand their return but H
       and W refuse. Who has superior claim to these missing items?

       Decision: _____

       Rule of Law: _____
       _____

CHAPTER 47

Bailments and Documents of Title

SCOPE NOTE

Transferring possession of goods is an everyday occurrence. The proverbial "may I borrow a cup of sugar" illustrates the pervasive influence bailments have in our private and public lives. The Chapter focuses upon the obligations that parties to a bailment owe one another, both as created by themselves and as imposed through operation of law. Explained in Chapter 47 are the general types of bailments recognized by law, how bailments are created and the rules of liability applied to the various types of bailment. Also discussed in the Chapter are two special cases of bailments, freight transporters and lodging operators.

With the increased national focus of America's economy, interstate flow of goods and people has expanded. Along with this development, the area of law controlling legal relationship between hotelkeepers and guests, owners and storers of goods as well as carriers and shippers has grown in importance. What is the hotelkeeper's obligation to protect the safety and property of patrons? To what extent are hotel guests responsible for their own protection? What restrictions are placed on a carrier's choice to discriminate among potential passengers and shippers? What liabilities are faced by storers of goods? These and related concerns are also discussed in Chapter 47. The Chapter closes with an examination of the types and functions of documents of title.

EDUCATIONAL OBJECTIVES

1. Define and discuss the importance of bailments.

2. Identify characteristics of a bailment that distinguish it from other property transactions.

3. Differentiate the rights/duties of parties to a bailment associated with the various types of bailments.

4. Describe classes of bailments and the related degrees of care required by the parties associated with them.

5. Distinguish among common possessory liens on personal property.

311

6.   Identify the type of and rationale for a hotelkeeper's protective duty to guests and their property.

7.   Discuss the differences between common law and statutory definitions of hotelkeeper liability.

8.   Explain definitional and liability differences between private and common carriers of goods.

9.   Outline the breadth of and defenses to common carrier liability for freight damage during transit as well as warehousers liability for stored goods.

10.   Discuss the role played by title documents in sales transactions.

11.   Identify the two most common documents of title used in sales of goods and the rights/duties of parties under those documents.

12.   Discuss the significance of negotiability and the rights/duties of the parties related to the process of "due negotiation."

CHAPTER OUTLINE

I.   Bailments
       A.   Types of Bailments
             1.   Sole benefit of bailor
             2.   Sole benefit of bailee
             3.   Mutual benefit of both parties
       B.   Essential Elements of a Bailment - transfer of possession of personal property between bailor and bailee
             1.   Delivery of possession - bailee exercises control
             2.   Personal property - tangible
             3.   Possession for a determinable time - contrasted to sales and other title transfers
             4.   Restoration of possession to the bailor - at end of bailment; bailment terminates by mutual assent, breach, destruction of property
       C.   Rights and Duties of Bailor and Bailee
             1.   Bailee's duty to exercise due care - degree of care required to protect goods; type of bailment
             2.   Bailee's absolute liability - return undamaged property; presumption against bailee; liability for misdelivery
             3.   Bailee's rights to compensation - reasonable payment for work in connection with bailment
       D.   Special Types of Bailments
             1.   Pledges - personal property transfered to secure a debt
             2.   Warehousing - storage of goods
             3.   Carriers of goods - common carrier/private carrier; consignor/consignee
                   a.   Duty to carry - to public (common carrier) or to contract party (private carrier)
                   b.   Liability for loss or damage - type of carrier
                   c.   Duty to deliver to the right person
             4.   Innkeepers - liability for damage or loss; common law v. statutory law
II.   Documents of Title - written document representing ownership
       A.   Types of Documents of Title - goods being shipped or stored
             1.   Warehouse receipts - goods in storage

            a.   Duties of warehouseman - reasonable care to prevent loss, damage
            b.   Lien of warehouseman - against goods for payment
        2.   Bills of lading - goods being shipped
            a.   Duties of issuer of bill of lading - delivery as per terms of document
            b.   Through bills of lading - connecting carriers
            c.   Lien of carrier - against goods for payment
    B.   Negotiability of Documents of Title - negotiable (to order of bearer) contrasted with non-
          negotiable (specifically named recipient)
        1.   Due negotiation - purchaser, in good faith, without notice, in regular course of
              business
        2.   Rights acquired by due negotiation - transferor's rights or greater (from document
              itself)
        3.   Rights acquired in the absence of due negotiation - transforor's rights only
        4.   Warranties - genuineness; no knowledge of defect; rightful negotiation
        5.   Ineffective documents of title - rightful contrasted to wrongful delivery
        6.   Lost or missing documents of title - issuance of substitute document

TRUE-FALSE: Circle true or false.

Answers

T   F   1.   A negotiable bill of lading provides for the delivery of goods to the bearer or to the
                    order of the named person.

T   F   2.   Carriers have a lien for unpaid charges which may be enforced by public or private
                    sale of the goods shipped.

T   F   3.   Warehousemen are statutorily prohibited from limiting their liability through
                    contractual provisions.

T   F   4.   Finders of abandoned property and donees of gifts are bailees.

T   F   5.   A bailment presumes separation of ownership and possession between different people.

T   F   6.   When bailed goods are destroyed, the law presumes that the bailor negligently caused
                    the damage.

T   F   7.   An owner of a document of title has ownership of the goods covered only if
                    accompanied by actual, physical possession of the goods.

T   F   8.   Both private and common carriers have an absolute duty to deliver goods to the
                    correct person.

T   F   9.   A warehouseman has no separate, enforceable right against goods to secure and
                    enforce payment for services.

T   F   10.   Extraordinary bailees are generally insurers of the safety of the goods bailed.

T   F   11.   The carrier of goods subject to a bearer or order title document has no further liability under the shipping contract once the goods are delivered at the destination point, regardless of whether the carrier obtains possession of the document.

T   F   12.   Naming in a negotiable title document the person to receive notice upon the arrival of goods does not limit the document's negotiability.

KEY TERMS - MATCHING EXERCISE: Select the term which best completes each statement below and write the corresponding number in the ANSWERS column.

Column I	Column II	Answers
1. The person to whom goods are to be delivered by a carrier.	1. Extraordinary	1. _____
	2. Warehouser	2. _____
2. The relationship created when a person parks a car in a parking lot, pays a charge, receives a ticket, locks the car and takes the keys.	3. Bailee	3. _____
	4. Consignee	4. _____
3. The person to whom property is transferred under a bailment.	5. Lease	5. _____
4. Title document issued by a carrier or transporter of goods.	6. Bill of Lading	6. _____
	7. Abandoned	7. _____
5. A bailment for the purpose of securing payment on a debt.	8. Possession	8. _____
	9. Common	9. _____
6. A transaction in which possession of personal property is delivered without a transfer of title.	10. Custody	10. _____
	11. Bailment	11. _____
7. A bailee who receives compensation for storing goods.	12. Pledge	12. _____
8. A transporter of goods offering services and facilities to the public indifferently and not in a casual or individual manner.	13. Private carrier	13. _____
	14. Common carrier	14. _____
	15. Negotiation	15. _____
9. One carrying another's goods only on isolated occasions, serving a limited number of customers under single, long term contract.	16. Non-negotiable	
	17. Good faith purchaser	

10. Method of transferring rights to title documents under which the transferee can acquire rights greater than the assignor.

11. A document of title made out to "bearer" or "order" of a named person.

12. A document of title under which delivery of goods, without surrender of the document, completely discharges the carrier or warehouser from further contractual liability.

13. Bills of lading which specify connecting carriers.

14. One taking an interest in goods sold to enforce a lien free of any rights of the persons against whom the lien was valid.

15. Written document representing ownership in goods.

18. Document of title

19. Negotiable

20. Through bills

MULTIPLE CHOICE: Select the alternative which best completes each statement below and write the corresponding letter in the ANSWERS column.

Answers

1. Transferors for value of documents of title warrant (a) the genuineness of the document (b) the rightfulness of the transfer (c) no knowledge of any fact impairing the validity of worth of the document (d) all of the above.

1. _____

2. A bailment in which the bailee must exercise greater care than a reasonably prudent person is a bailment for the benefit of the (a) bailee (b) bailor (c) bailor and bailee (d) third person.

2. _____

3. A non-negotiable document of title is transferable only by (a) negotiation (b) the process of laches (c) assignment (d) ratification.

3. _____

4. Property subject to bailment includes (a) promissory notes (b) corporate bonds (c) treasury bonds (d) all of the above.

4. _____

5. Unauthorized use of the bailed goods by the bailee is considered (a) misappropriation (b) trespass (c) assumption of risk (d) immaterial if the possession is lawful.

5. _____

6.   A document of title issued by a carrier who promises to deliver goods to
       the named consignee is a (a) straight bill of lading (b) destination receipt   6. _____
       (c) delivery order (d) sub-bill.

7.   A bailment is not automatically terminated by (a) mutual consent (b)
       breach of the agreement by the bailor (c) destruction of the goods (d)   7. _____
       accomplishment of the purpose of the bailment.

8.   The liability a private carrier owes to the goods transported is that of (a)   8. _____
       an insurer (b) a bailee (c) a reasonable person (d) slight care.

9.   Essential elements to a bailment include (a) transfers of real property (b)
       parties known as buyer and seller (c) conveyance of title but not   9. _____
       possession (d) none of the above.

10. . When a document of title is lost, the claimant of the goods (a) may seek
       an issuance of a substitute document from courts (b) must find the
       document or surrender right to delivery (c) has lost all delivery rights
       (d) can use the doctrine of detrimental reliance to gain possession of the   10. _____
       goods.

11.   Code requirements for "due negotiation" of title documents include all of
       the following except (a) purchase for value (b) in good faith (c) as   11. _____
       settlement or payment of debt (d) none of the above.

12.   Duly negotiating documents of title (a) cuts off defenses and claims
       valid against the transferor (b) creates new rights in the holder (c)
       facilitates credit extensions based on such documents (d) all of the   12. _____
       above.

13.   Persons who cut off transferee rights under transfer of a non-negotiable
       title document include (a) bailee creditors (b) transferor creditors (c) any   13. _____
       good faith purchase for value (d) all of the above.

CASE PROBLEMS - SHORT ESSAY ANSWERS: Read each case problem carefully.   When
appropriate, answer by stating a Decision for the case and by explaining the rationale - Rule of Law -
relied upon to support your decision.

1.   T, a thief, bails goods stolen from owner O with carrier C and, in return, receives a negotiable bill
       of lading. The bill, transferred several times, is eventually duly negotiated to H. H and original
       owner O both claim the goods. Who wins and why?

       Decision: _____

       _____

       Rule of Law: _____

       _____

2.   Cheesemaker C sues warehouseman W for damage done to C's stored cheese, asserting W's
       negligence as the cause. The warehouse receipt C received from W provided: "All stored property

is at the owner's risk of loss or damage from riot, fire, water, deterioration, leakage, frost, the goods being perishable or otherwise inherently defective." W failed to keep an even temperature in the storage rooms and the cheese became moldy. W argues that the warehouse receipt exempts any liability for the damage to the cheese. Who prevails? Discuss.

Decision: _____

Rule of Law: _____

_____

3. A hires B to deliver a stove to a certain address. B accidentally delivers it to the wrong house which B cannot later locate. Is B liable for this loss? Discuss.

Decision: _____

Rule of Law: _____

_____

4. A lends B $50 and takes B's gold watch in exchange as collateral. A sells the watch to C fully informing C of the situation. Is A guilty of conversion? Explain.

Decision: _____

Rule of Law: _____

_____

5. Ms. Guest spends a night at Innkeeper Hotel. Guest has with her a $2,500 Swiss watch. Innkeeper has a hotel safe for protecting customer valuables. No notice of its availability is posted at the registration desk or in any of the individual guest rooms. When Guest registers, Innkeeper fails to mention the safe. Sometime during the night, following Guest's check-in, a thief enters her room and steals the watch. Who bears the loss of the watch and why?

Decision: _____

Rule of Law: _____

_____

Interests in Real Property

SCOPE NOTE

The legal doctrines relating to the ownership use and transfer of interests in land are discussed in Chapters 48 and 49. This is an extremely technical and complicated area of law due partly to the fact that the basis for our system of real property law lies in the highly formalized, intricate structure of feudal land-tenure which dominated English law during the 13th and 14th centuries. Chapter 48 introduces the study of real property law by discussing the types of ownership interests in real property. The terms and doctrines associated with freehold and non-freehold interests in land are examined.

Chapter 48 continues by contrasting ownership of land held by one person (ownership "in severalty") to ownership shared by several people (ownership in co-tenancy). Possessory interests in real property (reducible to control and occupancy) are distinguished from non-possessory (incapable of control and occupancy) interests. The essential doctrines associated with forms of concurrent (multiple) ownership are developed. Also examined are the legal principles which control the legal relationship of co-owners (co-tenants) of real property. The Chapter closes with a discussion of the types of interests one may hold in another's land and the nature of the reciprocal rights/duties among the parties to such a legal relationship.

EDUCATIONAL OBJECTIVES

1. Define real property and differentiate freehold from non-freehold interests in land.

2. Identify, outline the essential characteristics of, and explain the means of creating recognized fee simple estates.

3. Describe the unique characteristics of, the methods for creating, and the purposes served by a life estate.

4. Explain the types of future interests associated with qualified or conditional estates.

5. Contrast vested with contingent future interests and how they are affected by the Rule Against Perpetuities.

6.   Distinguish the various classes of leasehold estates and how they are created.

7.   Discuss the methods used and the consequences of parties to a leasehold transferring their respective interests to other individuals.

8.   Outline the rights/duties of the parties to a rental agreement and how they are influenced by such factors as condition of the premises, presence of government regulation and acts of the parties.

9.   Contrast common forms of concurrent ownership in terms of their definitional characteristics, method of creation and purposes served.

10.   Compare the types of easements and discuss how they are created.

11.   Differentiate between profits aprendre and licenses.

CHAPTER OUTLINE

I.   Freehold Estates - immediate possession and ownership at least for life
      A.   Fee Estates - immediate possession
            1.   Fee simple - absolute ownership; transferable and inheritable
            2.   Base or qualified fee - certain conditions restrict title
      B.   Life Estates - terminable at death
            1.   Conventional life estates - created by agreement; life tenant and remainderman
            2.   Life estates established by law - followed death of a spouse; existed under common law
                  a.   Dower - held by surviving wife
                  b.   Curtesy - held by surviving husband
      C.   Future Interests - not immediately possessory; takes effect in future
            1.   Reversions - held by grantor/grantor's heirs; tied to life estate
            2.   Remainders - held by person other than grantor/grantor's heirs
                  a.   Vested remainders - no condition other than termination of intermediate estate
                  b.   Contingent remainders - possession subject to specified condition
                  c.   Rule Against Perpetuities - limit on length, complexity of contingent remainder
II.   Leasehold Estates - landowner grants possession rights to another for definite time
      A.   Creation and Duration - usually by agreement
            1.   Definite terms - automatic termination at end of specified term
            2.   Periodic tenancy - indefinite succession of specific term
            3.   Tenancy at will - terminates by act of either party at any time
            4.   Tenancy at sufferance - possession without a valid lease
      B.   Transfer of Interests - original parties to lease (landlord and tenant) seek replacement by a third party
            1.   Transfers by landlord - tenant's lease valid under time of original agreement
            2.   Transfers by tenant
                  a.   Assignment - tenant transfers all interest; has no reversion; tenant still has payment obligation
                  b.   Sublease - tenant transfers less than full interest; sublessee liable to tenant, not landlord
      C.   Tenant's Obligations - rent payment; no damage, loss to unit
            1.   Destruction of the premises - lease usually calls for landlord to repair; suspension of

rent until unit usable
2. Eviction or abandonment - landlord orders tenant to leave or tenant leaves prior to expiration of rental term
   a. Dispossession by landlord for breach of covenant - lease terminates upon landlord's rightful eviction
   b. Wrongful abandonment by tenant - rent payment duty ends upon re-entry, re-letting
   c. Wrongful eviction by landlord - landlord breaches quiet enjoyment right; tenant's duties are terminated
D. Landlord's Obligations
1. Quiet enjoyment
2. Fitness for use
3. Repair - duty arises from statute or contract; applies to areas remaining under landlord's control
III. Concurrent Ownership - ownership held by two or more persons (co-tenants)
   A. Joint Tenancy - survivorship characteristic; four unities requirement
   B. Tenancy in Common - estate of inheritance; unity of possession
   C. Tenancy by the Entireties - joint tenancy held by husband and wife
   D. Community Property - by statute in some States; applies to marital property
   E. Condominiums - ownership of single unit; tenant in common for rest of facility
   F. Cooperatives - group owns whole and leases back separate units to shareholding tenants
IV. Nonpossessory Interests - limited rights in another's land
   A. Easements - use of another's land for specific purpose
      1. Types of easements - in gross (personal to parties) or appurtenant (runs with land)
      2. Creation of easements
         a. Express grant or reservation - written agreement between parties
         b. Implied grant or reservation - arises from established use and division of land
         c. Necessity - arises through operation of law to preserve use
         d. Dedication - public use
         e. Prescription - arises through adverse use
   B. Profits A Prendre - right to remove "valuables" (trees, minerals, etc.)
   C. Licenses - slightest permission to use land; protection against trespass

TRUE-FALSE: Circle true or false.

Answers

T   F   1. A fee simple estate is of indefinite duration and could therefore last forever.

T   F   2. By statute in most States today, joint tenancy can be created by a conveyance "to A and B and their heirs."

T   F   3. "To A and his heirs" is the only language that can effectively create a fee simple estate today.

T   F   4. At common law, landlords had no obligation to keep rented residential premises in habitable/tenantable condition.

T   F   5. Survivorship refers to the interest of a joint tenant passing to his heirs at his death.

T   F   6.   Concurrent ownership does not mean two or more persons owning specific and separate portions of property.

T   F   7.   A license, like an easement, creates an interest in real property.

T   F   8.   Where a tenant has expressly agreed to pay rent in the rental agreement, an assignment of the lease to another person does not free the first tenant from further rent payment obligation.

T   F   9.   Most courts hold that when a tenant wrongfully abandons rented premises and the landlord rerents the premises to another, the abandoning tenant's obligation to pay rent ceases.

T   F   10.   Divorce automatically terminates a tenancy by the entireties.

T   F   11.   When a lease does not mention time for rent payment, rent is due and payable at the end of the rental term.

T   F   12.   Under a contingent remainder, the remainderman has rights to immediate possession upon termination of the preceding estate.

KEY TERMS - MATCHING EXERCISE: Select the term which best completes each statement below and write the corresponding number in the ANSWERS column.

Column I	Column II	Answers
1. A future interest held by one not the grantor or the grantor's heirs.	1. Periodic tenancy	1. _____
2. Failure to care properly for property which is held for only a limited time.	2. Life estate	2. _____
3. Easements which create rights and duties pertaining to the land itself and not personal to the parties that created them.	3. Appurtenant	3. _____
	4. Waste	4. _____
	5. Remainder	5. _____
4. The interest retained by a grantor or his heirs when no disposition is made of the balance of a life estate.	6. Partition	6. _____
	7. Vested	7. _____
5. A type of co-ownership recognized in some States creating a one-half undivided interest between spouses in property acquired during marriage.	8. Constructive eviction	8. _____
	9. Reversion	9. _____
	10. Assignment	10. _____
6. The parcel of land which is benefitted by an easement.	11. Profit aprendre	11. _____

7. The doctrine which allows a tenant to abandon rented premises and terminate a lease when a landlord has failed to meet the terms of the lease.

8. The right to harvest the crops from the land of another.

9. The act of changing undivided interests in land into separate and divided interests.

10. A future interest which has as its only condition to possession the termination of the preceding estate.

11. Common law life estate surviving husband had in deceased wife's real property.

12. Tenant's holding land after expiration of a lease.

13. Someone who has temporary use and possession of another's land.

14. Holding land for an indefinite period subject to termination by either party to the agreement.

15. Life estate held by a wife in deceased husband's real property.

12. Dominant estate   12. _____

13. Contingent   13. _____

14. Possibility of   14. _____
    reverter
                             15. _____
15. Community property

16. Tenant

17. Tenancy at sufferance

18. Dower

19. Tenancy at will

20. Courtesy

MULTIPLE CHOICE: Select the alternative which best completes each statement below and write the corresponding letter in the ANSWERS column.

Answers

1. When a tenant under an eight-year lease transfers the premises to another person for a five-year period, the transfer is called a/n (a) conditional apportionment (b) assignment (c) sublease (d) equitable allocation.

1. _____

2. A tenancy in common may be created by (a) operation of law (b) an ineffective attempt to create a joint tenancy (c) more than one instrument (d) all of the above.

2. _____

3.   A wife's dower right in her husband's property (a) is an example of a conventional life estate (b) passes to her all of his real property when he dies (c) is an example of a life estate created by operation of law (d) stems from statutory law.

3. _____

4.   An in gross easement is (a) personal to the parties that created it (b) similar in purpose to a zoning restriction (c) nothing more than a negative covenant (d) much like a constructive trust.

4. _____

5.   The purpose of the rule against perpetuities is to (a) discourage any transfer of property within the immediate family (b) allow States to heavily tax property in lower income neighborhoods (c) facilitate easy transfer of land by eliminating clouds on title stemming from contingent future interests (d) tax equally inherited and income producing property.

5. _____

6.   The type of co-ownership by which a buyer acquires separate title to a purchased unit while also becoming a tenant in common vis-a-vis the common facilities of which the unit is a part is called a (a) condominium (b) cooperative (c) tenancy by estoppel (d) unified severalty.

6. _____

7.   Creation of concurrent ownership by the same instrument is an absolute requirement of (a) community property (b) tenancy at will (c) tenancy in common (d) joint tenancy.

7. _____

8.   Among the four "unities" that exist, the only one required of a tenancy in common is the unity of (a) possession (b) time (c) title (d) interest.

8. _____

9.   A rental agreement covering a definite period of time (a) expires automatically at the end of the stated rental term (b) terminates only upon one of the parties giving notice (c) is automatically renewed if no termination notice is given (d) none of the above.

9. _____

10. Under common law, a tenant must repair (a) damage caused by ordinary wear and tear (b) extraordinary damage even though caused without fault (c) damages which are caused by fault (d) all of the above.

10. _____

11. _____ is an indirect form of co-ownership which gives shareholders leasehold rights to individual units (a) tenancy by entireties (b) cooperative (c) tenancy by estoppel (d) condominium.

11. _____

12. Easements are created by (a) estoppel (b) eviction (c) reservation (d) all of the above.

12. _____

13. Landlord's obligation not to disrupt the tenant's possession and use of the premises is known as the covenant of (a) repair (b) habitability (c) no disposition (d) quiet enjoyment.

13. _____

CASE PROBLEMS - SHORT ESSAY ANSWERS: Read each case problem carefully. When appropriate, answer by stating a Decision for the case and by explaining the rationale - Rule of Law - relied upon to support your decision.

1.   A, B, and C are joint-tenant owners of Greenacre. C conveys an interest in the land to D. Following this action, A dies. What form or forms and percentage of concurrent ownership exist between the surviving parties? Explain.

Decision: _____

Rule of Law: _____

2.   A conveys land "to B so long as the property is used for church purposes." B sells the property to C, who builds a liquor store on the property. A and B are dead. A's heirs, B's heirs and C claim the property. Who prevails? Discuss.

Decision: _____

Rule of Law: _____

3.   H is a tenant in common owner of a dairy farm with A, a joint tenant owner of a ranch with B, and a life tenant of a poultry farm. When H dies, what dower rights would his surviving wife have in these three property interests? Explain.

Decision: _____

Rule of Law: _____

4.   A has a right to cross neighbor B's land. When B sells the land to C, may C stop A from crossing the land? Explain.

Decision: _____

Rule of Law: _____

5.   A conveys, by deed, an undivided one-half interest in Blackacre to B and wills the other one-half interest in the same land to C, stating in both documents that C and B are to hold as "joint tenants." A dies. Are B and C joint-tenant owners of Blackacre? Explain.

Decision: _____

Rule of Law: _____

Transfer and Control of Real Property

SCOPE NOTE

Title to real property may be transferred in many ways. Ownership may pass to government (through tax default, escheat, dedication or eminent domain) or out from government (through grants and tax sales). Events (marriage, movement of air and water) may trigger the passage of title. Acts by the present owner (sale, gift) or inaction by the present owner (adverse possession, mortgage foreclosure proceedings) may pass title. In Chapter 49, the legal principles controlling methods of acquiring title to real property are discussed in the context of purchase agreements, security interests in land and adverse possession.

As a general rule, owners of real property enjoy the benefits of ownership according to their own wishes with little outside interference. Under various circumstances, however, public (government regulation) and private (contractual controls) limitations are placed on the manner and degree to which one may enjoy the incidents of real property ownership. To protect and promote the general welfare of society as well as to effectuate the intent of contractual provisions, are reasons for restricting how one may exercise title interests on land. Chapter 49 also focuses on the conflicting goals involved in facilitating enjoyment of the incidents of title on the one hand and promoting the general welfare of society through public and private controls on ownership on the other.

EDUCATIONAL OBJECTIVES

1.   Outline the major steps involved in purchasing real property.

2.   Explain formation requirements for valid land sales contracts.

3.   Define and discuss the significance of marketable title.

4.   Discuss the importance of deeds and distinguish among the various types of deeds.

5.   List execution requirements for a valid deed.

6.   Develop the importance of delivery and recording deeds in terms of their effectiveness.

7.   Define and explain the significance of adverse possession.

8.   Discuss the purpose and execution requirements of mortgages.

9.   Identify the rights/duties of parties to a mortgage and how their legal relationship is affected by transfers of the mortgage interest.

10.   Outline various issues and problems related to discharge, foreclosure and redemption of mortgages.

11.   Define and discuss the importance of eminent domain.

12.   Specify how the public use, just compensation and due process doctrines relate to eminant domain.

13.   Describe the purposes served by zoning ordinances.

14.   Distinguish among the various ways of avoiding zoning limitations.

15.   List the types and ways of creating private controls over land.

16.   Discuss how restrictive covenants are interpreted and how they are terminated.

CHAPTER OUTLINE

I.   Transfer of Real Property
       A.   Contract for Sale
            1.   Formation - written agreement: names; description; time; deed; price
            2.   Marketable title - implied duty of seller; free from certain defects
            3.   Implied warranty of habitability - suitable for human use
       B.   Deeds - written document conveying title
            1.   Types of deeds - extent of liability of grantor for title defects
                  a.   Warranty - grantor assures no defects
                  b.   Special warranty - grantor assures no conduct that impairs title
                  c.   Quitclaim - grantor makes no title assurances
            2.   Formal requirements - valid, enforceable deed
                  a.   Consideration - usually not required (gift)
                  b.   Description of land - clear, certain identification
                  c.   Quantity of the estate - title interest transferred
                  d.   Covenant of title - undisturbed (quiet enjoyment) ownership in buyer
                  e.   Execution - protection against competing interests
       C.   Secured Transactions - land used as security in credit extension; involves debt, creditor interest in specified land
            1.   Form of mortgages - writing; parties named; land described
            2.   Rights and duties - lien contrasted to title approaches: ownership and possession
            3.   Transfer of mortgage interests - purchaser of mortgaged land and liability for transferor's debt; contrast purchases "subject to" with "assumption of" outstanding mortgage
            4.   Foreclosure - regaining property following default; deficiency judgments
       D.   Adverse Possession - title passages without deed or regular formality; hostile use to owner; statute of limitation restrictions

II.   Public and Private Controls - restrictions on property use and ownership
    A.   Zoning - public control over land use
        1.   Enabling acts and zoning ordinances - regulate land use in local areas
        2.   Variance - avoid regulations based on hardship
        3.   Non-conforming uses - reasonable time to adjust to new restrictions
        4.   Judicial review of zoning - grounds for court invalidating zoning ordinance
            a.   Invalidity of zoning ordinance - unreasonable application of authority; no reasonable relation to protecting health, safety, etc.
            b.   Zoning amounts to a taking - restriction prevents any beneficial use
    B.   Eminent Domain - power to convert private property to public use
        1.   Public use - condemnation power is delegatable
        2.   Just compensation - fair market value
    C.   Private Restrictions Upon Land Use - contractual, deed clauses restrict land use
        1.   Nature of restrictive covenants
        2.   Type and construction of restrictive covenants
        3.   Termination of restrictive covenants
        4.   Validity of restrictive covenants

TRUE-FALSE: Circle true or false.

Answers

T   F   1.   Most States follow the common law rule that after the land sales contract is made, risk of loss to the real property passes to the seller.

T   F   2.   A quitclaim deed could convey as much interest in land as a warranty deed.

T   F   3.   A warranty deed does not transfer an after-acquired title.

T   F   4.   The contract for the sale of land impliedly requires that the seller convey a marketable title to the buyer.

T   F   5.   Recording a deed is always necessary for title to pass from the grantor to the grantee.

T   F   6.   A mortgagor may generally assign the mortgage to a third person without having to receive the mortgagee's consent unless the mortgage agreement provides otherwise.

T   F   7.   The police power of government may be employed to regulate property use as well as to take property.

T   F   8.   The power of eminent domain may not be delegated to private enterprise.

T   F   9.   Compensation for property taken under eminent domain is determined on the basis of market value of the property condemned.

T   F   10.   The usual method for enforcing restrictive covenants is a suit for money damages.

T   F   11.   In real estate secured transactions, the creditor is the mortgagee and the debtor the mortgagor.

T   F   12.   Most states have adopted the "lien" approach to mortgage law.

KEY TERMS - MATCHING EXERCISE: Select the term which best completes each statement below and write the corresponding number in the ANSWERS column.

	Column I		Column II		Answers
1.	A method for freeing property from zoning restrictions in cases of "particular hardship."	1.	After acquired title	1.	_____
		2.	Variance	2.	_____
2.	The statutory basis of authority for city zoning powers.	3.	Eminent domain	3.	_____
		4.	Warranty deed	4.	_____
3.	A constitutional principle protecting the interests of private property owners from unreasonable exercises of eminant domain powers.	5.	Quitclaim deed	5.	_____
		6.	Adverse possession	6.	_____
4.	A third person who receives a deed from the grantor and holds it for the grantee for a certain time period.	7.	Escrow agent	7.	_____
		8.	Due process	8.	_____
5.	Private limitations placed upon how land may be used.	9.	Deficiency judgment	9.	_____
6.	A method of transferring title to land involuntarily.	10.	Conveyance	10.	_____
7.	A deed under which grantor assumes all liability for any title defects.	11.	Enabling laws	11.	_____
		12.	Trust deed	12.	_____
8.	Document in a secured real estate transaction conveying property to a third person to hold for the benefit of the creditor.	13.	Allonge	13.	_____
		14.	Restrictive covenant	14.	_____
9.	The power to convert private property to public use.	15.	Allocation	15.	_____
		16.	Foreclosure		
10.	An action taken by the mortgagee against the mortgagor to recover any balance still owing on the debt when foreclosure proceedings are insufficient to satisfy the full debt owing.	17.	Title theory		
		18.	Police power		
		19.	Confiscation		
		20.	Redemption		

11. Common law doctrine giving ownership
     rights and possession to the
     mortgagee in secured real estate
     transactions.

12. Mortgagor's right to remove a
     mortgage lien by paying off the
     debt in full.

13. Mortgagee's debt satisfaction rights
     following mortgagor's default.

14. Regulatory action resulting in
     property owner's being deprived of
     any and all beneficial use of
     their land.

15. Regulatory authority of government to
     protect public health, safety and
     morals.

MULTIPLE CHOICE: Select the alternative which best completes each statement below and write the
corresponding letter in the ANSWERS column.

Answers

1.   Private property may be taken by the government if (a) private use is to
     be made of the property (b) the owner is reimbursed the purchase price
     paid for the property (c) due process has been followed in condemnation
     proceedings (d) an equitable trust is established in the owner's name.   1. _____

2.   The disputed level of just compensation accompanying condemnation is
     determined by (a) a jury in equity (b) administrative law judges (c) state
     compensation boards (d) court of law.   2. _____

3.   Acknowledgement of the deed is necessary to (a) bind the grantor and
     grantee (b) record the deed (c) have it be effective against an escrow
     agent (d) all of the above.   3. _____

4.   Which of the following is not necessary for the valid transfer of land (a)
     delivery of the deed (b) the grantor's intention to make a transfer (c) a
     title search (d) grantor's issuing a deed.   4. _____

5.   Of the following, which is not an absolute requirement for adverse
     possession to ripen into title (a) open and continuous possession (b)
     constructive possession (c) possession for a required statutory time period
     (d) possession without owner's consent.   5. _____

6.   A marketable title is free from (a) all encumbrances except mortgages
     (b) all encumbrances except easements (c) zoning restrictions (d) title
     defects appearing in the chain of title available through land records.   6. _____

7.   Compensation for condemned property is given to (a) holders of
       contingent remainders (b) owners of the property taken (c) wife for her
       dower interest in her living husband's land (d) none of the above.   7. _____

8.   A purchaser of mortgaged real property is not personally liable for the
       mortgage debt unless (a) the mortgage note is pledged (b) the property is
       taken "subject to" the mortgage (c) the mortgage is "expressly assumed"
       by the purchaser (d) notice is given to the assignor.   8. _____

9.   The primary tool for public regulation of private land use is a (a) zoning
       ordinance (b) restrictive statute (c) court decision (d) condemnation
       proceeding.   9. _____

10.   Which of the following is not an example of restrictive covenant (a) a
       covenant that limits the use of property to residential purposes (b) a
       restriction specifying the minimum cost of each house that is built in a
       given area (c) a covenant against encumbrances (d) a covenant
       prohibiting the sale of intoxicating beverages.   10. _____

11.   In a lien theory state (a) mortgagee has title (b) mortgagor has possession
       and title (c) mortgagee has possession (d) none of the above.   11. _____

12.   Clause in mortgage contract allowing mortgagee to sell the property
       without a court order is a (a) strict redemption (b) judicial sale (c)
       equitable deficiency (d) power of sale clause.   12. _____

13.   Secured real estate transactions are governed by (a) State statute and
       common law (b) the U.C.C. (c) Federal real estate laws (d) none of the
       above.   13. _____

CASE PROBLEMS - SHORT ESSAY ANSWERS: Read each case problem carefully.   When
appropriate, answer by stating a Decision for the case and by explaining the rationale - Rule of Law -
relied upon to support your decision.

1.   A restrictive covenant banning the sale of cigarettes within the village of Bloomfield has been in
       existence for fifty years. For the past ten years, two tobacco shops and three pharmacies have
       been selling cigarettes in the village. When Frank Cooper decides to sell cigarettes from vending
       machines in his general store in Bloomfield, will he be prohibited by the covenant? Explain.

       Decision: _____

       _____

       Rule of Law: _____

       _____

2.   Wing and Wang Chan, husband and wife, are recent arrivees from China. Desiring to settle
       quickly, they hire a real estate agent and start looking for a home. They find a "priced-right"
       dream house and submit a purchase offer. Their bid is refused and upon further inquiry they
       learn that no homes in the area may be sold to persons of Asian descent according to the dictates
       of the original deed from the first owner of the tract development. Dismayed, the Chans seek

your advice. What can you tell them?

Decision: _____

_____

Rule of Law: _____

_____

3.   A has been operating a junk yard within the city limits of Springfield for the past 35 years. The Springfield City Council passes a zoning ordinance forbidding the presence of junk yards within the city limits.   The city demands that A shut down his junk yard immediately and A refuses. The city then sues A. Who wins and why?

Decision: _____

_____

Rule of Law: _____

_____

4.   L owns an undeveloped 2 acre lot in a run down area of mixed residential and light commercial use. The city adopts an urban renewal plan for the area which provides for the location of a park on L's site.   State and Federal officials have not yet approved the plan nor has funding or a developer been located.   As part of its plan, the city states that landowners who build on lots scheduled for condemnation will not be compensated for the loss of those buildings when condemnation proceedings commence.   L believes the city's plan is unfair and asks for advice. What advice will you give?

Decision: _____

_____

Rule of Law: _____

_____

5.   Railroad Company R.R. wants to increase the width of its roadbeds which abut A's land. R.R. approaches A, requesting to purchase land from A.   A refuses to sell the land arguing that widened roadbeds are not necessary. Railroad company fears loss of business if its tracks are not widened. Can the company force A to give up the land? Explain.

Decision: _____

_____

Rule of Law: _____

_____

CHAPTER 50
Trusts and Wills

SCOPE NOTE

At various times during our financial lives, we might find it necessary and worthwhile to transfer control of property we own to another person to manage for our own benefit or for the benefit of a third party. Such arrangements are called trusts. Under what circumstances are trusts useful devices? What formalities are associated with the creation of a trust? What is the nature of the legal relationship between the parties to a trust? Chapter 50 focuses upon these and other matters in its discussion of the law of trusts, its vocabulary, and essential doctrines. Chapter 50 also provides a general overview of the law of testate and intestate succession and how property passes following the death of its owner. Attention is placed on the benefits/costs of dying without a will. Also discussed in the Chapter is the process of property distribution following death.

EDUCATIONAL OBJECTIVES

1.   Explain the nature and purpose of trusts.

2.   Discuss the requirements for establishing a valid, enforceable trust.

3.   Identify the parties to a trust and outline their individual and mutual rights and duties.

4.   Describe how the existence of a trust may come to an end.

5.   Differentiate the various types and classes of trusts.

6.   Differentiate testate and intestate succession.

7.   Explain the nature and purpose of a will.

8.   Identify the requirements for drafting a valid will.

9.   List the types and respective characteristics of recognized wills.

10.   Discuss the events and acts associated with altering/revoking a will.

11.   Understand under what circumstances an apparently valid testamentary instrument will not be

enforced.

12.   Know the rights of beneficiaries and the spouse of the decedent under a will.

13.   Define and identify the problems associated with abatement and ademption.

14.   Explain the purpose and role of the Uniform Probate Code.

15.   Discuss how and to whom property passes when its owner dies without a valid enforceable will.

16.   Outline the probate duties of a personal representative.

17.   Describe the tax consequences of death.

CHAPTER OUTLINE

I.   Trusts
    A.   Types of Trusts
        1.   Express trusts - an oral or written trust established by voluntary action.
            a.   Charitable trusts - any trust that has for its purpose the improvement of humankind.
            b.   Spendthrift trusts - a provision in a trust instrument under which the trust estate is removed from the beneficiary's control and from liability for her individual debts.
            c.   Totten trusts - is a joint bank (savings) account opened by the settlor of the trust and payable to the beneficiary on death of the settlor.
        2.   Implied trusts - a trust imposed upon property because of acts of the parties.
            a.   Constructive trusts - are imposed upon property by the equity court to rectify fraud or to prevent unjust enrichment.
            b.   Resulting trusts - serve to carry out the true intent of the parties in cases where the intent was inadequately expressed.
    B.   Creation of Trusts
        1.   Settlor - the person who creates the trust.
        2.   Subject matter - the trust property which must consist of any definite and specific real or personal property.
        3.   Trustee - an individual or institution that is legally capable of holding title to and dealing with property.
            a.   Duties of the trustee - three primary duties are listed.
            b.   Powers of the trustee - are determined by the settlor and State statutes.
            c.   Allocation of principal and income - trusts often specify how the trust property or funds shall be allocated.
        4.   Beneficiary - there are very few restrictions on who (or what) may be a recipient of trust property.
    C.   Termination of a Trust - as a general rule a trust is irrevocable unless the power of revocation is reserved by the settlor.
II.   Decedent's Estates
    A.   Wills - the legal document that determines to whom the assets of a decedent will be distributed after death.
        1.   Mental capacity

      a.   Testamentary power and capacity – the power to make a will is granted by the State; the capacity refers to limits placed upon particular persons because of personal mental deficiencies.

      b.   Conduct invalidating a will – includes duress, undue influence, and fraud.

2.   Formal requirements of a will

      a.   Writing – a basic requirement of a valid will.

      b.   Signature – a will must be signed by the testator.

      c.   Attestation – a will must be attested (certified) by witnesses, usually two or three as required by statute.

3.   Revocation of a will

      a.   Destruction or alteration – tearing or burning will revoke the will and in some States erasure or obliteration may.

      b.   Subsequent will – the execution of a second will does not itself revoke an earlier will.

      c.   Operation of law – common law and the UPC differ on the effect marriage and divorce have on a will.

      d.   Renunciation by the surviving spouse – of the decedent spouse's will is set by statute.

      e.   Abatement and ademption of a bequest – both have serious implications for beneficiaries of a will.

4.   Special types of wills

      a.   Nuncupative wills – are oral wills.

      b.   Holographic wills – a completely handwritten will.

      c.   Soldiers' and Sailors' wills – may be valid but cannot pass title to real estate.

      d.   Conditional wills – a will that takes effect only on the happening of a specific condition.

      e.   Joint and mutual or reciprocal wills – are types of wills involving two or more persons.

5.   Codicil – is an addition or revision of a will.

B.   Intestate Succession

1.   Property which descends – to the intestate's heirs includes all vested property interests of the intestate.

2.   Course of descent – are the rules of descent set by State statute.

C.   Administration of Estates – the statutory rules and procedures that control the management of the decedent's estate.

TRUE–FALSE: Circle true or false.

Answers

T   F   1.   Each trust has a settlor, a trustee, and a beneficiary.

T   F   2.   A will takes effect only upon the death of the testator; in other words, a will is revocable at any time during life.

T   F   3.   Fraud, undue influence, or duress may invalidate a will since they reflect an intent other than the testator's.

T   F   4.   A beneficiary's interest in a non-spendthrift trust may be attached by creditors.

T   F   5.   A second will automatically revokes the first will.

T   F   6.   A resulting trust is often used to rectify fraud or to prevent unjust enrichment.

T   F   7.   Stepchildren inherit from an intestate decedent to the same extent as natural children (heirs).

T   F   8.   As in contract law, consideration is an essential element of an enforceable trust.

T   F   9.   Even though legally created, a trust is generally revocable.

T   F   10.   Legally adopted children inherit to the same extent as natural children (heirs) of the adopting parents.

T   F   11.   Mutual or reciprocal wills are those in which the same instrument is made the will of two persons and is signed by them jointly.

T   F   12.   An inheritance tax is imposed by the Federal government on the privilege of an heir or beneficiary to receive property from the decedent's estate.

KEY TERMS – MATCHING EXERCISE: Select the term which best completes each statement below and write the corresponding number in the ANSWERS column.

Column I	Column II	Answers
1. A written or oral trust in which property is transferred to a trustee for the benefit of another.	1. Totten trust	1. _____
2. The act of witnessing a will.	2. Probate	2. _____
3. The legal effect of the intentional destruction of a will by the testator.	3. Attestation	3. _____
	4. Trust res	4. _____
4. A trust clause prohibiting the beneficiary from impairing the trust rights by an assignment of the rights.	5. Per stirpes	5. _____
	6. Express trust	6. _____
	7. Resulting trust	7. _____
5. The kind of trust that may be created when a settlor opens a joint bank account.	8. Escheat	8. _____
	9. Holographic	9. _____
6. The property that is the subject matter of the trust.	10. Per capita	10. _____
	11. Spendthrift	11. _____
	12. Charitable trust	12. _____

7.   Another name for an oral will.

8.   Any trust established for the improvement of mankind.

9.   Lineal descendents of predeceased children inherit from a decedent by representation of their parent.

10. The procedure for managing the decedent's estate.

11. The person named in a will to manage the administration of the decedent's estate.

12. An addition to or a revision of an existing will.

13. The statutory right of a surviving spouse to elect to take an intestate succession statutory share of the decedent's estate rather than the share left to the spouse in the decedent's will.

14. Another name for a handwritten will.

15. A reduction in the value of the estate of the testator after the execution of his will.

13. Codicil   13. _____

14. Nuncupative   14. _____

15. Revocation   15. _____

16. Executor

17. Ademption

18. Renunciation

19. Abatement

20. Administrator

MULTIPLE CHOICE: Select the alternative which best completes each statement below and write the corresponding letter in the ANSWERS column.

Answers

1.   Although no particular words are necessary to create a trust, one element that must be present is the (a) formal writing (b) intent to create a trust (c) designation of a trustee (d) all of the above.   1. _____

2.   The subject matter of a trust must be (a) definite and specific (b) real property (c) intangible (d) all of the above.   2. _____

3.   A trustee who by State law is required to invest only in those securities listed by the State, is controlled by a law that is (a) permissive (b) mandatory (c) invalid (d) tempered by reasonableness.   3. _____

4. If a person has obtained money by duress, the person will be treated as a trustee over a (a) constructive trust (b) resulting trust (c) express trust (d) precatory trust.

4. _____

5. The trustee must (a) carry out the trust's purposes (b) use prudence and care in the administration of the trust (c) be loyal to the beneficiary (d) all of the above.

5. _____

6. Which of the following is not an absolute necessity for all valid wills? (a) power (b) capacity (c) intent (d) intelligence.

6. _____

7. A codicil, like a will, must be (a) in writing (b) signed by the testator (c) witnessed (d) all of the above.

7. _____

8. A State inheritance tax is imposed upon the (a) decedent's estate (b) executor (c) recipient of the estate (d) attorney.

8. _____

9. A nuncupative will generally must (a) be handwritten (b) be made when no attorney is available (c) be made during the testator's last illness (d) dispose of real property only.

9. _____

10. Since a will can be renounced, the following person cannot be disinherited by the decedent, a surviving (a) parent (b) child (c) spouse (d) none of the above can be disinherited.

10. _____

11. A will may be revoked by (a) tearing or burning the will (b) operation of law (c) a subsequent will that is inconsistent with the original will (d) all of the above.

11. _____

12. The formal requirements for a will do not include the need for the (a) testator's signature (b) will to be recorded (c) will to be written (d) all of the above.

12. _____

13. The type of trust that is incorporated into a will and takes effect only on the testator's death is a (a) living trust (b) totten trust (c) testamentary trust (d) resulting trust.

13. _____

CASE PROBLEMS - SHORT ESSAY ANSWERS: Read each case problem carefully. When appropriate, answer by stating a Decision for the case and by explaining the rationale - Rule of Law - relied upon to support your decision.

1. A sets up a spendthrift trust for her son, B. C is a creditor of B's to whom B owes $800 for a motorcycle. Under what circumstances can C obtain payment?

Decision: _____

Rule of Law: _____

_____

2.   A appoints B trustee of a trust for the benefit of C and D. B dies. C and D petition the court to have the trust terminated. What result?

Decision: _____

_____

Rule of Law: _____

_____

3.   Ted dictated a will to his nurse. It was typed, signed, and attested. In it, he divided his entire estate among his wife and children. Ted dies. Eight months later, a son is born to Ted's widow. Does the new child share in the estate? Explain.

Decision: _____

_____

Rule of Law: _____

_____

4.   When Tom wrote his will, his estate was worth $35,000. Tom's will left $1,000 to A, $500 to B, and the balance to C. At the time of his death, Tom's estate was worth $1,500 after estate debts had been paid. What does C receive? Explain.

Decision: _____

_____

Rule of Law: _____

_____

5.   Abby's will left her business, a pizza parlor, to her nephew, H. One year before her death, Abby sold the pizza parlor for $50,000. Is H entitled to the $50,000 in lieu of the pizza parlor? Explain.

Decision: _____

_____

Rule of Law: _____

_____

CHAPTER 51

Insurance

SCOPE NOTE

In Chapter 51, the basic principles and terminology of insurance law are discussed. The nature and function of insurance as well as the regulation of the conduct and the contract of the insurance parties are addressed. The types of personal property interests that can be insured against loss are also focused upon.

EDUCATIONAL OBJECTIVES

1.   Define insurance and discuss the role it plays in our lives.

2.   Describe how the insurance industry is regulated.

3.   Distinguish characteristics of the various types of insurance companies.

4.   Contrast the various types of insurance.

5.   Identify the methods used to determine the cost (premium) of insurance.

6.   Outline the requirements for and the steps involved in creating a valid, enforceable insurance contract.

7.   Apply the Insurable Interest Doctrine to the various types of insurance coverage.

8.   Differentiate between waiver, estoppel, representations and warranties as they affect forfeiture and avoidance of an insurance contract.

9.   Explain the rules controlling party performance on and termination of the insurance contract.

CHAPTER OUTLINE

A.   Forms of Organization - the forms or kinds of insurance organizations are listed.
B.   Kinds of Insurance

1.   Life insurance - is a contract in which the insurer pays a specific sum of money to the beneficiary upon the death of the insured provided premiums have been paid.
    a.   Ordinary life - is a form of insurance protection plus savings.
    b.   Term life - is issued for a limited time period and is pure protection with no savings feature.
    c.   Universal life - is a form of ordinary life that invests and accumulates part of the premium.

2.   Endowment and annuity contracts - an agreement by the insurer to pay a lump sum of money to the insured at a certain age or to pay fixed sums at periodic intervals.

3.   Accident and health insurance - is insurance against losses due to accidents and sickness.

4.   Fire and property insurance - protects the owner of real or personal property against loss from fire and other perils.

5.   Casualty insurance - covers loss due to damage of personal property by causes other than fire.

6.   Collision insurance - protects the owner of an automobile against loss due to contact with other cars or objects.

7.   Liability insurance - covers loss due to liability of the insured who injures another person or her property.

8.   No-fault insurance - a statute that compensates victims of automobile accidents regardless of liability.

9.   Credit insurance - protects creditors against loss due to the insolvency of their debtors.

10.   Fidelity insurance - protects an employer against loss due to dishonesty of employees.

11.   Group insurance - covers a number of individuals under a single policy.

12.   Marine insurance - covers ship and cargo against "perils of the sea."

13.   Title insurance - protects against loss from defects in the title to real property or due to liens on the property.

C.   Nature of Insurance Contracts

1.   Offer and acceptance - the basic principles of contract law apply to insurance policies and it is the insured who makes the offer which can be accepted by the insurance company.

2.   Insurable interest - this concept's purpose is to eliminate gambling and lessen the moral hazard.
    a.   Property insurance - ownership creates an insurable interest in the property.
    b.   Life insurance - close relatives, creditors, and business associates or employers may take out insurance on another's life.

3.   Premiums - the money paid by the insured to the company for the insurance protection.

4.   Double indemnity - in the event of accidental death, the insurer pays twice the face amount of the policy.

5.   Defenses of the insurer - three closely related defenses are listed to induce an insurer to enter into a contract.
    a.   Misrepresentation - a false statement made by or on behalf of an applicant for insurance to induce an insurer to enter into a contract.
    b.   Breach of warranty - in insurance contracts, warranties operate as conditions which must exist before the contract is effective.
    c.   Concealment - is the failure of an applicant for insurance to disclose material facts that the insurer does not know.

6.   Waiver and estoppel - waiver is the intentional relinquishment of a known right; estoppel means that a person is prevented by conduct from asserting a position inconsistent with his acts.

7.   Performance and termination - most contracts of insurance are performed and thus the

insurer's obligations are terminated.

a.   Cancellation - of an insurance contract by mutual consent terminates it.

b.   Notice - after the occurrence of the insured event, the owner of the policy or the insured is required to give notice to the insurer.

TRUE-FALSE: Circle true or false.

Answers

T   F   1.   To rescind an insurance contract by mutual consent, all premiums paid by the insured must be returned by the insurer.

T   F   2.   The McCarran-Ferguson Act leaves regulation of insurance to the States instead of the Federal Government.

T   F   3.   Insurance companies can write only one type of insurance policy.

T   F   4.   Ordinary life insurance requires premium payments throughout the life of the insured.

T   F   5.   An annuity policy is an agreement by the insurer to pay a lump sum to the insured when the insured reaches a specific age.

T   F   6.   Casualty insurance policies are generally written to cover loss due to damage to real property.

T   F   7.   One person may take out a life insurance policy on another person's life if the other person is a close relative or partner.

T   F   8.   A representation by an applicant for insurance is generally not a part of the insurance contract.

T   F   9.   Most life insurance policies are written on a level premium, e.g., fixed rate, plan.

T   F   10.   In order to renew any life insurance policy, the insured must take and pass a new physical exam.

T   F   11.   The life insurance contract is created and is legally enforceable when the offer of the applicant is accepted by the life insurance agent.

T   F   12.   The basic principles of contract law apply to insurance policies.

KEY TERMS - MATCHING EXERCISE: Select the term which best completes each statement below and write the corresponding number in the ANSWERS column.

	Column I		Column II		Answers
1.	A system of compensating victims of car accidents regardless of liability.	1.	Double indemnity	1.	_____
		2.	Reinsurance	2.	_____

2.   The failure of an applicant for insurance to disclose material facts that the insurer does not know.

3.   The type of insurance that indemnifies against loss from defects in the title to real property.

4.   The rule that prevents a person from asserting a position that is inconsistent with the person's acts which have been relied on by another with justification.

5.   The authority of an agent which can make the insurance coverage effective immediately.

6.   An insurance policy in which the insurer will pay a lump sum of money to the insured at a specified age.

7.   A type of insurance that shares a loss due to fire between insurer and the insured.

8.   A type of insurance that covers loss due to an employee's dishonesty such as embezzlement.

9.   The consideration given in exchange for insurance coverage.

10.   Payment of twice the face amount of a policy if the insured dies accidentally.

11.   A specific time period, generally two years, after which an insurer may no longer challenge the existence and validity of a life insurance contract.

12.   The kind of fire that fire insurance policies cover.

3.   Endowment insurance   3. _____

4.   Fidelity insurance   4. _____

5.   Annuity insurance   5. _____

6.   No-fault insurance   6. _____

7.   Cash surrender value   7. _____

                                   8. _____
8.   Non-forfeiture
                                   9. _____
9.   Concealment
                                   10. _____
10.   Stock insurance
                                   11. _____
11.   Title insurance
                                   12. _____
12.   Binder
                                   13. _____
13.   Premium
                                   14. _____
14.   Co-insurance
                                   15. _____
15.   Estoppel

16.   Incontestability clause

17.   Friendly

18.   Hostile

19.   Collision insurance

20.   Insurable interest

13. An insurance contract in which the insurer agrees to pay fixed amounts to the insured at periodic intervals after the insured reaches a certain age.

14. A form of savings within an ordinary life insurance policy that enables the insured to borrow from the insurer after the policy has been in force for a given time.

15. The kind of fire that is not covered by a fire insurance policy.

MULTIPLE CHOICE: Select the alternative which best completes each statement below and write the corresponding letter in the ANSWERS column.

Answers

1. In an insurance contract, the insurance company is called the (a) insurer (b) insured (c) policyholder (d) none of the above.

   1. _____

2. Insurance premiums are paid only for a specified number of years in (a) an ordinary life contract (b) a term contract (c) a limited-payment contract (d) more than one of the above.

   2. _____

3. A single policy of insurance that covers a number of individuals having a common interest is (a) credit insurance (b) fidelity insurance (c) title insurance (d) group insurance.

   3. _____

4. Life insurance premiums are calculated on the basis of (a) interest (b) mortality rates (c) expense (d) all of the above.

   4. _____

5. An $8,000 fire insurance policy covers a $10,000 building, and there is an 80% co-insurance clause. If there is total destruction, the insured's recovery is (a) $8,000 (b) $2,000 (c) $10,000 (d) $6,400.

   5. _____

6. The insurable interest for property insurance must exist at the time (a) the property loss occurs (b) the policy is taken out (c) the property is purchased (d) none of the above.

   6. _____

7. To eliminate gambling by the use of insurance, there is the requirement of (a) a binding contract (b) materiality (c) using a valued policy (d) an insurable interest.

   7. _____

8. Defenses an insurance company can assert to an insurance contract include (a) breach of warranty (b) concealment (c) misrepresentation (d) all of the above.

   8. _____

9.   The intentional relinquishment of a known right is (a) estoppel (b)   9.   _____
     waiver (c) consideration (d) concealment.

10. The form of life insurance in which the entire premium is prepaid in
     one lump sum is (a) ordinary life (b) limited payment (c) single
     premium (d) none of the above.   10. _____

11. The kind of insurance in which an agent may have authority to make
     the insurance effective immediately is (a) fire insurance (b) casualty
     insurance (c) both A and B (d) none of the above.   11. _____

12. Damages caused by a hostile fire are covered by the standard fire
     insurance policy and include (a) smoke damage (b) water damage (c)
     heat damage (d) all of the above.   12. _____

13. A method used to increase coverage of a fire insurance policy to include
     benefits not provided in the standard policy is (a) a binder (b) an
     endorsement (c) a waiver (d) none of the above.   13. _____

CASE PROBLEMS – SHORT ESSAY ANSWERS: Read each case problem carefully.   When
appropriate, answer by stating a Decision for the case and by explaining the rationale - Rule of Law -
relied upon to support your decision.

1.   Thomas has a $50,000 life insurance contract with a double indemnity clause.   While playing
     Russian roulette, Thomas shoots himself and dies.   Must the insurance company pay $100,000 to
     Thomas' beneficiary?   Explain.

     Decision: _____

     _____

     Rule of Law: _____

     _____

2.   A wants to purchase a life insurance policy but suffers from diabetes.   A has B take the required
     physical exam in place of A.   B passes the exam, and the insurance company issues a policy to A.
     If the company learns of the impersonation, does the incontestability clause prevent the company
     from rescinding the policy and contract?   Explain.

     Decision: _____

     _____

     Rule of Law: _____

     _____

3.   Audrey has fire insurance on her $50,000 house.   The policy has an 80% co-insurance clause.   The
     policy has a face value of $30,000.   A fire damages the house in the amount of $24,000.   Can
     Audrey recover and, if so, how much?

     Decision: _____

     _____

     Rule of Law: _____

     _____

4.   W, the neighbor of B, secretly takes out a large amount of life insurance upon B's life, payable to W's son. Later, W causes B's death. W's son sues the insurance company for payment. Decide.

Decision: _____

_____

Rule of Law: _____

_____

5.   Frank, a farmer, sees a tornado approaching his farm. Frank has 800 acres of wheat ready for harvest, and he fears its loss. Frank calls his insurance agent in another town and obtains crop insurance to last for 30 days, just enough to harvest, he says. When the insurance company is presented with a claim by Frank for wind loss of 200 acres of wheat, what can it do?

Decision: _____

_____

Rule of Law: _____

_____

PROPERTY UNIT
RESEARCH QUESTIONS:

1.   Research your State's laws on intestate succession. If you were to die without a will, how and to whom would your property pass? Is that how you would want it distributed? Draft a will distributing your property in the manner (what, how and to whom) you desire. Is it the same as the plan of distribution under intestate succession laws? Explain.

2.   Assume you want to purchase a house. Trace the steps and complete drafting and processing the documents necessary for buying the home.

UNIFORM CPA EXAMINATION: INFORMATION ON BUSINESS LAW

To be certified, public accountants must meet competence standards prescribed by state examining boards. All states require that candidates pass the Uniform Certified Public Accountant Examination, administered by the American Institute of Certified Public Accountants (AICPA). The Uniform CPA Examination is given twice a year (in May and November). It consists of four separate sections: accounting practice; accounting theory; auditing; and business law.

The section of the CPA Examination dealing with business law usually lasts three and one-half hours and consists of objective and essay questions. The format is a series of sixty one point multiple choice questions and four ten point essay questions. Essay questions are written to test candidate knowledge of different business law rules and concepts. These questions consist of a statement of facts involving legal issues. The exam writer is asked to address these issues while determining the liability of the parties to the case. Multiple choice questions are similar to those in this Study Guide.

Considerable knowledge of business law is required to pass the CPA Examination. Specific information on the substantive content and various percentages given to the areas of law examined is explained in the guidelines adopted by the Board of Examiners of AICPA. The revised guidelines (effective in May, 1986) state:

"The Business Law section tests the candidate's knowledge of the legal implications inherent in business transactions particularly as they may relate to accounting and auditing. The scope of the Business Law section includes the CPA and the law, business organizations, contracts, debtor-creditor relationships, government regulation of business, Uniform Commercial Code, and property. Many of the subjects on the examination are normally covered in standard textbooks on business law, auditing, taxation, and accounting. However, some subjects either are not included in such texts or are not covered in adequate depth. Important recent developments with which candidates are expected to be familiar may not yet be reflected in some texts. Candidates are expected to recognize the existence of legal implications and the applicable basic legal principles, and they are usually asked to indicate the probable result of the application of such basic principles.

"The Business Law section is chiefly conceptual in nature and broad in scope. It is not intended to test competence to practice law nor expertise in legal matters, but to determine that the candidate's knowledge is sufficient to recognize relevant legal issues, recognize the legal implications of business situations, apply the underlying principles of law to accounting and auditing situations, and seek legal counsel, or recommend that it be sought, when appropriate.

"This section deals with federal and widely adopted uniform laws. Where there is no federal or appropriate uniform law on a subject, the questions are intended principally to test knowledge of the majority rules. Federal tax elements (income, estate or gift) may be covered where appropriate in the overall context of a question.

"**Business Law - Content Specification Outline**

I.   The CPA and the Law (10%)
      A.   Common Law Liability to Clients and Third Persons
      B.   Federal Statutory Liability
           1.   Securities Acts
           2.   Internal Revenue Code

       C.   Workpapers, Privileged Communication, and Confidentiality

II.   Business Organizations (20%)

       A.   Agency

            1.   Formation and Termination

            2.   Liabilities of Principal

            3.   Disclosed and Undisclosd Principals

            4.   Agency Authority and Liability

       B.   Partnerships and Joint Ventures

            1.   Formation and Existence

            2.   Liabilities and Authority of Partners and Joint Owners

            3.   Allocation of Profit or Loss

            4.   Transfer of Interest

            5.   Termination, Winding Up, and Dissolution

       C.   Corporations

            1.   Formation, Purposes, and Powers

            2.   Stockholders, Directors, and Officers

            3.   Financial Structure, Capital, and Dividends

            4.   Merger, Consolidation, and Dissolution

       D.   Estates and Trusts

            1.   Formation and Purposes

            2.   Allocation between Principal and Income

            3.   Fiduciary Responsibilities

            4.   Distributions and Termination

III.   Contracts (15%)

       A.   Offer and Acceptance

       B.   Consideration

       C.   Capacity, Legality, and Public Policy

       D.   Statute of Frauds

       E.   Statute of Limitations

       F.   Fraud, Duress, and Undue Influence

       G.   Mistake and Misrepresentation

       H.   Parol Evidence Rule

       I.   Third Party Rights

       J.   Assignments

       K.   Discharge, Breach, and Remedies

IV.   Debtor-Creditor Relationships (10%)

       A.   Suretyship

            1.   Liabilities and Defenses

            2.   Release of Parties

            3.   Remedies of Parties

       B.   Bankruptcy

            1.   Voluntary and Involuntary Bankruptcy

            2.   Effects of Bankruptcy on Debtors and Creditors

            3.   Reorganizations

V.   Government Regulation of Business (10%)

       A.   Regulation of Employment

            1.   Federal Insurance Contributions Act

            2.   Federal Unemployment Tax Act

            3.   Workmen's Compensation

B.   Federal Securities Acts
1.   Securities Registration
2.   Reporting Requirements
3.   Exempt Securities and Transactions
VI.   Uniform Commercial Code (25%)
A.   Commercial Paper
1.   Types of Negotiable Instruments
2.   Requisites for Negotiability
3.   Transfer and Negotiation
4.   Holders and Holders in Due Course
5.   Liabilities, Defenses, and Rights
6.   Dischage
B.   Documents of Title and Investment Securities
1.   Warehouse Receipts
2.   Bills of Lading
3.   Issuance, Transfer, and Registration of Securities
C.   Sales
1.   Contracts Covering Goods
2.   Warranties
3.   Product Liability
4.   Risk of Loss
5.   Performance and Obligations
6.   Remedies and Defenses
D.   Secured Transactions
1.   Attachment of Security Agreements
2.   Perfection of Security Interests
3.   Priorities
4.   Rights of Debtors, Creditors, and Third Parties
VII.   Property (10%)
A.   Real and Personal Property
1.   Distinctions Between Realty and Personalty
2.   Types of Ownership
3.   Lessor-Lessee
4.   Deeds, Recording, Title Defects, and Title Insurance
B.   Mortgages
1.   Characteristics
2.   Recording Requirements
3.   Priorities
4.   Foreclosure
C.   Fire and Casualty Insurance
1.   Coinsurance
2.   Multiple Insurance Coverage
3.   Insurable Interest"*

These AICPA specifications do not state the emphasis placed upon the various topics within the major areas of business law that are examined. These proportions vary from examination to examination.

CONCLUDING THOUGHTS

Understanding contract law is very important to accountants. Unit II in Smith and Roberson's *Business Law, Seventh Edition* and this *Study Guide* should be studied carefully, since nearly 15% of the CPA Business Law Examination covers topics relating to contracts. Other topics that are likely to appear on CPA examinations include commercial paper, federal securities legislation, corporations, partnerships, sales and secured transactions, property and other major business law areas.

*The Revised Business Law Content Specification Outline for the Uniform Certified Public Accountant Examination (effective May, 1986), Copyright 1985 by the American Institute of Certified Public Accountants, Inc. Reprinted with permission.

CROSS REFERENCES TABLE
Business Law Topics Appearing on CPA Examinations
Text and Study Guide Chapters

TOPIC, ESTIMATED AICPA EMPHASIS & GROUP CHAPTERS IN STUDY GUIDE:

ACCOUNTANTS AND THE LAW (10%)   45

BUSINESS ORGANIZATIONS (20%)

A. Agency   17 and 18
B. Partnerships and Joint Ventures   29-32
C. Corporations   33-36
D. Estates and Trusts   50

CONTRACTS (15%)

A. Introduction to Contracts   7
B. Mutual Assent   8
C. Invalidating Assent   9
D. Consideration   10
E. Illegal Bargains   11
F. Capacity   12
G. Statute of Frauds   13
H. Parol Evidence Rule   13
I. Third Party Rights   14
J. Performance, Breach and Discharge   15
K. Remedies   16

DEBTOR-CREDITOR RELATIONSHIPS (10%)

A. Secured Transactions   37
B. Suretyship   38
C. Bankruptcy   39

GOVERNMENT REGULATION OF BUSINESS (10%)

A. Employment Law   43
B. Federal Securities Acts   44
C. Antitrust   41
D. Unfair Competition   40

UNIFORM COMMERCIAL CODE (25%)

A. Commercial Paper   24-28
B. Documents of Title   47
C. Sales   19-23

PROPERTY (10%)

A. Real and Personal Property   46-49
B. Mortgages   49
C. Fire and Casualty Insurance   51

FUTURE CPA EXAMINATIONS

Scheduled Uniform CPA Examinations:

1988   May 4, 5, 6; November 2, 3, 4

1989   May 3, 4, 5; November 1, 2, 3

1990   May 2, 3, 4; November 7, 8, 9

1991   May 8, 9, 10; November 6, 7, 8

Students planning to take the examinations should obtain copies of *Information for CPA Candidates* issued by AICPA. Copies are available from:

The American Institute of Certified Public Accountants
1211 Avenue of the Americas
New York, NY   1036

ANSWERS TO CHAPTER 1 - Introduction to Law

TRUE-FALSE:

1.	T	4	4.	T	12	7.	F	9	10.	T	6
2.	T	9	5.	F	10	8.	T	15	11.	F	13
3.	F	11	6.	T	9	9.	F	14	12.	T	13

KEY TERMS - MATCHING:

1.	4	9	5.	14	12	9.	3	14	13.	2	13
2.	6	8	6.	7	12	10.	5	8	14.	18	14
3.	9	9	7.	13	6	11.	20	14	15.	19	12
4.	15	11	8.	10	9	12.	8	12			

MULTIPLE CHOICE:

1.	d	12	5.	d	6	8.	d	8	11.	a	8
2.	d	15	6.	c	14	9.	b	9	12.	b	12
3.	a	14	7.	d	12	10.	d	9	13.	d	9
4.	c	14									

CASE PROBLEMS - ESSAY ANSWERS:

1. This landmark U.S. Supreme Court decision would be found in the following two source books: first, in Volume 347 of the United States Supreme Court Reports at page 686, and second, in Volume 74 of the Supreme Court Reporter at page 686. This is an example of a case citation. p. 12

2. No. This is a trial in equity, and equity courts do not allow jury trials. p. 10

3. No. The state has not proven beyond a reasonable doubt that Horn caused the fire, and they are charged with the burden of proof. p. 6

4. If Baker owns personal property (e.g., a car), Anita may have it legally seized and sold. p. 4

5. Society may condemn John's failure to attempt a rescue as morally wrong, but the law generally imposes no legal duty on him to act. p. 5

All answers are keyed to page numbers in the main text.

ANSWERS TO CHAPTER 2 - Legal Process

TRUE-FALSE:

1.	F	29	4.	F	23	7.	T	35	10.	T	31
2.	T	23	5.	T	30	8.	F	33	11.	T	20
3.	T	19	6.	T	26	9.	T	19	12.	F	35

KEY TERMS - MATCHING:

1.	6	20	5.	10	35	9.	2	33	13.	3	36
2.	5	29	6.	11	30	10.	13	23	14.	17	35
3.	14	32	7.	8	29	11.	12	30	15.	9	30
4.	15	32	8.	4	30	12.	20	30			

MULTIPLE CHOICE:

1.	d	26	5.	a	20	8.	b	22	11.	d	25
2.	a	19	6.	c	20	9.	d	23	12.	c	29
3.	c	32	7.	d	22	10.	d	30	13.	d	34
4.	d	22									

CASE PROBLEMS - ESSAY ANSWERS:

1. Remand means the original decision by the State district court is reversed by the Supreme Court. The case will now be re-tried in the original trial court, i.e., the district court. p. 33

2. Yes. The Constitution states that the U.S. Supreme Court has original jurisdiction in cases affecting ambassadors. p. 20

3. No. Generally, State court decisions are not binding upon another State's courts. p. 27

4. Yes. If Malcolm is a citizen of Colorado, the Federal district court would have jurisdiction because (1) Malcolm could sue for over $10,000, and (2) "diversity of citizenship" exists, i.e., the parties are citizens of different states. p. 26

5. No. A decision of a Federal Circuit Court is not binding upon other circuit courts. pp. 26, 27

ANSWERS TO CHAPTER 3 - Constitutional and Administrative Law

TRUE-FALSE:

1.	T	46	4.	T	51	7.	T	48	10.	F	51
2.	F	46	5.	F	53	8.	T	62,63	11.	T	48
3.	F	49	6.	F	60	9.	T	62	12.	F	48

KEY TERMS - MATCHING:

1.	3	47	5.	7	55	9.	1	59	13.	17	63
2.	6	52	6.	9	56	10.	10	57	14.	19	62
3.	12	49	7.	11	48	11.	4	47	15.	14	48
4.	13	51	8.	15	53	12.	20	62			

MULTIPLE CHOICE:

1.	c	47	5.	d	59	8.	d	57,58	11.	a	48
2.	d	48	6.	b	60	9.	c	60	12.	b	48
3.	a	48	7.	c	57	10.	d	57	13.	d	58
4.	b	46									

CASE PROBLEMS - ESSAY ANSWERS:

1. President Nixon contended that the separation of powers doctrine precluded the judicial branch of the government from reviewing the executive branch, i.e., the President's claim of executive privilege. The Supreme Court rejected this claim and ruled that it is the "province and duty of the judicial department to say what the law is" in this case. p. 48

2. Datsun. The commerce clause and the import-export clause of the Constitution immunize from State taxation goods that have entered the stream of commerce whether they are interstate or foreign and whether as imports or exports. p. 51

3. Our Constitution divides the government into three distinct and independent branches: executive, legislative, and judicial. The purpose of the doctrine is to avoid excessive power in any branch of government. p. 48

4. Tenth Amendment. This amendment states, "the powers not delegated to the United States by the Constitution, nor prohibited by it to the States, are reserved to the States respectively, or to the people." p. 49

5. The U.S. Supreme Court applies the strict scrutiny test whenever legislation affects fundamental rights or involves suspect classifications which include those made on the basis of race or national origin. Thus the Court ruled in the Brown case that segregated public schools violated the equal protection guarantee. p. 58

ANSWERS TO CHAPTER 4 – Criminal Law

TRUE-FALSE:

1.	F	81	4.	F	90	7.	T	95	10.	F	89
2.	T	81	5.	F	90	8.	T	81	11.	T	82
3.	T	88	6.	T	94	9.	T	85	12.	F	84

KEY TERMS – MATCHING:

1.	6	86	5.	1	83	9.	8	91	13.	2	95
2.	5	93	6.	9	96	10.	4	94	14.	18	93
3.	12	82	7.	11	82	11.	20	94	15.	19	93
4.	13	83	8.	15	91	12.	17	94			

MULTIPLE CHOICE:

1.	d	93,95	5.	b	95	8.	d	91	11.	c	94
2.	d	89	6.	b	95	9.	c	95	12.	d	83
3.	c	95	7.	c	81	10.	d	96	13.	c	96
4.	a	95									

CASE PROBLEMS – ESSAY ANSWERS:

1. Entrapment. Melvin was induced to commit the crime by Allen, the F.B.I. agent. p. 93

2. Carol loses. The U.S. Supreme Court has ruled that the use of a six-member jury in a criminal case does not violate the Constitution. p. 96

3. Indictment. A grand jury, on the basis of probable cause, could vote a "true bill" and indict (charge) her with the commission of the crime. p. 94

4. Howard is guilty. Although most crimes require criminal intent, some statutory crimes do not. If a person voluntarily becomes intoxicated, the person cannot use intoxication as a successful defense. pp. 82, 92

5. The Supreme Court held that depriving the defendant, Gideon, of the assistance of a lawyer in a felony trial is a denial of due process. p. 96

ANSWERS TO CHAPTER 5 - Intentional Torts

TRUE-FALSE:

1.	T	116	4.	F	124	7.	F	120	10.	T	128
2.	F	117	5.	F	129	8.	F	116	11.	T	117
3.	F	120	6.	T	127	9.	F	121	12.	T	124

KEY TERMS - MATCHING:

1.	7	127	5.	9	119	9.	13	125	13.	17	122
2.	1	116	6.	11	121	10.	5	126	14.	16	123
3.	4	118	7.	6	125	11.	20	116	15.	2	121
4.	8	118	8.	12	124	12.	19	121			

MULTIPLE CHOICE:

1.	d	117	5.	b	117	8.	a	127	11.	c	124
2.	a	121	6.	c	122	9.	d	128	12.	d	128
3.	d	124	7.	d	126	10.	c	126	13.	d	124
4.	d	125									

CASE PROBLEMS - ESSAY ANSWERS:

1. B wins. B's consent does not extend to intentional acts of violence beyond the rules of the game. p. 128

2. Potentially, B could be guilty of battery. However, if B reasonably believed A was about to inflict death or serious bodily harm to B, then B is privileged to use even deadly force as self-defense. pp. 128, 129

3. Yes. The "publication" requirement of defamation (in this case, specifically, libel) and the "publicized" requirement of invasion of privacy have both been met. pp. 121, 124

4. The tort is slander. Slander is the oral publication of a defamatory statement which is not true and which injures a person's reputation. p. 121

5. B wins. A is liable for the tort of emotional distress. p. 120

ANSWERS TO CHAPTER 6 – Negligence and Strict Liability

TRUE-FALSE:

1.	T	144	4.	T	158	7.	T	156	10.	F	154
2.	T	145	5.	F	157	8.	F	148	11.	F	149
3.	F	146	6.	F	157	9.	T	144	12.	T	145

KEY TERMS – MATCHING:

1.	6	144	5.	1	150	9.	8	154	13.	3	156
2.	13	157	6.	14	152	10.	5	149	14.	10	155
3.	11	155	7.	2	144	11.	20	150	15.	9	158
4.	4	150	8.	7	150	12.	19	153			

MULTIPLE CHOICE:

1.	a	158	5.	c	152	8.	c	148	11.	d	149
2.	d	150	6.	a	145	9.	d	157	12.	d	150
3.	d	157	7.	b	146	10.	c	155	13.	a	152
4.	b	157									

CASE PROBLEMS – ESSAY ANSWERS:

1.   Sarah wins.   Joelene was flying the plane negligently and is liable to Sarah for this tort, i.e., negligence. p. 144

2.   Yes. As the person responsible for Kathy's care, Mark would have a duty to act and would be liable for not taking action. p. 148.

3.   No. Abner's act of leaving Baker unconscious in the middle of the street could "normally result" in additional injury to Baker. It is also foreseeable that Baker would be struck by a car, and Abner has a duty of affirmative action when there is danger of further harm to the unconscious person. At the very least, Abner should have carried or dragged Baker out of the street. pp. 148, 153

4. $45,000. The amount of the judgment award is determined by multiplying the percentage of the defendant's negligence times the amount of damage, e.g., 90% times $50,000, which is $45,000. p. 155

5.   This is an example of strict liability because this activity is so inherently dangerous to the public that absolute liability is imposed regardless of fault. p. 156

ANSWERS TO CHAPTER 7 - Introduction to Contracts

TRUE-FALSE:

1.	T	175	4.	F	176	7.	F	178	10.	T	179
2.	T	175	5.	T	177	8.	F	178	11.	T	177
3.	F	175	6.	F	178	9.	T	178	12.	F	179

KEY TERMS - MATCHING:

1.	15	175	5.	3	178	9.	9	179	13.	20	177
2.	5	177	6.	7	179	10.	2	175	14.	4	177
3.	12	178	7.	8	178	11.	18	176	15.	19	179
4.	1	175	8.	6	178	12.	16	177			

MULTIPLE CHOICE:

1.	a	175	5.	c	178	8.	d	174	11.	a	175
2.	d	177	6.	d	179	9.	c	175	12.	b	178
3.	d	179	7.	b	178	10.	c	175	13.	c	177
4.	b	178									

CASE PROBLEMS - ESSAY ANSWERS:

1. An implied contract is created. Sara requested and accepted Mary's services, and Sara's estate must pay Mary a reasonable amount for the services. p. 177

2. Yes. The moment Julie purchased the microscope, an implied, unilateral contract existed. p. 178

3. Yes. It is clearly understood from the statements of both parties that they were making and exchanging mutual promises. The parties need not use the actual word "promise" to create a bilateral contract. p. 178

4. A false statement that is material to the contract agreed upon by the parties is fraud. Fraud makes the contract voidable to the defrauded party, Joyce. p. 178

5. Yes. This is an example of a quasi contract. p. 179

ANSWERS TO CHAPTER 8 - Mutual Assent

TRUE-FALSE:

1.	T	185	4.	T	186	7.	F	186	10.	T	195
2.	T	185	5.	T	192	8.	F	196	11.	T	187
3.	F	197	6.	T	193	9.	T	190	12	T	192

KEY TERMS - MATCHING:

1.	15	193	5.	10	188	9.	9	196	13.	20	185
2.	11	192	6.	1	185	10.	4	194	14.	6	190
3.	14	196	7.	12	189	11.	16	189	15.	18	185
4.	2	185	8.	3	190	12.	19	191			

MULTIPLE CHOICE:

1.	d	193	5.	d	197	8.	d	186	11.	d	186
2.	d	190	6.	d	190	9.	b	195	12.	d	190
3.	a	185	7.	b	192	10.	a	185	13.	c	192
4.	d	186									

CASE PROBLEMS - ESSAY ANSWERS:

1. Sam wins. The U.C.C. and the Restatement would require that Jerome accept by registered mail, as requested by Sam, in order for Sam to be bound. p. 195

2. B wins. Today, such unsolicited items, e.g., the candy, would be considered a gift. p. 196

3. A wins. The option is a binding promise not to revoke for one year and is enforceable against B's executor. p. 193

4. No. Statements made under circumstances of emotional stress are not offers since they lack contractual intent. p. 188

5. No. This is an example of the parties engaging in preliminary negotiations. B's letter is the actual offer, not the acceptance of an offer. p. 187

ANSWERS TO CHAPTER 9 – Conduct Invalidating Assent

TRUE-FALSE:

1.	T	212	4.	F	212	7.	F	211	10.	F	218
2.	T	214	5.	T	218	8.	T	216	11.	T	215
3.	F	210	6.	F	211	9.	T	217	12.	T	213

KEY TERMS - MATCHING:

1.	5	211	5.	12	218	9.	9	213	13.	6	212
2.	7	214	6.	8	219	10.	13	210	14.	10	210
3.	1	215	7.	2	216	11.	14	210	15.	19	215
4.	3	217	8.	15	211	12.	11	215			

MULTIPLE CHOICE:

1.	c	210	5.	a	214	8.	b	213	11.	c	219
2.	a	211	6.	d	214	9.	d	212	12.	d	211
3.	b	212	7.	b	213	10.	d	216	13.	d	218
4.	a	212									

CASE PROBLEMS - ESSAY ANSWERS:

1. Yes. One may have a duty of disclosure because of prior representations innocently made but which are later discovered to be untrue before making a contract. Abner's lack of disclosure is fraud. p. 213

2. No. This is an example of duress. p. 210

3. Yes. Ignorance through negligence such as not reading the document will not relieve a party from contractual obligations. p. 218

4. No to both questions. A prediction is normally not a factual statement and does not form the basis for fraud. p. 214

5. No. If the subject matter of the contract (potatoes) is destroyed without fault of either party before the risk of loss passes to the buyer, then, if the loss is total, the contract is avoided. p. 217

ANSWERS TO CHAPTER 10 - Consideration

TRUE-FALSE:

1.	T	231	4.	F	233	7.	T	232	10.	T	236
2.	T	231	5.	T	232	8.	F	235	11.	T	236
3.	F	231	6.	T	237	9.	F	234	12.	F	238

KEY TERMS - MATCHING:

1.	13	236	5.	7	232	9.	6	234	13.	16	239
2.	2	239	6.	4	233	10.	10	238	14.	14	240
3.	3	239	7.	5	234	11.	1	237	15.	18	240
4.	12	239	8.	11	234	12.	20	237			

MULTIPLE CHOICE:

1.	d	231	5.	c	232	8.	d	240	11.	d	239
2.	a	232	6.	c	237	9.	c	239	12.	d	240
3.	b	235	7.	c	235	10.	d	239	13.	c	237
4.	d	232									

CASE PROBLEMS - ESSAY ANSWERS:

1. I would argue that the fund had already substantially relied on the pledge, and normally courts will uphold these charitable subscriptions as an exception to the requirement of consideration. p. 239

2. Ray wins. Because Samantha knew the check was tendered as full payment of a disputed debt, and because she cashed it, she would probably be unable to collect the remainder. p. 237

3. Under Section 2-209(1), the U.C.C. would hold that a good faith agreement modifying a contract for the sale of goods needs no new consideration to be binding. p. 237

4. No. Past consideration is no consideration. Bill's promise to pay is for a past transaction. p. 237

5. Courts will usually hold that William has given up a legal right; hence, legally, his forbearance is a legal detriment, and the uncle must pay the $10,000. p. 233

ANSWERS TO CHAPTER 11 - Illegal Bargains

TRUE-FALSE:

1.	F	250	4.	F	251	7.	F	252	10.	F	259
2.	T	250	5.	T	251	8.	T	253	11.	F	256
3.	F	251	6.	T	252	9.	F	256	12.	T	252

KEY TERMS - MATCHING:

1.	9	257	5.	8	259	9.	5	253	13.	3	255
2.	10	255	6.	12	251	10.	15	257	14.	19	255
3.	7	256	7.	2	251	11.	11	251	15.	1	251
4.	6	252	8.	14	252	12.	16	253			

MULTIPLE CHOICE:

1.	b	252	5.	c	252	8.	c	255	11.	c	250
2.	c	251	6.	d	252	9.	d	258	12.	d	258
3.	a	251	7.	d	252	10.	a	253	13.	c	254
4.	c	251									

CASE PROBLEMS - ESSAY ANSWERS:

1. No. The maximum rate of interest in state Z is 8% or $80 per year on a $1,000 loan. A and B agreed to $72 interest and thus no usury. p. 252

2. Barbara wins. The statute was for revenue purposes only and not for protection of the public. p. 251

3. No. Where one person has a superior bargaining position which enables that person to impose an exculpatory clause upon another person as part of their contract, the courts tend to nullify the clause. p. 257

4. C loses. The issue is whether or not the restraint is reasonable. Since a barber shop is localized business, a restraint that prohibits a barber business anywhere in the county for a period of five years is unreasonable. p. 253

5. B loses. Since the contract is a violation of a criminal statute, it will be held unenforceable. p. 250

ANSWERS TO CHAPTER 12 – Contractual Capacity

TRUE-FALSE:

1.	F	271	4.	T	273	7.	F	274	10.	F	275
2.	F	271	5.	F	273	8.	T	275	11.	F	273
3.	T	272	6.	F	274	9.	F	276	12.	F	274

KEY TERMS – MATCHING:

1.	10	275	5.	1	274	9.	9	274	13.	11	271
2.	8	276	6.	2	274	10.	7	272	14.	20	275
3.	15	274	7.	3	273	11.	5	272	15.	16	275
4.	12	271	8.	4	271	12.	19	271			

MULTIPLE CHOICE:

1.	d	272	5.	b	271	8.	d	275	11.	d	275
2.	a	272	6.	d	272	9.	d	274	12.	c	276
3.	b	272	7.	b	273	10.	b	275	13.	d	273
4.	d	272									

CASE PROBLEMS – ESSAY ANSWERS:

1. The majority view is that even though a minor (Mary) misrepresents her age, she may nevertheless disaffirm the contract. p. 274

2. Contracts entered into by persons judged insane are void and have no legal effect. p. 275

3. No. A minor may disaffirm a contract for the sale of a chattel within a reasonable time after reaching majority age. Continued use after reaching majority age is an implied ratification. pp. 272, 273

4. A wins. An intoxicated person who is uanble to comprehend the nature and effect of a contract can avoid the contract. p. 276

5. A minor is not liable for anything, including necessaries, unless they are actually furnished to the minor or used by the minor. Also, the minor is not liable if the minor is already supplied or is being supplied with the items (necessaries) by someone else such as the minor's parents. pp. 271, 272

ANSWERS TO CHAPTER 13 – Contracts in Writing

TRUE-FALSE:

1.	T	289	4.	T	292	7.	T	291	10.	F	300
2.	T	290	5.	T	296	8.	T	292	11.	T	299
3.	T	291	6.	F	289	9.	T	294	12.	T	300

KEY TERMS - MATCHING:

1.	9	291	5.	2	300	9.	4	295	13.	19	290
2.	11	296	6.	15	294	10.	1	298	14.	5	291
3.	12	290	7.	3	291	11.	20	290	15.	17	292
4.	7	300	8.	13	300	12.	10	289			

MULTIPLE CHOICE:

1.	b	294	5.	d	292	8.	b	295	11.	b	291
2.	c	296	6.	a	295	9.	a	292	12.	b	293
3.	d	297	7.	d	301	10.	d	301	13.	d	301
4.	c	291									

CASE PROBLEMS - ESSAY ANSWERS:

1. No. The parol evidence rule does not apply whenever parties to an existing contract subsequently agree to cancel it. p. 301

2. No. Neither the Statute of Frauds nor the U.C.C. would allow this memo to bind the parties since the subject matter and quantity are not clear. pp. 296, 297

3. Probably not. This is a contract for the sale of an interest in land and thus it is unenforceable. However, A may recover damages for the work done and damages would be the appropriate remedy. p. 299

4. A loses. The Code states that oral contracts for goods specifically manufactured for the buyer and which are not suitabe for resale in the ordinary course of business are enforceable. This contract is not within the Statute of Frauds. p. 297

5. Allen loses. The party to be charged, i.e., Bernard, has not signed the letter. p. 296

ANSWERS TO CHAPTER 14 – Rights of Third Parties

TRUE-FALSE:

1.	T	322	4.	F	321	7.	T	325	10.	T	327
2.	F	327	5.	T	327	8.	F	325	11.	T	328
3.	F	322	6.	F	326	9.	T	326	12.	T	330

KEY TERMS – MATCHING:

1.	11	327	5.	12	326	9.	2	330	13.	17	323
2.	6	323	6.	9	328	10.	4	327	14.	3	324
3.	13	328	7.	14	326	11.	8	321	15.	18	322
4.	15	326	8.	10	328	12.	19	322			

MULTIPLE CHOICE:

1.	d	324	5.	d	325	8.	a	330	11.	b	321
2.	d	324	6.	c	330	9.	b	326	12.	c	322
3.	d	324	7.	a	328	10.	d	326	13.	d	327
4.	b	327									

CASE PROBLEMS – ESSAY ANSWERS:

1. Y is a donee beneficiary and may recover; it does not matter that Y was unaware of the policy. p. 328

2. Because C is only an incidental beneficiary, C has no rights under the contract and cannot sue. p. 330

3. Since the risk assumed by the appliance company was with A, the assignment to B would be an entirely different risk to the company, and they need not take it. p. 324

4. X wins. Because E made a contract with X for a personal service, E does not have the right to delegate the duty to another. p. 327

5. The majority view says Y wins because Y was prior in time. A minority view would give the wages to T because T gave first notice. p. 326

ANSWERS TO CHAPTER 15 - Performance, Breach, and Discharge

TRUE-FALSE:

1.	T	340	4.	F	341	7.	F	347	10.	F	349
2.	T	340	5.	F	341	8.	F	346	11.	T	343
3.	F	341	6.	T	342	9.	T	343	12.	T	343

KEY TERMS - MATCHING:

1.	7	344	5.	15	347	9.	4	342	13.	5	343
2.	9	345	6.	1	346	10.	8	344	14.	14	347
3.	11	347	7.	2	345	11.	16	343	15.	20	343
4.	13	346	8.	3	350	12.	18	347			

MULTIPLE CHOICE:

1.	a	346	5.	d	340	8.	a	342	11.	b	343
2.	b	348	6.	d	341	9.	b	343	12.	c	345
3.	d	344	7.	c	341	10.	a	346	13.	b	347
4.	c	350									

CASE PROBLEMS - ESSAY ANSWERS:

1. Decision for A because this situation presents an impossibility for which neither party was responsible. This is the frustration of purpose doctrine. p. 348

2. War discharges the contract either due to subsequent illegality or impossibility. p. 347

3. Yes. By novation, Z has become the new debtor and is liable for the debt. p. 346

4. Y wins. This is an example of mutual rescission. p. 346

5. B wins. The law will imply a condition concurrent whereby A and B have a duty to perform the acts of delivery and payment at the same time. The remedy of specific performance would only be granted for non-performance or failure to tender performance and, in the case of the sale of personal property, only when the property is unique. p. 342

ANSWERS TO CHAPTER 16 – Remedies

TRUE-FALSE:

1.	T	360		4.	F	369		7.	F	366		10.	T	364
2.	F	360		5.	F	365		8.	F	363		11.	T	367
3.	F	360		6.	F	361		9.	T	361		12.	F	366

KEY TERMS – MATCHING:

1.	4	360		5.	13	364		9.	6	366		13.	16	363
2.	9	361		6.	14	367		10.	10	367		14.	2	364
3.	11	363		7.	3	369		11.	20	360		15.	18	365
4.	15	364		8.	12	366		12.	17	362				

MULTIPLE CHOICE:

1.	b	361		5.	a	364		8.	b	364		11.	d	368
2.	c	366		6.	b	364		9.	c	366		12.	d	369
3.	a	368		7.	c	361		10.	d	368		13.	a	365
4.	b	363											

CASE PROBLEMS – ESSAY ANSWERS:

1.   You might sue for lost profits, but under the reasoning of Hadley v. Baxendale, you would have to have told Ace of your need specifically to render them liable. pp. 361, 363

2.   Possibly. Although punitive damages are not generally recoverable for breach of contract, if the conduct constituting the breach is also a tort (fraud), punitive damages may be obtained. p. 364

3.   Probably not, because the courts would look at this as a penalty rather than a valid liquidated damage clause since the $2,000 would not bear a reasonable relationship to the amount of probable loss. p. 364

4.   For all the lawnmowers A built after the repudiation, B would probably not be liable, because A could have mitigated the damages by not continuing to build. p. 365

5.   Yes. B can ask for the remedy of specific performance from A because the car is unique. p. 366

ANSWERS TO CHAPTER 17 – Relationship of Principal and Agent

TRUE-FALSE:

1.	T	382	4.	T	384	7.	T	387	10.	F	391
2.	F	385	5.	F	382	8.	T	390	11.	F	383
3.	T	387	6.	T	386	9.	F	388	12.	T	391

KEY TERMS - MATCHING:

1.	7	383	5.	15	386	9.	12	390	13.	19	385
2.	6	383	6.	10	383	10.	5	390	14.	17	382
3.	9	384	7.	13	390	11.	20	388	15.	18	390
4.	1	386	8.	3	391	12.	16	388			

MULTIPLE CHOICE:

1.	c	385	5.	b	383	8.	a	385	11.	d	389
2.	a	386	6.	d	389,90	9.	b	384	12.	c	389
3.	b	385	7.	d	385	10.	c	381	13.	a	390
4.	a	385									

CASE PROBLEMS - ESSAY ANSWERS:

1. No. This would be considered a contract for personal services, and A cannot delegate them. This case is beyond the scope of agency purposes. p. 383

2. Yes, because A has breached the fiduciary duty to P. Agents who are employed to buy may not buy from themselves. p. 387

3. No. An agent has a duty not to make any secret profit while dealing for the principal. p. 387

4. No. The authority of the agent to perform a specific act is terminated when the act is performed. A could not sell the second painting without new authority from P. p. 389

5. When war occurs which puts a principal and an agent in the position of hostile enemies from countries at war, the agency relationship is terminated due to supervening illegality. Thus, D no longer has authority to represent T since their agency contract has been terminated through operation of law. p. 391

ANSWERS TO CHAPTER 18 – Relationship with Third Parties

TRUE-FALSE:

1.	T	407		4.	T	407		7.	T	415		10.	T	412
2.	F	407		5.	T	412		8.	F	414		11.	F	408
3.	F	417		6.	F	417-18		9.	F	413		12.	T	413

KEY TERMS – MATCHING:

1.	14	417		5.	2	415		9.	4	407		13.	16	407
2.	7	407		6.	11	415		10.	5	407		14.	20	412
3.	9	412		7.	8	413		11.	1	407		15.	17	412
4.	15	407		8.	13	407		12.	19	407				

MULTIPLE CHOICE:

1.	b	413		5.	a	419		8.	d	415		11.	b	419
2.	a	413		6.	d	413		9.	a	417		12.	a	412
3.	c	415		7.	b	418		10.	c	418		13.	b	412
4.	d	417											

CASE PROBLEMS – ESSAY ANSWERS:

1.   Probably not. A pattern of conduct has been established, based on A's five year purchases, where C has continuously done business with P. C may assume, having no knowledge otherwise, that the established purchase pattern will continue. The apparent authority of A to act, coupled with C's lack of knowledge that C is not so authorized, gives C a right of recourse against P. p. 408-9

2.   Yes. Agents are liable for their own wrongful and negligent acts whether or not the principal is also liable. p. 420

3.   No. An agent who makes a contract with a third person on behalf of a disclosed principal has no right of action against the third person for breach of contract. p. 420

4.   No. A third person can proceed to trial against both the principal and agent but if, before the entry of judgment, the third person elects to obtain a judgment against the principal alone and does obtain a judgment the third person could not seek another judgment from the agent. An election to obtain judgment against one party irrevocably binds the third person to that choice. p. 419

5.   Normally a principal is not liable for the torts of an independent contractor unless they arise from breach of non-delegatable duties that are imposed by law. Usually, dangerous activity falls within non-delegatable duties. Since the duty to act safely is imposed by law and dynamiting is a dangerous activity, P is most likely liable for X's dynamiting. T can sue P. p. 417

ANSWERS TO CHAPTER 19 - Introduction to Sales

TRUE-FALSE:

1.	T	437	4.	T	441	7.	F	436	10.	F	449
2.	F	447	5.	T	447	8.	T	438	11.	T	436
3.	F	442	6.	F	446	9.	T	443	12.	F	441

KEY TERMS - MATCHING:

1.	4	436	5.	15	437	9.	13	439	13.	19	438
2.	7	436	6.	10	440	10.	6	438	14.	17	443
3.	11	439	7.	8	446	11.	1	443	15.	18	446
4.	9	438	8.	2	444	12.	16	447			

MULTIPLE CHOICE:

1.	c	436	5.	d	441	8.	b	436,438	11.	c	441
2.	d	436	6.	b	440	9.	d	439	12.	d	442
3.	b	446	7.	a	448	10.	a	442	13.	b	448
4.	d	444									

CASE PROBLEMS - ESSAY ANSWERS:

1.   Yes. Under U.C.C. 2-205, a merchant's written offer containing a statement that it will remain open for a specified period is irrevocable during the stated time.   p. 443

2.   No. The U.C.C. holds output and quantity contracts valid. An objective standard, based on the good faith of the parties, drawing upon prior agreements, course dealings and usages of trade, is used to supply the miasing term.   p. 442

3.   Yes. The unequal bargaining positions of the parties to the contract and the $800 purchase price for an item with a $180 fair market retail value render the agreement "unconscionable." Under section 2-302 of the U.C.C., courts have the authority to deny or limit enforcement of such unfair, harsh and indecent contracts.   pp. 439-440

4.   A contract exists and Penny's additional terms are not a rejection or counter offer. Under U.C.C. 2-207, Penny's acceptance, definitely and seasonably made, is effective. Since both parties are merchants, her additional terms will become part of the contract because the offer was not expressly limited to its terms and the additional terms probably do not materially alter the terms of the offer unless Yummy objects to them in writing within a reasonable time.   p. 444

5.   Wally loses. The Code states that oral contracts for goods specifically manufactured for the buyer, which are not suitable for resale in the ordinary course of business, are enforceable. This contract is not within the Statute of Frauds.   pp. 447-448

ANSWERS TO CHAPTER 20 - Transfer of Title and Risk of Loss

TRUE-FALSE:

1.	T	465	4.	F	462	7.	F	468	10.	T	470
2.	F	461-2	5.	T	462	8.	T	470	11.	T	470
3.	T	465	6.	T	470	9.	F	464	12.	F	466

KEY TERMS - MATCHING:

1.	8	460	5.	5	463	9.	14	466	13.	16	467
2.	9	464	6.	12	465	10.	1	470	14.	19	467
3.	7	462	7.	3	466	11.	20	462	15.	18	460
4.	11	464	8.	13	467	12.	17	462			

MULTIPLE CHOICE:

1.	c	462	5.	d	461	8.	c	466	11.	a	465
2.	c	462	6.	a	463	9.	b	466	12.	c	466
3.	d	471	7.	a	463	10.	b	465	13.	d	469
4.	b	471									

CASE PROBLEMS - ESSAY ANSWERS:

1. For the purchasers. A's violation of the Code does not invalidate the sale at the auction. A is personally liable (to the extent of the net proceeds from the sale) to the creditors for the improper auction procedures. The creditors have no resource against the g/f/p/v/ at the auction.   p. 472

2. For C. B's leaving the goods with merchant S is an act of "entrusting" under the Code. C, a buyer in the ordinary course of business, will therefore prevail.   pp. 464-5

3. A has lost title to the coat and has no rights against C. By "entrusting" the fur coat to merchant dealer B, A has given the latter power to transfer all of her rights to a buyer in the ordinary course of business which C was. A's only recourse is money damages against B.   p. 464

4. Buyer suffers the loss. When goods, held by a bailee, are sold to another and the goods are covered by a negotiable title document, risk of loss passes to the buyer on the latter's receipt of the document. Since grain owner had delivered the title document to buyer, buyer suffers the loss.   p. 468

5. In a contract calling for shipment and delivery "ex ship," title and risk of loss pass to the buyer only when the goods are off the ship at their destination point. Thus, S still has title and bears the risk of loss for the sunken goods.   pp. 467-68

ANSWERS TO CHAPTER 21 – Products Liability: Warranties and Strict Reliability in Tort

TRUE-FALSE:

1.	T	492	4.	F	487	7.	F	494	10.	T	492
2.	F	485	5.	F	488	8.	T	493	11.	F	487
3.	T	484	6.	T	490	9.	F	495	12.	T	494

KEY TERMS - MATCHING:

1.	8	485	5.	6	493	9.	15	490	13.	16	487
2.	12	490	6.	10	492	10.	3	497	14.	5	492
3.	7	486	7.	14	490	11.	4	487	15.	20	498
4.	9	486	8.	2	496	12.	18	487			

MULTIPLE CHOICE:

1.	a	494	5.	a	497	8.	d	489	11.	d	489
2.	c	496	6.	c	498	9.	c	487	12.	a	485
3.	a	486	7.	b	493	10.	d	484-5	13.	b	491
4.	b	490									

CASE PROBLEMS - ESSAY ANSWERS:

1. No. Strict liability in tort does not apply to an occasional seller not in business of selling the defective product. p. 492

2. B may revoke acceptance and seek damages from S based upon a breach of the implied warranty of merchantability. The car is obviously not fit for ordinary driving purposes. p. 488

3. A manufacturer has a duty to warn of potential hazards or foreseeable dangers arising out of the normal or probable use of a product. Where a consumer has misused a product, the manufacturer has no duty to warn about dangers therefrom and faces no liability. For the manufacturer. p. 498

4. It depends. Assuming that the rods were warranted, the seller must be notified of any breach within a reasonable time after a defect is or should have been discovered. If B fails to notify S, no damages are recoverable. If B does seasonably notify S, damages are $300: the difference between the value of the goods as accepted and the value they would have had had they been conforming to the contract. p. 491

5. C loses. Since the inedible ingredient in question, the bone, was both natural to the food consumed and its presence could have been reasonably expected, C will have to bear her own loss, based on either the natural substance or the reasonable expectation test. p. 488

ANSWERS TO CHAPTER 22 - Performance

TRUE-FALSE:

1.	T	510	4.	T	516	7.	T	516	10.	T	517
2.	F	511	5.	F	514	8.	F	516-17	11.	F	520
3.	F	521	6.	T	518	9.	F	511	12.	T	517

KEY TERMS - MATCHING:

1.	7	510	5.	12	518	9.	10	512	13.	19	511
2.	3	515	6.	5	514	10.	11	516	14.	17	520
3.	6	512	7.	9	521	11.	20	517	15.	18	510
4.	15	516	8.	1	511	12.	16	516			

MULTIPLE CHOICE:

1.	a	511	5.	c	516	8.	c	516	11.	d	516
2.	d	514	6.	b	515	9.	d	516-17	12.	a	515
3.	d	512	7.	a	518	10.	b	512	13.	c	515
4.	b	518									

CASE PROBLEMS - ESSAY ANSWERS:

1.   Probably not. Assuming that the masks were specified and identified to the contract when it was made, their total loss during the flood, before risk of loss passed to B, avoided the contract. p. 520

2.   For B. Although this is a breach of an installment contract with commercial units and therefore gives rise to a cause of action, S may not treat the one-day delayed payment as a material breach striking at the heart of the contract. The one-day delay is not justification to cancel the entire contract. p. 515

3.   B probably wins. For H.H. to effectively revoke her acceptance, the defect in the non-conforming rifle must substantially impair the value. Arguably, the scratches and nicks do not detract from the usefulness or performance capacity of the rifle and are therefore not substantial value impairments. However, since the test for value impairment is subjective - personal to the buyer - H.H. could argue that she intended to use the gun as a showcase collector's piece as well as for hunting and the blemishes, foreclosing the showcase capacity, are substantial value impairments. p. 517

4.   Decision for S. A merchant buyer, who has possession of rightfully rejected goods, must make reasonable efforts to resell the goods if they are perishable even if the seller gives the buyer no instructions. Failure to comply with the Code makes merchant buyer B liable for losses stemming from holding the perishable bananas and not selling them on seller's account. p. 516

5.   S probably wins. Ordinarily, impossibility of performance (in this case, the trade embargo) does not excuse performance on the contract. But, where the parties understood when they entered their contract the performance would depend upon a certain event or condition (availability of Australian widgees), the non-occurrence or termination of that presupposed basic condition (trade embargo on Australian goods) will excuse duties of performance. p. 520

ANSWERS TO CHAPTER 23 – Remedies

TRUE-FALSE:

1.	T	533	4.	F	537	7.	T	542	10.	F	539
2.	T	534	5.	T	538	8.	F	542	11.	T	532
3.	F	534	6.	F	542	9.	F	536	12.	T	533

KEY TERMS – MATCHING:

1.	1	533	5.	6	542	9.	12	536	13.	16	538
2.	13	534	6.	7	542	10.	4	539	14.	19	534
3.	2	537	7.	9	536	11.	20	532	15.	18	532
4.	5	540	8.	10	536	12.	17	535			

MULTIPLE CHOICE:

1.	b	533	5.	b	539	8.	c	536	11.	d	534
2.	d	535	6.	a	539	9.	c	535	12.	b	542
3.	c	537	7.	a	536	10.	b	533	13.	c	537
4.	c	538									

CASE PROBLEMS – ESSAY ANSWERS:

1. Since the seller is usually never accountable to the buyer for any profit made on a resale of the goods, B recovers nothing. p. 534

2. Since the difference between the cost of the goods purchased by B's "cover" and the contract price resulted in a $1,000 "better deal" for B, all that B might recover are incidental or consequential damages less expenses saved as a result of S's breach. p. 537

3. B should exercise a right of recovery against S for the identified goods in which B holds a special property interest. The Code gives a buyer the right to recover goods from an insolvent seller when the seller becomes involvent within 10 days of the first installment payment on the sales contract. To perfect this special interest in the goods, B must tender the remaining $7,500 to S. pp. 538-9

4. B may store the nails for the seller's account, reship them to the seller or resell them for the seller's account. By disposing of them, B is neither converting them nor accepting them. B would be liable to the seller for any excess over his security interest in the goods. p. 539

5. Because the painting in this case is unique, a court of equity will issue a decree of specific performance requiring delivery of the painting from C to A rather than a money damages judgment. p. 539

ANSWERS TO CHAPTER 24 - **Form and Content**

TRUE-FALSE:

1.	T	563	4.	F	562	7.	T	567	10.	T	567
2.	F	566	5.	T	565	8.	T	566-7	11.	T	560
3.	T	560	6.	F	567	9.	F	565	12.	F	558-9

KEY TERMS - MATCHING:

1.	5	558	5.	4	558	9.	3	566	13.	19	565
2.	2	564	6.	8	556	10.	1	558	14.	16	556
3.	14	563	7.	11	564	11.	9	558	15.	18	560
4.	12	560	8.	15	558	12.	17	560			

MULTIPLE CHOICE:

1.	b	563	5.	b	565	8.	a	556	11.	b	558
2.	d	562	6.	d	561	9.	c	566	12.	b	560
3.	d	560	7.	d	556	10.	a	565	13.	a	567
4.	b	558									

CASE PROBLEMS - ESSAY ANSWERS:

1.   S wins.   Where words and figures on an instrument are in conflict, the words, unless unclear themselves, are controlling. B must come up with the $810 difference. p. 568

2.   None. Provisions in commercial paper granting the obligor the option to extend the maturity date for a definite time period do not affect negotiability. p. 566

3.   Yes. Auxiliary clauses of this nature do not affect the sum certain due on the instrument. The note is therefore negotiable. p. 564

4.   Yes. Any symbol is sufficient as a signature so long as the person signing has adopted it and intends it to be their authentic signature. p. 562

5.   No. A bare indebtedness acknowledgement, such as an "I.O.U.," is not a a negotiable instrument carrying with it an obligation of payment to its holder. M has made no promises of payment at all. p. 562

ANSWERS TO CHAPTER 25 – Transfer

TRUE-FALSE:

1.	T	577	4.	F	578	7.	T	580	10.	F	581
2.	F	579	5.	T	581	8.	F	580	11.	T	578
3.	T	581	6.	F	580	9.	T	580	12.	F	577

KEY TERMS - MATCHING:

1.	4	579	5.	15	577	9.	12	581	13.	16	578
2.	14	579	6.	13	580	10.	7	577	14.	6	577
3.	5	579	7.	10	580	11.	18	560	15.	19	581
4.	1	577	8.	2	577	12.	20	581			

MULTIPLE CHOICE:

1.	d	577	5.	c	579	8.	b	579	11.	a	577
2.	c	580	6.	b	579	9.	d	581	12.	b	579-80
3.	d	579	7.	d	579	10.	c	581	13.	d	580
4.	a	581									

CASE PROBLEMS - ESSAY ANSWERS:

1. For X. Indorsees under a conditional indorsement have no rights to payment until the stated condition is met. The maker of a note conditionally indorsed is not discharged from the instrument if payment is made inconsistent with the stated restriction. Since the note in question was presented for payment three days prior to the occurrence of the event which would trigger X's obligation to pay, X may properly dishonor Z's presentment for payment. pp. 580

2. An indorsement which conveys less than the entire amount of a note is not an effective negotiation. The type of indorsement is effective only as an assignment. p. 579

3. Only if X's signature appeared on the note. Since the bearer paper became order paper through P's special indorsement, any further negotiation of the note would require X's indorsement. M may rightfully refuse payment to F if the note does not contain X's signature. p. 578

4. Yes. Anyone who possesses bearer paper is a holder entitled to payment. p. 577

5. To protect the interest in the instrument, B can convert the blank indorsement to a special indorsement by writing over A's signature any restriction not contrary to the type of indorsement. Thus, B may write "Pay to the order of B" to protect the interest. p. 580

ANSWERS TO CHAPTER 26 – Holder in Due Course

TRUE-FALSE:

1.	T	593	4.	F	595	7.	T	603	10.	T	603
2.	T	591	5.	T	594	8.	F	598	11.	F	598
3.	F	591	6.	F	597	9.	T	594	12.	F	590

KEY TERMS - MATCHING:

1.	4	589	5.	6	598	9.	1	596	13.	18	597
2.	2	593	6.	13	601	10.	12	598	14.	17	594
3.	7	592	7.	10	599	11.	19	589	15.	9	597
4.	3	598	8.	11	597	12.	16	599			

MULTIPLE CHOICE:

1.	d	597	5.	d	597	8.	b	598	11.	a	591
2.	a	601	6.	b	599	9.	d	604	12.	b	594
3.	d	593	7.	c	589	10.	c	594	13.	c	598
4.	a	596									

CASE PROBLEMS - ESSAY ANSWERS:

1.   H is holder of the full $1,000 face value of the note. A holder is not required to pay the full face amount to give value, but only the amount agreed upon with the transferor. p. 591

2.   No. One, not a holder in due course, cannot cleanse paper which is held by transferring the paper to and re-acquiring it from a holder in due course. P cannot use the shelter rule to profit from wrongdoing. pp. 596-7

3.   S's alteration is not a material one which would operate to discharge M on the instrument. Changing figures to comply with the controlling written number is not a material change. p. 599

4.   Probably not. Under the Code, notice must be received in a timely manner sufficient to provide a reasonable opportunity to act on it. Such is not the case here. p. 593

5.   No. Based on a F.T.C. regulation effective May 1976, holders of commercial paper issued in connection with consumer credit transactions acquire the paper subject to all claims, defenses and demands, including fraud and defective goods, which the consumer debtor could have asserted against the payee on the instrument. p. 603

ANSWERS TO CHAPTER 27 - Liability of Parties

TRUE-FALSE:

1.	T	618	4.	F	620	7.	F	625	10.	T	631
2.	T	618	5.	T	623	8.	T	627	11.	T	626
3.	F	621	6.	T	623	9.	F	629	12.	F	631-2

KEY TERMS - MATCHING:

1.	4	621	5.	9	625	9.	13	633	13.	16	622
2.	11	620	6.	7	627	10.	12	628	14.	20	627
3.	14	627-8	7.	2	629	11.	18	618	15.	17	635
4.	8	621	8.	6	622	12.	16	618			

MULTIPLE CHOICE:

1.	c	618	5.	c	624	8.	a	626	11.	c	619
2.	d	621	6.	a	623	9.	b	618-9	12.	b	629
3.	b	622	7.	c	629	10.	d	636	13.	a	629
4.	b	625									

CASE PROBLEMS - ESSAY ANSWERS:

1. M can collect on the instrument from the drawer, A, to the original tenor of $500. When certification is at the request of the drawer, the drawer is not relieved of secondary liability on the instrument. p. 621

2. A's willingness and ability to pay at the specified place, i.e., the bank, is the equivalent of tender of payment. A is liable for the face amount and interest accrued at the time payment was due, but not for additional interest thereafter or for subsequent costs and attorney's fees. p. 634

3. No. H's actions constitute improper presentment. The drawee can require the holder to adhere to the terms of the instrument (presentment only at the main office of the drawee) without causing a dishonor. p. 623

4. M is liable. By having failed to identify P, P is not obligated on the instrument to H, and M is solely bound to make payment. p. 619

5. For H. Since the maker, M, is in the best position to know the original amount of the instrument, when M pays the altered amount to the innocent party, H, M absorbs the loss. p. 632

ANSWERS TO CHAPTER 28 - Bank Deposits and Collections

TRUE-FALSE:

1.	T	647	4.	F	649	7.	T	655	10.	T	655
2.	F	647	5.	F	654	8.	F	650	11.	F	649
3.	T	653	6.	T	654	9.	F	650	12.	T	649

KEY TERMS - MATCHING:

1.	1	647	5.	14	651	9.	2	655	13.	18	657
2.	3	647	6.	15	653	10.	6	652	14.	16	649
3.	13	647	7.	8	656	11.	17	648	15.	19	655
4.	7	649	8.	11	650	12.	20	655			

MULTIPLE CHOICE:

1.	a	650	5.	b	653	8.	a	657	11.	d	657
2.	d	652	6.	c	652	9.	d	649	12.	c	658
3.	c	655-6	7.	b	652	10.	a	653	13.	b	649
4.	c	650									

CASE PROBLEMS - ESSAY ANSWERS:

1. For C. A payor bank receiving an item properly payable from a customer's account which lacks sufficient funds to cover the designated amount may pay the item, charge the account, and seek reimbursement from the customer for both the overdraft created by the item and any service charges connected with its handling. p. 653

2. Cathy will be liable for only $50 of the withdrawals if she notifies her bank of the card's disappearance within two days after she knows of its absence. After two days, she will be liable for the full amount of Frank's withdrawals up to a maximum of $500 if she notifies the bank within 60 days of the card's absence. pp. 657-8

3. H may bring an action for payment against B because a stop payment order does not automatically relieve the drawer of liability to the holder. Since H is a holder in due course of a negotiable instrument arising from a non-consumer transaction, the personal defense of failure-of-consideration may not be used by B to avoid payment to H. p. 654

4. Under the U.C.C., a bank may fix a time at or after 2:00 p.m. as a cut-off hour for handling items and making appropriate entries on its books. This rule permits the bank to extend the banking day until a later hour without starting the running time for the midnight deadline. An item having been received after the cut-off time is deemed to be received at the opening of business on the next banking day. In this case, the next banking day is Monday and the midnight deadline is thus on Tuesday. Here, the bank did not act until Wednesday. Therefore it did not act seasonably. p. 650

5. For P. The payor bank's authority to honor checks drawn by its customers is not affected by the incompetence of a customer at the time collection is undertaken and payment made when the bank is in fact not aware of the adjudication of incompetence. The bank may make payment without incurring any liability. p. 654

ANSWERS TO CHAPTER 29 - Nature and Formation

TRUE-FALSE:

1.	F	674	4.	F	673	7.	F	680	10.	T	672
2.	T	673	5.	T	679	8.	T	675	11.	F	682
3.	T	673	6.	F	679	9.	F	673	12.	T	682

KEY TERMS - MATCHING:

1.	13	675	5.	7	674	9.	3	672	13.	18	675
2.	12	674	6.	10	673	10.	2	681	14.	5	674
3.	1	673	7.	14	674	11.	20	679	15.	9	674
4.	4	674	8.	8	678	12.	16	675			

MULTIPLE CHOICE:

1.	a	681	5.	b	680	8.	d	680	11.	d	673
2.	d	680	6.	c	673	9.	d	681	12.	d	674
3.	a	679	7.	b	675	10.	c	674	13.	c	675
4.	a	674									

CASE PROBLEMS - ESSAY ANSWERS:

1. Yes. They have an agreement to share the profits and continue to manage the business. This constitutes a partnership. p. 679

2. Yes. C is an ostensible partner and is liable to persons who have extended credit in good faith relying that C is a partner. p. 674

3. No. An adjudicated incompetent person's contracts, including a partnership agreement, are void. p. 678

4. C is a dormant partner since C is both a secret and a silent partner. p. 674

5. No. The Statute of Frauds requires that a contract to form a partnership to continue for a period longer than one year requires a writing to be enforceable. p. 675

ANSWERS TO CHAPTER 30 – Duties, Rights and Liabilities

TRUE-FALSE:

1.	T	692	4.	F	694	7.	F	695	10.	T	692
2.	T	694	5.	T	700	8.	F	699	11.	T	697
3.	F	695	6.	T	695	9.	F	700	12.	T	697

KEY TERMS – MATCHING:

1.	8	695	5.	4	698	9.	11	692	13.	7	696
2.	1	695	6.	9	696	10.	6	694	14.	10	695
3.	2	696	7.	15	698	11.	20	694	15.	19	693
4.	3	692	8.	14	698	12.	17	695			

MULTIPLE CHOICE:

1.	a	695	5.	a	698	8.	b	696	11.	d	693
2.	d	698	6.	a	698	9.	c	699	12.	b	694
3.	d	692	7.	d	695	10.	d	694	13.	c	694
4.	c	698									

CASE PROBLEMS – ESSAY ANSWERS:

1. B and C win. P does not become a partner and is not entitled to participate in the management of the partnership. P is only entitled to receive her share of the profits and to participate in the event of liquidation. p. 695

2. Q wins. Unanimous agreement among all the partners is required when a matter involves changing the terms of the partnership agreement. p. 695

3. The Uniform Partnership Act provides that, unless otherwise agreed, no partner is entitled to compensation for acting in the partnership business. p. 695

4. The partners prevail. The transfer is outside the scope of the partnership. A lacked authority to act alone. The Uniform Partnership Act provides that the assignment of partnership property for the benefit of creditors must be authorized by all partners to bind the partnership. p. 698

5. No. A partner may not sue the partnership for damages, but the partner may sue in equity for an accounting. p. 696

ANSWERS TO CHAPTER 31 – Dissolution, Winding Up, and Termination

TRUE-FALSE:

1.	T	712	4.	F	713	7.	T	716	10.	T	715
2.	T	712	5.	T	711	8.	F	711	11.	T	710
3.	F	710	6.	T	712	9.	F	714	12.	F	710

KEY TERMS - MATCHING:

1.	8	712	5.	4	714	9.	11	712	13.	12	711
2.	1	714	6.	9	715	10.	6	710	14.	13	711
3.	7	711	7.	5	711	11.	20	716	15.	17	713
4.	3	712	8.	14	711	12.	16	716			

MULTIPLE CHOICE:

1.	a	712	5.	a	712	8.	b	716	11.	d	715
2.	d	711	6.	a	711	9.	d	711	12.	c	714
3.	b	711	7.	d	714	10.	d	711	13.	b	710
4.	a	711									

CASE PROBLEMS - ESSAY ANSWES:

1. Yes on both counts. If the partnership agreement allows X and Y to continue the business, they may, and Z may be discharged from her liabilities to existing creditors by a novation. pp. 712, 715

2. Z must give actual notice of her retirement to persons with whom the partnership regularly does business and give notice by newspaper publication to the general business community. p. 716

3. C will receive $15,000. The total value of the firm's assets ($100,000) is reduced by the amount of outstanding debts, leaving $60,000 available for distribution to the partners. Capital contributions ($5,000 per partner) must be subtracted from this amount. This leaves $45,000 to be divided equally among three partners. p. 713

4. Yes. A partner can apply for dissolution by court order since partner A is guilty of conduct prejudicial to the business and has willfully breached the partnership agreement. p. 711

5. X wins. Even though C retired with the consent of the other partners, who agreed to assume full liability for all old partnership debts, C is still liable to creditors whose claims arose prior to dissolution. C's recourse would be to seek indemnification from A and B for their failure to live up to the agreement. p. 716

ANSWERS TO CHAPTER 32 – Limited Partnerships

TRUE-FALSE:

1.	F	725	4.	T	734	7.	F	726	10.	F	730
2.	F	726	5.	F	732	8.	T	726	11.	T	728
3.	T	734	6.	T	731	9.	T	729	12.	T	733

KEY TERMS – MATCHING:

1.	5	726	5.	10	726	9.	7	732	13.	12	730
2.	8	728	6.	13	733	10.	15	734	14.	17	728
3.	6	732	7.	1	733	11.	20	730	15.	19	728
4.	9	734	8.	2	733	12.	4	731			

MULTIPLE CHOICE:

1.	d	733	5.	d	731	8.	a	734	11.	c	726
2.	d	725	6.	b	728	9.	b	732	12.	c	728
3.	c	730	7.	c	734	10.	c	728	13.	d	733
4.	d	726									

CASE PROBLEMS – ESSAY ANSWERS:

1. No. Absent a provision in the partnership agreement, a limited partner has limited personal liability and does not share in the losses of the partnership beyond her capital contribution.   p. 730

2. C can sue both A and B. A limited partner whose name is used as part of the partnership name renders the limited partner liable as a general partner to any creditor who did not know of the limited partnership. In addition, since the words "limited partnership" must be in the partnership name, B is also liable for this reason.   p. 728

3. No. The death of a joint venturer, who is not the manager of the joint venture, does not necessarily dissolve the joint venture.   p. 733

4. Yes. If all partners, general or limited, agree in writing, the new general partner may be added. p. 730

5. The certificate shall contain the name of the limited partnership, the purpose of the business, the location of the business, the names and residences of each general and limited partner, the term of existence, the capital contributions of each limited partner, the time for return of contributions of limited partners, and the share of the profits of each limited partner.   p. 726

ANSWERS TO CHAPTER 33 - Nature, Formation, and Power

TRUE-FALSE:

1.	T	752	4.	F	760	7.	T	749	10.	F	749
2.	T	762	5.	F	764	8.	T	751	11.	F	749
3.	T	757	6.	T	766	9.	F	750	12.	T	757

KEY TERMS - MATCHING:

1.	3	751	5.	8	757	9.	9	766	13.	1	751
2.	2	760	6.	7	755	10.	11	752	14.	19	752
3.	5	758	7.	14	765	11.	17	752	15.	16	751
4.	6	762	8.	12	758	12.	18	754			

MULTIPLE CHOICE:

1.	c	755	5.	a	755	8.	d	766	11.	d	751
2.	a	751	6.	c	760	9.	d	766	12.	d	752
3.	d	750	7.	b	764	10.	c	757	13.	d	751
4.	c	757									

CASE PROBLEMS - ESSAY ANSWERS:

1. Yes. If the business is operated as a corporation, the business' debts can be satisfied only from assets of the corporation. C's personal assets would be protected. p. 751

2. Possibly. A corporation may be liable for crimes committed by its agents and punished for the violation by a fine. p. 766

3. Contracts made by a promoter for a corporation not yet formed are binding only on the promoter. The corporation becomes liable if it ratifies the contract after the corporation is formed. p. 755

4. No. A promoter has a fiduciary duty to the shareholders and the corporation and cannot retain secret profits resulting from this relationship. p. 755

5. No. The case illustrates the formation of a de facto corporation. The corporation would be liable to the customer. A, B, and C would not be personally liable. Only the State can challenge the existence of a de facto corporation. Under the Revised Act, liability is imposed on persons who purport to act as a corporation only if they know there is no proper incorporation. A, B, and C did not know and are not personally liable. p. 762

ANSWERS TO CHAPTER 34 – Financial Structure

TRUE-FALSE:

1.	F	778	4.	F	786	7.	F	784	10.	T	793
2.	T	783	5.	F	786	8.	F	791	11.	T	781
3.	F	785	6.	F	778	9.	T	793	12.	F	786

KEY TERMS – MATCHING:

1.	7	779	5.	8	780	9.	10	778	13.	17	780
2.	6	791	6.	5	793	10.	14	784	14.	18	785
3.	2	793	7.	12	781	11.	20	781	15.	19	786
4.	4	793	8.	9	780	12.	16	779			

MULTIPLE CHOICE:

1.	d	791	5.	d	790	8.	d	792	11.	c	787
2.	d	782	6.	a	791	9.	c	793	12.	a	786
3.	b	787	7.	d	793	10.	d	791	13.	d	792
4.	b	784									

CASE PROBLEMS – ESSAY ANSWERS:

1. No. The majority position follows Section 19 of the Model Act which states that in the absence of fraud, the judgment of the board of directors as to the value of the consideration received for shares shall be conclusive. p. 783

2. Yes. If provided for in the articles of incorporation, a corporation does have the power of redemption. To protect creditors, however, most States have statutory restrictions upon redemption which may overrule the articles of incorporation (charter). p. 787

3. Yes. A corporation becomes the debtor of its shareholders when a cash dividend is properly declared. The shareholders may enforce their claims as unsecured creditors in a court of law. p. 789

4. B wins. A has breached A's warranty that the transfer is effective and rightful. Neither party is owner of the stock. p. 793

5. A wins. An issuer who registers the transfer of a certificated security upon an unauthorized indorsement is subject to liability for improper registration. p. 794

ANSWERS TO CHAPTER 35 – Management Structure

TRUE-FALSE:

1.	T	815	4.	T	816	7.	T	823	10.	F	809
2.	T	804	5.	T	817	8.	T	815	11.	T	804
3.	F	813	6.	F	814	9.	F	811,816	12.	F	823

KEY TERMS – MATCHING:

1.	15	812	5.	11	821	9.	2	810	13.	7	815
2.	4	815	6.	12	821	10.	14	809	14.	18	810
3.	8	820	7.	9	815	11.	16	819	15.	5	817
4.	10	820	8.	6	822	12.	20	817			

MULTIPLE CHOICE:

1.	a	820	5.	b	815	8.	d	814	11.	d	804
2.	d	817	6.	c	817	9.	d	809	12.	d	807
3.	d	807,814	7.	a	815	10.	a	821,823	13.	d	818
4.	d	814									

CASE PROBLEMS – ESSAY ANSWERS:

1. Because the vote is cumulative, X has 30 votes. X may give all 30 votes to one director or apportion the 30 votes between two or among all three of the candidates. p. 809

2. No. Because of an officer's fiduciary duty and the "corporate opportunity" doctrine, A must make full disclosure of the opportunity to the corporation before A purchased the land. pp. 820, 821

3. No. Unless all the directors signed a consent in writing to vote without a meeting, they do not have the power to bind the corporation when acting individually. p. 815

4. X wins. Absent fraud, a court will not hold X liable for damages if X is using good judgment which later proves to be financially unsound. pp. 818, 819

5. X is liable. Either directors or officers may be held liable for not fulfilling their duty of diligence to the corporation. p. 819

ANSWERS TO CHAPTER 36 – Fundamental Changes

TRUE-FALSE:

1.	F	838	4.	T	840	7.	F	841	10.	F	845
2.	F	838	5.	F	840	8.	T	837	11.	F	837
3.	T	840	6.	F	845	9.	T	843	12.	T	845

KEY TERMS – MATCHING:

1.	3	840	5.	9	836	9.	12	840	13.	1	840
2.	2	841	6.	6	843	10.	13	845	14.	11	843
3.	15	836	7.	7	845	11.	20	839	15.	17	845
4.	4	840	8.	8	842	12.	16	842			

MULTIPLE CHOICE:

1.	d	844	5.	d	845	8.	b	845	11.	d	837
2.	d	837	6.	d	844	9.	d	845	12.	b	837
3.	d	845	7.	d	845	10.	d	844	13.	b	844
4.	d	845									

CASE PROBLEMS – ESSAY ANSWERS:

1.   Upon dissolution, the assets of the corporation are liquidated and used first to pay creditors and the expenses of liquidation. A will be paid ahead of all the shareholders. p. 845

2.   No. The Model Act, Section 81, requires a written demand for the money on a form provided by the corporation within a time period set by the corporation. Unless Abby makes the demand within that time period, she is not entitled to payment for her shares. p. 843

3.   No. Only the dissenting shareholders of the subsidiary corporation have the right to obtain payment for their shares from the parent corporation. p. 840

4.   Merger, consolidation, the purchase of the assets of one corporation by the other, or dissolution of one corporation are all possible remedies. pp. 838, 844

5.   Yes. When one corporation becomes the parent over another, no change is made in the legal existence of either, i.e., the separate existence of both corporations is not affected by the exchange. p. 839

ANSWERS TO CHAPTER 37 – Secured Transactions in Personal Property

TRUE-FALSE:

1.	F	860	4.	T	867	7.	T	863	10.	T	860
2.	T	861	5.	F	868	8.	F	880	11.	F	864
3.	F	867	6.	T	871	9.	T	861	12.	F	869-70

KEY TERMS - MATCHING:

1.	5	862	5.	1	868	9.	12	863	13.	15	862
2.	7	861	6.	13	864	10.	3	862	14.	20	864
3.	9	867	7.	8	863	11.	19	861	15.	18	880
4.	10	871	8.	2	862	12.	16	861			

MULTIPLE CHOICE:

1.	c	873	5.	c	875	8.	c	868	11.	d	863
2.	b	861	6.	c	860	9.	d	873	12.	a	868
3.	d	861	7.	a	874	10.	b	868	13.	c	877
4.	b	863									

CASE PROBLEMS - ESSAY ANSWERS:

1. Under a conditional sales contract, the seller retains "title" in the goods as a security until they are fully paid for. When the buyer defaults on the contract, the seller may usually recover the goods. For S. p. 861

2. L has incorrectly identified the collateral. The books are likely equipment under the U.C.C.'s broad definition of this term. p. 862

3. Unless the agreement between debtor and creditor provides otherwise, the secured creditor has rights to sale proceeds upon transfer of the collateral. Assuming the agreement between L and B did not speak to this issue, B may assert a claim against the $1,000. p. 867

4. L has priority since that security interest was perfected first and C could have found out about it by checking the recorded financing statement. p. 874

5. Assuming that following default, B did not sign a written waiver of any rights, S's actions are improper since B has paid at least 60% of the original $2,500 debt. S must therefore sell the repossessed unit within 90 days after repossession and reimburse B for any amount of the sale proceeds that exceed the debt balance plus expenses associated with repossession and resale. p. 880

ANSWERS TO CHAPTER 38 - Suretyship

TRUE-FALSE:

1.	F	895-6	4.	F	898	7.	T	900	10.	T	898
2.	T	896	5.	T	898	8.	F	897	11.	T	898
3.	F	896	6.	F	900	9.	T	898	12.	F	900

KEY TERMS - MATCHING:

1.	6	894	5.	2	897	9.	13	898	13.	8	897
2.	15	894	6.	4	898	10.	14	896	14.	17	900
3.	1	896	7.	10	897	11.	20	895	15.	18	896
4.	11	896	8.	12	896	12.	16	896			

MULTIPLE CHOICE:

1.	a	894	5.	d	899	8.	c	896	11.	a	898
2.	b	894	6.	d	900	9.	a	896	12.	c	895
3.	c	897	7.	b	900	10.	d	900	13.	d	898
4.	a	896									

CASE PROBLEMS - ESSAY ANSWERS:

1.   Unless Samantha has knowledge of this extension, consents to it, or Casper has expressly reserved his remedies against her, she is discharged from the agreement and has no further payment liability. p. 900

2.   Probably not. Absent the application of the main purpose doctrine to this case, the general rule under the Statute of Frauds controls. Since Bea's promise was not in writing, it is not enforceable. p. 896

3.   Cindy wins. When the debtor, owing several loans to one creditor, makes an undesignated payment, the creditor may apply the money to any of the debts in any manner. Thus, the full $5,400 is still owing and Cindy may seek that from Cecil. p. 900

4.   Sal is released from the contract since sureties are discharged from their payment obligations to the extent of the value of security interests released or impaired by the creditor. p. 899

5.   Cityville may enforce Sally's payment obligation since bankruptcy discharge of the principal debtor does not release the surety. p. 898

ANSWERS TO CHAPTER 39 – Bankruptcy and Relief of Debtors

TRUE-FALSE:

1.	F	909	4.	T	914	7.	F	911	10.	T	911
2.	T	910	5.	F	915	8.	T	921	11.	T	914
3.	F	913	6.	F	913	9.	T	924	12.	F	924

KEY TERMS - MATCHING:

1.	12	908	5.	5	912	9.	15	920	13.	19	915
2.	3	927	6.	1	915	10.	8	926	14.	17	922
3.	4	928	7.	2	914	11.	20	912	15.	18	926
4.	11	909	8.	7	926	12.	16	914			

MULTIPLE CHOICE:

1.	c	910	5.	d	909	8.	d	913	11.	b	927
2.	b	912	6.	c	917	9.	b	920	12.	a	921
3.	b	916	7.	a	915	10.	c	922	13.	d	918
4.	a	911									

CASE PROBLEMS - ESSAY ANSWERS:

1. No. Student loans are non-dischargeable debts for five years after they become due. p. 915

2. No. Since the agreement was made after D's discharge, it is unenforceable under 1978 Bankruptcy Reform Act. p. 914

3. Creditors 1, 2, and 3 hold some degree of priority claims. The portion of their debts given priority status must be fully satisfied before any general unsecured creditors receive payment. Accordingly, Creditor 1 receives $10,000, Creditor 2 $2,000, and Creditor 3 $6,000, totalling $18,000 of priority claims satisfied. This leaves $27,000 to apply to the remaining $36,000 in unsecured debt: $7,000 to Creditor 1; $6,000 to Creditor 2; $12,000 to Creditor 4; and $11,000 to Creditor 5. Creditor 6 will not share in debtor's estate since they failed to list their claim with the court. The $27,000 will be divided pro rata among Creditors 1, 2, 4, and 5. Each will receive 75% (27,000/36,000 or 3/4) return on the debt owed them: Creditor 1 receives $5,250; Creditor 2 receives $4,500; Creditor 4 receives $8,250; and Creditor 5 receives $9,000. pp. 912-13; pp. 918-19

4. Dingle's transfers constitute a fraudulent conveyance. It can result in Doodles being denied discharge as well as the trustee avoiding the transfers and bringing the boat and car back into Doodles' estate. p. 917

5. The transfer is legal since before it can be a voidable preference, Paddywack must be insolvent or the transfers must make him insolvent. Here, Paddywack is solvent (assets exceeding liabilities). p. 916

ANSWERS TO CHAPTER 40 – Unfair Competition and Business Torts

TRUE-FALSE:

1.	T	940	4.	F	952	7.	T	948	10.	F	950
2.	T	947	5.	T	950	8.	F	942-3	11.	T	941
3.	F	950	6.	F	946	9.	T	952	12.	F	943

KEY TERMS – MATCHING:

1.	14	940	5.	2	948	9.	6	945	13.	18	946
2.	1	943	6.	7	950	10.	3	947	14.	19	948
3.	15	942	7.	4	948	11.	17	942	15.	16	951
4.	9	944	8.	10	952	12.	20	942			

MULTIPLE CHOICE:

1.	b	940	5.	a	952	8.	a	942	11.	d	948
2.	d	947	6.	c	947	9.	b	951	12.	c	952
3.	c	942	7.	c	942	10.	a	951	13.	b	945
4.	b	946									

CASE PROBLEMS – ESSAY ANSWERS:

1. Probably not. Since "Lantern" is related to the function and purpose of Larry's lamps, he cannot tie up the word for exclusive application to his lamps. p. 948

2. Toys Mfg., Inc. may restrain A and B, through an injunction, from using the special knowledge and skills they developed while employed at Toys for the benefit of Playthings. If Toys were not allowed to so protect its trade secrets, Playthings would gain an unfair competitive advantage at Toy's expense. p. 947

3. Probably not. Natural substances are not patentable. Discovering the usefulness of an already existing and known bacteria does not meet the requirement of a human made or modified invention. Only if Dr. Science's efforts amount to genetically engineering the bacteria could it be patentable. p. 952

4. The Puffers. By failing to register their copyright, the Eskimos are foreclosed from bringing an infringement action against the Puffers. p. 950

5. Depending on whether Hook's statements are fraudulent or not, Cappy may pursue either out-of-pocket damages of $13,000 if no fraud was present or benefit-of-the-bargain damages of $18,000 if fraud was present. p. 946

ANSWERS TO CHAPTER 41 - Antitrust

TRUE-FALSE:

1.	T	969	4.	T	966-7	7.	T	979	10.	F	973
2.	T	973	5.	F	977	8.	F	966	11.	T	966
3.	F	973	6.	F	972	9.	T	971	12.	F	968

KEY TERMS - MATCHING:

1.	3	973	5.	14	971	9.	6	972	13.	16	973
2.	7	972	6.	13	979	10.	12	970	14.	11	974
3.	15	967	7.	4	971	11.	17	969	15.	5	976
4.	9	967	8.	10	967	12.	20	970			

MULTIPLE CHOICE:

1.	d	976	5.	a	972	8.	c	977	11.	a	972
2.	b	979	6.	c	974	9.	b	968	12.	c	972
3.	d	969-70	7.	a	979	10.	d	970	13.	b	976
4.	c	979									

CASE PROBLEMS - ESSAY ANSWERS:

1. This is an example of an exclusive supply contract which might be a violation of anti-trust statutes (Section 3 of the Clayton Act) if it results in a considerable reduction of competition or has the effect of establishing a monopoly. pp. 973-4

2. This is an example of resale price maintenance (vertical price fixing). This practice was once legal under State Fair Trade Acts but is now a per-se violation of the Sherman Anti-Trust Act when interstate commerce is affected. p. 970

3. Probably. Since the contract between Home Furnishings and the distributor calls for lower prices then competitors of Home Furnishings pay, this could amount to the type of price discrimination prohibited by Section 2 of the Robinson-Patman Act. For the price differentials not to be vilations, they would have to be justified on the basis of legitimate business reasons. p. 977

4. Yes. Since Pewtrid raised the price on the paint to be purchased and the sales price for the three gallons of paint was more than the usual retail price for two gallons, the ad campaign was deceptive by referring to the third gallon as "free." p. 979

5. Yes. Since the practice of law is professional commerce, and lawyers are sellers of professional services, agreements between these sellers to establish minimum prices at which their services are sold is prohibited under the Act. pp. 969-70

ANSWERS TO CHAPTER 42 - Consumer Protection

TRUE-FALSE:

1.	F	1004-5	4.	F	1004	7.	F	1002	10.	T	997
2.	T	1000	5.	F	996	8.	F	1005	11.	F	997
3.	T	1002	6.	T	998	9.	F	999	12.	T	1004

KEY TERMS - MATCHING:

1.	5	980	5.	9	1006	9.	4	998	13.	17	1002
2.	7	996	6.	12	999	10.	1	1001	14.	13	1002
3.	8	999	7.	10	1003	11.	19	998	15.	18	1004
4.	15	1001	8.	14	1006	12.	16	1000			

MULTIPLE CHOICE:

1.	c	1002	5.	c	996	8.	a	1001	11.	b	1004
2.	b	1001	6.	b	1000-1	9.	b	1001	12.	d	1006
3.	d	1002	7.	d	999	10.	c	1004-5	13.	a	1003
4.	a	1001									

CASE PROBLEMS - ESSAY ANSWERS:

1. Jackson is not liable for any of the $250. Since the card was neither requested nor accepted, the entire loss for its unauthorized use falls on Plakton Petroleum as provided for under the FCCPA. p. 1004

2. According to provisions in the FCCPA, an employer may not fire employees simply because creditors of employees have exercised a right of wage assignment or garnishment against them. In this case, E's threat of discharge is improper and illegal. p. 1005

3. The final $1,600 payment is called a balloon payment. In such cases, a debtor unable to meet the amount is not automatically in default with the possibility of losing the goods. In some States, balloon payment clauses are void and prohibited. In others, B may refinance the $1,600 on the same terms as the prior payment of $5,600 without any penalty. p. 1003

4. The Magnusson-Moss Act applies only where written warranties accompany the sale of goods or services. The Act does not require that such warranties be given. Since, in this case, no warranty was given by S, B has no rights under Magnusson-Moss. p. 1000

5. Under the Federal Interstate Land Sales Full Disclosure Act, purchasers of land through an interstate promotional campaign must be provided a "statement of record" or property report prior to entering a contract of sale with the real property seller. When sellers fail to provide such a statement, buyers may cancel their conracts with the seller anytime within two years after the contract was signed. Since in this case H and W were never given a report from S, I would advise them to exercise their revocation rights as allowed under the ILSFDA. p. 1001

ANSWERS TO CHAPTER 43 - Employment Law

TRUE-FALSE:

1.	T	1020	4.	T	1023	7.	T	1026	10.	F	1030	
2.	F	1020	5.	F	1023	8.	T	1030	11.	T	1025	
3.	F	1021	6.	F	1024	9.	T	1031	12.	F	1029	

KEY TERMS - MATCHING:

1.	4	1021	5.	15	1024	9.	13	1030	13.	17	1024	
2.	7	1021	6.	10	1029	10.	6	1030	14.	19	1025	
3.	11	1022	7.	8	1029	11.	16	1021	15.	18	1027	
4.	9	1022	8.	2	1031	12.	20	1022				

MULTIPLE CHOICE:

1.	d	1020	5.	b	1024	8.	c	1029	11.	d	1023	
2.	c	1021	6.	b	1024	9.	b	1031	12.	d	1027-28	
3.	a	1023	7.	a	1029	10.	a	1031	13.	c	1022	
4.	c	1023										

CASE PROBLEMS - ESSAY ANSWERS:

1. Probably not. Since stock clerks and yard attendants are most likely different with different responsibilities, they may have different salary scales without violating the Equal Pay Act. p. 1023

2. Aerospace wins. Federal age discrimination laws apply only to persons at least 40 years old. p. 1026

3. Forty wins if his opinions carry no direct reprisal or threat of coercion against his workers. This falls under the employer free speech section of the Taft-Hartley Act. p. 1022

4. Charlene wins. OSHA forbids discharge of employment based on employees exercising their rights under the Act. p. 1029

5. Folsum wins. The union's action is a prohibited secondary boycott under the terms of Taft-Hartley and amounts to a union unfair labor practice. p. 1022

ANSWERS TO CHAPTER 44 – Securities Regulation

TRUE-FALSE:

1.	F	1050	4.	T	1056	7.	F	1059	10.	F	1051
2.	F	1051	5.	F	1058	8.	T	1050	11.	T	1051
3.	T	1052	6.	T	1052	9.	T	1065	12.	T	1053

KEY TERMS – MATCHING:

1.	15	1050	5.	3	1060	9.	9	1054	13.	16	1053
2.	5	1051	6.	7	1063	10.	10	1054	14.	18	1062
3.	12	1051	7.	8	1062	11.	20	1050	15.	19	1064
4.	1	1053	8.	6	1050	12.	17	1052			

MULTIPLE CHOICE:

1.	a	1051	5.	d	1053	8.	a	1057	11.	d	1064
2.	c	1052	6.	c	1051	9.	c	1060	12.	d	1064
3.	d	1051–2	7.	d	1055	10.	b	1058–9	13.	a	1065
4.	a	1053									

CASE PROBLEMS – ESSAY ANSWERS:

1. No. Under Regulation A, although Ajax is exempt for registration purposes, it still must file a notification and an offering circular with SEC. p. 1052

2. Since this transaction meets the definition of "short-swing" trading by "insiders," Brown is liable for the profits to the corporation and its shareholders. p. 1061

3. No. Under Section 3 of the 1933 Securities Act, securities marketing by non-profit organizations are exempt from registration requirements. p. 1053

4. Yes. Since an untrue statement was made by Explorations in its registration statements, I is entitled to a return of his investment plus interest. Because Sammy and Edith were named as directors in the registration, they are liable to I unless they can apply the defense of due diligence to their case. p. 1057

5. No. Since XYZ's assets are less than $5 million and the class of equity securities shareholders is less than 500, it does not have to register these securities. p. 1059

ANSWERS TO CHAPTER 45 – Accountants' Legal Liability

TRUE-FALSE:

1.	T	1082	4.	F	1084	7.	T	1085	10.	F	1085
2.	F	1083	5.	T	1085	8.	F	1085	11.	T	1082
3.	T	1083	6.	F	1085	9.	T	1086	12.	F	1083

KEY TERMS - MATCHING:

1.	9	1083	5.	2	1086	9.	4	1085	13.	18	1082
2.	11	1083	6.	15	1086	10.	1	1084	14.	14	1083
3.	12	1083	7.	3	1083	11.	16	1086	15.	20	1083
4.	7	1083	8.	13	1085	12.	17	1082			

MULTIPLE CHOICE:

1.	c	1082	5.	c	1085	8.	b	1085	11.	d	1084
2.	a	1083	6.	d	1085	9.	c	1086	12.	c	1085
3.	d	1084	7.	a	1086	10.	a	1082	13.	b	1086
4.	b	1085									

CASE PROBLEMS - ESSAY ANSWERS:

1. Since accountant explicitly agreed to furnish a final report by May 15th and time was of the essence, failure to meet this deadline constitutes a material breach which discharges client's payment obligation. p. 1083

2. Accountant's failure to follow up on the discrepancies may constitute negligence opening liability to the parties as "forseeable plaintiffs" for compensatory damages. But since no fraud was involved on accountant's part, no basis for punitive damages exists. p. 1084

3. Accountant wins. As owner of the working papers, accountant is not obligated to give them over to client. p. 1085

4. Accountant has substantially performed on the contract. As such, contractually agreed upon compensation is due from client reduced by damages caused by accountant's delay. p. 1083

5. Prosecutor wins. Accountant must testify since Federal law does not recognize an accountant-client privilege. p. 1085

ANSWERS TO CHAPTER 46 – Introduction to Real and Personal Property

TRUE-FALSE:

1.	T	1106	4.	T	1111	7.	T	1111	10.	T	1109
2.	T	1109	5.	F	1111	8.	T	1110	11.	F	1109
3.	F	1110	6.	F	1111	9.	F	1108	12.	T	1108

KEY TERMS - MATCHING:

1.	3	1107	5.	4	1107	9.	1	1110	13.	20	1110
2.	7	1109	6.	5	1109	10.	15	1111	14.	17	1106
3.	9	1107	7.	8	1111-2	11.	18	1110	15.	19	1106
4.	12	1107	8.	11	1107	12.	16	1110			

MULTIPLE CHOICE:

1.	b	1107	5.	b	1110	8.	d	1108	11.	b	1106
2.	d	1109-10	6.	a	1112	9.	a	1109	12.	d	1107
3.	a	1110	7.	d	1109	10.	c	1108	13.	a	1111
4.	c	1110									

CASE PROBLEMS - ESSAY ANSWERS:

1. This is an example of title transfer through accession. Since Ragmuffin's taking of the fabric pieces was based on the innocent mistaken belief that they were abandoned, and through Ragmuffin's work, the value of the pieces has increased and their identity substantially changed, Ragmuffin will own the coat. Josephine's only remedy is reimbursement for the value of the pieces of cloth in their original, not improved, state. p. 1111

2. Sam probably must keep the money. The law generally presumes that donees accept gifts when the property does not impose a burden on them and they are benefitted from it. Since Sam remained silent for six months after receiving the money order, he is presumed to have accepted it. p. 1110

3. Since the ring was on the floor when it was discovered, it would probably be considered lost and not misplaced. Therefore, Brown, the finder, would have superior rights to the ring vis-a-vis Smith. Brown wins. p. 1111

4. Probably B. Although a building merely resting on land is normally regarded as real property, with a tenant having no right of removal even though the building is not firmly attached to the land, if B can show that the store's use was peculiar to his business, then the building would be a retainable "trade fixture" and B could remove it. p. 1109

5. M and F probably have superior rights to the items in question. The goods are most likely fixtures since they have been so firmly attached to the home as to lose their identity as personal property and have become part of the home. In addition, they most likely cannot be removed without material damage. Therefore, they were sold with the house to M and F. pp. 1108-9.

ANSWERS TO CHAPTER 47 – Bailments and Documents of Title

TRUE-FALSE:

1.	T	1127	4.	F	1121	7.	F	1126	10.	T	1123-4
2.	T	1127	5.	T	1119	8.	T	1125	11.	F	1128
3.	F	1126	6.	F	1122	9.	F	1126	12.	T	1128

KEY TERMS – MATCHING:

1.	4	1125	5.	12	1124	9.	13	1124	13.	20	1127
2.	5	1120	6.	11	1119	10.	15	1128	14.	17	1127
3.	3	1119	7.	2	1124	11.	19	1128	15.	18	1125
4.	6	1126	8.	14	1124	12.	16	1128			

MULTIPLE CHOICE:

1.	d	1129	5.	b	1123	8.	b	1125	11.	c	1128
2.	a	1122	6.	a	1127-8	9.	d	1120	12.	d	1129
3.	c	1128	7.	b	1121	10.	a	1130	13.	b	1129
4.	d	1121									

CASE PROBLEMS – ESSAY ANSWERS:

1. For the owner. The holder of a negotiable bill issued to a thief following bailment of stolen goods acquires no right to the goods as against the true owner, regardless of intervening due negotiation. A thief who delivers goods to a carrier and receives a negotiable document cannot extinguish the true owner's title. p. 1129

2. For C. U.C.C. 7-204(1) holds W's obligation to C as that of a reasonably careful warehouseman. In this case, reasonable care would have avoided the damage to the cheese. Although W may limit by contract the extent of liability by fixing a damages maximum, the duty of reasonable care cannot be completely waived. p. 1126

3. Yes. B, as the bailee for hire, has an absolute duty to deliver the goods to the right person. The innocent misdelivery is a conversion of the goods and B is not excused from liability. p. 1123

4. No. Since the transaction between A and B is a pledge and not a bailment, the pledgee, A, is free to transfer or assign the interest in the goods to another, even without obtaining the pledgor, B's consent beforehand. p. 1124

5. Innkeeper suffers the loss. By statute, innkeepers may avoid their common law strict liability for the belongings of their guests by providing a safe for guest use and posting notice of its existence. Here, however, no notice was given Guest of Innkeeper's safe. Innkeeper is therefore the insurer of Guest's watch under common law. p. 1125

ANSWERS TO CHAPTER 48 – Interests in Real Property

TRUE-FALSE:

1.	T	1139	4.	T	1147	7.	F	1152	10.	F	1149
2.	F	1148	5.	F	1148	8.	T	1145	11.	T	1145
3.	F	1139-40	6.	T	1148	9.	T	1146-7	12.	F	1142

KEY TERMS - MATCHING:

1.	5	1142	5.	15	1149-50	9.	6	1148	13.	16	1143
2.	4	1140	6.	12	1150	10.	7	1142	14.	19	1144
3.	3	1151	7.	8	1148	11.	20	1141	15.	18	1140
4.	9	1141	8.	11	1152	12.	17	1144			

MULTIPLE CHOICE:

1.	c	1145	5.	c	1142	8.	a	1149	11.	b	1150
2.	d	1149	6.	a	1150	9.	a	1143	12.	c	1151
3.	c	1140	7.	d	1149	10.	c	1145	13.	d	1147
4.	a	1151									

CASE PROBLEMS - ESSAY ANSWERS:

1. Initially, A, B, and C each have a one-third undivided interest in the land. Upon C conveying a one-third interest to D, D becomes a tenant in common with A and B, who remain joint-tenant owners of Greenacre for their two-thirds interests. When A dies, B acquires A's undivided one-third interest by right of survivorship and, as a result, holds a two-thirds interest as a tenant in common with D, who has an undivided one-third interest. pp. 1148-9

2. A's heirs. The qualification which limited the fee estate in the land runs against all subsequent owners. When the property no longer is used for the specific purpose mentioned, it automatically reverts to the grantor or the grantor's heirs through "possibility of reverter." p. 1141

3. H's wife has dower or inheritance rights only in real property held in fee simple or its equivalent by H. Since H's interest in the dairy farm is the only estate of inheritance (held in fee simple), his wife will have no rights or interests in the joint tenancy property (ranch) or the life tenancy property (poultry farm). W will only receive H's interest in the dairy farm. pp. 1140, 1148, 1149

4. It depends. If A's land is the dominant parcel of an appurtenant easement, then it is not necessary to refer specifically to that easement in the deed from B to C in order to give A the ongoing use of the easement over C's land. But if A's easement is in gross, then it must be mentioned in the deed from B to C, otherwise it is extinguished. p. 1151

5. No. Since B and C acquire their interests by different instruments which take effect at different times, the unities of time and title are lacking from the "four unities" required for joint tenancy. B and C are therefore tenants in common. p. 1149

ANSWERS TO CHAPTER 49 - Transfer and Control of Real Property

TRUE-FALSE:

1.	F	1164	4.	T	1164	7.	F	1170	10.	F	1173
2.	T	1165	5.	F	1167	8.	F	1172	11.	T	1167
3.	F	1165	6.	T	1168	9.	T	1172	12.	T	1168

KEY TERMS - MATCHING:

1.	2	1171	5.	14	1172	9.	3	1171-2	13.	16	1169
2.	11	1170	6.	6	1169-70	10.	9	1169	14.	19	1171
3.	8	1171-2	7.	4	1165	11.	17	1168	15.	18	1170
4.	7	1166-7	8.	12	1168	12.	20	1168			

MULTIPLE CHOICE:

1.	c	1171-2	5.	b	1170	8.	c	1168-9	11.	b	1168
2.	d	1170	6.	d	1164	9.	a	1170	12.	d	1169
3.	b	1166	7.	b	1172	10.	c	1173	13.	a	1167
4.	c	1166									

CASE PROBLEMS - ESSAY ANSWERS:

1. Due to the two tobacco shops and three pharmacists selling cigarettes in violation of the dictates of the restrictive covenant, Frank can persuasively argue that the character of the area has changed and that the covenant has been abandoned. There would thus be no justification for enforcing the covenant against him. p. 1173

2. Racially based restrictive covenants are invalid and therefore unenforceable stemming from 1947 U.S. Supreme Court decision. Advise the Chans to resubmit the bid and if they are turned down again for the same reason, bring action against the sellers to invalidate the restriction. p. 1173

3. A prevails. Zoning ordinances may not be used to immediately end a lawful use of property which had been existing prior to the passage of the ordinance. A will be permitted to operate the junkyard for a reasonable time. p. 1171

4. Zoning ordinances which result in a "taking" of property without compensation are invalid. If the effect of a zoning restriction is to render nearly any beneficial use of property impossible, then the ordinance is an invalid confiscation. The city is not certain whether its urban renewal plan will ever go into effect. During the interim, L is essentially barred from pursuing beneficial development of the site given the plans' building compensation restriction. L should therefore argue that this part of the plan amounts to a confiscation and seek to invalidate it. p. 1171

5. Possibly. The power of eminent domain can be delegated to R.R. if the increased width of the tracks would result in improved service to the public and therefore constitute promoting a "public purpose." p. 1172

ANSWERS TO CHAPTER 50 – Trusts and wills

TRUE-FALSE:

1.	T	1189	4.	T	1191	7.	F	1198	10.	T	1198
2.	T	1192	5.	F	1195	8.	F	1189	11.	F	1197
3.	T	1193	6.	F	1189	9.	F	1191	12.	F	1199

KEY TERMS – MATCHING:

1.	6	1186	5.	1	1188	9.	5	1198	13.	18	1195
2.	3	1194	6.	4	1189	10.	2	1199	14.	9	1196
3.	15	1195	7.	14	1196	11.	16	1199	15.	19	1196
4.	11	1187	8.	12	1187	12.	13	1197			

MULTIPLE CHOICE:

1.	b	1189	5.	d	1190	8.	c	1199	11.	d	1195
2.	a	1189	6.	d	1193	9.	c	1196	12.	b	1194
3.	b	1190	7.	d	1197	10.	c	1195	13.	c	1189
4.	a	1188									

CASE PROBLEMS – ESSAY ANSWERS:

1.   If properly created, creditors of a beneficiary of a spendthrift trust cannot attach the trust fund or its income but must wait to obtain payment until the income is received by the beneficiary. p. 1187

2.   The death of the trustee does not terminate the trust. Nor will the court terminate the trust simply because all beneficiaries ask for it. The court will decide according to the trust purposes of the settlor. p. 1192

3.   Yes. The birth of a child after execution of a will may revoke the will at least as far as that child is concerned. p. 1195

4.   Nothing. This is an example of abatement. Specific gifts must be satisfied first. p. 1196

5.   No. This is an example of ademption; the will provision is impossible to perform. p. 1196

ANSWERS TO CHAPTER 51 - Insurance

TRUE-FALSE:

1.	T	1218	4.	T	1211	7.	T	1215	10.	F	1212
2.	T	1210	5.	F	1212	8.	T	1216	11.	F	1214
3.	F	1211	6.	F	1213	9.	T	1215	12.	T	1214

KEY TERMS - MATCHING:

1.	6	1213	5.	12	1215	9.	13	1215	13.	5	1212
2.	9	1217	6.	3	1212	10.	1	1216	14.	7	1211
3.	11	1214	7.	14	1213	11.	16	1216	15.	17	1212
4.	15	1217	8.	4	1214	12.	18	1212			

MULTIPLE CHOICE:

1.	a	1210	5.	a	1213	8.	d	1216	11.	c	1215
2.	d	1212	6.	a	1215	9.	b	1217	12.	d	1212
3.	d	1214	7.	d	1215	10.	c	1212	13.	b	1212
4.	d	1215									

CASE PROBLEMS - ESSAY ANSWERS:

1. No. Playing Russian roulette has been held not to be accidental. p. 1216

2. No. The incontestability clause does not prevent rescission in this case. p. 1216

3. Audrey recovers $18,000. She is under-insured and must bear a proportionate share of the loss. p. 1213

4. The company wins. W had no insurable interest in B's life. p. 1215

5. Argue that Frank has concealed material facts. The nondisclosure must normally be fraudulent as well as material to invalidate the policy. p. 1217